THIRD EDITION

Group Counseling

Strategies and Skills

Related Titles

Theory and Practice of Group Counseling, Fourth Edition
  Gerald Corey

Student Manual for Theory and Practice of Group Counseling, Fourth Edition
  Gerald Corey

Group Techniques, Second Edition
  Gerald Corey, Marianne Schneider Corey, and Patrick Callanan

Groups: Process and Practice, Fifth Edition
  Marianne Schneider Corey and Gerald Corey

Critical Incidents in Group Therapy
  Jeremiah Donigian and Richard Malnati

Systemic Group Therapy: A Triadic Model
  Jeremiah Donigian and Richard Malnati

Face to Face: The Small Group Experience and Interpersonal Growth
  Gerard Egan

*Interpersonal Living—A Skills/Contract Approach
to Human-Relations Training in Groups*
  Gerard Egan

Group Dynamics, Second Edition
  Donelson R. Forsyth

Advanced Group Leadership
  Jeffrey A. Kottler

Understanding Group Therapy: Process and Practice Video Series, Volumes 1–3
  Irvin D. Yalom

THIRD EDITION

Group Counseling

Strategies and Skills

Ed E. Jacobs

West Virginia University

Robert L. Masson

West Virginia University

Riley L. Harvill

University of North Texas

Brooks/Cole Publishing Company

 I(T)P® *An International Thompson Publishing Company*

*Pacific Grove • Albany • Belmont • Bonn • Boston • Cincinnati • Detroit • Johannesburg • London
Madrid • Melbourne • Mexico City • New York • Paris • Singapore • Tokyo • Toronto • Washington*

Sponsoring Editor: *Eileen Murphy*
Marketing Team: *Jean Vevers Thompson, Deanne Brown, and Christine Davis*
Editorial Assistants: *Lisa Blanton and Susan Carlson*
Production Editor: *Laurel Jackson*
Manuscript Editors: *Mary Anne Shahidi and Jane Somers*

Permissions Editor: *Cathleen Collins Morrison*
Interior and Cover Design: *Lisa Thompson*
Interior Illustration: *Jennifer Mackres*
Typesetting: *Joan Mueller Cochrane*
Cover Printing: *Phoenix Color Corporation*
Printing and Binding: *The Maple-Vail Book Mfg. Group*

For more information, contact:

BROOKS/COLE PUBLISHING COMPANY
511 Forest Lodge Road
Pacific Grove, CA 93950
USA

International Thomson Publishing Europe
Berkshire House 168-173
High Holborn
London WC1V 7AA
England

Thomas Nelson Australia
102 Dodds Street
South Melbourne, 3205
Victoria, Australia

Nelson Canada
1120 Birchmount Road
Scarborough, Ontario
Canada M1K 5G4

International Thomson Editores
Seneca 53
Col. Polanco
11560 México, D. F., México

International Thomson Publishing GmbH
Königswinterer Strasse 418
53227 Bonn
Germany

International Thomson Publishing Asia
221 Henderson Road
#05-10 Henderson Building
Singapore 0315

International Thomson Publishing Japan
Hirakawacho Kyowa Building, 3F
2-2-1 Hirakawacho
Chiyoda-ku, Tokyo 102
Japan

Printed in the United States of America

10   9   8   7   6   5   4   3   2   1

Library of Congress Cataloging-in-Publication Data

Jacobs, Edward E., [date]
    Group counseling : strategies and skills / Ed E. Jacobs, Robert L. Masson, Riley L. Harvill. — 3rd ed.
        p.   cm.
    Includes bibliographical references and index.
    ISBN 0-534-34486-0
    1. Group counseling.   2. Leadership.   I. Masson, Robert L., [date]
    II. Harvill, Riley, L., [date]   .   III. Title
BF637.C6J34   1997
158'.35—dc21
                                                                97-8769
                                                                CIP

Ed E. Jacobs is an associate professor at West Virginia University in the Counseling, Counseling Psychology, and Rehabilitation Department. He is also the founder and director of Impact Therapy Associates. He teaches courses in techniques, theories, group, and addictions and conducts workshops throughout the United States, Canada, and Europe on group counseling and impact therapy. He has written two other counseling books: *Impact Therapy* and *Creative Counseling Techniques: An Illustrated Guide*. In addition, he enjoys traveling, softball, racquetball, tennis, biking, skiing, and visiting with friends all over the country.

Robert L. Masson is a professor at West Virginia University in the Counseling, Counseling Psychology, and Rehabilitation Department. He teaches courses in techniques, theories, group, and rehabilitation counseling. Bob enjoys spending time with his wife, Kathy; sailing; biking; and traveling.

Riley L. Harvill is an associate professor at University of North Texas in the Counselor Education Department. He teaches courses in individual and group counseling. He is also the co-founder of The HarBeck Company, a human resource training and consulting firm located in Dallas, Texas. In addition, he enjoys spending time with his family, biking, and traveling. Riley also enjoys the challenges of creative writing and technical writing.

CONTENTS

Group Counseling Strategies and Skills, Third Edition, provides an in-depth look at group counseling with an emphasis on practical knowledge and techniques for effective group leadership. This book is for counselors, social workers, psychologists, and all others who lead groups of one kind or another. Our active approach to group leadership reflects our belief that the leader is primarily responsible for the planning and implementation of the group. We have found that in most settings—schools, hospitals, rehabilitation facilities, mental health centers—the leader must take an active part in facilitating the group. Therefore, we discuss many different kinds of groups and describe both basic and advanced skills. The examples, which include sample dialogue from groups, help the reader understand how an effective leader applies these skills. In this edition, we added more examples because we continue to receive feedback regarding their usefulness.

The purpose of this text is to integrate traditional theories and concepts of group process with thoughtful strategies and specific exercises. We recognize that group leadership is one of the most difficult types of professional work undertaken by therapists, school counselors, drug and alcohol counselors, correctional counselors, nurses, and others in the helping professions. Our goal is to bridge the gap between theory and practice with a sophisticated how-to approach for both beginning students and experienced practitioners. In this edition, we have included many references and suggestions regarding leading groups with members from diverse populations because American society is becoming increasingly multicultural. We have also added to this edition more discussion of group process.

Organization

The three opening chapters provide an overview of group leadership. In these chapters, we examine various kinds of groups, leadership styles, uses of current theories, group dynamics, therapeutic forces in groups, group process, and purpose of groups. In Chapter One, we introduce our approach to group leadership based on the principles of impact therapy, an active, multisensory approach to counseling. Also in Chapter One, in our discussion on leadership style, we present a clear picture of different approaches to leading groups. We discuss in detail the differences between the interpersonal and intrapersonal approaches to leading. For this edition, we split the chapter on purpose and focus to allow for better coverage of each topic; Chapter Three is now devoted entirely to the purpose of groups.

Chapters Four, Five, and Six cover a range of both basic and advanced leadership skills for planning and implementing a group, as well as specific strategies and skills for initiating the first and second sessions of a group. Among the skills discussed are summarizing, clarifying, and using one's eyes and voice effectively. Sample plans, with detailed discussion of each plan, are included in the chapter on planning. Chapter Five, which focuses on the first and second sessions of a group, describes what a leader must consider in the first sessions, and we provide many examples of how to begin various kinds of groups. We also present techniques for introducing members and for the introduction of a new member during the second or subsequent sessions.

Chapter Seven affirms the importance of establishing, holding, and deepening the focus in a group. We present creative ways to "get the focus" and a discussion of the depth chart, a tool for monitoring the depth of a session. Chapter Eight offers techniques for skillfully drawing out quiet members and cutting off members who ramble or otherwise diffuse the group's focus. In this edition, we have added more examples of techniques for cutting off group members.

In Chapter Nine, we outline the essential uses of rounds and dyads and illustrate our points with numerous examples. We discuss other exercises extensively in Chapters Ten and Eleven. Written, movement, fantasy, and creative exercises are among those reviewed, and we have added many new and unique exercises involving movement and the use of creative props. We also present techniques for introducing and processing the exercises, together with ethical considerations and specific cautions about using particular exercises.

Chapter Twelve is devoted to the strategies and skills needed during the critical middle sessions of a group. We offer a way for the leader to prepare for dealing with topics during the middle sessions, especially issues related to sex, the need for approval, religion, and self-esteem. We also discuss trust and commitment, common mistakes that some leaders make during this period, and various strategies for increasing the group's effectiveness. Chapter Thirteen focuses specifically on skills and techniques essential for leading therapy groups; it has been completely revised to clarify our model for conducting therapy in groups. We also discuss the leader's role and responsibilities, the process of therapy, specific techniques, and common mistakes. In addition, we outline ways of conducting therapy with one member of a group while involving all the other members.

Chapter Fourteen contains techniques for closing sessions and groups. Chapter Fifteen offers strategies for handling problem members (such as chronic talkers and negative members) and situations (such as resistance, sexual feelings, and conflicts between members). Chapter Sixteen deals with issues specific to certain populations, such as children, adolescents, couples, older people, and those who are chemically dependent, divorced, survivors of sexual abuse, and adult children of alcoholics. Chapter Seventeen offers thoughts on co-leading, legal and ethical issues, research, and evaluation techniques. We also discuss the training of group counselors and the future of group work.

For ease of reading and for a nonsexist presentation, we have used both *he* and *she* to represent leaders and members. We also use the terms *counseling* and *therapy* interchangeably.

Acknowledgments

We wish to express our appreciation to the many friends and students who contributed ideas and insights to the third edition of this book. We also want to express our appreciation to the workshop participants who shared with us the difficulties inherent in leading groups in the field.

The reviewers who encouraged us to assess various sections of the book also deserve recognition. As a result of their efforts, we consider the third edition significantly more contemporary and relevant to the needs of practitioners today. Our sincere thanks to Joyce Clohessy, Westmoreland County Community College; Aaron W. Hughey, Western Kentucky University; Fran Mullis, Georgia State University; and Peterann M. Siehl, Bowling Green State University.

We also want to thank Laurel Jackson, our production editor, for making sure the book got published in a timely fashion. Special thanks go to Jane Somers and Mary Anne Shahidi, whose hard work as the copy editors made the book more readable, and to indexer Karen Randolph. Finally, we want to thank Eileen Murphy for her support and for our energizing conversations about this project. It is a pleasure working with Eileen and with all the people at Brooks/Cole.

Ed E. Jacobs
Robert L. Masson
Riley L. Harvill

CHAPTER ONE

Introduction

If you are a new group leader or a student studying group leadership, you may be thinking that you know very little about groups, especially if you believe you have never been in one. Actually, everyone has had some kind of group experience, be it in classes, orientation sessions, job training sessions, Sunday school meetings, staff meetings, or counseling or support groups. Depending on the leader's ability, some of these experiences were valuable and some were not.

If studying group counseling is new for you, you may be asking yourself several questions:

- ◆ What are the advantages of leading groups?
- ◆ What kind of groups are there?
- ◆ What happens in groups?
- ◆ How do I prepare for my group?
- ◆ What do I do if nobody talks?
- ◆ What should I do if someone talks too much?
- ◆ What leadership style should I use?

This book was written to answer these questions. In it, we provide a wealth of information and practical examples, hints, and techniques that will increase your understanding of group dynamics and enhance your effectiveness as a group leader. We believe that reading this book should improve your ability to lead all kinds of groups, trainings, and meetings. Our emphasis is on skills, techniques, and the art of leading.

In this chapter, we discuss a number of basic considerations: who should lead groups, reasons for leading groups, kinds of groups, group versus individual counseling, use of theories, group counseling in a multicultural context, group leadership styles, leadership functions, what makes an effective leader, and potential group problems.

Who Should Lead Groups?

Knowing how to lead groups is beneficial to anyone in a helping, teaching, or supervisory role. Professionals such as counselors, psychologists, social workers, psychiatrists, ministers, managers, and teachers can all use groups to enhance their work with people. As Gladding (1996) says, "Groups are an economical and effective means of helping individuals who share similar problems and concerns. Counselors who limit their competencies to individual counseling skills limit their options for helping" (p. 327). Conyne, Harvill, Morganett, Morran, and Hulse-Killacky (1990) discuss how counselors and therapists in the 21st century will need to be competent in leading counseling groups, psychotherapy groups, prevention groups, and community development teams. Currently, more and more administrators in schools and agencies are requiring their counselors to lead groups.

Reasons for Leading Groups

Corey (1995) opens his text on group counseling by saying, "Although there is still a place in a community agency for individual counseling, limiting the delivery of services to this model is no longer practical, especially in these tight financial times. Not only do groups let practitioners work with more clients, but the group process also has unique learning advantages" (p. 3). There are many valid reasons for using a group approach. Two reasons are common to practically all groups: groups are more efficient, and groups offer more resources or viewpoints. Other reasons for using a group approach include the feeling of commonality, the experience of "belonging," the chance to practice new behaviors, the opportunity for feedback, the opportunity for vicarious learning by listening and observing others, the approximation to real-life encounters, and the pressure to uphold commitments.

Efficiency

Having several clients meet as a group for a common purpose can save considerable time and effort. For instance, a school counselor who is responsible for 300 students will barely be able to see each student once during a school year using only a one-to-one format. However, by having groups for advising, values clarification, personal growth, support, and problem solving, the school counselor can meet the needs of many more students. Groups provide a framework that promises to deliver services to the largest number of students, with the most efficient use of time (Phillips & Phillips, 1992; Roland & Neitzchman, 1996). In situations where there is a need to orient residents, patients, or prisoners to policies and procedures, groups can certainly save time. If a supervisor finds that her staff has different opinions about an issue, bringing the people together for one meeting is more efficient than having individual meetings. In most agencies and schools, professionals are incorporating groups into their overall program to help handle the ever increasing case loads. They no longer have the luxury of just working with individuals.

Experience of Commonality

Many people have feelings they believe to be unique to them. Having people get together in a group allows them to discover that they are not the only ones having similar thoughts and feelings. As group members share personal concerns, thoughts, and feelings, they are often amazed that others in the group have similar concerns. Yalom (1995) uses the term *universality* when he discusses the value of people getting together. Following are some examples of groups where the experience of commonality can be helpful:

- Parents whose children have died
- Pregnant teenagers
- Children new to a school
- Recently divorced persons
- AIDS patients

Greater Variety of Resources and Viewpoints

Whether they are sharing information, solving a problem, exploring personal values, or discovering they have common feelings, a group of people can offer more viewpoints, and hence more resources. Shulman (1984) uses the phrase *sharing data* to describe the interaction of the multiple resources present in groups. Group members often relate that one of the most helpful aspects of being in a group is the variety of viewpoints expressed and discussed. When only two people get together, it is possible they will possess similar information, values, or ways of seeing the world. Usually this is not the case in a group setting—members will have a variety of opinions and ideas, thus making the experience interesting and valuable.

Sense of Belonging

Writers in counseling and psychology have pointed out the powerful human need to belong (Adler, 1927; Berne, 1964; Maslow, 1962). This need can be satisfied in part by being in a group (Kottler, 1994; Trotzer, 1989; Yalom, 1995). Members will often identify with each other and then feel part of a whole. Groups where the sense of belonging has proven beneficial are groups for veterans, women, men, ex-convicts, addicts, addicted teenagers, people with disabilities, and the elderly. Members of these groups have said that the experience of being accepted was one of the most important features of the group. This is especially true for teenagers, which accounts for why groups are very popular in the middle and high schools.

Skills Practice

Groups provide an arena for safe practice (Corey, 1996; Gladding, 1995; Yalom, 1995). Members can practice new skills and behaviors in a supportive environment before trying them in real-world situations. The range of new behaviors to explore is nearly infinite; members can practice interviewing for jobs, learning how to make friends, being more assertive, asking for a raise, or talking to significant people in their lives. They may share personal facts about themselves, confront others, talk about difficult subjects, look at others when they talk, cry in front of others, laugh with others, sing with others, or disagree with others. Practicing these interactions and skills will greatly enhance members' chances for more effective living. Assertiveness, communication, parenting, marital enrichment, employer-employee relations training, and police riot-training groups are all examples of groups in which members might experiment with new behaviors.

Feedback

Groups provide an opportunity for members to receive feedback. Group feedback often is more powerful than individual feedback because when only one person is giving feedback, the receiver can dismiss that person's viewpoint. When six or seven people are saying the same thing, it is difficult to deny the accuracy of what is being said. In groups where behavior rehearsal is a major component, the suggestions, reactions, and perceptions of others can be valuable.

There are many kinds of feedback and ways of giving feedback in a group. Gladding (1996) states, "Feedback is a multidimensional process that consists of group members' responding to the verbal messages and nonverbal behaviors of one another. It is one of the most important parts of any group experience" (p. 343). Frequently, members will have the opportunity to hear both first impressions and updated impressions. Hulse-Killacky and Page (1994) have been studying how and when to conduct feedback activities. They have developed an instrument for studying how members feel about giving and receiving feedback. Because feedback can be such a valuable part of group counseling, we have devoted an entire section to feedback exercises and how to deliver effective feedback (see Chapter Ten).

Vicarious Learning

A number of authors (Bandura, 1977; Kottler, 1994; Posthuma, 1996) have discussed the positive value of vicarious learning in groups. Members frequently have the opportunity to hear concerns similar to their own. On countless occasions members say such things as, "That's exactly the same problem I have." Other members say, "Listening to you has really made me aware of the fears and hang-ups I have."

Often a member will sit in silence, yet learn a great deal by watching how fellow members resolve their personal concerns. A good example of this comes from a group that we led. In a group consisting of five women living in the same college residence hall, one member said very little throughout the eight sessions. We felt we had not reached her at all. About 6 months later, we got a short note from her saying she had changed a number of things in her life because of the group. She thanked us for allowing her to be in the group even though she participated very little verbally.

Real-Life Approximation

Groups replicate real-life situations better than one-to-one counseling. Different writers have discussed groups as a microcosm or reflection of society (Dinkmeyer & Muro, 1979; Gazda, 1989; Yalom, 1995). Trotzer (1989) calls groups "mini societies." The group setting becomes a temporary substitute for the community, family, work site, or organization. In the comparatively safe atmosphere of the group, emotions, human behaviors, and attitudes such as confrontation, rigidity, fear, anger, doubt, worry, and jealousy can be identified and discussed. Being exposed to these in a group environment enables individuals to learn methods of relating and coping that may extend into their everyday living.

The social context of the group experience is valuable in many other ways. Not only are maladaptive emotions and behaviors scrutinized and worked on, but members also are given the opportunity to discover how people honestly react to them over a period of weeks or months.

Commitment

Commitment to work on specific concerns often has more strength when made in a group setting. Although such commitments are often made in one-to-one situations (counselor-client, nurse-patient, supervisor-supervisee), the motivation to honor them seems to be stronger when they are made to a number of people. This is one of the most helpful aspects of such groups as Alcoholics Anonymous, Weight Watchers, Gamblers Anonymous, and groups that help people stop smoking, find a job, or become more assertive. In these groups, members make at least an implied commitment to stop, start, or change certain behaviors. The combination of support, subtle expectations, and the desire not to let down the group is often a powerful motivation for behavioral change.

Kinds of Groups

Some people think the term *group* refers exclusively to a counseling or therapy group for troubled individuals. In fact, there are many different kinds of groups with a variety of purposes. A group is two or more people who have come together for the purpose of some designated interaction (Gladding, 1996). A leader may form a group to discuss or decide something, to explore personal problems, or to complete a specific task or achieve a specific goal. During your professional career, you most likely will have the opportunity to lead many different kinds of groups. The techniques discussed in this book can apply to all kinds of groups and also to meetings, workshops, classes, and family counseling.

Educators have classified groups differently. Trotzer (1989) divides groups into six major categories: guidance and life skills groups, counseling groups, psychotherapy groups, support and self-help groups, consultation groups, and growth groups. The Association for Specialists in Group Work (ASGW), which is a national division of the American Counseling Association, sets forth training standards for four kinds of groups: guidance/psychoeducational, counseling/interpersonal problem-solving, psychotherapy/personality reconstruction, and task/work groups (1991). Gladding's (1995) list of kinds of groups includes group guidance, group counseling, and group psychotherapy, along with some additional traditional and historical categories. (If you are interested in an excellent history of group work, starting from before 1900, see Gladding [1995].)

We have created seven categories of groups, based on their different goals. Some goals reflect what the members gain from the group and others what the members will do in the group.

1. Education
2. Discussion
3. Task
4. Growth and experiential
5. Counseling and therapy
6. Support
7. Self-help

Education Groups

Often, helping professionals are asked to provide clients with information on various topics. Examples would be the following:

- Rehabilitation clients learning how to use a wheelchair
- Students learning study skills
- People with diabetes acquiring information on nutrition
- Women learning how to protect themselves from being raped
- Managers learning how to better supervise employees
- Sixth-graders learning about the harmful effects of drug use

In each of these groups, the leader provides information and then elicits reactions and comments from the members, thereby serving sometimes as an educator and other times as a facilitator of discussion. It is very important for the leader to conceptualize this dual role. There is no set formula for how much one should be in either—it will depend on the amount of information to be covered, the amount of knowledge the members already have, and the amount of time available. Likewise, there is no set format for the number of sessions or length of meetings. Often, education groups are held just once for 2 to 8 hours. Others meet for a number of weeks, 1 or 2 hours per week.

◆ E X A M P L E S

This group is composed of eight students who want hints on how to study more efficiently. It is 20 minutes into the first session.

Leader: OK, let's talk about the different ways of going about studying a chapter in a text. What are the ways that you do it?

Jerry: Well, I just read the chapter and underline.

Bill: I do the same thing.

Kevin: I try to outline 'em, but it takes me too long.

Bobbi: I just read it twice and hope for the best.

Leader: Let me give you some ideas. One of the best things you can do is to sit down and skim the chapter for the main idea of what you are going to read. Often, there is a summary at the end of each chapter. Then decide the kinds of questions that the professor might ask. If you can, look over your other tests and try to get a sense of the kind of questions you have been asked before. How does that sound?

Becky: Well, I never thought of skimming the chapter.

Jim: I like that idea.

Chu: Me, too. Would you suggest underlining or taking notes or what?

Leader: It's quicker to either underline or mark in the margin. Many people, however, don't learn from underlining.

Kevin: That's true for me. It's not helpful for me to underline. But when I take notes as I read, I remember.

Jim: Yeah, I like that idea. I've been underlining too, but it hasn't helped. I think I'd better take notes or try something else.

The leader's role in this group is to offer helpful suggestions and ideas concerning ways of studying and to get members to share methods of studying that do and do not work for them.

This group is composed of five women who each weigh over 200 pounds. The purpose of the group is to educate the women about behavior modification methods of losing weight. It is the second meeting, and it's 10 minutes into the session.

Leader: Get out your list of things other than food that are reinforcing for you—let's talk about them.

Rhonda: I realize that I do like to read, although I don't do it, and there are three or four TV shows that I like. I also put on my list that I have two friends who live back in Missouri that I would like to call but don't.

Phyllis: Gosh, that's strange. I also put down I have some friends who live in California that I would like to call. The other thing I like to do that would be good for weight control is walking early in the morning. I'll bet I haven't gone for a good walk in the morning for over a year.

Sally: Oh, I'd go with you! I get up early, but I just sit around and watch the news.

Leader: I hope the two of you will talk after the meeting about doing that. How about others? Margie, what about you?

Margie: My list doesn't make sense.

Leader: Do you mean that the activities you listed are strange or that you did not do it exactly right? I'm not sure what you mean.

Margie: Well, I've got things like sleeping, exercising, washing my car, cleaning my house—you know, dumb things like that.

Leader: I don't really see those as dumb. In fact, let's talk more about how you can use your "reinforcer list" to help you. Let me go into a little more theory. . . .

In this example, the leader is both educating by providing information and facilitating interaction by bringing up topics, clarifying comments, and getting members to share.

Discussion Groups

In a discussion group, the focus is usually on topics or issues rather than any member's personal concerns. Its purpose is to give participants the opportunity to share ideas and exchange information. The leader serves mainly as a facilitator because she does not necessarily have more knowledge than the members do about the subject. Following are some possible examples of discussion groups:

- ◆ Book club
- ◆ Current events group
- ◆ Bible studies group
- ◆ Life styles group

◆ EXAMPLES

This group is composed of students discussing "How the Family Is Changing."

Leader: Let's list all the different forms in which families exist in our town. Each of you make a list. *(After a couple of minutes)* In looking at your list, what stands out to you?

Lynn: I never realized how many families aren't just the regular kind—that is, a mom, a dad, and some kids.

Don: You know, I think we need to be more accepting of all these kinds of families.

Hector: I agree, because I'm currently living with just my mom, and I remember that last year I was kidded about it.

Lewis: Yeah, I think there is too much bullying of other kids. How do we stop bullies from having so much power?

Leader: *(Intervening) Wait, let's discuss the different kinds of families today. Maybe some other time we can talk about the bully problem.*

Billy: The thing I wonder about is all those single fathers. What do they know about babies?

Sarah: I saw on TV just the other day a good show about. . . .

The leader's role in this group is to generate discussion on the topic of the changing family. Since it is a discussion group, the leader did not let Lewis shift the focus of the group to dealing with bullies.

It is the monthly meeting of the Reading Club. The book being discussed is titled *Love and Addiction.*

Leader: Let's do a quick round of 1 to 10. If you liked the book a whole lot, give it a 10; a 1 means you did not like it at all.

Leslie: I'd give it a 7.

Ralph: 9.

Steve: 10.

Tuyen: 7.

Cindy: 8.

Lendon: 9.

Fred: 6.

Leader: Since most people did like it, let's talk about what stood out for you. What were two or three points that really hit you?

Steve: There was just so much in there that helped me to understand the crazy relationship I'm currently in. I felt the authors were talking directly to me. I thought it was really interesting the way they described how people get into bad relationships.

Tuyen: It reminded me of the Bible and some of its passages. Don't you think the Bible is good for learning about relationships?

Leader: Let's save that discussion to the end or later. Let's, for now, focus on this book.

Ralph: I thought the description of kinds of relationships was excellent. It really helped me to think through an old relationship that I'd had. On page 27—everyone look at that for a minute. . . .

In this group, the leader used the 1 to 10 ratings to generate discussion. Once the discussion got going, he kept members involved by seeing to it that the discussion was relevant and meaningful. He did not let the discussion shift to the Bible.

Task Groups

The task group is one in which a specific task is to be accomplished, such as discussing a patient on a psychiatric ward, resolving conflicts among house residents, or deciding policies for a school. It is called a *task group* because its purpose is very specific. This kind of group usually meets once or just a few times and ends when the task is completed. Staff meetings, faculty meetings, organizational meetings, planning sessions, or decision-making meetings are examples of task groups. In the field of business, a *focus group* is a kind of task group that is used to evaluate products or perceptions of products. The following list should give you a better idea of task groups:

- Members of a club choosing a slate of officers
- Houseparents deciding rules and policies
- Professionals all involved in the treatment of one student (for example, a counselor, two teachers, a social worker, and a special education coordinator)
- Professionals collaborating on a year-end report
- Citizens wanting to do something about drunk drivers
- Students or teachers talking about ways to curb violence on the playground
- Students or teachers trying to change some policies at their school

The leader's role in a task group is to keep the group on task and to facilitate discussion and interaction. In some task groups, the members stay focused on their own; thus, the leader's role is more facilitative. In other task groups, discussion becomes unfocused or conflict breaks out among members. In such instances, the leader intervenes and then brings the group back to the task.

◆ E X A M P L E S

The purpose of this group is to discuss Oswaldo's living situation. (The child is currently residing in an emergency crisis shelter.) A houseparent, Oswaldo's mother, a social worker, and a counselor have been brought together. The leader of the group is the social worker.

Mother: I want Oswaldo at home! He's my boy, and that's where he should be!

Houseparent: Oswaldo has not been cooperative here, and I don't think he's ready to go home.

Mother: *(In a condescending voice)* I don't care what you think. I think the program here is terrible. He should be allowed to call home whenever he wants. And the policy about visitations should absolutely be changed. Let's talk about that!

Leader: *(Seeing that they're off the task)* Wait a minute. Let's get back to our task, which is deciding whether Oswaldo is ready to go home.

Counselor: I have seen Oswaldo for five sessions, and he's still a very angry kid. My own opinion is he will not do well at home.

Leader: Why don't you elaborate on why you feel that way and what you think would be helpful for Oswaldo?

The purpose of this group is to select one of three applicants to fill a vacant position in a small community agency. To make the decision, the director has brought together her staff of six to discuss the interviews.

Montel: I feel that we need a female, so I think we should hire Sarah.

Sheri: I agree we need another female.

Tom: *(Angrily)* Hold on just a minute! That's a bunch of crap. Why did we interview two guys if we were going to hire a woman? We never said anything about hiring a woman.

Director: *(Recognizing a potentially volatile situation)* Let's talk about what we do need. I think both points are well taken. We never did decide we needed a woman. However, all things being equal, I think hiring a woman would be in our best interest. Let's go over each candidate's strengths and weaknesses.

Filip: I didn't like the fact that Sarah smokes. None of us smoke. In fact, I think we should get the secretary to stop smoking.

Tom: Oh, I agree. Let's do that. Let's make a policy about smoking. *(Turns to the director)* How do we pass such a policy? I would like to make a motion.

Director: *(Realizing that the group is off the intended task)* Wait! We're here to decide on the three candidates. We need to choose one of them. At the next meeting, we can set policies on smoking or whatever. Let's go over each candidate, listing strengths and weaknesses.

In each of these groups, the leader made clear what was the task and kept the group working on the task.

Growth Groups and Experiential Groups

Growth groups consist of members who want to experience being in a group and who have the motivation to learn more about themselves. T-groups, or *training groups,* were the first popular kind of growth group; the first one was held in Bethel, Maine, in 1947. Sensitivity groups, awareness groups, and encounter groups would all be considered growth groups. Corey (1995) discusses structured growth groups in some detail. He describes social competence groups for youngsters, self-esteem groups, anger-control groups, groups that engage in adventurous activities, and many other structured growth groups.

Growth groups are conducted in settings such as schools, colleges, community centers, and retreat centers. In these groups, members are given the opportunity to explore and develop personal goals and better understand themselves and others. The goals include changes in lifestyle, a greater awareness of oneself and others, improved interpersonal communications, and an assessment of values—all accomplished in an atmosphere of sharing and listening. Depending on the specific goal of the group, the leader may need knowledge of a broad range of issues such as parenting, sex, religion, need for approval, etc. In growth groups, quite often considerable counseling will take place as different issues come to the surface.

One form of growth group is the experiential group, in which the leader designs experiential activities for the members. Often these are conducted outdoors and involve physical challenges, risk taking, and cooperation among members. Perhaps the best known is the "ropes course," where members are challenged on a number of activities that involve ropes.

◆ E X A M P L E S

This group is composed of ten teenagers who are out on the ropes course. They have just completed two activities.

Leader: What have you learned so far?

Buz: That fear is more in the mind!

Eden: I agree. I never thought I could do the "Pamper Pole," but when I saw Amiel do it, I thought, "I can do it."

Steve: The group support has been what stood out for me. I was really scared, but everyone kept telling me I could do it. That really helped.

Leader: I want us to talk about the value of group support, but first let me pick up on what Buz is saying about fear often being in the mind.

The purpose of this group is to examine values. (This kind of group could meet in a school, a church, or a community center.)

Leader: Today we are going to take a look at some of the things you value. First, let me have everyone stand up and get in a line behind Serj. *(Everyone is now standing in the center of the room in a straight line, with the leader standing in front where everyone can see him.)* On the count of three, I am going to ask you to move to the position that is most like the way you are. Toward the wall to your left is "spender," and toward the wall to your right is "saver." That is, if any time you have money you spend it, you would move all the way to the wall to your left. If you spend some and save some, you may want to position yourself in the middle, and so on. Everyone understand? *(Everyone nods)* Okay, on three. One, two, three. *(Everyone moves)*

Leader: Any comments?

Doug: I am glad to see I am not the only spender because my mom says I spend, spend, spend.

Toni: I wish I could spend. I always feel like I must save my money. That's why I'm up against this wall. Have you spenders always been able to spend?

Leader: *(After letting several members comment)* The main point of doing this is to see that people are different and to help each of you get a better understanding of why you are the way you are. Let's now talk about why you are the way you are and whether you want to change.

In each of these examples, the leader initiated activities that focused members on relevant self-exploration and personal growth.

Counseling and Therapy Groups

Counseling and therapy groups are different from growth groups in that the members come to the group because of certain problems in their lives. School counselors often lead counseling groups for students who have various problems at home, at school, or with friends. The leader focuses the group on different individuals and problems; then members try to help one another with the leader's guidance. The leader will, at times, play a dominant role in that he directs the session in order to make it more productive.

Therapy groups are for members who have more severe problems. Examples of therapy groups include:

- Patients diagnosed as having emotional disorders
- Teenagers in an institutional setting
- People with an eating disorder or some other addiction
- People who suffer from panic attacks
- People who were sexually abused

It is important to realize that group experts do not agree on how counseling and therapy groups should be conducted. Opinions vary widely on the role of the members, the role of the leader, the appropriate tone, and the use of theory in the group. Some believe that members should be responsible for the majority of the therapy, with supportive probing and encouragement from the leader (Rogers, 1970; Yalom, 1995). Others feel that a confrontive, aggressive approach works best, such as in positive peer culture groups (Vorrath, 1974) or Synanon groups (Casriel, 1963). Some believe that individual therapy by the leader, while the majority of the group observes, is very beneficial (Dyer & Vriend, 1980; Perls, 1969). Some leaders strictly follow one of the theoretical models, such as rational emotive behavior therapy (REBT), transactional analysis (TA), or psychoanalytic theory. Others use none of the individual counseling theories as their theoretical base, but rather believe it is the power of the group interaction—sharing, involvement, and belonging—that serves as the main agent for change (Yalom, 1995).

Our leadership model for counseling and therapy groups is based on impact therapy (Jacobs, 1994), which is an active, creative, multisensory, theory-driven approach to counseling. In our approach, the leader is primarily responsible for making sure that individuals working on issues get the best help possible. The leader will do whatever is most helpful—sometimes using other members' input and sometimes conducting therapy while the other members listen, watch, and periodically share. Later in this chapter and throughout the book, we discuss how to use an impact therapy approach and why this approach is well suited for most group counseling situations.

◆ EXAMPLES

This group consists of five women whose husbands routinely physically abuse them. It is 20 minutes into the second session.

Leader: A number of you have talked about your poor self-concept. Rather than us just talking about self-concept, I'd like for someone to volunteer to work on her self-concept. The rest of us will listen and try to be helpful.

Katelyn: I will because I feel terrible about myself, but I'm sort of scared.

Leader: I think all of us understand your fear. Why don't you start by telling us more about how you felt growing up?

Katelyn: I always felt like a nothing. My parents definitely favored my brother and sister. They even told me that if they'd known I was going to be so much trouble, they would have never had me. (*Starts to cry*)

Jodi: My cousin who lives in Cleveland told me she felt the same way. The other day she told me this story. She said. . . .

Leader: (*With a kind voice*) Jodi, let's stay with Katelyn. How many of you have felt like Katelyn? (*All four raise their hands.*)

Sue Lin: Katelyn, I cried myself to sleep every night, it seemed like, when I was growing up.

Katelyn: You did? So did I. I always felt everything was my fault. . . .

This group consists of five teenagers who all recently attempted suicide. It is 15 minutes into the third session, and the members have been discussing their relationship with their parents.

Carl: At least your parents care! Hell, my old man hasn't been to see me since he brought me here. When he left, he said to me, "I'm done with you!"

Dione: At least you have a dad. My mom has all these men over all the time. I can't stand it.

Leader: (*In a caring tone*) Look, we could sit here and talk about how bad things are, but I am not sure that is the most helpful thing. What do the rest of you think?

Trudy: I think we have to learn to feel good about ourselves no matter what our parents say and do. Like you said last time, we all need to learn how to cope with our feelings.

Leader: Let's focus on the feelings you have about yourself and talk about how you can change your feelings by changing some of the negative "self-talk" that is in your head. I want each of you to think of the negative things you tell yourself throughout the week. I am going to write your thoughts here on the wipeboard and then show you how you tell yourselves all kinds of negative things that are not true.

In the first example, no specific theory was demonstrated, although the leader was most likely thinking in terms of Adlerian, rational emotive behavior therapy, or transactional analysis. In the second example, the leader was using impact therapy and rational emotive behavior therapy to help these teenagers examine their poor self-concept. (If you are a beginning student, you may not be familiar with the approaches mentioned, which is not important at this point.

The crucial thing to note is that the leaders of counseling or therapy groups use some kind of theory and do not just "wing it.")

Support Groups

A support group is composed of members with something in common and meets every day, once a week, once a month, or twice a month. In this type of group, members share thoughts and feelings and help one another examine issues and concerns. According to Corey (1995), the two terms self-help group and *support group* are often used interchangeably. However, in this text we separate the two terms and discuss support groups as groups that are led by a professional like yourself. Support groups enable members to learn that other people struggle with the same problems, feel similar emotions, and think similar thoughts. The following are examples of support groups:

- Victims of a natural disaster, such as a flood or tornado, who share feelings about the loss of loved ones, loss of property, or survivor's guilt
- Elderly people confined to convalescent centers
- Those whose loved ones are dying
- Individuals with a disability coming together to share their feelings and fears
- People with AIDS, Hepatitis C, cancer, herpes, or some other disease
- Stepparents who find it helpful to share the specific difficulties experienced in a stepfamily
- Teenage fathers who are actively involved with their children

The role of the leader in a support group is to encourage sharing among participants. Ideally, the interactions are personal, and members speak directly to one another. It is important for leaders of these groups to keep in mind that sharing is the group's purpose and goal. It cannot be achieved if the leader or any member dominates.

◆ EXAMPLES

This group is composed of members of a community that has recently experienced a disaster: a fire in a local movie theater killed 50 people. Of the ten members present in the group, some were in the theater and managed to escape, and some lost loved ones in the fire. It is 45 minutes into the third session.

Leader: How are you sleeping?

Joe: I'm still not sleeping through the night. I have this anger at God, and I don't know what to do with it.

Sherita: I have the same feeling. I haven't been to church since the fire, and I don't know if I'll ever go back.

Leader: *(Seeing that Bill is shaking his head "no")* Bill, you seem troubled by what Sherita and Joe said.

Bill: *(In a tentative, gentle manner)* Well, I am troubled. I guess my faith in God has been the thing that has pulled me through this. I don't know why it happened, but I guess He had a reason. I wish Sherita and Joe could see their way clear to go back to church.

Leader: Does anyone else want to comment on that?

Jack: A priest gave me a book to read that helped me cope. The main point in the book was that you just have to go on and not ask "why." I guess that book really has helped, and I did sleep last week for the first time.

At this point, the leader's purpose is not to work therapeutically with the members' anger toward God, but rather to facilitate interaction and let people hear how others are coping. Now the leader invites another member into the discussion.

Leader: Zach, what has helped you the most?

Zach: I'm staying busy. I'm back at work, and at night I've made it a point not to be alone, at least in the early evening. I've arranged to eat meals with friends and family. I've also planned weekends well, and I'm making myself do things even though they don't seem to have much meaning. A friend of mine said, "Zach, you've just gotta start living again." He was right!

Joe: You know, hearing you say that is helpful. I think that's what I need to start doing. I guess I haven't really thought about it, but I'm not trying to live in the present; I'm just staying in the past.

Hein: Joe, I hope you'll start living now because it's true for me, too. Just a week or so ago, I started living again, and it really made all the difference. I really do believe that as long as we're here on earth we've got to focus on our life and not on why it was *our* husband or son or loved one who died. *(Pauses and says with pain)* But believe me, it's not easy.

Leader: You know, I do have to agree with Hein and Zach that focusing on the present and future is really the way to go. Does anyone else want to comment?

The leader is doing an excellent job of leading the group by allowing members to share and learn from each other. Notice that the leader is not overly involved in the discussion. Many leaders make the mistake of talking too much, which prevents members from sharing.

This group is composed of eight elderly people living in a convalescent center. It is the third meeting.

Carl: Nobody came to visit me this weekend.

Three members simultaneously: They didn't?

Carl: *(Dejectedly)* They called at the last minute and said something else came up and they weren't going to be able to come.

Claude: That's too bad. I didn't check on you this weekend because I thought you were gone.

Wayne: I wish you had come down to my room. I certainly would have spent time with you.

Bob: We oughta get up a system to check on each other during the weekends. You know, they're the hardest.

Bertha: Boy, that's for sure.

Jim: I guess I'm beginning to count on this group more than on my family.

Claude: You know, I enjoy this group because you all care. It's not that my family doesn't care; it's just that it's a burden for them to come here. Yeah, I do like this group.

Leader: *(Realizing that Leona hasn't talked)* How about you, Leona? Are you feeling better about the group? I know the first couple of times you weren't sure if you were going to like it.

Leona: Oh, I think I like it. We just talk. I guess I was afraid people were going to tell me what to do. It feels good here.

The leader understands that the purpose of this group is to generate member-to-member interaction so that they feel cared for by other members. Because this appears to be happening, he is staying out of the discussion except to draw out comments from quiet individuals or generate discussion if the interaction starts to decline. Eventually the leader may initiate discussion of Bob's suggestion that they develop a system to check on each other during weekends.

This group is composed of eight teenage girls who all are at least 6 months pregnant. It's the second meeting.

Leader: Let's talk about two things today. First, the reaction you're getting from peers and family; second, any decisions you have made regarding keeping the baby or giving it up for adoption.

Julie: Can I start?

Leader: Sure.

Julie: Well, the decision is so hard. I thought I knew for sure that I was going to keep the baby, and then I saw a show on TV about a teenager giving up her baby. Did anyone see that movie?

Paige, Linda, and Rebecca: I did.

Julie: The movie got me thinking about giving up the baby.

Linda: I want to give up the baby, but my mom is like the mom in the movie. She doesn't want me to give it up. She thinks giving up the baby would be a horrible thing to do. *(Turns to leader)* What do you think?

Leader: No doubt the decision is a tough one, especially when your family is putting pressure on you one way or another. I hope that what we can do is take a look at all the forces that come into play in this decision and then try to help each one of you. I hope you realize that although each of you is in the same situation, you must make your own decision. I hope what we do in the group will be helpful and supportive.

Cindy: But what do you do when you have pressure from your mom and dad? They want me to keep the baby, but I really don't want to be reminded of this period of my life. This has been horrible for me. There are lots of people wanting to adopt babies, and I don't want a baby.

Leader: *(Knowing that Cindy is a fairly strong person, she decides to spend a little time with her, believing that the others will benefit)* Cindy, what is the thing you are most afraid of if you give up the baby?

Cindy: I'm afraid of how mad my parents are going to be. Other than that, I see it as a good idea for me. I'm not saying you all should do this.

Leader: Okay, can you deal with your parents being mad at you—and how mad would they be?

Cindy: Well, they would be real mad, and I am not sure if I could handle their anger. I feel so bad when they are mad at me.

Leader: Cindy, I want to help you and everyone understand more about where feelings come from. *(Leader teaches Cindy and the rest of the group that thoughts can cause feelings.)*

This vignette is an example of how one kind of group will sometimes overlap with another kind. Even though some education and counseling is taking place, it is mainly a support group.

Self-Help Groups

The last kind of group we want to discuss is the self-help group, which is now very popular (Corey, 1995; Gladding, 1995). Self-help support groups are groups led by laypeople who have a similar concern as those at the meeting. Alcoholics Anonymous is the most well-known self-help group. Millions feel their lives have been changed by attending AA meetings. Many other self-help groups follow the AA model, using the Twelve Steps. We realize that not everyone is helped by attending these groups, but we do believe that all counselors should be aware of these groups because they have been of tremendous value to so many people throughout the world. Students of ours are required to attend AA meetings as part of a course on addictions. They report that the experience was one of the best learning activities of their entire master's program.

Since these groups have no permanent, professional leader, and the purpose of this text is to improve group leadership, we will not focus on self-help groups.

However, if you are not familiar with these groups, we encourage you to attend some meetings and read about them. The *American Journal of Community Psychology* (1991), in a special edition, has a number of articles on self-help groups. Corey (1995) discusses attitudes toward self-help groups and the differences between self-help groups and therapy groups.

Group versus Individual Counseling

Many people ask us, "Which is better, group counseling or individual counseling?" Sometimes one or the other is best, and sometimes the combination of individual and group counseling produces the most benefit; but this is difficult to answer since people and situations are so different. For most people, groups can be quite valuable. For some people, group counseling is better because members need the input from others, plus they learn more from listening than talking. In many instances with teenagers, group counseling is better than individual counseling because teenagers often will talk more readily with other teenagers than with adults. For those stuck in the grief process, groups have been found to be very valuable (Price, Dinas, Dunn, & Winterowd, 1995).

While there are many advantages to group counseling, it is important to realize that group counseling is not for everyone (Corey, 1995; Yalom, 1995). Administrators often do not understand this and, consequently, force members into groups. Individuals who do not want to be or are not ready to be in a group can disrupt it or be harmed because group pressure may cause them to take some action or self-disclose before they are ready (Gladding, 1996). Another disadvantage of group counseling is that individuals' problems sometimes are not dealt with adequately in a group setting due to constraints of time. When group leaders recognize that a member needs more than group counseling can provide or that the member is going to be disruptive, they should encourage the member to consider the option of individual counseling instead.

Use of Theories

Many of our students have asked us if there are any specific group counseling theories. The answer is no. Although labels have been given to many groups—encounter, T, sensory awareness, here-and-now, psychodrama—these names simply describe what takes place in the groups and are not specific group counseling theories. However, this does not mean that a leader does not use theory when working with growth, support, or counseling/therapy groups. Theories originally developed for individual counseling—such as rational emotive behavior therapy (REBT), transactional analysis (TA), behavioral, Adlerian, or reality therapy—have been successfully adapted for groups.

Throughout this text, and especially in our discussion of counseling and therapy groups, we mention various counseling theories. To cover them in detail is beyond the purpose of this book. If you desire further information about specific theories as they apply to group work, see Corey (1995) or Gladding (1995).

We cannot stress enough the importance of being able to use counseling theory when leading counseling, therapy, or growth groups. Those who do not have a good working knowledge of at least one theoretical perspective often lead a very shallow group; that is, the group never goes below surface interaction and sharing. If the members do become more involved, the leader who does not have a theoretical base is usually overwhelmed. Gladding's position is that "Overall, multiple theoretical models provide richness and diversity for conducting groups" (1996, p. 333).

On the other hand, certain kinds of groups do not require the use of counseling theory. Discussion, education, and task groups require, instead, that the leader possess a variety of basic leadership skills in order to monitor and direct the flow of conversation and interaction.

For human relationships training groups, there are some organization and development theories that may apply. Kormanski (1991) discusses these and presents a strong argument for the use of theory with training groups.

Our Approach to Groups: Impact Therapy

Our approach to groups is based on the principles of *impact therapy*, which is a multisensory approach that recognizes that change or impact comes from not only verbal but also visual and kinesthetic exchanges (Jacobs, 1994). "Impact therapy is an approach to counseling that shows respect for the way clients learn, change, and develop. The emphasis is on making counseling clear, concrete, and thought-provoking, rather than vague, abstract, and emotional" (p. 1). Impact therapy is a theory-driven approach using primarily REBT, TA, Gestalt, Adlerian, and reality therapy, and many creative techniques from *Creative Counseling Techniques: An Illustrated Guide* (Jacobs, 1992). Four core beliefs of impact therapy are:

- People don't mind being led when they are led well.
- Counseling should never be boring.
- Counseling should be clear and concrete.
- The counselor is primarily responsible for the therapy but not ultimately responsible for the outcome.

The impact therapy model gives leaders permission to lead their groups. As we do workshops all over the country, many participants express how relieved and thankful they are to be hearing that it is okay to be active and verbal when leading groups. We believe the counselor should feel in charge and actively lead most groups using theories and techniques that make the sessions interesting and productive.

Group Counseling in a Multicultural Context

More and more counseling programs are emphasizing multicultural counseling—many are also requiring courses on the subject. Certainly in today's society, understanding cultural differences is a must, especially for counselors who are leading groups with diverse populations. Corey (1995) states, "Multicultural group work involves strategies that cultivate understanding and appreciation of diversity in such areas as culture, ethnicity, race, gender, class, religion, and lifestyle" (p. 16).

Since this is a book about an active leadership approach, we want to emphasize that the leader must always consider the different cultural backgrounds of the members. For instance, counselors working with Asian students will need to be aware that they may be quiet at first out of deference to authority figures. Using nonthreatening questions in the beginning may be very helpful (Cheng, 1996). The leader needs to be aware of issues pertaining not only to cultural matters but also to gender, age, and sexual orientation. Ethically, we have an obligation to acquire the knowledge and skills necessary to work in a multicultural context (Corey, 1995; Ibrahim & Arredondo, 1990). Corey discusses in detail group work as it applies to a multicultural population, covering such topics as the need for a multicultural focus, the challenges and rewards of a multicultural perspective, and transcending cultural expectations. Throughout this book, we make numerous references to multicultural issues. If you feel you are not well versed in multicultural issues and counseling considerations, we strongly encourage you to seek out course work, workshops, reading, and life experiences that will broaden your understanding.

Group Leadership Styles

Much has been written regarding leadership style (Capuzzi & Gross, 1991; Johnson & Johnson, 1991; Posthuma,1996). We believe that the style or role of the leader will always depend on the purpose of the group. As Gladding (1995) states, "Most effective group leaders show versatility" (p. 51). However, some people are taught only one style of leadership, regardless of the kind of group they are leading. Many model their group leadership style after the style of a group leader they had in graduate school. This may not be a good idea because the groups in an academic program very often differ greatly from those in a school, rehab, or mental health setting.

The major leadership debate seems to center on how active, directive, and structured the leader should be. Until recently, many group educators hesitated to tell students to be active and directive. A similar situation existed in the 1960s regarding individual counseling, when educators debated the relative merits of directive and nondirective counseling. Now most educators encourage their students to be active and reasonably directive in their individual counseling.

For group counseling, our position is that an active style of leadership works best for most groups. Repeating the core belief from impact therapy, we want to emphasize that *people don't mind being led when they are led well*. The reason is that most members of most groups need some structure, organization, and direction. In fact, most members expect and want the leader to lead. This is especially true in schools, hospitals, prisons, mental health and rehabilitation centers, and with issue-focused groups such as those concerning divorce, abuse, incest, or addiction.

Leader-Directed versus Group-Directed

A related question regarding leadership style is, Should the group be leader-directed or group-directed? Many writers express concern regarding the leader-directed approach (Capuzzi & Gross, 1991; Gladding, 1995; Posthuma, 1996; Starak, 1988). One concern is that the members will have to cater to the leader. The opposite is actually true—good leaders who follow the leader-directed model never demand that the members follow them as if they were gurus; rather, they lead in a manner that is valuable for the members. The leader-directed style of leadership does not mean that the leader is on an ego trip or that the group has to serve the personality of the leader. It simply means that the leader has an understanding of the members' needs and structures the group to meet those needs.

Leaders using the group-directed approach often will turn the group over to the members and have the members determine the direction and content. This can be quite valuable for some groups. However, there are times when this wastes much time, especially for a group that is meeting only once or for only a few sessions. Often the members don't know what they need. For example, parents of teens in a drug treatment center or victims of some kind of disaster often attend a group to find help, but they are not at all clear as to how the group can be helpful. A leader-directed style can be of great benefit by providing structure, thought-provoking questions, and group exercises. The question is not really whether the approach is group-directed or leader-directed, but rather who is primarily responsible for the group—the leader or the members? We believe the leader is responsible for the group. As Trotzer (1989) states:

> Leaders, because of their training and professional commitment, are remiss if they do not exercise their responsibility to prevent negative consequences in the group. Leaders can share responsibility to a very large degree, but they can never abdicate their responsibility. Doing so completely undermines the nature of the helping profession and is detrimental to positive therapeutic intervention. Leaders must be willing to divert topic and conversational trends that seem to be shaping into negative and damaging content (Blaker & Samo, 1973). They must be willing to intervene to protect members and to serve as a reality check if the group does not do so. As Lakin (1969) noted, responsibility must be consciously exercised and modeled by the leader if the group is to qualify as a professional therapeutic venture. (p. 218)

Even though the leader is responsible, the amount of leading will depend on the kind of group and the composition of its members. For certain groups, the leader may primarily want the members to direct the group; for other groups, the leader will want to assume much of the directing. It is important for the leader to remember that the amount of active leading can vary according to the stage of the group. In the middle stage of many kinds of groups, the members are fully aware of how the group should flow and therefore should be actively involved in choosing the topics and the direction.

Interpersonal versus Intrapersonal Leadership Styles

Another way to view leadership style is as a continuum from focusing on the group as a whole to focusing on the individuals in the group (Shapiro, 1978). Corey (1995) states that the *interpersonally oriented* leader "emphasizes the here and now, the interactions among the members, the group as a whole, the ongoing group dynamics, and the obstacles to the development of effective interpersonal relationships within the group" (p. 82). The *intrapersonally oriented* leader focuses primarily on the needs and concerns of the individual members.

Understanding both styles of leadership is very important. Leaders must be able to adapt a style along this continuum, depending on the kind of group, the needs of the members, and the dynamics occurring within the group. You might want to think of the continuum as a 1–10 scale:

Interpersonal									*Intrapersonal*
Focus on group process								Focus on personal issues	

1	2	3	4	5	6	7	8	9	10

When the purpose of the group is to improve relationships among members or to accomplish a task, the leader will probably use an interpersonal leadership style within the 2–5 range. For growth groups, the leadership style will depend on the purpose of the group—some growth groups benefit from a 2–5 range and others benefit from a 6–8 range.

On the continuum, we feel that for most counseling and therapy groups, leaders should use a style that falls between 6 and 8. The intrapersonal model (6–8 on the continuum) is better because members in most of these groups have intrapersonal conflicts they need to deal with. In most therapy groups, the members need to address issues such as unfinished business from the past, problems with parents or lovers, sexual abuse, abandonment, low self-esteem, fear of failure, guilt, shame, or need for approval. The intrapersonal perspective seems better suited for helping clients obtain a better understanding of these issues. The intrapersonally oriented leader will address these issues directly, whereas the interpersonally oriented leader will wait until the issues emerge and then may focus on them only as they apply to the here-and-now experience within the group. For these reasons, we find the interpersonal leadership style somewhat limited.

In using a style ranging from 6 to 8 on the continuum, the leader primarily will encourage members to share with the group their personal issues, concerns, and feelings. Once a member discloses a concern, the leader would use techniques and theories to help the disclosing member. He would involve the other members in many different ways when focusing on a member or an issue. Those leaders operating at a 9 or 10 on the continuum usually only do one-on-one counseling while other members watch (Perls, 1969). Leaders using a style in the 2–4 range focus more on what is happening in the group in the present moment and less on pressing personal issues or the past.

Even though we feel that, for most counseling and therapy groups, a style of 6–8 on the continuum is best, we want to qualify this by saying that *at all times the leader must be flexible.* There will be times when the leader will need to focus on the group dynamics and interaction rather than on an individual's personal problem.

It should also be pointed out that some experts (Carroll, 1986; Rogers, 1970; Yalom, 1995) believe strongly in the interpersonal model (1–3 on the continuum) for counseling and therapy groups. Group leaders who follow this model place strong emphasis on the stages of the group and on the members being the primary agents of change.

Another important point is that for some groups the leadership continuum will be of little importance. For instance, leaders of education and discussion groups will primarily use various leadership skills and techniques to generate discussion and not be concerned about the group having either an interpersonal or intrapersonal focus.

Leadership Functions

Another way to view leadership style is to consider leadership functions. Yalom (1995) states that the leader may provide emotional stimulation, caring, praise, protection, acceptance, interpretations, and explanations. The leader also may serve as a model through self-disclosure and as a person who sets limits, enforces rules, and manages the time. In other words, depending on the kind of group, the leader may perform many different roles and functions.

Gladding (1995) writes, "There are both *content* and *process* functions that the leader must address throughout the life of the group" (p. 65). *Content* is defined as the task or purpose of the group, and *process* is defined as the relationship between members and how members participate in the group (Hulse-Killacky, Schumacher, & Kraus, 1996). (The terms *group dynamic* and *group process* are used interchangeably throughout the book since they mean basically the same thing.) In discussing process and content, Hulse-Killacky et al. point out that the terms are mutually interactive, and attention must be paid to both because exclusive focus on content eliminates any focus on important process material, and too much focus on process can blur the purpose of the group and leave members frustrated. The following list of different groups and possible leadership behaviors may clarify this point. (We also discuss the balancing of process and content in the next chapter and throughout the entire book because it is such a major concept.)

♦ In a group of elementary school children who fight with each other, the leader would want to focus more on process than content. The leader may want to use structured exercises to help the children talk about the fighting and ways of preventing it.

♦ In a task group for assigning work duties in a residential treatment setting, the leader would want to focus on both the content and the process of how the decisions are being made. The leader would also set some limits and enforce certain rules.

♦ In a group of angry adults who are meeting to deal with racial issues in the community, the leader would want to facilitate members' sharing, focusing both on content and process. The leader would pay particular attention to the process to make sure that the tension does not escalate. Also, the leader would want to be aware of the multicultural issues that may be present.

♦ In a group of adult children of alcoholics who feel they are still affected by growing up in an alcoholic family, the leader would want to focus on content because ACOAs have many issues. The leader could use group exercises to help members recognize and experience some well-hidden but intense feelings. In addition, the leader might model self-disclosure if he or she grew up in an alcoholic home. Also, the leader would want to pay attention to process since talking about the family may be difficult because the ACOAs may have grown up with the "don't tell family secrets" mandate.

What Makes an Effective Leader?

Numerous writers have described what makes an effective counselor and group leader (Cavanaugh, 1990; Corey, 1996; Egan, 1994; Gladding, 1996; Hackney & Cormier, 1994). Among the characteristics discussed are caring, openness, flexibility, warmth, objectivity, trustworthiness, honesty, strength, patience, and sensitivity. Each of these characteristics is important, and we suggest you refer to the works cited or to any other beginning counseling text if you desire further clarification of ideal helper characteristics.

Additional leadership characteristics include comfort with oneself and others; a liking of people; comfort in a position of authority; confidence in one's ability to lead; and the ability to tune in to others' feelings, reactions, moods, and words. Another very important characteristic of an effective leader is sound psychological health. Leading is so demanding that personal issues are likely to surface if they have never been resolved. Corey (1995) and Yalom (1995) both strongly suggest that leaders be actively involved in their own personal growth.

Leading groups successfully requires a great deal from the leader. Often people lead groups when they simply do not possess the necessary leadership characteristics. Aside from those already mentioned, six other traits warrant further discussion.

Experience with individuals Effective leaders have spent considerable time talking with all kinds of people, not just those like themselves. The broader the leader's range of life experiences, the greater the chances for understanding the diverse members of a group. More and more groups have a multicultural membership for which the leader should be prepared (Corey, 1995; Newlon & Arciniega, 1992).

The effective counseling or therapy group leader has not only general experience with people but also considerable experience in one-to-one counseling. This is necessary because all types of situations arise while leading these groups, and the more experience the leader has working with individuals, the easier it will be to work with an individual and the group simultaneously. Without individual counseling experience, one would very likely find leading counseling and therapy groups very difficult.

Experience with groups In the development of any skill, practice and experience increase one's effectiveness. Beginning leaders can learn from their mistakes with each group experience and should not be overly self-critical. When possible, it is advisable to begin by leading education, discussion, support, or task groups and restricting the number of members to four or five. Once comfortable, beginning leaders can increase the number of members or try a growth group centered on topics familiar to them. When novice leaders feel they can comfortably facilitate growth groups, they might try co-leading several counseling or therapy groups before leading one on their own.

Planning and organizational skills Effective leaders are good planners. They can plan a session or a series of sessions in such a way that the group is interesting, beneficial, and personally valuable. When leading discussion, education, task, or growth groups, effective leaders give considerable thought to relevant topics and to activities and exercises that pertain to those topics. Effective leaders organize sessions in such a way that the topics are covered and there is a flow from topic to topic. Because planning is essential to effective leading, we devote all of Chapter Four to it.

Knowledge of the topic In almost any kind of group, the leader who is well informed will naturally do a better job of leading than the one who lacks information. The leader can use information to stimulate discussion, clarify issues, and share ideas. Unfortunately, too often leaders are asked to lead groups on topics about which they have very little knowledge or understanding.

A good understanding of basic human conflicts and dilemmas A group leader must be prepared to deal with a number of human problems and multicultural issues (Corey, 1995; Newlon & Arciniega, 1992). This is especially true in growth, counseling, and therapy groups in which issues such as guilt, fear of failure, self-worth, parents, anger, love relationships, and death often emerge. Effective leaders have an understanding of these issues and know several ways to help those who are struggling with them.

A good understanding of counseling theory Even though we discussed this earlier, we feel that it is important enough to briefly comment again on the importance of knowing a theory. Knowledge of counseling theory is the key to understanding people and the world in which we live. Theories of therapy—such as rational emotive behavior therapy, transactional analysis, reality therapy, Adlerian, and behavioral therapy—help counselors understand why people do what they do in their lives and in groups. Theories offer group leaders a variety of ways to comprehend what people are saying and doing. Corey and Corey (1992) state, "Group leaders without any theory behind their interventions will probably find that their groups never reach a productive stage" (p. 7). If you do not feel you have a good working knowledge of the various counseling theories, seek out workshops and books that relate to the theories. Study a few of the theories until you master them and feel confident in their application.

Potential Group Problems

So far, we have discussed basic issues that pertain to the general field of group work. To give you an idea of some of the challenges that arise when leading groups, we have compiled a partial list. Some of these challenges occur in certain kinds of groups; others, in all kinds of groups. This list of problematic member behaviors and situations further illustrates the need for learning effective leadership skills. Group members might do any of the following:

- Skip from topic to topic
- Try to dominate the discussion
- Be "chit-chatty" rather than personal and focused
- Attend sporadically
- Be shy and withdrawn
- Get angry at the leader
- Get angry at each other
- Try to force others to speak
- Try to preach morals and religion to the group
- Be resistant because of forced attendance
- Dislike other members
- Stop attending the group

As you can see, leaders must be able to deal with all kinds of members and situations. In the remainder of this book, we teach ways of approaching not only these situations, but many more.

Concluding Comments

Counselors, psychologists, social workers, ministers, and others who work with people should learn to lead groups. The advantages of group work include efficiency, more viewpoints, belonging, feedback, vicarious learning, and practicing in a setting that is close to real life. There are seven kinds of groups: education, discussion, task, support, growth, counseling/therapy, and self-help. It is important for leaders to identify what kind of group they are leading so that the purpose is clear. There are many approaches to leading groups but no actual theories. Understanding leadership style is very important. It is essential to understand the difference between an interpersonal and intrapersonal group leadership style. A leader should be flexible because different kinds of groups have different purposes and require that leaders adjust their style accordingly. Our approach to group counseling is based on the impact therapy approach to counseling, which is an active, multisensory, theory-driven approach. We concluded with a portrait of the effective leader and a list of difficult situations that typically arise in groups. Throughout the book, many of the topics covered in this chapter will be elaborated on, so if you are feeling overwhelmed by the material, relax and enjoy the rest of the book. By the end, you will have a good understanding of kinds of groups, leadership styles, and group leadership skills and techniques.

CHAPTER TWO

Stages of Groups, Group Process, and Therapeutic Forces

In the literature on group counseling, three aspects are frequently addressed: stages of group, group dynamics or group process, and therapeutic forces. In this text, we use the terms *group process* and *group dynamics* to refer to the attitudes and interaction of group members and leaders. Writers sometimes define these terms differently, but all agree that they are similar. We agree with Posthuma (1996), who states, "Because of this concurrent, intimate, and ongoing relationship between the two, the two terms can be used interchangeably to mean the same thing" (p. 7). *Therapeutic forces* are the factors that influence the group dynamics. In this chapter, we discuss the importance of understanding each of these aspects of group counseling and how they are interrelated.

Stages of Groups

Much has been written regarding the stages of groups, the characteristics of each stage, and how much time each stage takes (Corey, 1995; Gladding, 1995; Maples, 1988). If you are observing group interactions and want to study the development of the group, reading the literature on stages of groups will be quite valuable. However, some of the literature can become confusing when the more detailed description of stages is applied to certain groups, such as discussion, education, or task groups; our description of stages applies to any kind of group.

All groups go through three stages, regardless of the type of group or style of leadership: the *beginning stage*, the *middle* or *working stage*, and the *ending* or *closing stage*. Whether a group meets for 1 session or 15 sessions, it will go through these stages, and it is important that the leader attend to each.

The Beginning Stage

By *beginning stage*, we mean the time period used for introductions and for discussions of such topics as the purpose of the group, what may happen, fears, ground rules, comfort levels, and the content of the group. In this stage, members are checking out other members and assessing their own level of comfort with sharing in the group. For some groups, such as certain task, education, and discussion groups, whose topics or agendas have not been predetermined, this is the period when the members determine the focus of the group.

The beginning stage may last part of the first session, the entire first session, or the first couple of sessions. It is not uncommon for the members of certain groups to take more than two sessions to feel enough trust and comfort to share beyond the surface level. For instance, in groups in a prison or residential treatment center for teenagers, it may take as many as three sessions to develop an atmosphere that lends itself to productive group work. For groups in a residential setting, "agendas" between members must sometimes be worked through before the group can proceed to the working stage. For groups with a culturally diverse membership, the beginning stage may need to last a couple of sessions or even longer since members may initially be very uncomfortable and awkward sharing in front of others.

For some groups, the beginning stage lasts only a few minutes because the purpose is clear and the trust and comfort levels are high to begin with. For example, members who meet to share feelings about a recent suicide, death, or disaster can move through the beginning stage in just a few minutes if the leader structures the group so members can share their feelings. We have seen leaders spend far too long on this stage, conducting icebreakers and talking about ground rules and the purpose of the group. A leader who provides very little structure tends to create a group that stays in the beginning stage for several sessions, creating dynamics that could be avoided. On the other hand, we have seen leaders move too quickly into the working stage, causing members to feel uncomfortable and even angry. Chapter Five is devoted to the beginning stage of groups.

The Working Stage

The *middle* or *working stage* is the stage of the group when the members focus on the purpose. In this stage, members learn new material, thoroughly discuss various topics, complete tasks, or engage in personal sharing and therapeutic work. This stage is the core of the group process; it is the period when members benefit from being in a group.

During this stage, many different dynamics can occur because the members are interacting in several different ways. The leader will want to pay particular attention to the interaction patterns and attitudes of the members toward each other and the leader. This is the time when members decide how much they want to get involved or share. If multicultural issues exist in the group, the leader will want to pay close attention to group dynamics since the members may be acting and reacting in very different ways that can be misunderstood by others in the group. This stage is discussed in greater detail in Chapter Twelve.

The Closing Stage

The *closing* or *ending stage* is devoted to ending the group. During this period, members share what they have learned, how they have changed, and how they plan to use what they have learned. Members also say good-bye and deal with the ending of the group. For some groups, the ending will be an emotional experience, while for others the closing will simply mean that the group has done what it was supposed to. The length of the closing stage will depend on the kind of group, the length of time it has been meeting, and its development. Most groups will need only one session for this stage. The closing of groups is covered in great detail in Chapter Fourteen.

Additional Stages

Certain groups will go through more stages because of the kind of group or the style of the leader. Most of the literature describing numerous stages of group process has been written about groups in which the leader is mainly using the interpersonal, facilitator model (Gladding, 1995; Yalom 1995). One such stage has been called the *storming stage*, which occurs when there is tension in the group due to the nature of the group, the members' attitudes, and/or the ability of the leader. Gladding (1995) describes this stage in the following manner: "Storming is a time of conflict and anxiety. . . . Group members and leaders struggle with issues related to structure, direction, control, catharsis, and interpersonal relationships (Hershenson & Power, 1987; Maples, 1988)" (p. 104).

Although we recognize that some groups will go through a storming stage, we believe that certain leadership models may create this stage when it is not necessary. Groups will often go through a storming stage when the leader does not actively lead or does a poor job of leading. Leaders who use an active, creative approach to groups usually do not create a storming stage. Skilled leaders will curtail many of these occurrences because they will be trying to ensure that the members clearly understand the purpose of the group, and they make the group a valuable experience by making the sessions relevant, interesting, and meaningful. In certain kinds of groups, however, particularly task groups, there will be times when storming is a necessary stage—especially when the group is one where there is a mixture of powerful personalities and some disagreement as to how things should be done.

Corey (1995) discusses the *transition stage* as separate from the working stage. According to Corey, this is the period when the beginning stage is over, but members are not yet ready to share on a highly personal level. Members contribute and interact, but they are still checking things out. Many counseling, therapy, support, and growth groups may go through a transition stage. When it does occur, it is good for a leader to recognize it and refrain from pushing the group ahead too quickly, thereby causing discomfort.

Group Process

Group process refers to the interaction and energy exchange between members and leaders—how the leader reacts to the members, and how the members talk to each other and the leader. Group process has been studied by sociologists, social psychologists, therapists, and researchers. Our discussion here will focus on group dynamics as they relate to the kind of groups we outlined in Chapter One. If you are interested in a discussion of the sociological view of group dynamics and a brief history of the study of group dynamics, see Johnson and Johnson (1997); they discuss the contributions that Kurt Lewin made in this area.

Dynamics of Interaction Patterns

One of the most important group dynamics to observe is who talks to whom and how often each member speaks. It is not unusual in the beginning stage of a group for a couple of members to try to dominate. If this occurs, the leader should alter the pattern by using cutting-off and drawing-out skills discussed in Chapter Eight. Sometimes members will fall into the habit of talking only to the leader or selected members instead of to the entire group. The leader will usually want to change this dynamic and get members to address the entire group because otherwise it will not lead to group cohesion.

Silent members may or may not create negative group dynamics. In most groups, participation of all members is desirable. When a member is almost totally silent, some of the others usually become uncomfortable, especially if this pattern continues for several weeks and the group is a counseling, therapy, or support group. In certain education, discussion, and task groups, the silent member may not produce a negative dynamic because in these groups the members are not usually as sensitive to the silence. We discuss dealing with silence and silent members in Chapters Eight and Fifteen.

Another pattern the leader should watch out for is that of one member speaking, followed by the leader, then a second member, then the leader, then a third member, then the leader—rather than member-to-member interaction. The leader should avoid establishing a pattern of responding after each member's comment. Also, group dynamics may be affected by members' expectations if some members have been in a group before. If members have been in other groups, it is always a good idea to get some sense of how their groups had been conducted since they may expect the current group to be the same as their previous one. The leader should also be aware at all times of any cultural or gender issues that may be affecting group dynamics.

◆ E X A M P L E

Sam: I like my mother, but I don't feel close to her.
Leader: I hope that gets better for you.

Bill: My mom and I fight all the time. I can't talk to her about anything.

Leader: So it is hard for you to talk to her.

Nan: I feel that my mom favors my brother but she won't admit it. We have a terrible relationship.

Leader: So you feel hurt by your mom's favoritism.

This leader has made the mistake of responding to each member's comment. A more skilled leader would have let more members comment before commenting herself.

Other patterns that the leader wants to look for include the following:

*   Members "ganging up" on other members
*   Members arguing with each other
*   Members discounting each other's suggestions
*   Members presenting problems and others trying to rescue
*   Members presenting a problem and the rest of the group giving advice (It is important for the leader to realize that groups are not advice-giving sessions.)

◆ EXAMPLE

Larry: . . . so I don't know whether to call her or not.

Steve: I don't think you should call her for at least a week.

Nancy: I don't know. I think you could wait a week and then send her a nice card.

Sandy: Why not a funny card?

Craig: I personally think you should let her make the next move. Let me tell you what happened to me. . . .

In this example, the members are giving advice from their own frame of reference, which is probably not helpful. Sometimes advice and suggestions are beneficial, but often leaders mistakenly let the group turn into an advice-giving session. In this example, the leader would want to intervene and redirect the discussion.

Group Dynamics of Different Kinds of Groups

Any discussion of group dynamics has to take into consideration the kind of group and the style of leadership. If the leader does not play an active role, usually someone in the group will try to take the leadership role. Even with an active leader there can be a bid for power by one or more members. Members may challenge the leader's authority or competency. Throughout the book, we discuss skills for handling these dynamics if they arise. In this section, we discuss dynamics unique to the seven kinds of groups described in Chapter One.

Education Groups

In an education group, the leader usually is presenting some information. Although the members will probably interact with each other, this is not the most important dynamic. Often, those attending education groups are eager to learn the material being presented. In some education groups, however, the members are not interested in the topic because they have been forced to attend, such as those attending a DUI (driving under the influence) group. In these groups, if the leader does not plan well or is not energetic, the group more than likely will not go well.

The dynamics for an education group become difficult when members are at different levels of understanding regarding the subject matter or when some are much more comfortable with the topic than others. A good example would be in dealing with the topic of sex. The leader of a sex-education group must be aware that some members will be more open and comfortable than others. In a group with a diverse population, multicultural issues may create some powerful group dynamics. It is important for the leader to observe how the members are relating to the material and devote extra time if necessary to process any cultural issues.

Education groups usually will not go through long beginning or closing stages. The leader does, however, have to plan for these stages. Although this may seem obvious, we have observed beginning leaders who pay no attention to group process in their planning. The middle stage of an education group will include delivery of the content and discussion of the material. As members get to know each other, they will usually become more comfortable and willing to share their reactions, questions, and feelings. The closing stage of an education group usually includes a summary of the material covered and sometimes questions and reactions to the information.

Discussion Groups

Discussion group leaders will mainly want to be aware of any member who tries to dominate or distract the group. Leaders also want to pay attention to how comfortable members are in sharing because if many are not comfortable, only a few members will be contributing and a good discussion will not occur. Discussion groups are often led in conjunction with a workshop or class and are therefore one-time experiences that last anywhere from 15 minutes to an hour. The tone set at the beginning of a discussion group is usually crucial—the leader should try to set a positive, upbeat, interactive tone. If possible, the leader should try to get everyone to share something in the first few minutes. This gets members involved and gives the leader an idea of each member's energy for the topic. The closing usually will consist of a summary of what was said.

Task Groups

In a task group, the ways in which members interact may be the most important dynamic to monitor. This is especially true if the leader's task is one of team building. Often, task groups accomplish nothing because the members cannot get along well enough to work together. If this is the case, the leader must do some conflict resolution work or team building before getting to the task of the group. The leader will also want to be aware of the formation of cliques and plays for power and control.

Johnson and Johnson (1997) discuss core activities that leaders can use to assess effectiveness of the task group: (1) accomplishing its goals, (2) maintaining itself internally, and (3) developing and changing in ways that improve its effectiveness. Observing these dynamics is excellent for the leader of task groups. As Johnson and Johnson state, "A successful group has the quality and kind of interaction among members that integrate these three core activities" (p. 8).

The beginning stage of task groups is often brief. Usually, the task is clarified during this stage. Most of the group's time is spent in the middle stage—working on the task. The closing stage of a task group can be very brief, sometimes coinciding with accomplishment of the task. However, some task groups will require a longer closing stage.

Growth and Experiential Groups

This kind of group varies greatly. In groups whose purpose is values clarification or self-exploration, the most important dynamic would be how the members feel about one another since they will be sharing their thoughts and feelings. Also, members might become jealous of other members' growth or become angry with the leader and blame him or her for what they are learning about themselves.

In some growth and experiential groups, individual members' needs and expectations can vary so widely that negative forces are created. If this occurs, the leader will want to focus on issues and concerns that are relevant to the majority of the members. The leader will also want to look for members who are not appropriate for the group—those who would be better served in some other group experience or individual counseling.

In some experiential groups where the purpose is team building and cooperative interaction, struggles for leadership can occur. Also, members may form factions or cliques that create antitherapeutic forces. Competition among members may arise and can be a detrimental dynamic. If these dynamics occur, the leader may want to talk to members privately or bring it up in the group. This will depend on the dynamics, the intensity, and the purpose of the group. When conducting group exercises, sometimes members will angrily turn on other members or the leader as a result of frustration with the activity.

The beginning stage of a growth or experiential group will usually last only one or two sessions because the leader will probably engage the members in some activities during one or both of these sessions. Most members will become more comfortable as the group progresses, and the working stage will be reached fairly quickly. The closing stage will last no more than one session and will usually consist of people sharing what they have learned about themselves and how they have grown.

Support Groups

In this kind of group, the leader wants to create a safe environment where members can share. The leader also wants to make sure that members feel they have opportunities to share their ideas and concerns with the group. The leader should make sure that one member does not dominate. Trust, commitment, and genuine caring among members are important dynamics for this kind of group. When members do not trust one another or there are members who are at odds with each other, the support group will not be effective. If these dynamics occur, they must be worked through for the group to succeed. This may be done privately or in front of the group—depending on the nature of the problem.

One other dynamic that is important to watch for is lack of commonality. For instance, a leader might form a group to help students who recently moved to the area and are new to the school. Most of the members would welcome the support, but a member who is new to the school because he could not get along in his other school and was forced to come to the new school would probably not be a good member of a support group. A member who is new to the school because he is just returning from a 1-year drug treatment facility may not be good for a support group—his needs may be too great, and individual counseling plus a counseling group or a group for recovering students may be best. For a support group to work, members must feel a common bond.

The beginning stage of a support group usually will last one to three sessions. During this stage, the sharing is usually not as personal as in the middle stage, when sharing is more intimate and caring is greater because the members now know each other. The closing of a support group can be an emotional experience for its members. Some may even feel frightened by the loss of the group as a support system. Because of this, the leader will want to allow plenty of time for terminating the group—maybe as much as two entire sessions.

Counseling and Therapy Groups

In counseling and therapy groups, the leader must be keenly aware of how members feel about each other and the leader. Members may resent others for being too quiet, too open, or too "together." Because members of these groups vary in their degree of mental health, the chances for complex dynamics are far greater than in any other group discussed. To prevent the occurrence of some of the complex dynamics, we advocate screening through individual interviews of potential members whenever possible. (We discuss screening in Chapters Four and Thirteen.)

Some leaders mistakenly ignore the dynamics and lead the group as if everyone were comfortable with everyone else. This often results in a boring, superficial group whose members are not willing to share personally due to their lack of trust in other members, the leader, or both. Also, one negative or hostile member can create impossible dynamics unless the leader does something to neutralize the effect of the acting out member. This can be done privately, which is usually best, or in the group if the leader sees value in this kind of intervention.

Much skill, knowledge, and courage are needed to lead an effective counseling or therapy group. Because members are dealing with personal issues, attacks on the leader are not uncommon. Unfortunately, sometimes the attacks are warranted because the leader does not have the knowledge or skills necessary to lead the group but is doing so because it is part of the job. As we say throughout the book, *leaders should not lead groups they are not trained to lead!*

The beginning stage of a counseling or therapy group can last one, two, or three sessions. Although some therapeutic discussion or work will probably be done during these sessions, the members usually will still be warming up to the idea of sharing their problems with others. Depending on the members, the counseling/therapy group may go through a transition stage where members are sharing but still not going into real personal issues. The leader will want to be aware of these dynamics so that he does not push too much for sharing that is beyond the comfort level of the members; at the same time, the leader will want to make sure the group is having productive sessions.

During the working stage, the leader will want to be aware that some members may be uncomfortable because watching others work gets them in touch with the pain they are trying to avoid. The leader will want to try to make the group safe but also not so comfortable that members only bring up superficial concerns. Members also have the tendency to draw attention to other members' issues as a way to avoid focusing on themselves.

The closing stage usually lasts one session, although there may be occasions when the leader sees a need to allow more time. The leader should pay careful attention to members' feelings about ending the group, especially if being in the group has been a very emotional, supportive experience for some members.

Self-Help Groups

Many different dynamics can occur in self-help groups, and without a leader to resolve these dynamics, some groups will not be productive and can even be harmful. We strongly believe in the self-help group and feel that generally these groups are very helpful and supportive. However, we recognize that usually few restrictions exist in these groups and that all kinds of dynamics can arise among the members as a result. If you are involved in setting up self-help groups, you should be aware of several dynamics. Members may attack each other or may try to take over the group. Cliques often form, causing other members to feel excluded. Members may need individual therapy in addition to or instead of a self-help group.

Once self-help groups have been formed, they are usually ongoing, with new members coming and others leaving constantly. There is no trained leader in self-help groups. If you are in charge of establishing a self-help group, you may want to attend the first couple of meetings to ensure that they get off to a good start. We suggest that you then drop in periodically to see if the group is being productive. Sometimes the groups have strayed far from their intended purpose and need to be redirected.

Therapeutic Forces

It is important for leaders to realize that they must attend to much more than just the verbal exchange among members. Hansen, Warner, and Smith (1980) describe the "group dynamicist" as a person who closely observes the "potent group currents" that influence the members. Some of these currents are lack of trust, lack of commitment, power plays, conflicts between members, strong alliances between members, and attention-seeking behaviors. Awareness of these forces is essential for good leading. Ohlsen, Horne, and Lawe (1988) describe a number of the forces present in almost any group situation. Members want to (1) feel accepted by the group, (2) know what is expected, (3) feel they belong, and (4) feel safe. When these forces are absent, members tend to be negative, hostile, withdrawn, or apathetic. Negative forces create dynamics that require the leader's attention.

The leader can tune in to some of the group dynamics and therapeutic forces by considering the following questions:

How does each member feel about being in the group?
Do the members seem to know what is expected in the group?
Is each member clear about why he or she is in the group?
How does each member deal with being in the group?
Do the members seem to like one another?
Do the members seem comfortable with one another?
Do the members have a sense of belonging to the group?
Do the members seem comfortable with the leader?
Are there any power plays for the leadership role?

The answers to these questions can be very helpful in understanding how members are feeling about the group and the leader.

Yalom (1995) discusses therapeutic forces in terms of *curative factors* operating in groups. He cites a number of different factors, including altruism (giving to other members), catharsis (releasing feelings and emotions), identification (modeling after members or leader), family reenactment (feeling as if one is in a family and learning from the experience), and instillation of hope (feeling hopeful about one's life). Yalom's factors are especially helpful when looking at therapeutic forces in support, counseling, and therapy groups. If all these curative factors are operating in a group, the group more than likely is helpful to the members. On the other hand, if many of these are not operating, the group may be only minimally beneficial.

Following are descriptions of 16 forces that we feel the leader should attend to. These forces can be either positive (therapeutic), neutral, or negative (antitherapeutic). Groups that are not successful will have one or more antitherapeutic forces operating. As a way to understand this, think of any group you have ever led or been a member of; then go through the 16 therapeutic forces, considering if the force was positive, neutral, or negative for that group. You will find that if the group was successful, most of the forces were positive or neutral. If the group was not successful, one or more of the forces were negative. We say "one or more" because sometimes a single antitherapeutic force can destroy a group. The 16 forces are as follows:

1. Clarity of purpose for both the leader and the members
2. Relevance of purpose for the members
3. Size of the group
4. Length of each session
5. Frequency of meetings
6. Adequacy of the setting
7. Time of day for both the leader and the members
8. The leader's attitude
9. Closed or open group
10. Voluntary or nonvoluntary membership
11. Members' level of goodwill
12. Members' level of commitment
13. Level of trust among members
14. Members' attitudes towards the leader
15. The leader's attitude toward the members
16. The leader's experience and readiness to deal with groups

Clarity of Purpose

Probably the single most important therapeutic force is clarity of purpose; that is, the leader and the members clearly understand the purpose of the group. In unsuccessful groups, the leader often is unclear as to the purpose and thus confuses the members. For instance, a leader might say the group is educational but spends most of the time doing therapy, or the leader might say the group is for support but spends the majority of the time focusing on one person or on one topic that is not relevant for most of the members. Unfortunately, members are often not sure what the purpose is. It is important that the leader always makes sure that everyone clearly understands the purpose of the group. Much of Chapter Three deals with clarity of purpose.

Relevance of Purpose

Not only should the members and leaders be clear regarding the purpose, but the purpose must be relevant for the members. An antitherapeutic force is created when the leader establishes a group that has little or no interest for the members. Leaders of mandatory groups such as DUI (driving under the influence), prison, or dropout prevention groups often have to be creative to make the group relevant for the members because the members do not come to the group believing it will have any relevance to their lives. It is the leader's responsibility to show the members that the group is in fact relevant for them. This is no easy task! The same is true for groups made up of students who want to drop out of school or who are troublemakers—making the group interesting enough so that the members find it relevant is a very challenging and sometimes almost impossible task. If you have to lead these groups, try hard to tune into the members' needs and try to turn this antitherapeutic force into a positive one.

Group Size

Group size can definitely affect group dynamics, so the leader should pay much attention to the decision of how many members to have in the group. The size of the group will depend in part on its purpose, the length of time of each session, the setting available, and the experience of the leader. We suggest 5 to 8 as the ideal number of members for most groups. For multicultural groups, the leader and members may be more comfortable with groups of no more than 5. If the group is going to be 1 hour or less, the leader will want to keep the group relatively small (no more than 6), unless it is an education group. Education groups usually have from 5 to 15 members; discussion groups usually have from 5 to 8. Ideally, personal growth, support, and counseling/therapy groups have from 5 to 8 members, although there can be as few as 3 and as many as 12.

The size of the group can definitely be antitherapeutic. If the group is too large, members very often will hesitate to share or will not have time to share. Leaders form large groups out of necessity without realizing that an antitherapeutic force is being created. Groups that are too small can cause members to feel too much pressure to participate, creating an equally negative force. On the other hand, some small groups (2 or 3 members) with a specific focus, such as members who attempted suicide or members who had been raped, can sometimes be quite valuable.

Length of Each Session

For members to feel invested in the group and in one another, enough time must be allotted for each session. If a group session is not long enough, members may feel they did not get their chance to share. Another problem that arises when insufficient time is allowed is that the group never really accomplishes much and the sharing never gets very personal.

For education, discussion, and task groups, the usual session lasts from 1 to 2 hours; it can be longer in certain instances. Counseling groups in schools usually last one period, which is 40–50 minutes. For groups composed of children, the length of time may be much shorter; 30 to 45 minutes is usually a good length for younger children. For therapy, support, and growth groups, at least an hour and a half—usually not longer than 3 hours—is advisable. However, there may be times when the leader and members decide to meet for a more extended period—5 or 6 hours, or for as long as an entire weekend.

Frequency of Meetings

The number of meetings per month will depend on many different factors, especially the purpose of the group and the composition of the members. Groups in residential settings often meet daily or two to three times a week. Most outpatient groups meet once a week or once every 2 weeks. Support groups usually meet once or twice a month. The key to the frequency of meetings is that they not be so frequent that they become boring and not so infrequent that each meeting is like a first session. A leader should pay attention to the effect of the interval between sessions and, if possible, adjust the frequency so that it is a positive rather than negative force.

Adequacy of the Setting

There are a number of things to consider regarding where the group meets. One is convenience. Members will tend to come regularly if the location is easily accessible. Of course, the choice of location is not always within the leader's control, but when it is, the convenience factor should be weighed.

Another consideration is the privacy of the meeting room. Ideally, the group will meet in a room that is closed to any other traffic during the meeting time. Sometimes, especially in schools and some institutions, this is not possible. When faced with an inadequate setting, the leader must do as much as possible to ensure privacy, recognizing that an antitherapeutic force is operating. The leader should also continue impressing upon the administration the importance of having a private room for group work.

Other things the leader needs to consider about the setting are whether the room is comfortable, what the wall decorations are like, what the lighting is like, and whether the seating arrangements and chairs are comfortable. Any of these can affect the therapeutic forces.

The relative size of the chairs also must be considered. It is best when they are approximately the same size, especially in a counseling/therapy group, since members sitting at various heights may create a negative group dynamic. An option in such a case is to have everyone sit on the floor. The leader would only want to do this if there were a comfortable carpet to sit on and if the members agreed. More than likely, a leader would not use the floor for education, discussion, or task groups. In most group situations, it is best that the chairs not be lounge chairs because members tend to simply relax and not get involved in the process. Another consideration is whether to use tables. In most cases, it is better not to because tables tend to serve as barriers between members. But there will be times when the leader may want to have tables, particularly in certain education and task groups.

Once these details are taken care of, the leader still has some other factors to consider. Usually the best seating arrangement is a circle so that all members can see each other. The leader will want to be careful that some people are not blocked by others who are sitting up slightly. If this occurs, the leader can simply ask them to move back so that no one feels excluded. A tighter circle often creates a more intimate feeling, and members may tend to share more.

Time of Day

The time the group meets can be a negative force; if the group meets right after lunch or late in the day, the leader and the members may be tired. When setting up a group, the leader should choose a time that seems best for the majority of those involved. This may seem like a simple matter, but often leaders find themselves leading a group in which the members have little energy because of the meeting time.

The Leader's Attitude

The leader's feelings about leading a group definitely affect how the group will go. If the leader has a positive attitude, a positive force is created. On the other hand, an antitherapeutic force is created by the leader who dreads going to group. Too often this is the case with leaders who have hectic schedules or are required to lead many groups in a given week.

Closed or Open Groups

An important decision for the leader is whether the membership will be *open* or *closed*. Many groups are conducted as closed groups—that is, no new members are admitted once the group is established. Closed groups can be time limited and goal oriented. Groups are also conducted on an open basis—members join and leave periodically. The purpose of the group and the population being served usually dictate the leader's choice. In most cases—especially for support and counseling/therapy groups—a closed group is better because the members develop trust and comfort as the group evolves. The only time a closed group becomes a detriment is when the group is getting stale and additional members would add new life.

In some settings, such as hospitals or residential treatment centers where there are new arrivals weekly, groups with an open membership are mandated. This does not have to constitute a negative force if the leader's style is adjusted for this dynamic. The leader must keep in mind that the group will not evolve through various stages because members will always be at different places in their feelings about the group. The leader will want to develop ways of introducing new members that do not detract from the flow of the last session. Often leaders will spend too much time introducing and orienting new members, thus creating a negative force. We discuss ways of bringing in new members in Chapter Four.

Voluntary or Nonvoluntary Membership

Perhaps the most basic force to consider is whether the members are voluntary or nonvoluntary. Naturally, it would be nice if all groups could be held on a voluntary basis. However, the courts and settings such as correctional institutions, residential treatment centers, and schools often mandate group participation. When a leader must conduct a group where there are nonvolunteers, it is important to adapt to this dynamic. Both Yalom (1995) and Corey (1995) state that negative attitudes about being in a group can be transformed by the leader's ability to prepare members for the group. Corey further states that the leader also has to believe in the group process. Often some nonvoluntary members will change their negative attitude if the first couple of sessions go well. To make the first sessions successful, the leader must plan the group on the assumption that there will be negative attitudes. The following are three examples of what a leader might say to nonvoluntary members during the first session.

◆ EXAMPLES

Leader: I realize many of you do not want to be here and probably are thinking this is going to be a big waste of time. All I can say is that I hope you will at least give it a chance. I think I have some things planned that should be of interest to all of you.

Leader: Since you did not volunteer for this group, I imagine you may have some strong negative feelings about being here. You will have a chance to air those feelings in a few minutes, but first I want to tell you a little about what we will be doing in the hope that you will see that the group can be interesting and may be helpful to you.

Leader: Every time I lead one of these groups, there are members who fight being here at the beginning, but by the end they thank me for providing a place for them to share their thoughts and feelings. I know that some of you right now are angry about being forced to be in this group. All I can say is that these groups have helped some people, and they can help you if you let them. If you will give the group a chance for a couple of weeks, I will do all I can to make it a good experience.

There will be times when no matter what the leader does, some members will remain negative and antitherapeutic. When faced with this situation, the leader should accept that the group will not go as well as desired. It is sometimes a good idea, when possible, to divide the group and let those who are totally negative sit out of the circle of the group and do something else, such as read, rest, or sit quietly. Another strategy is to meet with the entire group for less time, then excuse the negative members and have those who are really interested remain. The point to remember and plan for is that, if you have nonvoluntary members, there will definitely be some negative group dynamics at the beginning of the group and perhaps throughout the sessions. Planning interesting and creative sessions is essential!

Members' Level of Goodwill

One of the forces to consider when thinking about the group is the members' level of goodwill. By goodwill, we mean the desire to be cooperative rather than resistant, disruptive, or hostile. It stands to reason that a group made up of members with goodwill will be much easier to lead than one of members with little goodwill. Goodwill usually produces a high level of commitment. Members lacking goodwill are those who are forced to be in the group or those who want to direct the group or be the center of attention. Such members have little or no commitment to the group.

How do you know if there is goodwill? The best way to assess this is simply to observe your members. You can nearly always tell how they feel about being in the group. If you are not sure, bring the topic up for discussion. Simply ask, "What is your feeling about being in the group?"

Members' Level of Commitment

As we have just suggested, the members' level of commitment is closely tied to the level of goodwill. When commitment is low, members will tend to get off track, show little interest, contribute very little, do disruptive things, argue with the leader, or attack one another. In other words, all kinds of negative group dynamics will occur when there is little commitment. As a leader, you must expect to have difficulty if you are leading a group of members who are not committed. In later chapters, we suggest some ways to deal with low commitment.

Level of Trust among Members

In groups whose members have goodwill and commitment, trust will usually develop over time if the group is moving in a positive direction. Problems of trust often occur when members have very different points of view or have negative relationships with each other outside of the group—such as living together, being in the same classes, working together, and so forth. If the group consists of members who do not like each other, the leader will need to try to change this by meeting with them privately to see if their differences can be resolved. The leader may even ask one or more members to drop out of the group. If the lack of trust does not change and, due to administrative policy, the members cannot be asked to leave the group, the leader will have to accept the fact that leading the group will be difficult.

In almost any group, the trust level increases or decreases as the group progresses, and it is important for the leader to pay attention to the evolving trust level. This increase or decrease is usually dependent on the ways members are reacting to one another. Obviously, if members are being hostile or are saying things that put other members down, the trust level will be low. Some members may not like each other, or cliques may have formed. Sometimes the trust level is low due to members' not trusting one or more members to keep disclosures confidential.

In counseling/therapy and growth groups, there is always the chance that some members will make some hurtful and judgmental comments to another member after some disclosure of an intimate detail of her life, such as an affair, an abortion, or sexual orientation. The leader's first concern needs to be for the disclosing member and to show that members will not be unfairly attacked for sharing comments or details of their lives. The leader needs to discuss these critical comments in such a way as to be supportive of the member under attack and, at the same time, not alienate the critical member or members.

◆ E X A M P L E

Jodi: I don't know how this happened. I didn't think this happened to people in their fifties. I thought only young people had affairs. Karl and I have nothing in common; and now with the kids being off at college, I am lonely. This guy at the place I work started eating lunch with me; and over the last six months, we have shared a lot. One thing led to another; and last week, we spent the afternoon at his place. Now, I feel so guilty and confused.

Bud: Jodi, I can't believe you would do that to your husband! You should have controlled yourself and not been so selfish. What about Karl? I think—

Leader: *(Using a firm but soft voice)* Bud, I want to stay with Jodi and help her with her pain. I want us to try to help her deal with her feelings and not be judgmental about her behavior. That is not what this group is for. Jodi, why don't you say some more and then we'll hear from others. I know that many can understand your feelings *(heads nod, indicating that the members understand)*.

If the leader allows negative statements to go by without clarification, trust becomes an antitherapeutic force; members will probably tend not to disclose much personal information for fear of being criticized. Ideally, the leader would be able to address the issue of being judgmental in the group and help members be more open-minded and less critical. This should be done only after helping the member who disclosed the personal information. Sometimes leaders get sidetracked and focus on the "judgmental" member or the topic of not being judgmental instead of focusing on the disclosing member who is in pain.

Members' Attitudes toward the Leader

The attitudes of the members toward the leader have to be considered when leading any group. Do they like him? Do they respect him? Do they trust him? Do they respect his group leadership skills? In most groups, members will have a variety of feelings toward the leader. Sometimes all the members may have negative feelings about the leader. In such a case, the leader needs to examine this dynamic, since it may have something to do with leadership style or ability. Often negative feelings are harbored by only one or two members. One person who is out to "get the leader" can definitely interfere with positive group dynamics.

◆ E X A M P L E

Leader: I would like to take a few minutes to discuss how you are feeling about the group.

Melvin: *(Angrily)* Why do you always ask us that? It's your job to know how we feel! Let's do something fun. All the things you have us do are boring!

In this situation, the leader would not want to focus on the negative member, especially if she knows that the member is mainly out to "get" her. The leader can deflect the negative dynamic by saying in a soft, firm voice something like this:

Leader: Melvin, I think most of the others feel differently. *(Turning to the rest of the group)* How are you feeling?

The most important thing for leaders to realize is that negative attitudes about them as leaders definitely affect the interaction and disclosures in the group.

The Leader's Attitude toward the Members

A force that is often overlooked but is of great importance is the leader's attitude toward the group members. During workshops on group leadership, it is common to hear group leaders express their dislike for some of their members. There are a number of reasons why this dynamic occurs. One is that members who are forced to be in the group devote their entire time to disrupting it. It is no wonder that leaders would not like this kind of member. If the group contains hostile, nonvoluntary members, the leader should try to figure out a way to exclude them. Otherwise, the leader will end up resenting and possibly arguing with them. This distracts from the purpose of the group and is rarely good for the group.

Another possible reason a leader might have a bad attitude is that the leader is being required to lead a group of people he does not like. If the leader cannot avoid leading the group and cannot change his feelings about the members, he may try adding a co-leader. If that is not possible, the leader should spend extra time planning the sessions in the hope that the exercises and activities will help make the group more interesting for both the members and leader. If the leader does not do this, the group surely will go poorly. If you ever find yourself in this situation, remember that trying to make it interesting certainly is to your advantage.

The Leader's Experience and Readiness to Deal with Groups

For those who are just starting out, the therapeutic force of experience needs to be mentioned. If the leader is new to leading groups, this may be an antitherapeutic force because the leader will be learning from the experience and will make mistakes. Also, the leader may be nervous. If this is the case, it is important to recognize and, if need be, mention it to the group. Along these same lines, in a counseling/therapy group, an antitherapeutic force will be present if the leader does not have much individual counseling experience. For a good counseling/therapy group to occur, the leader must be experienced in individual counseling and have knowledge about counseling theories.

Ideally, beginning leaders would work with a more experienced co-leader for a few groups before leading by themselves, but this usually is not the case. If you find yourself leading without the benefit of prior experience, do the best you can and learn from the experience by discussing your group with your supervisor or colleague.

Process and Content

We, along with Corey and Corey (1992), Donigian (1994), Gladding (1995), and many other writers, stress the importance of paying attention to the group process. Posthuma (1996) and Hulse-Killacky, Schumacher, and Kraus (1996) discuss the need for balancing process and content. In their discussion, they use the term *process* to include stages of group, group dynamics, and therapeutic forces. They use *content* to refer to the purpose or task of the group. They make an excellent point regarding how the leader needs to always be aware of both the content and process and focus the group on each, depending on the purpose and what is needed at the time. Hulse-Killacky et al. (1996) state, "process and content are mutually interactive and operate as two threads of one string" (p. 4). Mistakes are made in both directions; that is, there may be too much emphasis on content or too much emphasis on process. Although our approach tends to focus more on content, we want to make sure that you understand the importance of paying attention to both. *The skilled leader is always monitoring the content and the process during any session.*

Concluding Comments

In this chapter, we discussed the stages of groups, group process, and therapeutic forces that leaders must be aware of to be effective. All groups go through at least three stages: beginning, working, and closing. Some groups go through additional stages. It is important that leaders be aware that groups go through these stages even though the amount of time for each stage will depend on the kind of group and its purpose. *Group process* (also referred to as *group dynamics*) refers to the attitudes and interaction of members and leaders. *Therapeutic forces* refers to the many different elements operating in a group, such as its size, its setting, the time of day it meets, its member composition, the trust and commitment levels of its members, and the leader's attitude and experience. It is also important for the leader to be aware of both *process* and *content* during any session.

CHAPTER THREE

Purpose of Groups

Being clear about the purpose of the group is perhaps the most important group leadership concept to be learned. All of the other skills and tasks discussed in this book—such as planning a group, holding and shifting the focus, and cutting off and drawing out members—are based on the leader's having a clear understanding of the purpose of the group. Because we consider this concept so important, we discuss clarity of purpose in this separate chapter and continue to mention it throughout the book. *Purpose* refers to why the group is meeting and what the goals and objectives are. (The terms *goals* and *objectives* will sometimes be used in place of *purpose*.) When the leader fully understands the purpose of the group, it is easier for him to decide such things as its size, membership, session length, and number of sessions.

The purpose of the group serves as a "map" for the leader. Members and leaders must be clear about both the general purpose of the group and the specific purpose of each session. Sometimes the purpose is obvious, such as losing weight, quitting smoking, overcoming a phobia, or learning study skills. Often, however, members' needs will not be so specific. Leading groups of people with a variety of needs means that the leader will have to help the group decide which needs are reasonable and possible to address. *Clarity of purpose helps the leader keep the members "on course" by suggesting relevant activities, asking relevant questions, and cutting off irrelevant discussions.* Groups are often confusing, boring, or unproductive when the objectives are not well defined or when the leader does not follow the stated objectives. The following are examples of sessions in which the purpose is either unclear or is not adhered to by the leader.

◆ EXAMPLES

Purpose: Learning to survive the pain of divorce

It is the first meeting. Members have been talking about their loneliness, self-doubts, and fears. Alan interrupts abruptly and starts talking about his

50

children and how he plans to care for them when they visit in a couple of months. The leader says to the group, "What are your thoughts on how Alan can handle the upcoming visit?" For the next 30 minutes, the group gives Alan suggestions on how to handle the situation, with much of the talk centering on what to feed the kids.

This leader made a mistake by asking for comments on what Alan was saying. The stated purpose was support and therapy to survive the pain of divorce, so the leader should not have focused the group on one person by asking that particular question. Rather, the leader should have halted the discussion and redirected the group back to a discussion of the members' feelings about their divorces. Allowing the discussion to continue probably resulted in some members becoming bored and frustrated. Members might also have become angry and left the group or cut in on the discussion and attacked Alan or the group for being shallow and petty. Such responses could have been prevented had the leader been clear about the purpose and then used her skills to redirect the group. For example, the leader could have said something like, "Alan, that's an important topic; however, it does not fit with the purpose of the group at this time. If you feel the need to talk about this soon, let's schedule an appointment."

Purpose: Orientation to prison life

The group starts with the leader going over the procedures for meals, visits, and weekend passes. One man brings up the prison's policy of no passes for the first month. Another inmate chimes in about the lack of places to be alone when he has visitors. Another asks the group what they think of that situation. Different members offer their opinions and ideas about it. Following this, the leader brings the discussion back to the policies and procedures by discussing mealtime procedures. One inmate mentions that he is a vegetarian and two others ask him a number of questions about why he doesn't eat meat. Another inmate says he thinks the meals are terrible. The leader asks what other members think about the meals. Two inmates then start complaining about the food, the heating in the rooms, and the lack of television sets on the units. The group ends with very little having been said about procedures in the prison.

Because this leader did not stick to the purpose and was more worried about whether people would talk, he let the group wander. There is a good chance that some members will be resistant at the second meeting because the first one was boring and irrelevant. The leader should have stopped the discussion on the different side issues and brought the group back to its intended purpose by saying kindly but firmly, "The purpose of this group is to discuss the rules and procedures of the prison. I'd be more than happy to arrange a time to discuss these other matters. However, for now let's get back to our topics—let's talk about the procedures for having a visitor."

Purpose: Adult Sunday school discussion group on church-related issues

It is the fourth session, and the topic scheduled for discussion this week is "Ways the Church Can Be More Responsive to the Changing Family—The Single-Parent Family and the Stepfamily." The discussion has been interesting and relevant. Then a member asks, "Why is the divorce rate so high now?" The leader mistakenly throws the question open to the group and, for the next 25 minutes, four of the nine members argue about the many reasons. When the group returns to the original topic of the church being responsive, the other members have lost interest and have little energy for the original topic.

Again, the leader's lack of clarity caused this group to go awry. If the leader had been clear about the purpose of this meeting, she would not have let the members discuss the causes of divorce. Rather, she would have said something like, "That might be something we could discuss at a later meeting. However, let's stay with the topic for this week."

Determining the Purpose of the Group

When setting up a group, the leader must assess the potential members' needs and then decide which kind of group will be most helpful. For example, a leader working with a group of mentally retarded teenagers might decide on an education group covering such topics as sex, money, and job hunting, or a counseling/support group to help them explore their feelings. Gathering information about the members' needs, deciding which needs can be met by the group, and then conceptualizing the kind of group that will ideally meet those needs enables the purpose to become more clearly defined in the leader's mind. The next example illustrates the process of clarifying the purpose of a group by determining what kind it will be.

◆ E X A M P L E

A therapist has been asked to lead a group for pregnant teenage girls. First, she tries to find out if the group's goal has already been determined. The leader finds there is no predetermined purpose. She then gathers information about the members' ages, length of pregnancies, the attitudes of their parents, and reasons for wanting to be in a group. She finds that the five girls range in age from 14 to 17. They are all at least four months pregnant, and all plan to keep the baby. They've volunteered to be in the group because of conflicts at home and a desire for information. The leader also discovers that their needs range from dealing with their peers, handling guilt associated with religious beliefs, nutrition information, parenting skills, coping with pregnancy, planning for the baby, and seeking information regarding the effects of drugs, alcohol, and smoking on the fetus.

Given these needs, it appears that an education/support group is called for. The overall purpose, therefore, will be to educate the girls on various aspects of pregnancy, as well as to facilitate personal sharing in an effort to establish support among members.

During the first session of any group, the leader needs to clarify with the members what the purpose is. By doing this, the leader ensures that the purpose coincides with what the members want or expect. It is important to note that it is not always the leader who determines exactly what is to happen in the group—often the members have much to say about the purpose. However, the leader can and often does initially decide on the very broad purpose and kind of group, such as education, therapy, or support.

Common Questions about Purpose

Certain questions often come up regarding the purpose of groups. Although some of them may seem similar, each one addresses slightly different issues.

Can the Group Have More than One Purpose?

Yes. Many groups may have multiple purposes, such as providing support, information, and therapy. The pairing of values clarification with counseling or drug information is compatible and can set the stage for an effective and interesting group experience. A group for people just released from a state hospital could have at least two purposes: to provide support and to provide information on such subjects as budgeting and how to interview for a job. A group for teenagers who are in gangs could have multiple purposes of providing information about alternatives to gangs, conflict mediation, and counseling.

Sometimes leaders mix purposes in incompatible ways. For example, an unskilled leader in a group on child-rearing might mistakenly use 30 minutes of the group's time to do counseling with a woman complaining about her husband. Ideally, the leader would meet with the woman at the end of the session or the next day but not during the group, since the other members have come for a totally different purpose. In residential settings, such as halfway houses, juvenile centers, or prisons, incompatible purposes often emerge. In these settings, leaders sometimes try to deal in a single session with issues such as problems with parents, tensions among residents, house rules, and disciplinary procedures. The issues should be separated into two or three different meetings because each has a tone and agenda that does not really mesh with the others.

The first session of any group is another example of a multiple-purpose group session. The leader always has at least two purposes in mind. One is introducing the general content of the group (such as study habits, communications skills, increasing marital happiness), and the other is getting members clear about the group and how it will be conducted. There are also two purposes for the last session: finishing the content and finishing the group. The main thing to consider when developing multiple purposes for your group is whether they are compatible.

Must Each Session Have a Purpose?

Yes. A good group leader will have in mind the purpose or purposes of each specific session. So far, our discussion of purpose has mostly centered on the content of the group and the overall purpose. Purpose can be looked at more specifically. One purpose might be to clarify what the rest of the sessions will be like. Other purposes can be to give feedback to each other, to get to know each other better, or to discuss a specific topic such as religion, sex, or the need for approval. Sometimes the leader, the members, or both will decide beforehand what the purpose of the next session will be. The following is a list of possible purposes for a session or a part of a session.

- ◆ To have fun
- ◆ To be informative
- ◆ To build trust
- ◆ To increase commitment
- ◆ To be thought-provoking
- ◆ To discuss group process—that is, what is happening between members
- ◆ To discuss gender, race, or other cultural issues that exist in the group
- ◆ To accomplish a task

Each of these may serve either as part of a multiple purpose or the sole purpose for one or more sessions. For instance, a leader who discovers that the group lacks trust or commitment would probably want to focus part of the next meeting on those issues rather than on the overall purpose, such as personal growth, getting out of prison, living with cancer, or learning assertiveness. Following are some examples of the specific purposes of group sessions.

◆ EXAMPLES

It is the fourth session of a discussion group composed of high school students exploring postgraduate options. The predetermined topic of discussion is the military. The students have been asked to gather as much information as they can to share with the group.

This is a growth group consisting of three women and five men. The leader starts the session by saying:

Leader: Tonight I thought it may be helpful to discuss something that I have observed in the group. Ever since Gloria shared she was a lesbian, there has been an underlying tension or something, and I think the group could benefit from talking about this.

In the fifth session of a therapy group, Sandy starts rambling again. The leader decides that the group is far enough along to start giving feedback to one another. He says the following to the group and to Sandy:

Leader: Sandy, I want to pick up on something that I think will help you and the other members of the group. I want to do a feedback exercise where we tell each other how we experience them in the group. That is, for the next 45 minutes, we are going to give each other feedback. Here's what I'd like you to do. I need a volunteer to go first. We will spend 3 minutes talking about that person, first listing the person's strengths and then the things the person may need to change. Who will go first?

It is the third session of a support group composed of juveniles in a detention center. The leader notices that there is no energy, although the group began only 10 minutes ago. She decides, therefore, that the best purpose for this session is to work on commitment and trust. She says to the group:

Leader: On a 1 to 10 scale, with 10 being a lot and 1 being none, how much commitment do you have to this group?

After the information is gathered, the leader will focus the remainder of the session on why members are not committed and what would increase their commitment.

It is the third in a series of five sessions of an educational group whose overall purpose is to teach nursing supervisors new ways to deal with their staff. The leader starts by saying:

Leader: Today, we are going to focus on nonverbal behavior. I want to go over some of the latest research, which I found to be quite useful; then I'll ask for reactions and comments. Jefferson and Smith studied the nonverbal behavior of 22 nursing supervisors and found. . . .

A therapy group in its third session is composed of mental health patients with outpatient status. The leader opens the group by saying, "Who has something to bring up tonight?" Two of the seven members respond. Joe says he wants to talk about his mom and her desire to control him. Molly mentions her anxiety at work. The leader says to the group:

Leader: Tonight, we'll focus on Molly's and Joe's concerns, and then during the last hour we'll spend time talking about learning to control our feelings by paying attention to the things that we tell ourselves. Actually, their issues will probably get most of you focused on learning to control your feelings.

As you can see, a leader can establish the session's purpose in a variety of ways. The simple, direct approach is often a very good way to make the purpose clear.

Can the Purpose Change?

Yes. Groups often start out as education, support, or growth groups, and as they develop, the members begin to share on a more personal level. If the leader sees a need to shift to counseling, it is best for her to discuss this in the group. Probably the best way to make the change would be for the leader to explain how the group could alter its purpose. If the group decided to switch its emphasis, the leader would need to be aware that it will probably take one or two sessions to completely change the direction. *Often leaders make the mistake of shifting the purpose of the group without informing the members.* As a result, members feel frustrated, confused, fearful, or resentful. As we have said throughout this discussion, it is important that both leaders and members remain clear about the group's purpose, and the leader should reiterate the purpose whenever necessary. If the leader decides to shift the purpose, she must be sure that the members are aware of her intent and that they, too, desire the shift.

Can There Be No Purpose?

This is inadvisable. Groups without a purpose usually dissolve due to lack of interest and direction. While you may choose to bring together a group of people having no predetermined goal in mind, the purpose of the first meeting should be to decide what the purpose should be for the remainder of the meetings. In fact, a group with no purpose cannot really be termed a group. Rather, it is a social gathering.

If the Leader Is Clear, Will the Members Be?

Not always. Often, members have their own ideas of what the group should be about, and they try to steer it in that direction. In addition, some members will come to groups for reasons other than the stated purpose; that is, they come to complain, to preach, or to attack, and will not follow the leader's direction. Another reason members may not be clear about the group's purpose is that some find it hard to understand what is going on. Due to their anxiety, they are not able to listen well. By reiterating, the leader can do much to clarify the intent of the group for the members. If she sees that some of the members are working at cross-purposes, she will probably want to do one of two things: (1) meet with those members who seem confused, or (2) discuss the problem in the group. Often, this clears up the confusion.

Purpose in Single-Session Groups

Most of our comments have implied that groups meet for a number of sessions. Many groups meet only once. When leading a single-session group, clarity of purpose is even more essential. The leader will want to be very clear about why this group is meeting and then plan a group that will accomplish the desired objective in the time allotted. The group's purpose may be to staff a patient (discuss and determine a treatment plan), to resolve a conflict, or to plan an event. Being clear will help the leader use the time effectively and accomplish the desired outcomes. Often at single-session group meetings, little is accomplished because the members keep switching topics and the leader fails to keep the discussion within the boundaries of the purpose. Another problem is that the members may focus for half the meeting on something that is irrelevant, thus necessitating a second meeting. A good leader should be clear as to the purpose, what needs to be done, and how much time should be spent on introductions, warm-up, background information, and the various topics.

Concluding Comments

Being clear about the purpose is perhaps the most important factor affecting the outcome of a group. It also affects the leader's choice of the kind of group, membership makeup, topics, dynamics, depth of intensity, and the leader's role. Clarity of purpose is crucial no matter what type of group is being led. The purpose of the group serves as the map for guiding the leader in planning and in conducting the session. Many beginning leaders fail to be clear as to the purpose, or they do not stick to the purpose. Sessions have different purposes— sometimes more than one. Also, the purpose of the group can change as the group develops. Once you have mastered the process of clarifying the purpose, the next important aspect to understand about effective group leadership pertains to planning, which is discussed in the next chapter.

CHAPTER FOUR

Planning

The importance of carefully planning a group cannot be overemphasized. Corey (1995) states, "If you want a group to be successful, you need to devote considerable time to planning. In my view planning should begin with the drafting of a written proposal" (p. 85). We agree that there are two aspects of planning: *pregroup planning* and *session planning*. Both are very important.

Pregroup Planning

Many groups are not successful due to too little emphasis on pregroup planning. Gladding (1995) points out the necessity of pregroup planning: "The dynamics of a group begin before the group ever convenes" (p. 30). In Chapters One and Two, we discussed several considerations for the formation of a group: how large it should be, whether it should have open or closed membership, how long sessions should last, and where it should meet. Four additional decisions to be made when establishing a group include

1. How many sessions will the group meet?
2. When will the group meet?
3. Who should the members be?
4. How will the members be screened?

How Many Sessions Will the Group Meet?

Many groups will be established for a certain length of time. For instance, parenting, childbirth, assertiveness-training, certain growth and therapy, and many education groups are scheduled to meet for a specified number of sessions. Counseling, therapy, growth, task, and support groups sometimes begin with no set number of sessions planned. Usually it is best to set a limit because it gives members an idea of how long they have to complete any personal work. Another option is to leave the decision about the number of sessions up to the members and let them decide once the group has been meeting for a while. Often, the number of sessions is dictated by other considerations, such as the length of a school term, the leader's availability, the needs of the population being served, or the amount of educational information to be covered.

When Will the Group Meet?

Two factors must be considered: time of day and frequency of meetings. Ideally, the meeting time will not conflict with members' other activities. If the setting for the group is an agency, school, or hospital, the choice of meeting time should cause as little disruption as possible in the daily routine. Choice of meeting time is especially important in a school, where the students would be coming from classes. The leader will want to make sure the same class is not missed on a regular basis. This can be accomplished by having the group rotate periods each week.

The members' schedules also need to be considered when setting the time. If the members work, perhaps the evening is best, or maybe even early morning or noon. For groups in a residential center—such as a prison, hospital, or detention center—a careful examination of the daily routine is helpful. Beginning leaders often make the mistake of planning a group without fully considering the many factors that might make the group's meeting time inconvenient.

The leader's schedule is also important; she must always be available to lead the group, and certain times and days are better than others. Days when the leader tends to be very busy with such things as staff meetings, paperwork, or intakes should be avoided. In the case of therapy groups, it is inadvisable to lead one group right after another—it is too taxing. Ideally, any therapy group leader would lead no more than one group a day; the maximum should be three.

Besides deciding on the best time to meet, the leader will usually be the one to decide how often the group will meet. Some groups meet daily; others meet twice a week, once a week, or once every two weeks; still others meet once a month. The frequency of meetings depends on the kind of group, its purpose, and the availability of members and leader. There is no set formula for how often a group should meet, but the leader must ensure that the meetings are properly spaced. It is important that the group meet neither so often nor so infrequently as to defeat the overall purpose.

Who Should the Members Be?

Any time a group is being formed, a number of considerations arise regarding its membership (Corey, 1995). Once the population to be served is determined (schoolchildren, hospital patients, prisoners, clients of a mental health center, or interested persons in a community), another decision to be made is whether the entire population will automatically constitute the membership or whether the members will volunteer or be selected. For example, in an orientation group at a university residence hall, will the group consist of all 15 new students in a wing, or will it include only those who want to be in a group? In a unit in a hospital for mental patients, will the group be for everyone, or will only selected patients be allowed? There are no absolute guidelines for deciding whom to include; usually the purpose of the group, time constraints, and setting will help the leader decide how to limit membership.

Another consideration is whether to place members who are very different in age or background in the same group. Certainly, multicultural issues need to be considered when selecting members. In schools, counselors must decide whether to include students from one grade only or from different grades. Also, school counselors need to decide if the groups should consist of members of the same sex or a mix of boys and girls. In various hospital situations, patients in the same unit often include young and old people or people with varying educational or socioeconomic backgrounds. Sometimes mixing the ages or backgrounds is beneficial; at other times, it can be detrimental. If the leader were planning a group for the unemployed, it would not be beneficial to place college-educated individuals and high school dropouts in the same group because their needs would differ. In a marital-problems group, mixing ages and backgrounds would probably prove beneficial because members might benefit from hearing different views and ideas. Since each group is different, we are not saying that certain groups should have certain members, but we are saying that it is very important that the leader give thought to these variables when selecting members of a group.

How Will the Members Be Screened?

Closely related to questions about membership composition are decisions about screening members. One of the biggest problems faced by counselors in agencies and institutions is that administrators do not let them select the members, and therefore groups are often conducted with members who should not be in the group. We encourage you to lobby hard for the right to screen your members if it will benefit the participants. *Screening is essential because not everyone is appropriate for every group.*

With some groups, screening is either unnecessary or only slightly beneficial. As Corey (1995) says, "The key point is that screening needs to be done within the context of the type of group that a practitioner is offering. Whether a client is to be included or excluded has much to do with the purposes of the group" (p. 88). For education, discussion, and task groups, screening may not be necessary—it depends on the specific situation. It should be pointed out that in many situations screening is not possible. When it is both possible and desirable, the leader has several procedural options for screening.

The Personal Interview

The best screening method, though the most time-consuming, is the personal interview. It allows the leader to assess most easily the appropriateness of the member for the group, and it gives the leader a chance to make contact with potential members. The leader has an opportunity to inform the prospective member about the group—the content, the process, membership, the rules, and so forth. Also, the personal interview gives potential members the chance to ask questions about the group and gives the leader the chance to see if the group is right for them. Listed are a number of questions that can be asked in a personal interview or on a screening form.

- Why do you want to be in this group?
- What are your expectations of the group?
- Have your ever been in a group before? If so, what was it like?
- What concerns do you want help with?
- Is there anyone you would not want to be in a group with?
- How do you think you can contribute to the group?
- Do you have any questions about the group or the leader?

Individual contact with the potential member   Personal interviews permit the leader and member to meet each other before the group actually begins. It is important for the leader to make this experience more than just a question-and-answer session. The leader should realize that the interview is the beginning of his relationship with the member. He will want to use many of the same skills used in an individual counseling session: attending, listening, and some probing. The leader will not want to let the interview become a counseling session. Too often, leaders alienate candidates by making the interview too formal or by turning it into a therapy session. The interview should be as comfortable as possible while the leader assesses the potential member's needs and goals.

Informing the member about the group   During the screening interview, the leader can explain the purpose of the group, how it will be conducted, any rules, and any other relevant information. If the group is a counseling or therapy group, the leader can tell the member about the theories that may be used. If it is to be a support group, the leader can give the member examples of what might be shared. Some leaders show a videotape of a group so the prospective member can see what the group will be like.

Assessment of appropriateness   By asking questions relevant to the type of group being formed, the leader can determine whether the potential member is appropriate for the group. In the personal interview, the leader can often spot those people whose needs and goals differ from those of the planned group. For educational groups, the leader tries to determine if the individual knows either too much or too little about the subject matter. For support groups, the leader may find that a potential member needs individual or group therapy rather than a support group. Screening for counseling and therapy groups allows the leader to determine if the person's needs can best be met by group or individual counseling.

Written Screening

Another method of screening is to have prospective members complete a written form. This gives the leader information necessary to decide if the person is appropriate for the group. Sometimes the only information the leader needs is biographical: age, grade level completed, sex, marital status, diagnosis, length of illness, kind of illness, living situation, and age of children. When basing choices on written material only, the leader must remember to include all the pertinent questions. Questions that are sometimes overlooked include the candidate's availability for meetings and whether the candidate needs child care and transportation.

The questions outlined for the personal interview can be used as part of a written screening form. Naturally, the questions asked will depend on the purpose of the group. If the topics to be covered are sensitive ones—such as sex, death, divorce, or religion—the leader may want to list them and ask prospective members to comment on how they feel about talking about those subjects. Some leaders ask members to write a brief autobiography as a way to help with screening. The key to effective screening is to find out certain information in order to form a group of members who can share and learn together.

Screening by Referral Sources

Another type of screening occurs when the leader informs possible referral sources, such as teachers, other therapists, or hospital staff, about the group, its purpose, and the kind of member sought. These people, in a sense, do the screening by telling appropriate potential members of the availability of the group. The leader who uses this method of screening will want to make sure that those making referrals fully understand the purpose of the group and the kind of members desired.

Screening by Using a Comprehensive Group Program

A leader conducting several groups in the same setting—such as in a prison, hospital, company, or school—can "screen" by assigning members to any one of the groups. Assigning members according to their knowledge, age, experience, or some personality characteristic often increases the likelihood of the group being valuable to the members. The leader can also sort members according to their interaction style or level of mental health. The leader may choose to place some highly verbal members in a group with some nontalkers. At times, it is useful to mix certain characteristics in that way. There really are no absolute guidelines for making these decisions because each situation and purpose is so different. The main thing to realize is that these kinds of screening decisions can be instrumental in enhancing positive therapeutic forces.

Screening after the Group Has Begun

There may be times when a leader will need to screen members even after the group has begun. If prescreening is not possible or not thorough enough, the leader may state in the first session that after the group meets for a couple of times, he plans to meet with each member to discuss his or her ongoing participation in the group. This kind of screening can be an excellent way to screen out some members who are not right for the group.

Another kind of screening that can be done after the group has been meeting for a few weeks is to have the members write a couple of pages on why the group is important and what they want to gain from the group. The leader stipulates that only those who complete the assignment can be in the group for the remaining sessions. The leader would use this kind of screening only to weed out those who are not committed to working in the group. In Chapter Twelve, we discuss further when and how to screen out members during the middle sessions.

Additional Considerations for Pregroup Planning

The leader will want to ascertain whether any additional materials are needed for the group, any resource people must be contacted, or any permission forms must be signed. School counselors quite often are required to have a permission form signed by a parent or guardian. A simple form describing the group and its purpose usually is sufficient. It may also be useful to consider whether any kind of oral or written contract from members is needed or desired.

"Big-Picture" Planning

Another part of pregroup planning is what we call *"big-picture" planning*. By this, we mean giving thought to all possible topics that *need* to be covered and to all possible topics that *could* be covered. Too often, leaders think only about the first session and not the overall picture of what needs to be covered during the life of the group. We suggest the leader first list the possible topics and then later put them in some possible order to be covered during the beginning, early middle, and middle stages of the group. A good leader makes an extensive list of possible topics and then prioritizes the topics in order to gain a better idea of what is important to cover and what can be omitted. The following lists contain examples of possible topics that would then be prioritized.

ANGER MANAGEMENT GROUP (SIX SESSIONS)

Where anger comes from	Current anger
Who or what situations members	Past anger
think cause them to get angry	Anger at siblings, friends, and others

Guilt in regard to anger
Anger at parents
How members currently
 deal with anger
Better ways to handle anger
Anger as a habit

How different theories look at
 anger (REBT = self-talk; TA =
 child ego-state)
What members learned about anger
 as they were growing up
Anger as a cover-up for hurt

DIVORCE GROUP (EIGHT SESSIONS)

Children
Dating
Sex
Anger
Guilt
Blame/fault
Loneliness
Fears
Self-esteem

Feelings of failure
Money
Remarriage
History of other relationships
Hurt
What can be learned from the
 marriage experience
Unfinished business

After making these lists, the leader of each group would then go back and consider which topics would be best to bring up in the beginning stage, which ones should be brought up later, which ones need only brief coverage, and which may not need to be brought up at all. This kind of planning definitely helps the leader have a better understanding of what he perceives the group will cover. This big-picture understanding aids the leader during the first few sessions when he is helping members clarify how the group can be helpful and which topics may be covered.

For any group, the leader should do big-picture planning. For some groups, this may not be extensive because the topics tend to emerge as the group meets and develops. However, for most groups, considerable time should be spent. Talking with colleagues about possible topics, reading books and articles on the subject, and gathering information during the screening process can help with big-picture planning. This process needs to be done before the group begins. It also needs to be an ongoing planning activity since the group is always evolving and the need to cover new and different topics often emerges.

Session Planning

Planning a specific session involves deciding on the topics and group activities as well as delegating an approximate amount of time needed for each. Most groups require a good deal of planning, although only a minimum of planning is necessary for certain kinds of counseling, therapy, growth, and support groups after their initial sessions. Minimal planning is necessary when the members come to understand the purpose of their group and arrive at the sessions eager to discuss concerns important to them and relevant to others. But even in groups where the planning of exercises and topics is minimal, the leader will want to give considerable thought to the kinds of exercises and topics that would be helpful. Many beginning leaders make the mistake of coming to the group without thinking about what may be valuable for the members, and when the members have little energy, the group falls flat. Groups will require planning when the members do not tend to bring issues to the group to discuss but rather respond to exercises and other activities.

Discussion, education, and task groups are often more effective when thoroughly planned by the leader. The thoughtful leader can organize the session in a way that makes the group both interesting and productive. In the remainder of this chapter, we discuss the considerations that go into planning an effective group session.

Consider the Stage of the Group

One of the first things to consider when planning a session is whether the session is a first, second, middle, or closing session. Planning a first session is very different from planning a middle or closing session. During the first session, there are a number of things that the leader will need to do, such as having members introduce themselves, clarifying the purpose of the group, setting a positive tone for the group, helping members get over any uneasiness, and going over any guidelines or rules for the group. (We discuss the first and second sessions of a group in Chapter Five.) During the closing sessions, the leader will want to make sure the members are saying and doing the things necessary for ending the group (see Chapter Fourteen).

Another consideration is how many more sessions the group will meet. Some groups meet only for one session; the planning for that kind of session is obviously different from a group that will meet for 10 weeks. Planning the fifth session when only two sessions are left will be different from planning a fifth session when six more sessions remain.

Plan the Format for the Session

When planning a session, the leader will want to consider the format for the session. Some groups work well with the same format each week; for instance, progress reports, an exercise, discussion, then practicing a new behavior, and closing comments; or sharing personal problems the first hour and then discussing some assigned topic that members were given the week before. For other groups, a varied format seems advantageous because it keeps the interest level high. By a varied format, we mean that one session might consist of two different exercises and a discussion; the next session might include a written activity, personal sharing, and then some role-playing practice; and another session might consist of a short film. Doing different things keeps members interested and curious. When planning, the leader should always consider whether the format is getting stale.

A common way to vary format is by using exercises, but the leader will want to be sure that he does not plan too many and that enough time is allotted for discussing the members' thoughts, feelings, and reactions to any exercise. As a rule, leaders should vary the type of exercises for a session since some members will respond better than others to certain exercises.

Anticipate Problems When Planning

The leader also needs to anticipate potential problems when planning. For example, if she has asked members to read something for the session, she can anticipate that some members will not have done the reading and can plan ways of processing the material that will not alienate those members. It is sometimes valuable to plan activities with specific members in mind, but it is important to have a backup plan in case those members are absent. In fact, it is always a good idea to have a backup plan in case an activity, exercise, or discussion does not go well.

√ *Planning the Phases of the Session*

When planning, the leader needs to be aware that each session has three phases: the *warm-up* or *beginning phase*, the *middle* or *working phase*, and the *closing phase*. During the warm-up phase, the leader often has members comment on any thoughts or reactions since the last session. During this phase, the leader also tries to get a sense of the members' energy and interest for the session and any topics or issues they may want to talk about. In the middle or working phase of the session, members focus on the group's purpose. We call it the middle phase when referring to an education or discussion group and the working phase for other groups. The closing phase is devoted to summarizing and ending the session. During this phase, the leader plans summary-type activities that help members integrate what they have learned during the middle or working phase of the group.

There are specific planning guidelines for each phase of any given session. The process of leading members through each of the phases is covered in great detail in later chapters, but we will discuss here each phase in regard to planning.

The Beginning Phase

A leader should always plan how he is going to begin a session and how long the warm-up phase should be. The first few minutes are sometimes used to review the previous session. The leader will need to decide how much time to devote to review. Too often, leaders plan a beginning phase that lasts too long. The warm-up phase for most groups usually is less than 10 minutes and should not be more than 15 minutes, except for the first session, which may require a longer warm-up phase. With school groups, in which the sessions are 30–40 minutes, counselors will want to plan a brief beginning phase in order to have time for quality interaction during the middle phase.

Some groups require almost no warming up time—the members come ready to talk, learn, or work. In other groups, the leader must plan for getting members focused on being in the group. There are a number of ways for a leader to do this:

- Talk about the last session, mentioning the key issues that were discussed, and then discuss the plan for the current session.
- Ask the members to comment on their past week—any thoughts, feelings, reactions, or observations.
- Get members to talk about current events, the weather, movies, television shows, and so on, for about 5 minutes.
- Ask certain members (ones who seem ready to respond) to give progress reports on what they have been working on.
- Ask members if there are any questions they would like answered, and then spend the first 5 minutes answering them. This is common in education and discussion groups.

During the beginning phase, the leader plans activities, exercises, or discussions that allow him to assess how members are feeling about being in the group that day. He may plan additional time for warming up if he feels that the group needs more time. There may be times when the leader will want to extend the beginning phase by discussing such topics as trust, energy, commitment, or interest in the group instead of going directly to the purpose of the group, which may be accomplishing a task, personal growth, or counseling.

The leader has a number of options for beginning a session. Any of these options may be used, depending on the group's purpose and the members' need for warming up. Most of the examples below are for later sessions of a group. (The beginning phase of the first and second sessions often requires more warm-up than what these openings allow.) In the next chapter, we discuss the beginning phase of the first and second sessions.

Education or Discussion Groups

- Before we get started on today's subject, does anyone have any questions or comments about last week or about that handout I gave you?
- Today, we are going to talk about _____ . To get you thinking about the subject, I'd like you to do the following. . . .
- I'd like to talk for a few minutes about _____ , and then we'll discuss your reactions, feelings, and thoughts.
- We're going to start with a 15-minute film. Afterward, we'll discuss any questions or reactions.

Task Groups

- Let's start with progress reports from each of you. Who wants to go first?
- Let me review briefly where we are and what seems to be the next thing we need to decide. . . .

◆ Before we start, do any of you have something pertinent you want to share?

Growth or Support Groups

◆ How has the week been?
◆ Any reactions to the last session, progress reports, or updates?
◆ What would you like to talk about tonight—any particular topic or issue you would like to discuss?
◆ Let's start by thinking about the most significant thing that has happened to you since our last meeting. In a minute, we'll go around and let each of you share this. Who wants to go first?—we'll hear from everyone.

Counseling or Therapy Groups

◆ Let's begin. Last session, a number of you talked about some very important personal issues. I think it would be good if you shared any reactions or thoughts you've had since then. We might do that for a few minutes, then move on to other people and topics.
◆ I want to start the group a little differently. I want each of you to think about whether you have something you would like to talk about. In a second, we'll go around the room. I'm going to have you simply say "yes" or "no" if there is something you would like to bring up. This is just a quick way to find out how many of you have something on your mind. I hope many of you will have something you want to discuss, but it is perfectly OK to say "no."
◆ Let's start. First, does anyone have something they'd like to bring up?
◆ Let's start. I was talking with Sammy out in the hall just now, and he said he had something that was really bothering him. I hope we can help. Sammy, you said you wanted to tell the group what happened when you saw your dad.

In the last example, the leader decided not to stay with his planned opening because he realized that focusing on Sammy would be a good way to begin the group. *Some leaders make the mistake of being unable to adjust their plans when something arises spontaneously that is as good as or better than what was planned.* On the other hand, some leaders are overly spontaneous and allow members to go on tangents at the very start of the group, which makes refocusing on the planned activities more difficult. In the two examples that follow, the leader made the mistake of "going with the flow" instead of with the planned beginning; consequently, much of the session was spent in an unproductive way.

◆ EXAMPLES

This group is for recently divorced women. Its purpose is to help the women begin living a single lifestyle. It is the beginning of the third session, and after making brief comments about how the previous week was, the leader planned to discuss starting to date again. A couple of members have already commented.

Leader: Any other comments?

Myra: I had a real crazy week. My daughter said she wanted to go live with her dad. I didn't know what to say. She was mad because I wouldn't let her have a dog—I just don't need that now!

Jan: I've heard that pets are good for children, especially after a loss. Is that true?

Pat: My daughter spends more time with our cat than she ever did. It is interesting how pets may be able to help during this time.

Vicky: I would think that there are many reasons for that. I can think of at least three. First, . . .

If Vicky is allowed to discuss the reasons for children's positive reactions to pets, the leader may have a difficult time shifting the focus of the group from pets to dating.

It is the second of four sessions in a group for men who are not satisfied with their current occupation and who want a change. The leader planned to focus on ways to assess skills and how to research occupations that use those skills.

Leader: Today, I thought we would focus on what skills you have and what occupations would fit those skills.

Omar: Can I say something? I have never believed I was good at anything because my father always cut me down. I really think that had an effect on me.

Bill: My problem is my oldest brother. He could always do things better than me.

Ted: I think I put myself down because my wife has always wanted me to be more than I am. She really has been on my case.

Sam: Mine, too. My wife nags me constantly. The other day she was on my case about my salary, my car, and the mess in the garage. Let me tell you what happened the other day when I got home from work. . . .

Because the leader did not interrupt, the members are now focused on their wives. Since the group is only meeting four times, the leader needs to stick to the planned topic rather than to allow the members to discuss their past or their wives. At this point, the leader would want to use a cutoff skill and return to her plan. (In later chapters, we discuss how to cut off.)

Introducing a New Member during the Beginning Phase

When planning the opening moments of an open-membership group session, the leader will need to allot time and choose a method for introducing new members. The leader may introduce them, have them introduce themselves, or have the established members introduce themselves by sharing how the group has been valuable to them. Chapter Five contains several examples of how to introduce new members to the group.

Creative Activities for the Beginning Phase

The leader must always be thinking about the warm-up phase and the best way to get the group started. With school groups—and especially elementary school groups—there is limited time, and the kids are often excited and wound up. We saw this difficult situation handled in a very interesting and effective way. The counselor had the overactive group sit in a tight circle. She placed a garbage can in the center and had the members all lean in toward the garbage can and talk all at once about anything that was on their minds at the time. Every kid started talking feverishly into the trash can. After a couple of minutes, the leader stopped them and "officially" started the group. This seemed to help the members calm down and get started.

Creative beginnings can be fun and interesting, and can set a good tone for the session. A dramatic movie clip, a song, or a reading are examples of other kinds of high energy openings. We have purposely been a little late and "harried" to start a group on the topic of time management. We have staged a brief, heated verbal exchange before the group began when we were going to teach transactional analysis.

Energy Level for the Beginning Phase

When planning, the leader should give thought to the kind of energy level to use during the beginning phase. Some groups benefit from a high energy opening, while others need a calm opening—the need varies with the members and the purpose of the group. The examples in the preceding creative section are high energy openings. Energy can come from the kind of activities used or from the energy in the leader's voice. One elementary school counselor we know used a high energy opening by talking enthusiastically with her Attention Deficit Hyperactive Disorder (ADHD) group—but she quickly realized this was a mistake and in the next session began with a calm voice and a calming activity. She found this was much better for these kids. Each group is different, so we cannot say what kind of energy is best for certain groups, but we want to emphasize that the leader should always consider whether the energy level being used is best for the group being led.

The Middle or Working Phase

Good planning of the middle or working phase is very important since it is the time when meaningful interactions and discussions should take place. Planning for the middle phase will vary, depending on the type of group. We discuss planning concerns for each kind of group. Also, we present sample session plans later in this chapter that should give you a good idea of how to plan for the bulk of the session.

If the group has multicultural issues, planning for them is very important. Otherwise, the leader will plan the group as if it is homogeneous rather than diverse. Careful planning can make a big difference in eliminating negative group dynamics and allowing enough time to deal with diversity.

Discussion and Education Groups

Planning a discussion or education group session requires that the leader decide, first, what topics or information to cover, then the order of presentation, and then how the topics should be covered. Additionally, the well-prepared leader will estimate as accurately as possible the amount of time needed for each topic or activity.

A leader has many options for covering a topic. She can give a mini-lecture. She can introduce the topic for discussion and have the members discuss it as a group or in pairs. She can invite a guest speaker or show a videotape. (If a speaker is used, the leader should inform the speaker of the cultural diversity in the group.) She can use one or more exercises (see Chapters Ten and Eleven).

Task Groups

The planning of a task group depends primarily on its purpose. It is always the leader's responsibility to make each session relevant and productive. Topics and exercises may be useful for some task groups. For example, in a group meeting to improve communications between management and workers, the leader can plan various exercises that help members understand their own communication patterns and style. In a group deciding policies for a new treatment unit, certain exercises might be useful if the group has trouble focusing on the task; the leader can conduct a brainstorming activity or have the group break into two or three smaller discussion groups. *Planning increases the chances that the time will be well spent and the group will be productive.*

Support Groups

In some support groups, members come eager to share their common concern—whether it be drugs, divorce, weight problems, or their disability; therefore, little planning is needed. In other support groups, the leader may have to provide topics or exercises that encourage members to share. For instance, in a group for veterans with disabilities, the leader might introduce topics such as how members' disabilities affect family relationships, what the hardest times are, or how to handle stress. In a group for spouses of people with Alzheimer's disease, the leader may introduce topics such as accepting the illness, getting some relief time, or dealing with the loss of the partner as a companion. The important thing to remember in planning a support group is to make sure the topics are relevant and the topics vary from week to week. If the members are constantly bringing up new and relevant topics, very little planning will be necessary.

Growth or Experiential Groups

Since the purpose of growth and experiential groups is to explore some aspect of one's personality, values, or interaction style, it is the leader's responsibility to plan meaningful activities. The leader should plan to focus on either a number of topics or a specific topic, and decide whether the group should focus on individuals or on the whole membership. Although the leader will be the one to plan each session, the topics may be decided either by the group or the leader.

The leader needs to consider the various group dynamics and therapeutic forces when planning. For instance, if the trust level is low, it would be inadvisable for the leader to plan activities that deal with real personal sharing. He might rather plan trust-building activities. If the group consists of a couple of members who tend to talk all the time, the leader could plan to use some movement kinds of exercises and then have members share what they learned or experienced. Also, the leader has to consider any multicultural issues when planning the middle phase of a growth group since the group's purpose usually is to explore values and attitudes. For instance, in a group that is exploring relationships between men and women, the leader would need to be aware of the different cultural views among the members and allow extra time for discussion of those differences.

Some growth groups are designed to be intense while others are not, and it is very important that the leader understand this. The type of activities planned will most definitely affect the level of intensity. The leader needs to give thought as to how "heavy" or "intense" the group should be and how to structure the group so that it is maximally beneficial. School groups are not meant to be too heavy, whereas residential treatment groups may get very intense.

Counseling and Therapy Groups

The planning of counseling and therapy groups varies greatly. Some require almost no planning because the members are ready, willing, and eager to share their concerns. In other groups, members are in pain, but they need exercises and other activities to encourage them to share. In therapy groups that require planning, the leader will want to consider any multicultural issues that need attention and topics that have yet to be covered. The skilled leader sometimes will choose to cover certain topics, hoping to help one or two specific members. For instance, a leader who knows that a few group members are having trouble dealing with anger may plan an exercise that focuses on anger. Leaders will also want to plan exercises that focus members on specific issues.

The Closing Phase

Planning the closing phase is crucial; a common mistake is to fail to plan adequately for this phase. Some leaders mistakenly let the clock announce the ending; that is, when the designated time to stop comes around, the group ends. The leader should always allow 3 to 10 minutes for summarizing and "processing" the session. Leaders should give extra thought to planning the ending of the first and last sessions of any group. Having each person comment on what he or she has learned or what stood out is a good plan for the closing phase. Other closing activities include discussing briefly the topic for the next session, having members discuss in dyads what they learned, or having each member commit out loud to doing something different during the week.

Chapter Fourteen is devoted to ending a session as well as to ending a group. If you are currently leading a group, we suggest you turn to that chapter for ideas on how to end your sessions.

Sample Session Plans

This section contains sample plans for sessions in different kinds of groups. Note that an estimated time is given for each activity to help the leader gauge the flow of the group. This helps greatly during the session, because otherwise the leader has little idea whether too much time is being spent on a topic. It is important to allot specific amounts of time for exercises and activities, but realize *the plan can and often will need to be changed as the session progresses.* The purpose of planning is to help organize a session in a logical sequence.

As you read through the sample plans, you may see unfamiliar terms. Since our purpose here is to give you an idea of how to plan a session, it is not necessary that you completely understand each activity; these activities are explained in later chapters. We tried to include a variety of techniques and activities to show the many ways to plan a session. After each plan is a discussion of its features.

PLAN 1

The first session of a parenting group consisting of ten members: two couples, three mothers alone, two single mothers, and one single father.

4 min.	Introductions—round (name, age of children, why they came to the group).
6 min.	Discuss the group—format, purpose (stress that it is mainly an educational and support group and not a therapy group). Have members share their needs and any fears or questions about the group. Have them share cultural differences. (Sandwich in the ground rules of confidentiality, attendance, no attacking of others.)
4 min.	Dyads (pairs)—share problems and feelings as a parent.

6 min.	Have members share these in large group (use their examples in discussion below).
15 min.	Discuss Adlerian principles of child behavior (use charts and handouts). Get reactions, interactions, and discussion to each of the following concepts. All behavior is purposeful. Children are not bad—they are discouraged. Four goals of misbehavior. Natural and logical consequences.
8 min.	Triads (make sure members are getting with different people)—discuss their parenting in reference to the comments regarding the Adlerian approach.
8 min.	Discuss comments from the triads.
14 min.	Focus on the first goal of misbehavior—attention getting. Use short role plays to demonstrate. Discuss ways to deal with situations.
5 min.	Dyads—discuss this goal in relation to their children and how they may handle situations differently.
12 min.	Process dyads. (If not much time is needed, discuss the second goal of misbehavior.)
8 min.	Summarize—what stood out, feelings about the group, one thing they plan to do differently. Hand out reading material. Remind them of next meeting time.

In this plan, the introductory exercise is brief because it is for an education group and the group is meeting only for an hour and a half. Also, the leader knows that the members will be interacting in dyads and triads during the sessions, so they will have several opportunities to get to know each other better. The introductions and discussion about the group are useful because they allow members to share some important information and to mention their fears and expectations regarding the group. The plan also includes looking at cultural differences since that may be a factor in a parenting group. The purpose of the group and the format are clarified during the first 10 minutes. Group rules are minimal, so no specific time is established to review them; they will probably be mentioned during the first few segments. (We discuss rules and how to present them in the next chapter.)

The dyad used early in the session gives members a chance to share their individual problems with one other person (this helps some members get more comfortable and "warms them up"); the large-group processing allows the leader and other members to hear each member's concerns. In discussing the Adlerian principles, the leader can use examples from the processing of the dyads. Because it is the first session and the group consists of members who more than likely have plenty to say since the topic is parenting, the leader chooses to use three dyads and triads. Using dyads and triads instead of the entire group to discuss some topics enables members to talk more, and often in the early sessions, some members are more comfortable sharing in dyads or triads than in the large group.

The leader varies the format to keep members interested. Also, the leader's plan includes some interesting and immediately useful content that is relevant to the group's purpose. Too often, leaders mistakenly plan first sessions that have very little content; thus, some members do not return. This plan has a good balance between content and process. Since it is the first session, more time than usual is allowed for the summary. Ordinarily, the summary would take 5 to 8 minutes. Remember, time periods are approximate but are necessary to give the leader some idea of how long to stay on any one activity.

PLAN 2

The second session of a growth and support group for fourth- and fifth-graders who don't seem to make friends easily. There is one new member this week.

5 min.	Introduce new member to the group—have members tell their names and what they remember about last week. Leader comments about the group and its purpose. Also, remind members when they talk to look at others instead of the leader.
2 min.	Have members list things they can do to make friends.
3 min.	Discuss lists in dyads.
15 min.	List ideas on chalkboard.
	Discuss the ideas.
	Role play some of the ideas.
	Have each member practice.
3 min.	Have each member tell one thing he or she will try this week.
2 min.	Summarize—each member completes "One thing I learned . . ."

In this plan, the leader uses welcoming a new member as a way to review last week's session. The opening segment is short because the entire session lasts only 30 minutes. Next, the leader uses a written exercise because this is a good way to get the children focused and involved. For the middle phase of the session, the leader has thought of several interesting ways to focus on making friends. The use of dyads helps achieve one purpose of the session, which is learning how to interact with others. Dyads enable the group members to practice talking with other children. To close the session, the leader plans a simple but focused ending—having members commit to trying something new and asking them to comment on what they learned in the session.

PLAN 3

The third session of a 6-week assertiveness-training group with eight members.

10 min.	Progress reports, observations from the week, questions.
15 min.	Reenact some "assertiveness" situations from the week (this could last longer if there are a number of situations).
5 min.	Dyads—process thoughts from the reenactments.
15 min.	Present the "broken record" technique:
	Demonstrate.
	Practice.

9 min.	Reactions, comments, and questions.
1 min.	Round (1–10; 10 = very much): How guilty do you feel when you are being assertive?
15 min.	Discuss their numbers and how not to feel guilty—teach REBT. Show ABC model. Write on board their irrational self-talk and then rational self-talk.
5 min.	Dyads: Discuss the use of REBT when being assertive.
10 min.	Discussion: Things I plan to try this week regarding being assertive.
5 min.	Summary: What stood out for you today? Any wishes for anyone in the group?

Progress reports are helpful both for the member who shares and for the rest of the members who hear how others are using what they learn in the group. Also, progress reports help members see the continuity and flow of the group experience. Plan 3 includes a review, the introduction of new material, and periods of focus on the past, present, and future. The plan uses a varied format that includes a round, dyads, teaching, demonstrating, practicing, interacting, and committing to trying new behavior during the coming week. The leader also introduces a theory that members can use during the rest of the sessions. In closing, the leader asks the "wishes for anyone" question so that members can say encouraging things to each other and feel the support of other members; this helps build cohesion in the group.

PLAN 4

The third session of a weekly therapy group for outpatients of a mental health center; the group has six members.

5 min.	Progress reports—ask about Bob's mother's visit, Ruth's exercise program, Tandy's contract to talk with two people each day.
5 min.	Thoughts, comments, reactions to the week.
10 min.	Review Ellis's ABC model—use examples from their week.
60 min.	Personal work—do yes/no round of who wants to bring up something; if all no's, use backup plan—focus on love relationships: Rate love relationship on a scale of 1 to 10 (10 = great). Ask what keeps it from being a 10 (discussion and personal work should come out of this).
20 min.	Introduce TA model if it did not come up during the personal work or continue the personal work if others want to work.
10 min.	Share (in triads) reactions to TA model.
5 min.	Summarize—What stood out? How will they use REBT and TA?
5 min.	Write in journals (journals are left for the leader to read).

In this plan, the leader starts by having specific members report on some of the work they have done in group. This fosters continuity. Also, when members know they are going to report to the group, they tend to think more about the group. The leader asks about the week to see whether anyone has something to share. This allows members to share positive or negative things that happened. Personal work could be started here, but the leader wants to spend a few minutes reviewing the REBT model and uses the members' comments about the week to show how REBT can be helpful. The review is brief because the leader wants to allow enough time for individual work. In therapy groups, members often come wanting to talk about some concern. The round (an exercise in which everyone comments) helps the leader learn quickly how many members have something to discuss. Two things to note in this segment are that the leader has a backup plan and that an hour—plus more time if necessary—has been allowed for personal work. The leader introduces transactional analysis (TA) to the group because it is a theory that most patients find interesting and helpful. For the final activity, the leader has members write in a journal that they leave with him; this gives them a chance to express what they may have wanted to say in the group but for some reason did not.

Frequent Mistakes in Planning

We close this chapter outlining some typical mistakes leaders make in planning. Some of them have been alluded to earlier in the chapter.

Not Planning

The biggest mistake made in planning is not doing it. Very often, at the end of workshops that we give, group leaders comment that they now realize that many of the problems they have with their groups stem mostly from not planning. Unfortunately, some professionals still subscribe to the notion that planning will detract from the group. It is very important to understand this is not true. Good planning is the best way to ensure that the session will be valuable to the group members.

Planning Too Much

The opposite of not planning is planning too many activities for the session, which often results in superficial coverage of several important topics. It is better to cover a few topics in depth than to skim over several. Our students frequently make this mistake because they are afraid members will not talk, so they plan too many topics for the time period allowed. It is good to have backup plans and additional topics, but it is important for the leader to allow time in his plan to focus on topics long enough so that there is new learning and impact.

Irrelevant or Meaningless Content

Too often, leaders choose activities, exercises, or topics that do not interest the members. Leaders sometimes use introductory exercises that are irrelevant and thus fail to set the appropriate tone, or they conduct activities that are not related to the members' concerns. Leaders also introduce topics that relate to only one or two members; this causes the others to lose interest or become resentful. It is absolutely essential that the leader do everything possible to ensure that the session will be relevant and valuable to most or all of the members. The following are examples of *poor* planning.

- For the first session of a weight-loss group, the leader plans 30 minutes on the topic of organic gardening.
- In a group for teenagers, the leader plans to focus on how to select the right college to attend, even though only two members are planning to go to college.
- For a 1½-hour session for stepparents, the leader plans a 15-minute mini-lecture on society and the family.
- In a group for couples with marital problems, the leader plans 30 minutes on dealing with children. Only two of the five couples have children.

Inappropriate Exercises

Leaders will sometimes plan an exercise for which members are not ready. For example, during a first or second session, members usually are not ready for an exercise that involves sharing about sexual concerns, nor are they ready for certain kinds of feedback exercises.

Too Many Exercises

Another mistake leaders make is to plan too many exercises for a given session. This prevents members from having enough time to process and learn from the exercises, thereby robbing them of much of the value of the exercises. Also, the session will seem like a series of exercises rather than a group in which members can share and exchange reactions, feelings, and thoughts. Inexperienced leaders are especially prone to this error, perhaps due to not fully understanding the purpose of the exercise and how to process it, or their fear that members won't have things to say.

Poor Planning of Time and Order

Many beginning leaders make mistakes in planning their use of time. A common error is planning warm-up or introductory activities that last too long. These exercises, although important, can drastically reduce time available for more meaningful, productive work in the middle part of the session. It is imperative that the leader plan the group so that the most time is spent on the most important issues.

A good plan has a reasonable order to it. Some leaders forget this and plan topics or exercises that are not related to each other. For example, a leader would not want to conduct an exercise that focuses on fun followed by one that focuses on death. Also, leaders sometimes arrange the topics or exercises in a sequence that makes them less beneficial than they could be. For instance, it would be a mistake for the leader to plan a long feedback exercise followed by a discussion of how members see themselves. Rather, the order should be reversed because it would benefit members more to consider how they see themselves before hearing feedback from others.

Not Planning an Interesting Beginning

Some leaders fail to plan interesting warm-up phases. This is especially a mistake for groups in institutions, such as prisons or mental hospitals, where members tend to be negative. It can be a mistake to plan a few minutes for opening comments from group members since they will often offer some complaint about the institution or the program. Leaders will want to plan interesting openings that do not allow negative comments to surface at the beginning. The leader might even establish that the last few minutes of each session will be available for members to air their complaints.

Allowing Too Much Time for Warm-Up

We mentioned this and the next two mistakes earlier, but they are such common mistakes that we wanted to repeat them here. Some leaders mistakenly plan long openings to sessions as a way to review the previous session. The idea is good, but allowing as much as 15 to 20 minutes is usually a mistake because most people want to move on to new material. It is very important to make sure that the opening is productive and not so long as to bore the members.

Not Allowing Enough Time for Warm-Up

When leaders have much to cover in a session, they sometimes forget to plan for the warm-up phase. Members usually need some time to get focused, which is the purpose of the first few minutes of any group. Groups will vary as to how much time is needed for the beginning phase of the session, but it is important that the leader allot whatever time is needed. In the next chapter, we discuss the warm-up phase in detail.

Vague Plans

Many beginning leaders plan their groups too vaguely to be of much help. For instance, the leader will plan to deal with the subject of anger and will allow 45 minutes for the topic but will neglect to plan in detail how to introduce the topic and what exercises and activities will be used. The leader who plans well will plan how he is going to cover the topic and also will give thought to possible spin-off subjects, such as anger at parents, self-talk and anger, and ways to deal with anger.

Lack of Flexibility

Some leaders rigidly follow their plan even when members have raised issues that are more meaningful and appropriate than those planned. Other leaders fail to recognize when their plan is not working. *It is necessary to be flexible and to allow for deviation from a plan whenever it becomes clear that members are not benefiting from it.* Imagine the toll in group commitment and interest in the following scenario.

◆ E X A M P L E

The leader has planned two activities to improve family communication for a group of teenagers who live together in a detention center. The members tell the leader how angry they are at two of the residents who are not in the group. Their anger is due to a stealing and lying incident. Rather than changing the plan and focusing on their immediate needs, the leader forces the members to try the communication-skills activities. They listlessly role play their mothers and fathers.

❖❖❖

⌐ *Concluding Comments*

Planning consists of two parts—pregroup planning and session planning. Pregroup planning involves making decisions on the kind of group, when it meets, how long it meets, and whom the members should be. Screening is very important and can be accomplished in a number of ways, including personal interview, written forms, or referral from others.

A leader should plan the beginning, middle, and ending phases of any particular session. Planning should include not only the activities and topics, but the amount of time to be devoted to each. There are many things to consider when planning each phase of a session. Common mistakes in planning include lack of planning, too much planning, not enough attention to how time is allotted, inappropriate or too many exercises, and inflexibility. Remember that although we emphasize the importance of having a plan, an effective leader is never a slave to that plan. If a valuable new topic emerges during a session, the leader should more than likely alter the plan; if the plan is not working, the leader should abandon it and use a backup plan. An effective leader is always thinking, evaluating, and making decisions during the session.

Getting Started: The First and Second Sessions

The First Session

The first and second sessions of any group are often the most important and usually are the most difficult to lead. The first session is difficult because the leader has many different dynamics and logistics to manage: starting the group, introducing the content to the members, and monitoring the members' reactions both to being in the group and to the content. We discuss 18 different things to consider in the first session.

1. Beginning the group
2. Helping members get acquainted
3. Setting a positive tone
4. Clarifying the purpose of the group
5. Explaining the leader's role
6. Explaining how the group will be conducted
7. Helping members verbalize expectations
8. Drawing out members
9. Using exercises
10. Checking out the comfort levels of the members
11. Explaining the rules
12. Explaining any special terms that will be used
13. Assessing members' interaction style
14. Cutting off members
15. Focusing on the content
16. Addressing questions
17. Getting members to look at other members
18. Closing the first session

Beginning the Group

One of the most important considerations for the first session is how to begin the group. How the leader opens the session will have an important bearing on the tone of the group and the comfort level of the members. The leader should convey warmth, trust, helpfulness, understanding, and positive regard. This is the time when members form their impressions of the leader and assess whether they think the group is going to be helpful to them.

Unfortunately, members sometimes quit groups that could be helpful because the opening few minutes were boring or intimidating. Others may be put off if the leader inappropriately uses a formal, businesslike manner in the opening moments. For some groups, a formal or firm opening is appropriate, but for most groups, it is less effective. Some leaders make the mistake of opening with a mini-lecture and discussion on issues such as the rules, the meeting time for each session, and the frequency of meetings. When 10 or 15 minutes are spent discussing these issues, the session usually gets off to a poor start because the members are bored. Another common mistake is allowing the introduction of members to take too long. Some beginning leaders are afraid to cut off members, so they politely let each member go on for 3 or 4 minutes—this makes for a boring opening for most groups. Remember, the opening few minutes of a first session are very important!

Following are seven possible openings that include an overview of the group and the introduction of the members.

Options for Opening the First Session

1. *Start with a brief statement about the group; then conduct an introduction exercise.* This type of opening is perhaps the one most frequently used. The leader gives a brief (1- to 2-minute), well-thought-out opening statement and then has the members participate in an introduction exercise. This prevents members from settling into a "listening" frame of mind; they become active almost immediately and quickly feel that they are participants in a group rather than listeners in a class. This opening is especially useful for groups where the members do not know each other.

◆ E X A M P L E

This group is for teenagers whose parents have divorced or separated in the last 4 months.

Leader: I'm really glad you are here. As you know, this group is for sharing thoughts, feelings, and reactions to your parents' divorce or separation. It is my understanding that each of you has experienced your parents either divorcing or separating within the last 4 months. Through this group, I hope you will realize that you're not the only one feeling the way you do. Having your parents split up causes all kinds of feelings—chances are many of you are having a variety of those feelings. We'll explore them in this group. To get started, I thought we'd do an introductory exercise to learn about each other. I am going to ask each of you to share your name, how long your parents have been divorced or separated, and whom you are currently living with. We'll go around the group. Who wants to start?

Ted: I will. I am Ted. My parents are definitely going to divorce or at least I think so. Last week—

Leader: *(Using a caring voice)* Ted, let me interrupt. For now, just how long separated and whom you are living with.

Ted: Sorry. I am Ted, and I am living with my mom. They separated 4 weeks ago.

Melinda: I am Melinda. . . .

2. *Start with a long opening statement about the group and its purpose; then conduct an introduction exercise.* This type of opening is often used for education or task groups, although some leaders use a long opening statement for therapy and growth groups as well. By an opening statement, we mean that the leader will spend the first 3 to 5 minutes describing, in a pleasant, energetic manner, the purpose and format of the group and then will present an overview of the planned content for another couple of minutes. During this opening, the leader will usually give some background information about himself and his experience in leading groups similar to the present one. A practical reason for using a long opening is to capture the interest of the members who are present when other members have not yet arrived. It is important to understand that when using a long opening statement, it needs to be interesting and informative for the members. If it is boring, the leader can lose the members for the entire session. Leaders should be cautious about boring members with too lengthy an opening. On numerous occasions, we have heard of leaders who talked for 10 to 15 minutes at the beginning—this would be a major mistake.

◆ EXAMPLE

The group consists of teachers in a large school district. It is the first session in a series of four on teacher burnout.

Leader: I'd like us to begin. I am Sarah Daniels. I am a counselor at North High School. Over the last several years, I have been studying teacher burnout. As a result of my studies, I have developed what I think is a helpful way of understanding burnout. Over the next 4 weeks, I will be going over the material. Briefly, I'd like to share what each session will be about. Today we will start by . . .

After going over the material for 2 or 3 minutes, the leader concludes the opening statement.

Leader: I hope you now have an idea of what will take place here and how this group can help. Now, before getting started with definitions of burnout, I'd like to take a couple of minutes and let you introduce yourselves. I'd like each of you to tell us your name, how long you have been teaching, what you teach, and a sentence or two about why you came.

3. *Start with a long opening statement; then get right into the content of the group.* This opening can be used in discussion, education, and task groups where the members already know each other or in groups where personal sharing will be minimal. A long opening statement is used when the leader feels the members need an explanation or clarification of the group's content or purpose. The long opening statement would be similar to that in option 2, where the leader outlines the content and shares some information about himself. It differs from option 2 in that the leader does not plan an introduction of the members because the members know each other or because the group is too large.

◆ E X A M P L E

This group is for helping 14 unemployed people find a job. The leader opens the session.

Leader: I am glad you decided to attend the group. I think you will find the information helpful in getting you back into the workforce. The goal of these group sessions will be to give you information about how to find potential jobs, how to interview for jobs, how to fill out applications, and how to keep a positive attitude while looking. Before we get started, I want to tell you a little about myself and about each of the five sessions. . . . *(After going over the proposed content of the five sessions, the leader continues.)*

Leader: Now, let's get started on today's material. We're going to discuss how to find potential jobs. I want each of you to think of three ways that you go about looking for work.

4. *Start with a brief statement about the group; then get into the content.* This opening would be used when no introductions are needed (members already know each other) and the purpose of the group is already clear to the members. This is a good opening for many discussion, education, and task groups, especially if they are meeting for a short period, such as an hour.

◆ E X A M P L E

This group's purpose is to decide on policies for a new treatment unit for adolescents. The leader begins.

Leader: Let's get started. We have a number of policies to decide on regarding the new unit. The current plan is to meet each Tuesday for an hour and a half at this time for the next 4 weeks or until we feel we are finished. Why don't we begin by listing the kinds of policies we think need to be written? I'll write them as you call them out.

5. *Start with a brief statement about the group; then have the members form dyads.* This opening can be used when no introduction exercise is necessary. The leader describes the group briefly and then has members form dyads to discuss either the content of the group or why they have come to the group. This kind of opening is useful when the purpose is already clear to everyone and the members are comfortable being in the group. It is also useful in certain kinds of task, education, discussion, and support groups.

◆ E X A M P L E

This group is for parents who have learned that their children have been sexually abused at a day care center.

Leader: I am glad you came tonight. I think that all of you will benefit from sharing your feelings with each other. When something like this occurs, a group can be helpful in getting support and exchanging ideas for helping your child. Since you all know each other, I want us to start by pairing up. Do not pair up with your spouse, if he or she is with you, or with someone you know very well.

   Now that you have a partner, I want you to share the feelings that you have experienced since this incident and why you chose to come to the group—that is, what you hope to gain from being here.

6. *Start with a brief statement about the group; then have members fill out a short sentence-completion form.* When no introductions are needed, using a sentence-completion form is an excellent way to open certain kinds of groups because it tends to help members focus. This kind of opening is helpful in leading task groups, discussion groups, and some education groups. It can also be used in growth and therapy groups when the members already know one another.

◆ E X A M P L E

This group's purpose is to improve staff relations in a hospital unit.

Leader: As you know, the purpose of this meeting is to improve working relations within the unit. I'd like to start by having you fill out this form, which consists of five incomplete sentences. The sentences have to do with the unit: your feelings, your perception of the problems, and so on. I'll give you a couple of minutes to complete it.

7. Start with an introduction exercise. Starting with an introduction exercise instead of a statement about the group should only be done when the members have a clear idea of the group's purpose. If an appropriate introduction exercise is used, this type of opening can serve a dual purpose: Members can introduce themselves and begin immediately to focus on the content of the group.

◆ E X A M P L E

This group is for single fathers.

Leader: Why don't we begin? As a way of starting, I'd like each of you to introduce yourself and tell us the age of your child or children and in two or three sentences how you came to be a single father. Who wants to go first?

These examples illustrate that there are a variety of appropriate ways to open a first session. *Remember, the right kind of opening, combined with enthusiasm on the part of the leader, will have a strong positive effect on how a group starts.*

Helping Members Get Acquainted

In a first session, the leader will want to give thought as to how members will get introduced to one another. If members do not know one another, it is usually beneficial to have them get acquainted soon after the session begins. Members tend to feel more at ease after learning each others' names and spending some time getting to know one another.

The amount of time spent on introductions varies according to the purpose. In groups where personal sharing will take place, more time should be spent helping members get to know one another since members are curious about those with whom they will be discussing personal issues. In most education and discussion groups and in many task groups, only a minimal amount of time needs to be spent on introductions because members either know one another or will not be discussing personal issues. In groups consisting of members from diverse cultural backgrounds, more time will probably be needed for introductions and getting acquainted.

The size of the group can limit the options for the kind of introduction exercise chosen. If the group has more than ten members, the leader will probably not want to use an introduction exercise involving each member sharing about himself or herself for 1 to 2 minutes because it would take too long. When groups are meeting for a rather short period (an hour or less), the leader will not want to use any introduction exercise that lasts more than 5 minutes. This applies especially to education, discussion, and task groups and to groups meeting for only one session.

The purpose of the group is probably the most important factor in determining what kind of introduction exercise to use. With groups meeting for educational or discussion purposes, the leader may want to use an exercise that helps people remember names. In growth, task, support, and therapy groups, the leader may choose an exercise that gets members to share relevant information about themselves. The leader may also have members share their reasons for attending the group or their expectations of the session. For instance, in a group for patients with cancer, an introduction activity where the members share their names, the names of their family members, where they work, and their favorite hobby would not be relevant. Instead, the leader could have the members state their names, how long they have been receiving treatment, and one fear or feeling about having the disease.

The following are descriptions of several introduction activities.

The Name Round

The name round is probably the most frequently used exercise for learning people's names. In the name round, members simply introduce themselves, sometimes giving names only, but most of the time sharing additional information. Naturally, what is shared will depend on the purpose of the group. For instance, in a parenting group, the leader would have members state the number of children they have and their ages, and maybe one concern they want to address in the group; in a changing families group for children, members could tell how long their parents have been divorced, whom they live with, and maybe a word or phrase regarding how they feel about their parents' divorce.

One common mistake of beginning leaders is to have members share irrelevant information. We have heard stories of members being asked to introduce themselves and tell various irrelevant things about themselves. Most members of serious groups are not interested in "cute" openings. A "fun" introduction activity is appropriate for certain kinds of groups (school or church retreats, social groups for the elderly), but it is a mistake to use a "light" introduction exercise for groups that have a serious purpose—for example, groups dealing with such issues as abuse, addiction, AIDS, anger, or rape. Another mistake is to let members share for too long, thus turning the introduction of members into a 15- to 20-minute activity that tends to get boring.

The Repeat Round

The repeat round is a name exercise where the first member says her name, the next member says the first member's name and then his name, and so on. This exercise is good for helping members remember everyone's name. School kids tend to like this, and it does help with learning the names.

The Introduction Dyad

This activity consists of two members pairing up and telling each other certain things about themselves, usually based on suggestions from the leader. Then all the members come back together in a group, and each one introduces his partner to the group. For example, in a group for children who have trouble making friends, a member might say, "This is Carlos. He likes football and fishing. He has two younger stepbrothers. His favorite subject in school is math." This exercise teaches listening and gives members a chance to get to know one other member better.

Repeated Dyad

Members pair up with every other member and spend 2 to 5 minutes sharing such things as why they are in the group and what they hope to get from it. (This is good for certain kinds of support, growth, and therapy groups.) This exercise should only be used when there are fewer than six members and the session is at least an hour and a half long; otherwise, it would take too much time to allow each member to form a dyad with every other member.

Milling

For large groups (12 or more members), we sometimes have members mill around and meet each other during the first 4 to 5 minutes of the first group session. The instructions are usually quite simple, such as, "To help you get acquainted, I'd like you to stand up and mill about the room meeting the other group members. Try to learn everyone's name and why he or she is here." A simple activity like this provides an opportunity for members to have contact with one another and speeds up the process of getting acquainted. This is especially good when the leader is waiting for a couple of members to arrive and the others are sitting quietly by themselves.

These are just some of the ways a leader can help members get acquainted. The important thing to understand is the leader should always give thought to how introductions are going to be handled. A good introduction exercise is one that is appropriate for the kind of group and the amount of time the group is meeting. *Using large name tags is probably the easiest way to help members remember the names of other members.*

Setting a Positive Tone

Another important task for the leader during the first and second sessions is to establish a positive tone for the group. The tone is the prevailing atmosphere; it stems from several sources, including the leader's enthusiasm and the members' comfort and trust. The leader can establish a positive tone by being enthusiastic and drawing out members, cutting off hostile or negative interactions, holding the focus on interesting topics, and shifting the focus when the topics are irrelevant or only interesting to a couple of members.

It is very important that the leader not let the group focus on negative members or negative issues for a major portion of the first session. A member who is complaining about being in the group or questioning its value can establish a negative tone that may be difficult to alter. Allowing extended hostile or heated interaction between members also contributes to a negative tone. Certainly some time may have to be devoted to these dynamics, but the leader will want to make sure that most of the time is spent sharing and discussing in a positive way. If a negative tone is set during the first two group sessions, members will usually never come to trust one another enough to share personal information about themselves. Also, they may feel that the group is a place to "nail" other members and therefore will either focus on others or fear being attacked by the group.

Setting a good tone for some nonvoluntary groups (DUI, residential homes, inpatient facilities) is very important and also sometimes very difficult since the members can be very hostile and negative. The leader will want to have an opening that gets the members' attention and gets them interested immediately. One group leader we know put a garbage can in the center of a group for teenagers who had been caught using alcohol at school and said something like, "I know you don't want to be here, so I want you to get all your complaints out now and then we'll put a lid on them. You have 10 minutes to complain." At the end of that 10 minutes, she stopped them, put the lid on, and said, "Let's name our group," which ended up being called "The Beach Group," and they were nowhere near a beach! The point is that leaders of nonvoluntary groups need to be prepared for uncooperative and hostile members who may try to set a negative tone for the group. Also, the leader may need to be rather firm but also show concern and understanding.

Clarifying the Purpose

The leader wants to be sure that the purpose of the group is clarified during the first and second sessions. Clarification is particularly important if there has been no screening interview. Even if the leader has screened the members and has already spent time discussing the group's purpose, it is still a good idea to review the purpose in the group. The purpose of some groups may require more clarification than others. In a group that has been advertised as a smoking-cessation group, the purpose is probably clear to all members; on the other hand, a divorce group could be intended for support or therapy. Therefore, the specific purpose of the group will have to be clarified during the first session.

For any group in which the purpose may be confusing, it is a good idea to reiterate the purpose throughout the first two sessions. After the second session, it usually is not necessary to review the purpose unless new members are added to the group or the purpose changes during the life of the group.

Explaining the Leader's Role

During the first session, the leader should explain what her role will be throughout the sessions: a teaching role, a facilitative role, an active leadership role, a therapeutic role, or some of each. Offering an explanation helps members form a picture of what to expect from the leader.

◆ E X A M P L E S

- Let me take just a minute to explain my role to all of you. As you know, for the next 6 weeks, we will be meeting every Monday evening so that you can share your experiences as a single parent. My role in this group will be to facilitate sharing and provide some information. On some occasions, the situation may call for me to become more active and lead the group in counseling a member who is asking the group for some help.

- In this group, I mainly will help you share any problems you are having here at school, at home, or with your friends. I will make sure that this is a safe place to share any concerns you have and will help you learn how to problem solve. I will encourage you to share and will ask you to do some different kinds of group exercises that will help you focus on different areas of your life, such as problems with parents, peer pressure, or problems with schoolwork.

- In this group, I will be introducing you to the dangers of alcohol and drug use. To do this, I will present some information and then get you to share reactions, thoughts, and questions. I will mostly be trying to get you to express your thoughts and concerns and will not be teaching like a teacher does where all you have to do is sit and listen. This is meant to be a group for sharing so I will be asking all of you to participate.

- My role in this group is to see to it you make the decisions that we discussed need to be made. My participation will be minimal; that is, I will not offer my opinion or ideas since I do not work here and do not know your agency as well as you do. I will encourage you to be open and honest with each other, and I will try to get you to express how you feel about the issues.

Also, I will try to structure the time wisely so we can accomplish something each time we meet.

Explaining How the Group Will Be Conducted

Closely allied to explaining the purpose and the leader's role is explaining what will happen during a session. It is important to clarify during the first session how the leader plans to conduct the group. Describing the kinds of discussions and activities that will take place in the group will help ease tension and ensure the smooth functioning of the group. If there is a specific format for the group, the leader would want to explain this.

◆ E X A M P L E

Leader: Each session we will spend the first few minutes sharing comments or any relevant experiences since our last meeting. We'll then focus on anything that one of you wants to talk about. If no one has anything for that day, we'll focus on a new topic. We'll split our time between discussing different concerns you have and the topics that we decide we want to cover. We'll always spend the last few minutes sharing what we got out of the session and offering any encouragement to each other.

In certain kinds of groups, the leader will want to inform members that they will be asked to do certain group exercises and that, at times, the group may get rather intense. Also, he may want to explain how he intends to work with individuals who bring up concerns they want to work on. Hearing this explanation during the first and second sessions will give members a much clearer understanding of what will take place in the group.

A good reason for stating what will happen in the group is that after hearing a description, some members may decide they do not want to be in the group. If a member decides not to join the group, the leader will want to determine the reason. Depending on the reason, the leader may or may not encourage the member to stay. That is, the leader would not want to urge a member to stay who definitely wanted a different kind of group, but she might try to encourage a member who feared that something bad might happen to him in the group. Usually the discussion with the member wanting to quit is done in private, but sometimes the leader may see the value of discussing it with the entire group.

Included in the discussion of how the group will be conducted should also be a discussion of the potential risks involved in being in a support, growth, counseling, or therapy group since groups can present life-changing experiences. The ASGW Ethical Guidelines (1989) specify that leaders are responsible for explaining and discussing the risks of being in a group. Members need to know they may discover uncomfortable things about themselves or their pasts. Also, they need to be informed that they will be challenged to look at how they see themselves, how they cope, and how they interact with others.

Helping Members Verbalize Expectations

One first-session activity that is beneficial for certain kinds of groups is to have members share their expectations of the group. In this way, the leader learns what the members want, and he can further clarify the purpose of the group by commenting. At times, the leader will expand upon some of the expectations voiced if they are in line with the purpose. At other times, the leader will need to point out that certain expectations will not be met by the current group due to its structure and purpose.

◆ E X A M P L E

This group is for teenage girls who have had a baby in the last 3 months. The leader has just finished an introduction exercise and decides to use a round to get members to verbalize their expectations. Note also how the leader comments on some of the expectations as they apply to the group.

Leader: OK, now that we know a little more about each other, I want to talk about your expectations for the group. I want you each to think of what you are hoping to get from the group. We'll go around and hear from each of you.

Angela: I just look forward to talking to kids my own age about having a baby. Talking to grown-ups all the time isn't fun.

Leader: Certainly one of the main reasons for the group is just that—all of you will get a chance to share with one another, and you do have things in common, that's for sure.

Donna: I am overwhelmed. Trying to handle the baby, school, my boyfriend, friends! I don't know if I can do it, and I hope to get some ideas.

Leader: I think all of you will find that the group can really be of help. I think each one of us has some ideas that can help others, and that's the benefit of the six of us meeting.

Nelda: I came because it sounded like something I could learn from.

Tandy: I need help with child-rearing. I am scared that I will screw up my kid, and I don't want to do that.

Leader: We will spend some time each week talking about child-rearing since I think each of you probably wants to hear about that. We'll also spend time sharing about anything you want to that pertains to being a teenage mother.

❖❖❖

Sometimes members attend a first session having expectations that are not in line with the purpose of the group. If this situation arises, the leader will want to reiterate the purpose. If a member remains insistent that the purpose should be different, the leader may have members get into pairs and discuss why they came or some other relevant question while the leader pairs up with the insistent member—this avoids a long discussion or debate in front of the group that may create a negative tone.

◆ E X A M P L E S

In this first example, the member has an expectation that is not in line with the group's purpose, which is to help first-year college students with study skills. The students are expressing their expectations.

Bud: I want to learn how to prepare for essay exams. My high school was such a breeze, and all my tests were fill-in-the-blank or multiple choice.

Akira: I need help with my math problems—I don't understand equations, and the instructor said I should get a tutor, so when I saw the announcement about a study skills group, I thought I would give it a try.

Leader: Well, Akira, let me clarify something for you and for others of you. This group is not really for tutoring as much as it is for teaching you how to study. That is, we will not work on any specific course but will talk about how to study for certain courses, including math. I guess what I am saying is that, if any of you are looking for specific help in a course, then probably a tutor would be better. We are going to talk about how to take notes, how to prepare for exams, and basically how to study. Akira, now that you are here, you may want to stay, or you may really just be looking for math help. If you want a tutor, I'll help you find one.

In this example, one member's expectations are different from the others'. The purpose of the group is for parents to discuss what to do about the many teenage pregnancies in the community. Members are discussing their views of the goal of the group.

Carla: I think it's good that we are meeting. I don't want my daughter to become pregnant, but I don't know the best way to prevent it. So I am hoping that as a group we can come up with some good ideas for educating our kids about sex.

Betsy: That's why I came. To try to come up with something that either the school or community can do.

Dot: I can tell you what we have to do, and that's to stop these kids from having abortions! They gave some statistics about teenage abortions on television that horrified me. I am here to see to it that the school does something about all these abortions!

Leader: I really don't see this group as focusing on abortions. The purpose of this group is to decide how to prevent so many from getting pregnant.

Dot: I can't buy that. It is our moral duty to stop kids from even considering abortion!

Leader: *(In a very calm voice)* Let's do this: I want you to pair up with someone you don't know very well and discuss what you think are the different topics that we need to discuss in this group. Dot, I'll be with you.

The leader could tell that Dot was not going to let the issue die, and he did not want the group to focus on a side issue. By using dyads, the leader was able to keep members focused while talking to Dot about the purpose. The leader would want to be careful not to spend the next half-hour trying to convince Dot of the purpose. He probably should not spend more than 5 minutes, if for no other reason than the other members will likely run out of things to say. This is a situation in which the leader might ask Dot to leave if she insists on talking about the abortion issue.

A leader can make several mistakes regarding the expectations of the members. Some leaders spend as much as half or three-fourths of a session on the question "What do you hope to get from this group?" This usually happens when expectations are varied and the leader feels obligated to discuss each one. Probably no more than 8 or 10 minutes should be spent on expectations, and often they can be covered in 5 minutes or less.

A very common mistake leaders make is to ask members for their expectations when they really don't have any. This can be the case in groups where the members are required to attend or are attending in order to avoid some other activity, such as a class or work. The leader may want to ask about expectations but should be prepared for little or no response—or responses that are not in line with the purpose.

◆ E X A M P L E

This is a mandatory group at a 30-day juvenile crisis center. The leader should not have mentioned expectations or should have expected some negative reactions because the members did not volunteer for the group.

Leader: I'd like to hear from each of you about why you are in the group and what you hope to gain from it.

Don: Hey, man, I don't want anything—they made me come.

Alton: There's nothing the matter with me—I hate this group therapy crap!

Leader: This isn't crap. Hopefully, it will be helpful.

Mel: I want to talk about rock music—the houseparent said we can talk about anything we want to.

Leader: Come on, be serious. What can you get from this group?

The leader did not second-guess that there probably would not be many expectations. A better way to handle this would be to ask if anyone had expectations, and then quickly move to an interesting exercise rather than pushing the idea of expectations.

❖❖❖

Drawing Out Members during the First Session

It is advisable that during the first and second sessions, the leader try to make sure that everyone has a chance to contribute. The leader should not force each member to speak; rather, members should feel they may participate if they so desire. If the members believe they haven't had an opportunity to verbalize their thoughts, feelings, or ideas, they may feel left out.

During the first session of a growth, counseling, therapy, or support group, the leader should, if possible, get each member to share something since this tends to reduce anxiety about being in the group. It is also important because members are usually curious about one another, and disclosures usually help members feel more comfortable. Be aware, however, that some members will be so uncomfortable or fearful that they will not share very much during the first meeting.

Two of the best ways to get members to share during the first session are the use of written exercises and rounds. Introduction rounds, other rounds, and some written exercises usually will get each member to comment. Written exercises, such as sentence completions or lists, are excellent activities because members usually will feel fairly comfortable when asked to share what they have written. Rounds are good because every member is asked to respond in a word, phrase, or number to some question such as, "On a 1–10 scale, with 10 being very comfortable, how comfortable are you being here in group?"

Use of Exercises during the First Session

During the first session, certain exercises can be used to create comfort, interest, and member involvement. Following, we discuss three: rounds, dyads, and sentence completions.

1. *Rounds* are the most valuable exercise that we use in the first session since they get everyone to speak, which is important. Earlier in this chapter, we explained the *name round* and the *repeat round*. Other rounds consist of 1–10 scales on some issue or feeling, such as commitment to being in the group, how it feels to work in a certain occupation, or how much stress members feel in their lives. Rounds can be used during the beginning, middle, and closing phases of the

session; the possibilities are endless. We discuss the use of rounds and dyads in detail in Chapter Nine.

2. *Dyads* (pairs) are very valuable in the beginning stage of groups because they give members the opportunity to talk more personally with one other member. Members can be paired with one another to discuss their reactions, feelings, ideas, answers, or some other relevant point. Because everyone gets a chance to talk, people are usually comfortable and often energized for talking in front of the whole group. Common mistakes with the use of dyads include letting them last too long or doing too many in one session. Dyads rarely should last over 5 minutes because long dyads do not allow members to have contact with others, and the leader cannot be sure how members are going to connect since they don't know each other. A member may feel annoyed or intimidated by his or her partner and thus conclude that the group is not helpful.

3. *Sentence-completion exercises* have also proved very helpful in facilitating interaction during the first session. This kind of written exercise gives members a base from which to comment. Also, members are usually very interested in hearing how others responded to the same incomplete sentence. The following are examples of sentence stems that could be used.

In a new group, I feel most comfortable when _____.

In a new group, I am most afraid of_____.

In a new group, I will usually_____.

For a group on stress:

The biggest stress for me at work is_____.

The biggest stress for me at home is_____.

One way I cope with stress is_____.

For a group of elementary school children whose parents are divorced:

The hardest thing about my parents' divorce is_____.

The person I blame the most for the divorce is_____.

When I think of my parents' divorce, I am most angry about_____.

These are just a few examples of exercises that may be helpful during the first session. Certainly other exercises—written, experiential, or verbal—are beneficial. However, some exercises are not appropriate for the first session. Certain fantasy exercises—which help members get in touch with feelings of sorrow, guilt, anxiety, or fears—will not help members become comfortable and, in fact, may cause members not to return to the group. The leader should always keep in mind when selecting exercises for the first session that their purpose is usually to help members get acquainted and feel comfortable, or to focus on the content in a meaningful but not too intense way. A good rule to follow for exercises during the first session is not to use too many. Some leaders make the mistake of doing one right after another, which does not leave much time for interaction or for processing the exercises, and it gives the members the impression that the group is about doing exercises rather than interaction and sharing.

Checking Out the Comfort Level

Feeling apprehensive or uncomfortable during the first session of a support, growth, counseling, or therapy group is quite common. To help reduce this discomfort, the leader might spend a few minutes focused on the topic of comfort level. By inquiring about members' comfort level, the leader lets members know he is aware that there may be some anxiety and that it is to be expected. In addition, hearing that others are anxious often eases members' anxiety by showing them they are not alone. The leader may want to introduce the topic of comfort during the warm-up phase—that is, within the first half-hour—if members seem extremely uncomfortable. If the leader does not discuss comfort in the beginning, he can introduce it almost any time throughout the session by saying something like, "Let's focus for a few minutes on the topic of comfort in this group," then continue with any of the following:

♦ In terms of comfort in the group right now, what is the word or phrase that best describes how you are feeling?
♦ On a 1–10 scale, with 10 being very uncomfortable and 1 being very comfortable, how would you rate how you are feeling in the group right now?
♦ On a 1–10 scale, with 10 being very uncomfortable and 1 being very comfortable, how would you rate how you were feeling in the group when we started, and how would you rate your feeling now?
♦ Does anyone want to comment on how he or she is feeling about being in this group?
♦ I'd like you to pair up with a person whom you would like to get to know better and talk about how you feel about being in the group. Discuss your comfort level and why you feel the way you do. Naturally, some of you are more comfortable than others. You'll have about 3 minutes to do this; then we'll come back to the large group for discussion.

Any of these activities will help members talk about the comfort level in the group. Such discussions often help members feel more comfortable, both through sharing their feelings and hearing that others feel some discomfort. The leader also gains a better idea of the source of discomfort. The leader may choose not to draw out those who rate themselves as very uncomfortable because focusing on them could make them more so. The leader will want to make sure that he does nothing to increase the group's discomfort level at this point.

It is essential to be aware that the comfort level might be low if members know each other outside the group, such as in a school setting. In these groups, some members may feel that the others don't like them or believe that what they share may negatively influence a relationship outside the group. If the leader senses that group members are uncomfortable, she will want to spend extra time trying to increase the comfort level by discussing it in group or by using exercises, rounds, and dyads to get members to share.

Explaining Group Rules

There are a number of things to consider regarding rules for the group: what should the rules be, who makes the rules, when to discuss them, and how to discuss them.

What should the rules be? All groups have rules about attendance; lateness; being reasonably cooperative and sensitive to others; one person talking at a time; and eating, smoking, and drinking during the session. Most counseling, therapy, support, and growth groups have rules about attacking others, putting others on the spot, and keeping shared personal disclosures confidential.

Who makes the rules? In most cases the leader makes the rules because the leader understands groups and what rules need to be in place for the group to be successful. Sometimes, the leader uses the group discussion activity to decide the rules. This can be a mistake because certain rules that are necessary may be deemed unimportant by members. Also, this can take up valuable time that could be spent on the actual purpose of the group.

When should the rules be discussed? It is usually preferable to cover group rules as needed rather than opening up with a speech or discussion about them. For some groups, presenting them at the very beginning may be fine (especially for some elementary and middle school groups); but for others, it is a mistake because when the rules are covered in the initial moments of the group, members become bored or anxious for something to happen. Also, by presenting the rules right at the beginning, a negative tone may be set.

How should the rules be discussed? Any presentation or discussion of rules for the group should be done in a pleasant, positive manner. Rules regarding such things as no eating, drinking, or smoking during group sessions, attendance, and no attacking of others or putting others on the spot can be briefly discussed since they are rules that the leader has decided upon. Rules about the confidentiality of the information shared among members needs more attention since it is very important that everyone understands what it means, and that everyone agrees to keep things confidential. The leader will want to get some acknowledgment from each person that he or she agrees to keep material confidential.

The following examples show when and how to "sandwich" in the rules and how to focus on confidentiality.

◆ EXAMPLES

It is 30 minutes into the first session of a therapy group.

Jake: I want to hear what David thinks. He hasn't said anything about his problems.

Leader: Let me jump in here. I know that some of you may want to hear from other members, but one rule that I have in groups that I lead is that no one will be forced to talk. So, rather than putting David on the spot, you might say that you are curious about what others are thinking. The reason for this rule is that I want people not to have to worry about being attacked or singled out. Any comments on this? *(Lets a few seconds pass)* Let's go back to sharing concerns you are currently working on.

In this example, the leader saw the need to mention a rule and stated it in a natural manner. He also spared David by shifting the focus from him to the rule and then back to the topic. Introducing rules when they are relevant helps members remember them better.

This group is in the first half-hour, and the members are discussing fears about being in the group. They are using a sentence-completion form containing a sentence that reads "One thing I am afraid of in groups is _____."

Beth: I wrote that I am afraid of looking foolish.

Leader: That is a very common feeling. I would imagine that others feel the same way. *(Several heads nod.)*

Fern: I wrote that I am afraid of being attacked by other members for something that I say.

Leader: I want to comment on that. I'd like to establish a rule that no one is allowed to attack another member. We are here to listen and learn from each other, not to attack those who differ from us. How do all of you feel about having that as a rule?

The leader asks the question to hold the focus on "no member will be allowed to attack another member" because she feels it is a very important issue for the group.

It is early in the middle phase of the first session, and a member says he has something he would like to bring up. It is obvious that what he is going to say is very personal, and he is the first member actually to say that he wants to talk about a concern. Up to now, members have shared only "safe" things about themselves.

John: I think I want to share something that happened here at the plant that I have never told anyone.

Leader: John, before you do I want to mention something very important. In the beginning, we discussed briefly that we should keep things confidential. I want to emphasize that rule since John obviously is about to share something important and personal to him. It is imperative that we keep the content of these group meetings confidential if there is to be a feeling of trust. Is this suitable to everyone? (*Looks around the room*) I am going to ask each of you if you agree to keep things confidential. Chico?

Chico: Yes.

Carlos: Yes.

Abdul: Yes.

Thomas: I agree.

Leader: OK, John, let's get back to what you wanted to share.

In regard to rules, our point is that the leader should not spend an inordinate amount of time on the rules unless there is some reason to do so. If a member tries to argue about a rule that the leader feels is necessary, the leader should calmly explain why it is important for the smooth running of the group. Sometimes, it is best simply to say what the rules are and why they exist rather than opening them up for discussion. For example, if a leader decides that there will be no smoking or eating during the group, she can tell the group the reason.

Leader: Since the room is small and some of us are nonsmokers, there will be no smoking during the session. If you feel you have to smoke, you may excuse yourself for a couple of minutes. Also, I'm going to ask you not to eat or drink during the session since it can be distracting.

A common mistake made by beginning leaders is to discuss issues like the preceding ones for 15 to 20 minutes. This is usually not necessary and detracts from the purpose of the group. In many kinds of groups, it is appropriate and helpful for the leader to decide the rules and inform the group what they are.

Explaining Terms

If the leader plans to use special terms, she should explain them to the members. Some terms that might confuse members are *rounds*, *dyads*, and *exercises*. If the group is a counseling, therapy, support, or growth group, the leader will want to explain the terms she might be using, such as *private logic*, *REBT*, *TA*, *ego states*, or *alter ego*. The leader could explain the terms when she is explaining her role or at any other time that seems appropriate, such as the first time they naturally occur. Explaining terms and procedures in the first or second session reduces the chances of confusion or misunderstanding when they are used in later sessions.

Assessing Members' Interaction Styles

During the first session, the leader will want to note the different ways that members interact in the group. This is extremely helpful for leading the session and planning for future sessions. Every member has a certain style or manner. Some members may be very quiet; others may try to dominate; others may be supportive; and still others may be very critical. By observing these styles, the leader will be able to adjust the plan for the session. Any leader who fails to assess the interaction style of members will make the task of leading much more difficult.

Leaders assess interaction styles by paying attention to what members say, how they say it, and how often they say anything. Too often, a beginning leader will get caught up in the content of the group and fail to observe that not all members are participating or that certain members are dominating.

Cutting Off Members during the First Session

It is very important during the first session to not let a member dominate or attack other members. If the leader does not restrain those members, others will feel intimidated or upset because they did not have a chance to contribute. The leader has to be prepared to use cutoff skills. Sometime during the first session, the leader should explain that he will at times be interrupting members.

Leader: Something that I may do from time to time is interrupt if I feel you are off on a tangent or others are wanting to speak. Two of my tasks are to keep us focused on the purpose of the group and to give everyone a chance to talk.

We devote most of Chapter Eight to how and when to cut off members and how to tell them that you will at times be doing this. *Cutting off is an essential skill for group leading*, and a leader must be prepared to refocus any member who is being very negative or hostile or who is trying to dominate or focus the group on some irrelevant tangent.

Focusing on the Content

In this book, *content* means the topic being discussed in the group. All groups have a content area; some are very specific—such as assertiveness, coping with divorce, or study skills—while others are less specific—such as personal problems or personal growth. The leader will want to be sure to focus some of the first session on the content or purpose of the group. Devoting too much time in the first session to explaining rules, making introductions, getting acquainted, and explaining the leadership role will cause members to become bored and lose interest because their needs are not being met. To focus members on the content, the leader can use an introduction exercise that helps them to think about why they came to the group—as in the following example. As the round ends, the leader focuses on content by "spinning off" from one member's comment—taking the comment and elaborating on it. The leader then focuses the members on the elaboration.

◆ EXAMPLES

It is the first session of a group for battered women. The leader has briefly discussed the purpose of the group and has had each of the five women introduce herself and tell a little about her situation. The introduction round is on the next-to-last person.

Jane: I'm Jane. I have been married for 4 years. I have two children. My husband has beaten me five times, and each time has been worse than the others. He says it is my fault—I'm confused about whether it is my fault.

Diane: I'm Diane. My husband verbally and physically abuses me daily. I have been in counseling, but I always seem to let him sweet talk me into going back with him.

Leader: Diane, that's a good topic that we will discuss later. I was thinking that for now a good theme to talk about may be the one that Jane and a number of others alluded to about being confused about whose fault it is. I know many women often do think it is their fault that their man gets so out of control. What thoughts or feelings do you have about whether you think it is your fault?

In this example, the leader focuses the group on an important topic that everyone has feelings about. The discussion could last for 10 to 20 minutes and would probably be very helpful since it is definitely a relevant topic for all the members.

The purpose of this group is to provide help for students who are close to being expelled from school. The members are discussing their expectations of the group.

Barry: I hope that people here can help me stay out of trouble. I really want to stay in school—I like being with my friends.

Leader: I think what Barry is saying applies to all of you—that you want to stay in school. Is that right? *(Sees all the heads nodding)* Let's talk then about what it's going to take to stay out of trouble. What do you need to do to keep yourself out of trouble? Who wants to comment on that?

Rico: I will. I realize that I have got to . . . *(A valuable discussion follows for the next 10 minutes about all the things that can help them stay out of trouble: doing school work, not talking during class, not fighting, hanging out with different friends, and attending the group.)*

Leader: A while back, we were going over expectations and took off on what Barry said. Does anyone else have an expectation for this group that hasn't been discussed?

Martha: I do. I hope that the group can be a place where I can learn to say "no!" I really need to learn this.

Leader: That's a good thing to learn, and I think we can talk about that in here. How many of you also have trouble saying "no"? *(Looks around)* Seems like quite a few. We have about 15 minutes left; let's talk about that for a few minutes. I'd like you to think about who is the hardest person for you to say "no" to. We'll go around the group and get each of you to comment—Your friends? Your siblings? Your parents?

In each of the preceding examples, the leader has skillfully focused the group on an interesting topic. Another way to move from the process to the content is to introduce an issue or present some information. In a task group, the leader might say, "Why don't we start by discussing the different options that are available?" One other way to make the transition from process to content is to use a group exercise. The important thing to understand is that the leader should make sure that considerable time is spent on the content of the group.

Addressing Questions

In the first session, members will sometimes have a wide variety of questions that they want answered. Some of their questions will pertain to the purpose of the group, others to the meeting time and place, the leader's credentials, and other details. A common mistake occurs when leaders do not anticipate these possible questions and fail to allot time for members to ask what they consider to be important questions. Answering questions is good, but it is very important that the leader does not allow the first session to become a question-and-answer session. It is also a leadership mistake to take a long time to answer a question that only one member is interested in. If the leader feels too much time is being spent on specific questions that are not relevant to all the members, she can offer to stay to answer additional questions when the session ends.

Getting Members to Look at Other Members

Very often, members will speak mainly to the leader unless the leader encourages them to talk to the entire group. Getting members to look around can be helpful in building interest, getting members involved, building group cohesion, and creating an atmosphere of belonging. To get members to look at the entire group or to get them to avoid looking only at you, any or all of the following are appropriate:

- Tell your members you would like them to look at the group rather than exclusively at you when they are talking. You can explain this in the beginning or after someone has spoken directly to you. Ask the person talking and the rest of the members to look at everyone in the group.

- ◆ Explain to the members that you are not going to be looking at them all the time when they are speaking because at various times you will be scanning the group. You can also tell them to let your scanning serve as a signal to them to address the entire group.

- ◆ Scan the group, because the talking member will tend to seek eye contact with someone; if you are scanning, the speaker will usually look elsewhere.

- ◆ Signal the member to talk to everyone by making a sweeping motion with your hand. A sweeping motion consists of bringing your right hand to your left shoulder and then bringing it slowly around until it is more or less pointing to your right.

Sometimes the leader will need to be persistent in redirecting members. If they address only the leader, there is a good chance that a leader-member-leader-member interaction pattern will develop, making leading much more difficult. In most groups, the leader is trying to get members to work together and to feel support and concern for one another. Having a member look at other members when talking helps develop trust, concern, and cohesion.

Other First-Session Considerations

In many kinds of groups, the opportunity may arise during the first session to focus on one member's ideas, opinions, stories, or concerns. In certain education, discussion, and task groups, it is very appropriate to allow the focus to be held on one issue for an extended period of time. However, in most support, growth, counseling and therapy groups, it is usually not a good idea to spend more than 15–20 minutes focused on one member. The purpose of the first session is to get people involved and to give members a chance to share. Focusing on one member may cause others to feel left out. Another reason to be careful when focusing on a member during the first session is that members may not be ready for in-depth therapy to take place during the first session.

Discussion of certain topics may be inappropriate for the first session. Beginning leaders can make the mistake of focusing on any topic that arises or focusing on issues that require more trust and comfort than is present in a first session. For instance, in a group for helping members find employment, the leader would not want to focus on how to present oneself during an interview but rather would probably want to focus the group on skills assessment or how to locate places of potential employment. How to interview is a good topic but should not be discussed until later. Other examples of inappropriate topics for the first session of a growth or therapy group might be sexual issues or death. Usually the leader should wait at least two or three sessions before introducing topics such as these.

Closing the First Session

Closing the first session is similar to closing any other session except that the leader will want to allow more time to hear members' reactions and clear up any questions or other matters that need clarifying. Depending on the kind of group, the leader may want to ask some of the following questions during the closing phase of the first session.

- ◆ How was the session for you?
- ◆ How was it different from what you thought was going to happen?
- ◆ What stood out to you?
- ◆ Was there anything that happened that you didn't understand or didn't like?
- ◆ Do you have questions about the group, its purpose, or what is going to happen?
- ◆ What did you learn from group today?

During the close of the first session, the leader will probably want to summarize the session and comment again on the purpose of the group and what the possibilities are for the future. For a full discussion of how to close sessions and groups, see Chapter Fourteen.

The Second Session

The leader continues setting the tone of the group during the second session, being aware that some members may still be uncomfortable. In addition, the leader needs to give thought to the following issues:

- ◆ Opening the second session
- ◆ Planning for a possible letdown
- ◆ Ending the second session

Opening the Second Session

Two important considerations for opening the second session are the introduction of new members and the evaluation of the first session's success.

New Members

If new members join the group, it is usually a good idea to begin with introductions. Several methods can be used. In the following example, the leader introduces the new member in a manner that gives that person an opportunity to hear what happened in the previous session as well as to get to know the names of other members. This type of introduction also serves as a review for the other members.

Leader: This is Ralph. He was unable to make our meeting last week. I thought as a way to get Ralph caught up I'd ask each of you to take a minute to think of one or two things that stood out to you about what we discussed last week, and then I'll ask each of you to share that. Be sure to say your name also.

This method can be combined with one that gives the new members a chance to share their own situations. For instance, at the beginning of a recovery group, the leader could say:

Leader: Since Carol is new, and as a review, I thought we'd start by having each of you share how your week was. To help Carol, you may want to comment on what was most helpful last week in the group. Also share your name.

At the end of this round, the leader could say something like:

Leader: Carol, if you feel comfortable, you may want to share some of your story, or you may want to wait until later. It's up to you.

Certain kinds of groups will require no planning beyond having new members give their names and a little information about themselves.

◆ E X A M P L E

Leader: *(After asking members to get settled for the beginning of the group)* There are two new members joining us today. I have asked them to tell us their names and some relevant information about themselves.

Melvin: My name is Melvin Conrad, and I'm glad to be here. I am new in town. My family moved here from New York.

Leader: Okay, Melvin. *(Looks toward Rhonda)*

Rhonda: My name is Rhonda. I am here because I want to get over my fear of people, and my counselor said this was a good place to do that.

This is perhaps the simplest and briefest method of introducing new members. After the new members give a brief comment, a round can be used when the other group members tell their names.

Another method of introduction is for the leader to tell the group about the new members. This can only be done if the leader has had the opportunity to meet with the new members before the session has begun. The reasons a leader might choose this approach are (1) to keep the time spent on the introduction to a minimum, (2) to tell the group something specific about the member that the member might not include in the self-introduction, or (3) to help the new member who is very anxious about speaking and needs time to ease into the group. For example, if a new member were frightened, the leader might say:

Leader: This is Ted. He's going to be joining the group. Ted told me that he was really apprehensive about coming today, so I told him that he would not have to say anything if he didn't want to. Let's start by talking about any thoughts or reactions to last week's session. What thoughts or feelings did you have about coming back the second time? I'd like each of you to share something and also state your name.

The amount of time spent introducing new members will often depend on the kind of group. In most counseling, therapy, growth, and support groups, an introduction activity of 5 minutes or less is all that is necessary for new members. During this time new members can tell the group their names and a little bit about why they are there, what their interests are, and what they hope to gain from being part of the group. In task, discussion, and education groups, merely having new members give their names may be sufficient.

When new members come to the second session, the leader must decide how much time should be spent informing them of what happened during the previous session. Informing new members of the events of the first session helps them adjust more quickly to the group and keeps them from feeling in the dark when other members talk about something that happened during the first session. If there is a lot to explain, the leader should try to do so before the second session to prevent returning members from being bored by a lengthy recap of the first session.

The Evaluation of the First Session

If the first session was reasonably successful, with a positive tone set and most of the members seeming to like the session, the leader will plan a brief warm-up and then move on to the content. On the other hand, if it did not go smoothly, the leader will have to assess why. Possible reasons for an unsuccessful first session could be any of the following:

- Members were afraid to talk or share.
- Members were confused about the purpose of the group.
- The group was held at a bad time of day.
- Members came to the group late and disrupted what was going on.
- Cultural or gender issues inhibited members from fully participating.
- The leader was unclear about the purpose of the group or the members' needs.
- The room was not conducive to groups.
- Members were forced to attend the group.
- Members reacted negatively to the leader.
- The session was not planned well.
- The focus moved from topic to topic too quickly.
- The focus was held on a person or topic too long.
- Too much or too little time was spent on warming up.

Much thought needs to go into the planning of a second session when the first session was not good. It may be necessary to ask certain members not to return because they are not appropriate for the group. Changes may need to be made with the setting, meeting time, or content. Unfortunately, many beginning leaders do not take the time to fully understand why the group did not go well, and they go to the second session with no significant changes from the first session.

When planning for the opening of the second session following an unsuccessful first session, the leader may choose from three options: (1) restate the purpose of the group and make no attempt to verbalize any of the negative events of the first session; (2) address what went wrong in an effort to explain that future sessions will not be similar to the first one; or (3) elicit from members their reactions to the first session. The advantage of the leader's addressing what went wrong is that he honestly acknowledges that the first session was not a good one and can point out ways that future sessions can be better.

◆ E X A M P L E S

Leader: Okay, let's get started. I'd like to say something about the first session. When the group ended the other night, I was concerned that some of you may have left feeling discouraged. I realize that not enough people got to share since we focused so much on a couple of you. I sensed that some of you felt a bit frustrated because, as we were wrapping up, you asked if every group was going to be like this and whether you would get a chance to talk. Let me assure you that not every group will be like the first one. All of you signed up to be in this group because you felt a need to get support and hear ideas from people who are struggling with the same issues that you are. I know that the group will be most beneficial if you share your thoughts and feelings concerning your common situations. I will make sure that the group does not focus on only one or two members unless a majority of you indicate a desire to do so.

The leader is attempting to inform them that the first session was not indicative of the remaining sessions.

Leader: I want to begin this session by getting your reaction to the last one. I feel that our first session was okay, but I do believe these next sessions can be better. Please share honestly any reaction or questions that you had about what we did here last time.

In this example, the leader gives the members a chance to react so that he can comment on their reactions in a positive, clarifying manner.

Our point is that the leader needs to consider how the first session went when planning the second session. The leader will also want to remember that it is usually necessary and helpful to reiterate the purpose of the group during the second session. If the first session did not go well, the leader will definitely need to plan to counteract the bad beginning. One leader we know decided to use name tags on the chairs to break up the cliques of eighth-grade girls. She knew she could have a good group, but the first session did not go well because of where the girls were sitting. She assigned seats for the next few sessions and had a very successful group.

It is also helpful, when possible, for the leader to arrive at the second session early and talk informally to members before the group begins. This provides some idea of how members reacted to the first session. It also gives the leader a chance to answer members' questions about the group and to get to know the members a little better.

Planning for a Possible Letdown

A skilled leader will anticipate a letdown during the second session. A common mistake of beginning leaders is to think that the excitement exhibited among members during the first session is always present in the second session. He often fails to anticipate that there may be a different energy for the second session. One reason for the change in the members' energy is that much of the first session is spent on members getting acquainted with each other, discussing why they are there, what their expectations are, and the format and rules for the group. Given these topics, the first session is often filled with a lot of sharing and excitement. In the second session, the focus moves toward personal sharing, and members often experience anxiety about participating. They become hesitant to interact, thus causing a letdown. This letdown is often disconcerting to a beginning group leader. To help prevent the letdown, the leader can mention at the end of the first session that there is a strong possibility that members may not feel as enthusiastic the next time. If it is appropriate, the leader can give the members a task to accomplish before the next session. This may help to keep the second session interesting and create a higher level of energy among the members. *The most important thing a leader can do to prevent the letdown is plan a good session based on what she learned from the first session.*

Ending the Second Session

The leader should plan to spend an extra few minutes ending the second session. During the closing phase, the leader will want to hear what the members perceive as being helpful and unhelpful. A round asking the members to describe their positive and negative reactions to the group is a very valuable closing activity.

◆ E X A M P L E S

Leader: Let's take a few minutes to wind up the group. We're going to do a round in just a moment. I would like each of you to share what stands out to you the most about being in this group. In addition, if there is anything that you would like to see us do differently, please say so.

Timothy: The thing that stands out to me the most is that I get to hear other people struggling with the same issue that I am. I would also like to talk more in pairs like we did at the beginning of the session.

Pauline: I liked the movement exercise that we did today. It really made me stop and think about my situation. I would also like to do more stuff in pairs. I feel as though I get to know that person better when we talk in twos.

Bert: I'm still a little bit hesitant about speaking up. I've always had difficulty being in groups. I think the dyads help me feel a little bit more comfortable.

Leader: I want to take a bit more time to end the group today so that I can get some idea of how you are feeling about being in this group thus far. Think of how you would rate this group on a 1 to 10 scale. *(Leader explains the meaning of the scale)* If your rating is not a 10, think what it would take to move the group up to a 10.

Kevin: I give the group an 8. I think that to make it a 10 we just need to feel more comfortable with each other.

Becky: I give it a 10. I really like the way we shared with each other today. I feel a lot more comfortable, and I feel as though I know these people very well. I also liked the way you started the group with that exercise that got us to list things.

In both of these examples, the leader would spend time discussing the various responses, clarifying anything that needed clarification and answering any questions.

Concluding Comments

The first and second sessions set the tone for the other sessions. One very important component of the first session is how the leader opens the session. The leader has many choices, including a brief opening statement and then an introduction exercise; a long opening statement, then an introduction exercise; an introduction exercise with no opening statement; or no introduction exercise when members already know each other. During the first session, the leader needs to pay attention to both content (what the group is about) and process (the interactions, comfort level, attitudes of members, etc.). It is important that the leader not focus too long on one person during the first sessions. The leader wants to make sure the group is interesting and engaging and to set a positive tone if at all possible.

Rules, such as no put-downs or attacking other members, confidentiality, and attendance, need to be covered during the first session. Often, the best way to cover the rules is to let them emerge as the session unfolds. It is usually not necessary to spend much time on the rules. Another first session caution is to avoid "heavy" counseling or therapy work during the first session.

In planning for the second session, the leader needs to be prepared for the typical letdown. If the first session did not go well, the leader will want to prepare specifically to counteract any negative reactions. Also, the leader often will want to spend extra time during the closing of the first and second sessions to get reactions and answer questions.

CHAPTER SIX

Basic Skills for Group Leaders

Throughout the first five chapters, we have referred to various leadership skills but have not discussed them in great detail. In the next few chapters, we describe specific skills that we feel are essential for good leading. Some of these are basic human-relations skills that you may have developed through specialized training. If you have had some training in interviewing or counseling, you will recognize the names of many of these skills.

Active listening	Tone setting
Reflection	Modeling and self-disclosure
Clarification and questioning	Use of eyes
Summarizing	Use of voice
Mini-lecturing and information giving	Use of the leader's energy
Encouraging and supporting	Identifying allies
	Multicultural understanding

Active Listening

Active listening entails listening to the content, voice, and body language of the person speaking (Corey & Corey, 1992). It also involves communicating to the person speaking that you are really listening. Most of you have probably been trained to listen on a one-to-one basis. Active listening as a group leader is a much more complex task since you listen to more people. The skilled leader actually tries to listen to all the members at the same time and not just to the one who is talking. To the extent this is possible, the leader wants to be aware of what members are feeling and thinking even when they are not speaking. The main technique the leader uses for this is to scan the room for nonverbal gestures—especially facial expressions and body shifts. We hope you can appreciate the complexity of this skill. It is difficult to convey to the member who is speaking that you are really listening while you are, at the same time, communicating with other members by picking up on their silent messages. We urge you to practice this skill whenever you are with a group of friends, family, or colleagues. See if you can take in more than just the content of the person who is talking: Try to pick up on what the others are thinking and feeling. This skill, perhaps more than any other, is essential for good group leadership; yet many students try to become skilled leaders without first becoming active listeners.

Reflection

In counseling, to reflect a comment is to restate it, conveying that you understand the content, the feeling behind it, or both. As a group leader, you will find it helpful and necessary to use the skill of reflecting both content and feeling. The purpose of reflecting is twofold: (1) to help the group member who is speaking become more aware of what he is saying, and (2) to communicate to him that you are aware of how he is feeling. As a group leader, you will use reflection at times with individual members, at other times to reflect what two or more members may be saying about a topic or issue, and at still other times to reflect what the entire group is experiencing.

◆ EXAMPLES

Alicia: I'm not sure how I'll do here. I'm a little uncomfortable with all this, but I sure want to get started to make some changes in my life.

Leader: Alicia, you seem to be feeling that the group is both an exciting and a scary experience for you at this point.

Martin: Looking for work is tough on me. I hate going into places and feeling like I've got to beg for anything they can give me.

Randy: Yeah, that's how I feel about it. Some days I'd rather stay home. I dread the thought of having to face those pompous receptionists.

Leader: You both seem to be saying that one of the hardest things in looking for work is having to deal with the feeling of being one down.

If the leader is on target with her reflection, it is likely that other members can relate to it. The leader may follow up her reflection with something like this: "I wonder if other people here are having similar feelings as they go out job hunting." As she watches for responses, the leader may find that the reflection she has directed to two members has actually encouraged others to become aware of their similar feelings.

Anita, a member in a group of abused women, has been talking for 3 minutes about how she dislikes herself for having remained in an abusive situation. The members have been very attentive, and as Anita finishes, it is apparent that others are feeling strong emotions. The leader tries to reflect the entire group:

Leader: From your reactions, I'd guess that most of you are in touch with what Anita is experiencing right now. Some of you may be having similar feelings about yourself.

In summary, the use of reflection with a single member, several members, or the entire group clarifies and deepens members' understanding and communicates that the leader is in tune with what is happening. One word of warning comes from Corey and Corey (1992), who state that "many neophyte group leaders find themselves confining most of their interactions to mere reflections" (p. 21). The warning is a good one because in many instances the use of reflection does not cause members to delve more deeply into the discussion at hand.

Clarification and Questioning

Several authors have discussed clarification and questioning as necessary group skills (Corey & Corey, 1992; Posthuma, 1996; Trotzer, 1989). Often, the leader will find it necessary to help members clarify their statements. Clarification may be done for the benefit of the entire group or for the speaker's benefit—that is, to help the member become more aware of what he or she is trying to say. There are several techniques for clarification that you may find useful: questioning, restating, and using other members to clarify.

◆ E X A M P L E S

Stan: I don't think we should accept the proposal. It has too many hidden agendas.

Leader: Stan, can you tell us a little more about what you mean by that?

Here the leader is attempting to clarify by gathering more information. He is using an open-ended question to encourage the member to clarify his statement.

Ellen: There are times when I think I'm going crazy, and yet I know I'm just off balance because of my divorce. My mom says, "What about the kids?" Carla, my 8-year-old, was crying last night. It's my life, though! I have got to get out. I don't know how my husband will make it.

Leader: Ellen, you've just said a lot. I'd like to try to clarify how you might be feeling at this point—do tell me if I am off base. There is a part of you that says this divorce is right, and then there is a part of you that says, "Maybe I'm being selfish." Others of you may want to check yourself to see if you have some conflicting views.

In this example, rather than questioning further, the leader has taken jumbled information presented by a member and used a statement to reorder it in an attempt to clarify the key issues. This clarification helps Ellen and the others become more aware of what she now needs to work on. We cannot emphasize enough the importance of clarification. If a member's thoughts are vague, confusing, or incomplete—as they often are in moments of stress—the rest of the members will have difficulty understanding her. As a result, some members will lose interest, and their minds will start to wander.

Danny: I want a dog, but my mom says "no." I know it'd be good for me. She says I wouldn't take care of it—like the rabbit. But I was only 8 then, and I'm 11 now. I know I'd do better in school. I wish my mom wasn't so mean to me.

Leader: Does anyone think they know how Danny is feeling about his mom and about having a pet?

Sally: I think I do. Danny is lonely sometimes and feels like having a pet friend would help him. By having a dog, he would have someone to talk to and play with, and that would help him feel better. Then he would do better in school. He says he thinks his mom is mean, but I think he knows she's not—she just doesn't want to take care of the dog. She's probably like my mom and feels that kids are enough to take care of.

Leader: That sounds right, Sally. Danny, how did it sound to you?

The method of using another member serves the dual purpose of clarifying what the member was saying and also involving other group members, thus generating interest and energy.

The leader has the responsibility of trying to maintain clear communication in the group. Confusing messages create frustration and drain group energy if they are not adequately clarified. Clarification is extremely important when the group is made up of members from different cultures.

Summarizing

The skill of summarizing is a must for all group leaders. Groups often generate material from a wide range of viewpoints. Because members are busy listening and sharing during the session, they often do not pick up on or remember many of the details. Therefore, thoughtful and concise summaries are very helpful to the members.

There are several occasions in a group session when summarizing can and should be used. A summary may be helpful when you have allowed a member to speak uninterrupted for several minutes. Without a summary, members may pick up on small or irrelevant points. The summary tightens the focus and allows the leader to stay with the issue or move on, depending on the needs of the particular member. A concise summary is also useful in making a transition from one topic to another. The summary can highlight key points in a discussion or in the work done by a member and can serve as a bridge to the next activity in the group. A summary is especially important if the discussion has been diffuse or has involved overlapping points or ideas. A good summary will pull together the major points and can serve to deepen or sharpen the focus.

Leader: So far, we've been talking in general terms about changes we would like to make in our lives. Juan and Al both talked about job changes. Betty, you said you wanted to improve your relationship with your husband in some major ways. Someone said they wanted to go back to school. Margaret, I think that was you. A couple of other people wanted to be happier. Now, I would like each of you to take a minute to think about this change you want. . . . What is one thing you will have to give up to get what you want?

In this example, the summary serves to highlight each member's desire for change and sets the stage for the leader to deepen the focus.

A summary can also be used at the opening of a session and is especially helpful if there is unfinished work from the last session or a strong interest on the part of the members to continue the topic. However, the summary should serve to get the group focused on the current session rather than to encourage a rehash of the previous session.

Leader: A lot happened last session. We talked mainly about prenatal care. Betsy talked about smoking and Jane talked about drugs, and they both wanted to quit. Others talked about things they were doing that might not be good. We discussed stress, food, and exercise. We finished with a discussion of what to do during the ninth month. Today, I want us to continue talking about the ninth month, especially the last couple of weeks and the delivery. First, I want to report that I have been talking individually with Jane and Betsy, and they are doing great! *(Group cheers)*

Another good time to use summarizing is at the end of a session. Because many ideas will have been discussed during the session, a skillful summary can be helpful. In our discussion of ending a session in Chapter Fourteen, we address the different ways to summarize and how to use the members to summarize.

Mini-Lecturing and Information Giving

Sometimes the leader will need or want to provide information to the group. In educational groups, the leader most often is the person who provides the expertise on subjects such as diet, health, birth control methods, or types of post–high school education. In situations when you are the "expert," you will want to do several things when giving a mini-lecture:

- Make it interesting.
- Make it relevant.
- Make sure you have considered cultural and gender differences.
- Make it short (usually no more than 5 to 8 minutes).
- Make it energizing.
- Make sure you have current, correct, and objective information.

The purpose of giving information is to enable people to learn from you and from the discussion that follows. By keeping your comments relatively short, you can provide good information without turning your group into a class. Probably the key to successful mini-lecturing is to briefly provide new and interesting ideas. Very often, beginning leaders will be afraid to give any information or will give boring mini-lectures. In discussion, educational, and task groups, it is important that the leader be well-informed about the subject. In growth or counseling groups, the skilled leader needs to have information on all kinds of topics, such as guilt, marital affairs, children, the value of hobbies and pets, and so forth. In almost any group, there will be times during a session when a 2- or 3-minute mini-lecture on some subject will help focus the group, deepen the focus, or simply help members understand something about which they are confused. Our point is that providing information is helpful in many groups, and the skilled leader not only has beneficial things to say but knows when and how to say them.

◆ EXAMPLE

The focus of this group is marital enrichment for young couples who have been married less than 2 years. In the second session, a member asks a question.

Member: Can marriages go smoothly without working so hard? When does it get easy?

Leader: Let me comment about that. Most marriages require work, especially during the first couple of years as the partners get to know each other in a different way. Also, differences continue to emerge that have to be discussed. Having to work hard during these first 2 years does not mean it is not a good marriage. Let me tell you three or four ways that each of you can benefit from working on your marriage now. . . . (*Leader talks for a few more minutes*)

Encouraging and Supporting

Because you are interested in the helping professions, you have most likely already learned to provide encouragement and support to others. As a group leader, this ability will be especially important in helping members deal with the anxiety of being in a new situation and sharing their ideas or personal feelings with others. Members are often concerned with how they will appear to others and sometimes fear they will say something "wrong" or "stupid" in the group. In growth or therapy groups, members sometimes fear they will reveal something about themselves that they will later regret. The skilled leader must take the initiative in providing support and encouragement that will help put members at ease (Dyer & Vriend, 1980). Acknowledging that some discomfort is normal often eases members' anxiety. For example, a leader might make an encouraging statement like, "People in groups may feel a little nervous. That feeling usually goes away as we get to know each other better and learn more of what the group is about."

In addition to the content of what you say, it is important that you communicate your support with warmth in your voice, a pleasant facial expression, and an "open" posture. Your encouragement must be genuine and congruent with your actual feelings. As the level of personal sharing in a group increases, members may require additional encouragement in their struggle to talk about themselves. Members' primary concern often will be how the other people in the group will react to them if they reveal something very personal. Your encouragement can help members get over their "scared" feelings and can help them take risks that they otherwise might not take. The following is an example of an encouraging and supportive statement:

Leader: John, you started to tell us about the problems you have regarding sex. You seem somewhat scared about the prospect of sharing such personal things with us, which is certainly normal. I think you will find that we'll listen without criticism. We're not here to be critical of you or anybody—we're all trying to be helpful and supportive of each other.

In this example, the leader is supportive and delivers a message to the other members that criticism or judgment would be antitherapeutic. This is an additional form of protection that the leader provides as part of her role.

Tone Setting

"Tone setting is subtle but crucial to the atmosphere and attitude of the group" (Trotzer, 1989, p. 207). By tone setting, we mean the mood for the group. Some beginning counselors are not aware of the tone-setting dimension of group leading; thus, without realizing what they are doing, they set a dull or very "serious" tone. Other beginners, wanting to be liked, set a very "light" tone and end up frustrated because no one seems committed to the group. It is important to realize that the leader sets the tone by his actions, words, and what he allows to happen. If the leader is very aggressive, he will create an atmosphere of resistance and tension. A leader who allows members to attack and criticize others permits a fearful tone to emerge. If the leader encourages sharing and caring, a more positive atmosphere is established. The thing to remember is that the leader is responsible for setting the tone and should consider the following:

- Should the group be serious, light, or somewhere in between?
- Should the tone be confrontational, or supportive? (Some groups for addicts, juveniles, and certain kinds of criminals are conducted effectively with very confrontational tones.)
- Should the tone be very formal, or informal?
- Should the group be task-oriented, or more relaxed?

If you ask yourself these questions and then lead according to your answers, you will probably achieve the desired tone for your group. The following examples show how a leader can set different tones for the group.

◆ EXAMPLES

Serious Tone

Leader: Let's begin. Before we start, I'd like you to pull in so that we are not all spread out. Also, I'd like you to put away any food or drinks for now. *(Members do this.)* OK, let's start by having different members introduce themselves and tell why they are here.

Social Tone

Leader: Let's begin. *(Members remain spread out and continue eating.)* I'd like to start by having you tell a little bit about who you are. Tell anything that you think is important or anything you'd like.

Confrontational Tone

It is the first session of a group of teenagers who have been caught using drugs. Joe has been talking about how he does not think he has any problem with drugs.

Leader: Joe, it is clear that you have a serious problem! In this group, we can help each other by making sure that people are honest with themselves. *(In a rather confrontational voice)* How many of you feel that Joe has a problem?

Supportive Tone

Leader: Joe, I hope the group can be of value even though you don't feel that you have a problem. Others of you may feel the same way. Also, I believe some of you do realize that you have a problem. The purpose of the group is to be helpful, and I am hoping that you'll help each other by listening, sharing, and hopefully caring for one another. Admitting that you have a problem will be tough.

Formal Tone

Leader: I am Tom Smith. I'm from the mental health center and am here today to serve as the leader of this group. Before we get started, I would like to go over some of the ground rules for this group. The first thing that I would like you to do is to introduce yourself. State your name, where you work, and why you decided to attend the group.

"On Task" Tone

Leader: I'd like us to get started. We have a lot to cover and only an hour and a half to do it. First. . . .

In the preceding examples, we outlined a number of possible "tones" for a group. In workshops that we conduct, we ask participants to describe the tone of groups they have led or been members of and state whether the group was successful or not successful. Some of the tones reported for the unsuccessful groups are "hostile," "boring," "frustrating," "combative," "slow-moving," and "confusing." For the successful groups, tones such as "warm," "serious and caring," "interesting," and "energizing" were reported. One other aspect of tone setting that the leader should be aware of is paying attention to things such as the lighting, seating, and wall decorations—these things can make a difference in the tone that is set. Remember that the leader sets the tone, and without the proper tone, groups most likely will not be as effective as they can be.

Modeling and Self-Disclosure

As a group leader, you will find modeling and self-disclosure to be important skills. These skills are also useful for getting members to share thoughts and feelings. Corey and Corey (1992) state that "one of the best ways to teach desired behaviors is by modeling those behaviors in the group" (p. 16). Your style of effective communication, your ability to listen, and your encouragement of others will serve as a model for your members to emulate. Your energy and interest in a subject or in the group itself can serve as a model for others. If the purpose of the group involves more personal sharing, then your self-disclosure can be used to demonstrate how to disclose and that you are willing to risk and share yourself. Your self-disclosure can also indicate that you are human and that you have dealt with many of the same issues in your life that they are presently exploring, and serve as a model of what you want from the members.

◆ EXAMPLES

Leader: Now that you have had a chance to think about the three people who have the most significant impact on your life in terms of who you are now, let's begin sharing. I'll go first to show how this might work. The most significant person in my life was my mother. She was significant because she supported me and sort of protected me from my father, who was an alcoholic. My brother. . . .

Here, the leader demonstrates the depth of sharing that can take place and shows the members. Self-disclosure can be used to reveal past events, present events, and present feelings about the group or about some members.

The following examples show two different kinds of self-disclosure.

Leader: In my current relationship, my partner and I have some trouble with how we like to socialize. She likes to spend time with lots of people, whereas I really only enjoy one or two people at a time. I think this is one of many concerns that couples deal with. Does anyone have that concern or have other concerns about a relationship?

Leader: I want to share how I am feeling about the group tonight. I feel that people are holding back. I am not sure why. Does anyone else feel that?

It is not necessary for the leader to self-disclose on every issue or topic that is discussed in the group. Frequent self-disclosure may, in fact, be distracting and confusing to the members. In addition, self-disclosure by the leader should not be of such intensity that the leader becomes the focus of the group. The preceding excerpts are good examples of how leaders can self-disclose yet make sure that the group does not focus on them.

Use of Eyes

Knowing how to use your eyes is very important when leading groups. The leader needs to be aware of how his eyes can gather valuable information, encourage members to speak, and possibly deter members from speaking (Harvill, Masson, & Jacobs, 1983). The leader can use his eyes in four ways:

1. To scan for nonverbal cues
2. To get members to look at other members

3. To draw out members
4. To cut off members

Scanning for Nonverbal Cues

Leaders gather valuable information by scanning the group with their eyes. Although scanning seems easy, most group leaders find it difficult because when people are talking, it is natural to look at them. Picture a beginning leader leading a group of ten members. The member closest to the leader's left starts talking, and the leader naturally turns to look at the speaker. Let's say the member talks for 2 minutes about a personal situation. During those 2 minutes, the beginning leader will have made contact only with the speaker and perhaps with the next two members to the speaker's left. For the entire 2 minutes, the leader has made no observation of the remaining seven members. Here are some of the problems and difficulties this leader might have:

- Some of the other members may feel excluded because the leader did not make eye contact with them.
- The leader has no idea how most of the members were reacting to what was being said.
- The leader has no idea who may want to speak next.
- Some of the other members may have lost interest because the member talked only to the leader.

If the leader does what is natural, which would be to look exclusively at the person speaking, she misses information that is very helpful in facilitating the group. Seeing members' reactions and knowing who wants to add comments makes leading a lot easier. Most beginning leaders can learn rather quickly to scan the group while they are talking. However, *learning to scan when someone else is talking is a skill that takes practice.*

Of course, there are situations when you would want to attend almost exclusively to the talking member—but those situations should be the exception rather than the rule. The rule is to *keep your eyes moving*. Scanning is the best way to pick up the various immediate reactions of the members. Among the most important nonverbal cues to observe are head nods, facial expressions, body shifts, and tears.

Head Nods

It is very helpful to look for head nods indicating agreement or disagreement when someone is offering an opinion or describing some concern. The leader can facilitate discussion by saying something like, "Biff, you're nodding—what are your thoughts?" or "I notice that some of your heads are nodding in agreement and some in disagreement—let's continue the discussion, realizing that there are differences here." Picking up on head nods can also be useful for drawing out and linking one person with another: "Jodi, you were nodding when Diane was mentioning leaving—are you also having similar thoughts?"

Facial Expressions

While head nodding implies some degree of agreement or disagreement about an issue, facial expressions may mean that the member has had a similar experience or is in some way relating positively or negatively to the issue. Facial expressions can suggest disapproval, confusion, or some other reaction that the leader may want to clarify.

◆ E X A M P L E

Barbara: He really believes that I should be home from work at five o'clock and his dinner should be on the table by six o'clock. I am not obligated to make dinner!

Sue: I agree with you.

Jane: There are no wife's duties!

Leader: *(Picking up on Ann's expression)* Ann, by your expression I'm guessing that you might be having mixed feelings about what Barbara and the others are saying.

Ann: Well, ah, I am. You see, I'm all confused about this. I want to believe what's being said, and yet I sure was raised differently. And, also, there are things I like to do as a wife.

Dee: I feel the same way you do, Ann.

Ann: You do? I thought I was the only one here who was somewhat traditional.

If the leader had not picked up on Ann's reaction, Ann might not have volunteered her thoughts because she was afraid of being different.

Body Shifts

Members often express themselves through the way they sit and move. Body shifts during the group frequently indicate confusion, boredom, or irritation. By observing these reactions the leader can often become aware of what members are feeling and can devise some strategies for dealing with a member or a number of members. For instance, if two or three members are noticeably confused, the leader may want to use the skills of reflection and clarification, give a mini-lecture that may provide valuable information, initiate a group exercise, or even have the group take a 10-minute break. One body shift that is important to observe is the forward lean, which often indicates "I've got something to say." Beginning leaders frequently miss this and other signals from members; as a result, they may ignore those who are ready to speak and resort to calling on members who may have less to say.

Tears

A member's tears, or "tearing up," is an important clue for the leader. While some members may break into tears and sob audibly, often people merely tear up while they are listening to another. The leader needs to be aware of members' tears because they are usually indicative of strong feelings. Whether the leader deals with the tears directly by drawing the member out or chooses simply to acknowledge them or ignore them will depend on the purpose of the group and other factors such as the time remaining, who the member is, and the leader's guess about what is causing the tears. The skilled leader who scans the group will, on occasion, observe members who are expressing their pain silently through tears. Not scanning the group causes the leader to miss this valuable information.

Getting Members to Look at Other Members

The leader can use her eyes to signal members to look at others. It is helpful to tell the members you will not always be looking at them when they talk, and your looking at others should serve as a signal to them to look around. When the leader uses the skill of scanning, the talking member will tend to seek eye contact with other group members, which is helpful for group development.

Drawing Out Members

Another way a leader might use his eyes is to make eye contact with those whom he is trying to draw out. By scanning the entire group and contacting particular members, the leader's eyes can serve as an invitation to talk. Beginning leaders sometimes make the mistake of maintaining eye contact only with those who are talking and not with those who are silent. The leader's eyes can really encourage members to join in and share. Let's say you have a member who has not spoken much, and it is already the third session. Observation indicates this member is scared and shy. Your kind and encouraging eye contact may help this person venture into the group. Once drawn out, this type of member may speak only to you. You may want to allow this at first and then, as the member becomes more comfortable, ask him to talk to the entire group.

The leader's eyes can also be helpful when a member is revealing something very painful. Encouragement through eye contact and body language may be just what the member needs to fully disclose some previously hidden aspects. This is another example of an appropriate time for the leader to maintain eye contact with only one member for a longer period. Usually this does not result in others feeling ignored since members are very attentive when someone is doing intense personal work.

Another way for the leader to use his eyes to draw out a member is to make eye contact with that person a number of times while speaking to the group as a whole.

◆ E X A M P L E

The group has been in progress for 45 minutes, and the leader is aware that Claire has said very little. The discussion has been about people's different values. The leader decides to shift the focus and try to draw Claire into the group.

Leader: Okay, now that we've generated a list of different values, let's talk more about you and where your own values come from. *(While scanning the group, the leader intentionally has been holding eye contact with Claire a little longer than previously)* Think about different people or institutions, such as the church or scouts, that have had an impact on you. *(The leader, noticing that Claire nodded at the word* church, *decides to say more about religion while looking often at Claire)* For some, religion may be the major source of your value system. Some of you may be very religious. *(Claire nods, and the leader nods back)* Sharing that would be helpful in the group. Who would like to share about where values come from? Let's take the influence of religion first. *(The leader ends the comments while looking at Claire)*

Claire: My family was very religious. In fact, . . .

In this example, the leader intentionally ended his comments looking at Claire, increasing the likelihood that she would speak. Of course, sometimes this will not be effective, and you need to be aware that this technique should be used with care and concern for your members. Unfortunately, some beginners misunderstand the technique and end up using eye contact as a "spotlight," thus creating undue pressure on a member to respond.

Cutting Off Members

Often, there will be one member who tends to speak first on any issue or question. There may be times when the leader will want someone else to comment first—perhaps just for a change or because the talkative member is negative or long-winded. When the leader knows that he is going to pose a question to the group, he can use his eyes to control the talkative member. By looking at the member as he starts to ask his question and then slowly shifting his eyes around to other members, he can finish his comments totally *out of eye contact* with the talkative member. This technique subtly invites others to respond and avoids the talkative member's nonverbal overtures to comment. Certainly this does not work all the time, but it can be effective.

◆ E X A M P L E

The leader, wishing to get members to share their fears about leaving the hospital, starts by looking at Joe, an overzealous member on the leader's left.

Leader: All of you probably have some fears about leaving this hospital. I hope that a number of you will share those fears. *(Now scanning the middle of the group)* Who would share some of those fears, no matter how big or small? *(The leader's eyes are now fixed on the members on the right.)*

In this example, the leader is hoping that members in the middle or on the far right side of the group will comment first. By finishing the question with Joe outside his range of vision, the leader increases the chance of someone other than Joe initiating the discussion.

Leaders can also use their eyes to help cut off a member who is speaking. If a member has gone on for a while, a very subtle but often helpful cutting-off technique is for the leader to avoid making eye contact with the speaker. Members frequently will "wind down" sooner when the leader is not attending to their comments.

By moving your eyes, you will be in contact with your members and more aware of the energy of the group. By scanning the group, you will have a better sense of what to do next. All in all, the leader who scans will have much more data than the leader who doesn't. The following examples should help you further understand reasons for scanning the group when you or other members are talking; they are offered as a way of reviewing how the use of your eyes can be of great value to you as a group leader.

◆ **E X A M P L E S**

A Support Group for Cancer Patients

Carl is talking about his recent diagnosis of cancer and his family's denial of the whole matter. While scanning the group, the leader notices that Sue's head is nodding vigorously. He asks Sue to share, and she comments on her family's denial and how she dealt with it. Carl listens intently.

A Group for Elementary School Children Who Live in Stepfamilies

The leader is talking about how the first few months are hard because of the blending of two families. She notices that Mike, Karen, and Bob are nodding, and Jane is looking down. (The leader knows from Jane's teachers that Jane is having a hard time in her new stepfamily.) The leader then gets Mike, Karen, and Bob to talk about their hard times while she continues to observe Jane. Toward the end of Bob's comments, the leader notices that Jane seems more relaxed, so she invites Jane to share.

A Therapy Group for Alcoholics

Gloria is telling a long story about her history of drinking, one she has told twice before. By scanning, the leader notices that the members are not paying attention and are starting to drift off. He decides to cut Gloria off by saying in a gentle, caring voice, "Gloria, you seem to be losing us. Are you aware that people aren't listening? My guess is that they are not listening because you have told us this twice before. How can we help you?"

A Divorce Adjustment Group

Mary is talking about how things are better for her now—she and her ex-husband are even talking about possibly dating each other. In scanning, the leader notices some questioning looks and also notices that Betty is starting to tear up. The leader decides to shift to Betty, who reveals that her ex-husband told her yesterday that he was going to get married.

A Personal Growth Group for Graduate Students

The leader has just introduced an exercise on family of origin, and while scanning the group, she notices that one of the members looks somewhat confused. She asks the member about his confusion, and he tells the group he was raised in an orphanage.

Practice Activities

To conclude this section, try practicing the following two training exercises. They will help you develop more effective use of your eyes in working with groups. Try each several times. The key to these exercises is to make them fun and interesting. See what you can learn.

1. In a group (one you are actually leading or simply a group of as few as three people standing around talking), move your eyes comfortably from face to face. Study expressions and reactions to the speaker. See if you can guess who will speak next. Also, see if you can tell by the data you are gathering from head nods, smiles, and other facial expressions whether the other people are agreeing or disagreeing with the speaker. Try to guess whether the next person will maintain the topic or go off in a new direction.

2. In a group, move your eyes comfortably from face to face. Think about each person's expression. What feeling do you get from it? If you were to make a statement about each person based on his or her expression, what would it be?

Use of Voice

Use of voice is another skill that many leaders overlook. Our discussion here will cover how the leader's voice can be used to influence the tone and atmosphere of the group as well as its pace and content. In later chapters, the use of the voice to draw out and cut off members is explained.

Use of Voice to Help Set the Tone

A leader conveys how a group will be led both by the content of his words and the tone of his voice. Leaders using a very strong, stern voice may intimidate the members, causing them not to share as much. A nonassertive voice may cause members to not respect or believe in the leader. A warm, encouraging voice often helps the scared, troubled, or withdrawn member. The skilled leader is very much aware of her voice and realizes that different kinds of groups may need different voice patterns.

Listen to your voice pattern, perhaps using a tape recorder. You will want to develop more than one voice pattern, because, at times, you will need to vary the tone of the group, and your voice can help in that process. Your voice also can communicate a serious or a light tone.

Use of Voice to Energize the Group

The leader's enthusiasm will help to energize the members. Frequently, leaders who complain that their group is "dead" are those who have not learned to use their voice effectively. Discussion, education, and task groups can be ruined if the leader does not demonstrate by his actions and voice that he is interested in the topic and the group. An enthusiastic voice will affect most members in a positive way as long as the leader is sincere. Very often, at the beginning of a new group—and even at the start of a given session—the leader's voice can be a key factor in generating interest and energy. We suggest that you observe various teachers and group leaders and notice how the energy level of the leader usually affects the listeners' or members' energy levels. Also, we recommend that you listen to your own voice when leading and determine whether you are using it to energize the group. If you are not, you can practice using different energy levels in your voice, thus changing your voice patterns and habits. Although this will take some effort, you will find the effort worthwhile.

Use of Voice to Pace the Group

Closely linked to the tone and energy of the group is its pace, which can also be influenced by the leader's voice. Often, a very slow talking leader will influence members in such a way as to slow the pace down—perhaps to such a degree that the group moves too slowly. Although there are exceptions, it is best to assume that your voice is having some influence. At times, you will want the group to move faster or slower; by learning to manipulate your rate of speech, you may be able to regulate the pace of the members. Practice this, and evaluate your effectiveness as you are leading. You will likely be surprised at how much influence your voice can have.

The leader's voice pattern—which includes tone, pitch, volume, and rate—can be instrumental in leading an effective group.

Use of the Leader's Energy

So far, we have discussed several skills that a leader finds useful. Another skill—perhaps we should call it a characteristic—is the leader's energy. Good leaders have enthusiasm for what they are doing. Unfortunately, leaders often hold group sessions at the end of the day when they are very tired. If possible, leaders should take a break before a group session. Leaders need to be excited about leading, because if they are not excited, the group members probably will not be. There really is no way to practice increasing your energy level, but it helps to be aware that your energy level affects that of the group.

Identifying Allies

A very useful skill is discovering who your allies are in the group; that is, which members you can count on to be cooperative and helpful. It is important to identify them, for there will be times during a session when you will want someone to start a discussion or an exercise, or when you will need someone reliable to play a role or take a risk. Also, when leading therapy groups, you may encounter a situation where one member is working at a very intense level on some issue, and another member becomes very emotional and needs immediate attention. A good therapy group leader has to be prepared for such occurrences. One way to handle this so as not to disrupt the work in progress is to ask your ally to be with the member who is very upset. This allows you to feel confident that the member who has become very emotional is getting some support while you are dealing with the "working" member and the rest of the group.

There are some important things to know about identifying your allies. Some members start out being very cooperative and are seemingly allies, but as the group progresses they desire to take over the group or have the focus be on them. Sometimes your best allies are members who are quiet at first and don't stand out at the very beginning. It usually takes at least a couple of group meetings to identify the members who will be especially helpful and cooperative. In some groups, there really isn't a need to be concerned about allies, but in others it becomes very important to identify them. You will, however, want to be careful not to play favorites in the group.

Multicultural Understanding

Awareness of multicultural issues is very important in groups since most groups will be made up of diverse cultural backgrounds. DeLucia-Waack (1996) states in her editorial that multiculturalism is inherent in all group work. The leader needs to understand not only the different cultures of the group members but also how each member's culture affects his or her participation in group. Corey (1995) makes some excellent points in his discussion of multicultural issues as they apply to group counseling:

> Each individual must be seen against the backdrop of his or her cultural group, the degree to which he or she has become acculturated, and the level of development of racial identity.... Whether practitioners pay attention to culture variations or ignore them, culture will continue to influence both group members' and group leaders' behavior, and the group process as well. Group counselors who ignore culture will provide less effective services. (p.16)

Concluding Comments

In this chapter, we describe a number of basic skills for leading groups, such as active listening, reflection, clarification, summarizing, mini-lecturing, encouraging, and modeling. Beginning leaders often fail to realize that these fundamental counseling skills are also useful in group leadership. A skilled leader uses her eyes to draw members out, cut members off, and notice important nonverbal gestures. A good leader knows how to use his voice to influence the tone of the group, the energy of the members, and the pace of the session. Understanding different cultures is essential for the group leader in today's multicultural society.

CHAPTER SEVEN

Focus

In this chapter, we discuss the importance of knowing how to establish, hold, shift, and deepen the focus. We use the term *focus* primarily as a noun to refer to what is happening in the group. At any given moment in a session, the focus is either on a *topic* (love relationships, ways of dealing with parents, trust within the group), an *activity* (guided fantasy, a written exercise, blind trust walk), or a *person* (his concerns, issues, or problems). Throughout a session, the leader establishes the focus on certain topics, activities, or individuals, holds the focus, and/or shifts the focus. The leader should always be aware of the depth of any discussion or personal work and should, when appropriate, try to deepen the focus. The skilled leader understands that the focus moves from person to person and topic to topic, and it is the leader who is responsible for making sure the focus goes with the purpose of the group. *Knowing how to establish, hold, shift, and deepen the focus is absolutely essential for good leadership.*

Establishing the Focus

There are many ways that the focus is established in a group. The important thing to understand is that the leader is usually the person who establishes the focus. Discussion of methods for establishing the focus follows.

Use of Comments to Establish the Focus

Often, establishing the focus is accomplished by stating to the members what the topic or activity is going to be for the next few minutes.

- Let's focus on the topic of guilt for the next hour.
- Let's focus on Julio for the next 20 minutes, and try to help him with his dilemma.
- I'd like us to summarize what this last 30 minutes has meant.
- Let's really zero in on one of these topics. It doesn't matter which one, but let's pick one rather than trying to talk about all three.

◆ The topic for tonight is learning how to budget your time. Who wants to share what they learned from doing the homework on time management?

Use of Activities and Exercises to Establish the Focus

Using visual aids and having members write or draw something are excellent ways to get members focused. The following are just a few examples of the activities that can be used.

1. *Use posters, charts, or diagrams relevant to the topic or task of the group.* Visual aids tend to get the members involved both visually and auditorily.

2. *Use a chalkboard or a large pad to list items or characteristics.* For instance, if the group members are talking about drugs, you could go to the chalkboard and say, "Let's list the pros and cons of drug use." Or if you are leading a high school group and the topic is friends, you could say, "Let's list the characteristics of a good friend." While looking at the list on the board, members often get more focused by trying to generate new items to add.

3. *Use a chalkboard to draw pictures or visual analogies.* For example, group members are discussing all the ways they feel they are being held down. You could go to the chalkboard (or a large newsprint pad) and sketch a large hot-air balloon with various lead weights hanging off the sides. Each weight would be labeled in terms of pounds (200, 100, 50, 25, 10), and there would be space under each to fill in what that weight represented. This image might prove helpful to members and allow them to focus on what is holding them down and to what degree. Another drawing might be of a road with various roadblocks and choices on it. Having a drawing in front of them often helps members focus on a topic. The visual image also keeps members focused in that they continue to look at the image and think of new things to add or new meanings for the image.

4. *Have members list or write something.* A very helpful focusing technique is to have members write answers on sentence-completion forms. For example, a leader who wants the group to focus on the topic of parents could make up a list of five sentences for members to complete, such as the following:

When I think of my mom, I _____.

When I think of my dad, I _____.

I wish my dad _____.

I wish my mom _____.

The biggest problem I have with my parents is _____.

Another focusing technique that involves writing is to have each member make a list of something. For instance, the leader could have a group of first-year college students list their worries or have elementary school children list their favorite activities.

5. *Have members draw something.* Drawing such things as their favorite scene, the house they grew up in, or their earliest memory helps members focus on topics such as "what I like and value," "what my family was like," and "the impact of childhood on present-day living."

6. *Put a large piece of paper on the floor in the center of the group with a stimulus word or phrase on it.* This is a good way to get the members zeroed in on one concept. With this phrase in the center of the floor to stare at, they will usually stay focused. Some examples of words and phrases that you might put in the middle of the group are "Dad," "Mom," "work," "responsibili-ties," "fears I have," "changes I can make in my life," and "things that make me happy."

7. *Use handouts that contain information you want to cover.* Handouts give members something to look at and relate to. Also, they are useful in that the members can refer to them after the session is over.

8. *Place an empty chair in the center of the room.* The empty chair can represent many different people. If you want to focus on parents, you could have the chair represent one or both parents. If you want to focus on anger, you could have the chair be someone with whom they are angry.

9. *Place a small child's chair in the center of the room.* The small chair can represent the "free child," the "inner child," or the "hurt child." By having the chair present, members tend to focus on that part of themselves much more easily than if simply asked to imagine being the child.

10. *Stand on a chair.* The leader can usually get members focused on such issues as need for approval, whom they see as "above" them, or codependency by standing on an empty chair and asking a few questions about the people they have "above" them.

Other creative techniques include the use of shields, beer bottles, rubber bands, audiotapes, and videotapes. For a complete description of these and other creative techniques, see *Creative Counseling Techniques: An Illustrated Guide* (Jacobs, 1992), a book that encourages counselors to be creative and innovative when doing individual and group counseling.

When used properly, all of these techniques can prove very helpful to the leader. There are many direct and creative ways to get groups focused, and it is important to have a number of techniques to choose from. Different situations call for different techniques; through trial and error and experience you will learn which ones work best in particular situations.

Use of Rounds and Dyads to Establish the Focus

Rounds and dyads are two additional ways to establish the focus. (See Chapter Nine for a thorough explanation of rounds and dyads.) Rounds are very useful because they involve everybody and get members focused since members have to think of what they are going to say. Following are a few examples of how rounds can be used to establish the focus.

- Think of what has been the biggest change since your accident. In a minute, I'm going to have each of you comment briefly on this. Take a few seconds to think about it.
- How much effect do your siblings have on you today—a lot, a little, or none? Think about this, and then we'll do a round.
- In a word or phrase, what stood out to you the most about tonight?

Dyads help members focus on a topic by pairing members and instructing them to discuss various ideas. The following examples illustrate how dyads can be used to get members to focus on certain issues.

- Pair up and talk about ways you can benefit from the group.
- Pair up and talk about your reaction to the reading for the week.
- OK, I'd like you to pair up with someone and talk about your ideas for a solution to the problem.

Holding the Focus

Once the leader has the group focused, knowing how to *hold* the focus is essential since the focus rarely stays constant or clear for long periods of time without the aid of the leader. The leader must constantly decide whether to hold the focus or shift it to some other person, topic, or activity. Holding the focus means sticking with what is happening. For example, if Mac is discussing the pain he's experiencing over his wife's death, and Melvin interrupts and begins discussing his brother's visit, the leader holds the focus by directing the group back to Mac. Another example would be if a valuable discussion is taking place concerning feelings of insecurity regarding dating, and someone asks a question about the five best places to go with a date. The trained leader does not let the topic shift to "places to go," but rather holds the focus on insecurities.

There are three considerations to keep in mind for holding the focus: when to hold it, how long to hold it, and how to hold it.

When to Hold the Focus

Focus on a Topic

The following questions are helpful in determining whether to hold the focus on a topic. (By *topic*, we mean such things as parents, vanity, the value of staying in school, how to budget money, or any other subject the group is discussing.)

- Is the topic relevant to the purpose of the group? If it is not relevant to the purpose, usually the leader will want to shift the focus to a more relevant one.
- Are the members interested in the topic? If most members are not interested, the leader will probably want to shift the focus, although there are times when the leader may decide to stay with it a little longer.

- Has the focus been on the topic too long? This will usually depend on how much the leader planned to cover in the session. If there are five major issues to discuss, and the group is still on the first one with only half the session remaining, the focus should probably be shifted.
- Has the group discussed the topic before? Sometimes a group will go over the same issues week after week.

The answers to these questions will give leaders a sense of whether to hold or shift the focus. When the leader is unsure about whether to stay with a topic, doing a "quick 1 to 10" will help him decide. The leader can say, "I want to get a quick reading from you on whether we should continue to discuss the issue of _____. On a 1 to 10 scale, with 10 being very interested and 1 being very disinterested, what number best describes your attitude?" Usually the numbers will indicate whether there is enough interest. If all are low numbers or high numbers, the decision is obvious. If there is a range, a number of things can be done. The leader may ask those who indicated high interest what they specifically would like to discuss, then focus the group there with a time limit of 5, 10, or 20 minutes. She could split the group and let those with high interest meet for 20 minutes (depending on the time remaining) while the others discuss another topic. Splitting the group would be appropriate only in educational or discussion groups, where group cohesion is not a major goal. Leaders would rarely do this in a growth or therapy group. The leader could also give a break to those who rated their interest as low while the high-interest members continued with the topic. As you can see, the quick 1–10 round can offer information that generates a number of options for the leader.

Focus on a Person

In any group, the focus can easily be on one person. When this happens, it is the leader who decides whether to hold the focus on the person or to shift it to another person or to a topic. The leader must consider a number of things when this happens.

Does focusing on one person serve the purpose of the group? Some groups meet for the purpose of doing therapy or personal growth work; in such groups, focusing on one person is appropriate. Other groups meet for discussion, sharing, or accomplishing a task; thus, to focus on one person would be inappropriate.

Is the person benefiting from having the focus? If the person is benefiting and most of the other members are also, then the leader would want to hold the focus. If the person is benefiting, but most of the other members are not, then the decision to hold the focus is more difficult. Rarely will the leader want to hold the focus when only one or two members are involved in what is being said. If the leader cannot engage most of the members, he may decide to meet with the person individually since the issue is not one that other members can relate to.

Who is talking, and how much "air time" has the speaker had recently? If the person talking has not spoken in a while, or has spoken very little throughout the group's life, it is usually beneficial to hold the focus on that individual. If, on the other hand, the person has had the group's attention often in the past, the leader may choose to shift the focus.

How Long to Hold the Focus

One question you may be asking is, "How long is the focus held on a person or topic?" There is no single answer because it depends on the purpose of the group, which session it is, what happened in the previous sessions, and how much time is left in the current session. Also, different factors must be considered depending on whether the focus is on a person or on a topic.

Focus on a Person

The amount of time to hold the focus on a person depends partly on the kind of group being led. For therapy, growth, and support groups, where holding the focus on one person is appropriate, the upper limit is probably 30 minutes. Naturally, there will be exceptions: Sometimes the leader may stay with one person for an hour or more—however, this should be the exception rather than the rule. In other kinds of groups (discussion, education, or task), a good rule of thumb would be not to hold the focus longer than 5 minutes on any one person since you would probably want an exchange of ideas or information from all the members.

Holding the focus for a long period of time also depends on which session it is. Leaders do not want anyone to dominate the first couple of sessions because they are trying to get people to feel comfortable being in the group. If one person dominates, other members may tend to sit back and listen rather than think and contribute. Beginning leaders often make the mistake of focusing for too long on one member in early sessions, probably due to their own nervousness and/or not knowing how to cut off or draw out other members.

Focus on a Topic

How long to hold the focus on a topic depends on a number of things. If the group is an education, discussion, or task group where there are a number of things to be covered, the leader will want to budget the time wisely. Many beginning leaders get so caught up in the content or interaction that they forget that other topics need to be covered. Also, leaders have to be aware when the interest in the topic is waning. It is usually best to shift the focus to another topic before the majority of the members get bored and tune out the group.

Focusing on a "heavy" issue in the early stages of a group is usually not wise. Also, topics such as sex or death should not be focused on unless there is ample time to discuss them. A discussion of death can stir up a number of feelings, memories, and fears, so it is probably wise not to hold the focus on death if it comes up during the last 30 minutes of the session. The leader would probably want to say something like, "Let's hold off discussing the topic of death until next week since we really don't have enough time to fully discuss it, and I wouldn't want us to get started on something that might leave some of you hanging."

How to Hold the Focus

When the group is flowing and the focus starts to shift, the leader has access to several skills and methods for holding the focus. The main skill is cutting members off. (See Chapter Eight for a complete discussion.) Whether you are using that skill or one of the methods described in this section, remember that the most important thing is to *act quickly*. The longer you wait before bringing the group back to the topic or person, the harder it will be, since the members' energy and attention will have become invested in the new person or topic. The most common method for holding the focus is to address the group directly. The following examples should give you some idea of what to say.

- Let's stay with Sandy.
- I want to go back to what Joe was saying. Joe, when did you start feeling that way?
- Can we put that on hold until Karen finishes with her list?
- I believe we may have left Manuel, and I think we need to stay with him a little longer—Manuel, do you want to say more about that situation?
- Let's finish this topic before we start a new one.
- I think if we're not careful, we'll get too many things going at once—let's go back to the topic of. . . .

If you decide that you want the group to stay with a certain topic or person for a while, it is sometimes helpful to verbalize this. If, for example, your group has been discussing aspects of daily living, you might say, "Let's spend the next 10 minutes talking only about what is difficult for you on a daily basis."

Another way to hold the focus is to conduct a group exercise or use a prop. For instance, if the members were discussing their fears about cancer and the focus shifted to financial concerns, the leader could bring them back to the topic of fears by saying, "I'd like to list *(stands and goes to the chalkboard)* the different fears that you are experiencing. Financial fear is one; what are some others?" Or imagine a task group where eight members are trying to resolve their differences on how the probation office and welfare office can work together. The discussion has turned momentarily to the local judge and how her recent rulings have been inconsistent. Seeing the need to hold the focus on the task, the leader could say to the members, "I'd like to do something a little different. I want each of you to pair up with someone from the other office and come up with a list of suggestions for improving the working relationship of your two offices."

The possible techniques for holding the focus are actually unlimited. With experience, you will develop more techniques. Until then, try to use some of the ideas provided in this section plus others you will learn later on in this book.

Shifting the Focus

Although holding the focus and shifting the focus are very much tied together, it is important to conceptualize them as separate skills. Leaders consciously shift the focus when they decide that there is a need for a change in the group. The shift can go in many directions:

- From a topic to a person
- From a topic to another topic
- From a topic to an activity
- From a person to another person
- From a person to a topic
- From a person to an activity
- From an activity to a topic
- From an activity to a person

It is important to notice that "from an activity to another activity" is not listed, since this kind of shifting of the focus is usually not appropriate. *One of the biggest mistakes that beginning leaders make is to conduct one activity after another.* Group exercises need to be followed by discussion and not just done consecutively. We discuss processing exercises in Chapter Eleven.

When to Shift the Focus

There are two main ways to conceptualize shifting the focus: (1) as a shift *away* from some person, topic, or activity, or (2) as a shift *toward* some person, topic, or activity. The leader shifts the focus when one of the following is the case:

- The focus has been on one person for too long.
- The focus has been on one topic for too long.
- The focus does not fit the purpose of the group.
- The time left dictates the need for change.
- The leader feels the members need a change to reenergize the group.
- The leader wants to draw another member into the group.
- The leader wants to introduce a new topic or activity.

Shift from a Topic to a Person

Leaders often want to shift the focus from a topic to a person in counseling, therapy, and growth groups—but certainly may also do so in all kinds of groups.

◆ E X A M P L E S

The group has been discussing jealousy, and a number of members have commented on how they handle it. The discussion has been going on for 3 or 4 minutes. The leader decides to focus on one person for a few minutes rather than continue to let the interaction go from one member to another. Here are two ways the focus can be shifted to a person:

Missy: I just can't help it—I'm a jealous person. If Frank is talking to some woman at a party, I lose it.

Bill: But why? My wife does that to me, too. I don't like it at all.

Ted: I'm a lot more jealous than my wife. In fact, I don't think she gets jealous, and that makes me mad sometimes!

Leader: Missy, I'm wondering if you would want to explore your jealousy further. You seem to be bothered by it, and I think I detect a desire on your part to get better control of it.

Using the same example, the leader merely indicates the desire to shift to a person but does not focus on any one individual.

Leader: Would anyone like to spend a few minutes talking specifically about their concerns with jealousy? It is apparent to me that many of you are concerned about it. Ted, you and Missy and Bill all have talked about how jealousy is interfering in your relationships.

Some additional comments that leaders can make to shift to a person include:

- I'd like each of you to consider what we have been talking about for the last few minutes. Does anybody want to work on anything regarding this issue?
- Who wants to take this issue deeper? There seem to be several things that you could work on.
- This discussion is good; however, I feel that some of you may have something personal that you want to discuss. Does anyone have something they would like to bring up?

In the last example, the shift would not only be to a person but possibly to a new topic. If the leader doesn't want the topic to shift, a comment like the first example, which is more specific, should be used.

Shift from One Topic to Another

In discussion, task, and education groups, the leader will usually need to shift the focus from time to time to cover the necessary material or accomplish the task. To shift the focus, the leader might say any of the following:

- Let's take a minute or two to finish this topic because we need to move on to something else.

- We seem to be about finished with this issue. Who has some other issues or points to bring up?
- We have a lot to cover tonight, so let's go on to something else.
- I would like to change the discussion to focus on what Kay was talking about. She mentioned the effects of the decision. Let's talk about what the rest of you think the effects would be.

In task groups and education groups, there is often certain material to be covered. The leader can help shift the focus by letting the members know the agenda and an estimate of the time needed to cover the topics. For example, the leader could say:

- Today, we are going to talk about diet and exercise as they relate to stress. We'll spend approximately 45 minutes on each topic.
- First, we need to decide which proposal we want to accept. Then we need to decide who will do what, and discuss the necessary schedule changes that will be required. We only have an hour and a half, so we'll need to watch the time.

In each of these examples, telling the members what the agenda is helps the leader. It will still be the leader's responsibility to budget the group's time and to shift the focus when needed, but the clock can be used to do so—that is, by allowing so many minutes for each topic, and, when the time has run out, the leader can say to the group, "We need to move on because of time." Here are some additional ways that leaders can shift to a new topic:

- We have a lot to cover today, so let's move on to the next chapter.
- Let's turn to another issue that is equally as important as the one we are now discussing.
- There are two more topics that we need to cover today. Let me throw them out to you, and then let's decide which one we want to do next.

Shift from a Topic to an Exercise

Often, when the group is discussing a topic, a group exercise may be useful to further the discussion or get members more involved. The leader introduces the exercise by saying something like, "I want us to stay with what we are discussing, but I think an exercise could be helpful now." Or the leader can say, "I want to change the format a little bit. There is a group exercise that fits in with what we are talking about." Leaders often use a round exercise to shift from a topic. For instance, if the group has been discussing a topic for some time, the leader might say, "In a word or phrase, what are you thinking about right now? Let's do a round and hear from everyone." Another round that leaders use after a discussion is, "What are two things that stood out to you? We'll quickly go around the room and hear from each of you." Another easy way to shift from a topic to an activity is to have members form dyads to further discuss the topic that was being explored in the large group.

Shift from One Person to Another

If the leader has determined that the focus needs to shift to another person, there are a number of possible things to say. Following are some examples of different situations and different responses:

- Lori, I think it would be good to let you just think about what you have been saying these last 15 minutes; then maybe we'll come back to you later on. What did this bring up for the rest of you? Who wants to explore their reactions or feelings?
- Joe, I'd like to shift to Cindy. *(The leader turns and addresses Cindy)* You seem to really be relating to this. I noticed a couple of times that you wanted to say something. Do you want to share that now?
- Avid, we'll stay with you for another couple of minutes; then I'm going to give others a chance to share their ideas.

In these examples, the leader addresses the person who has the focus and then shifts it. The leader who wants to cut off the member who has the focus will address the group directly. In such situations, the leader might say something like this:

- Does anyone want to comment on what Joe has been saying?
- Let's not focus on Joe, but rather on yourselves. Any thoughts or feelings?
- Cindy, how about you? You seem deep in thought.
- Can anyone relate to what Lori has been saying? (The leader would look away from Lori and would have some idea of who might want to speak.)

Shift from a Person to a Topic

There will be times when the leader will want to focus on the topic that a person is addressing. This may be because the topic is one that he thinks is relevant for most of the members, or because he wants to subtly shift the focus from the member who currently has it. Here are some examples:

- Dean, I want to pick up on what you've been talking about. I think the issue is a good one, and I want to hear how others think and feel about it. What do others of you think about the issue—how do you deal with it and what reactions have you gotten? (Throwing out so many different questions invites discussion, which in this case is the intention.)
- Carol, you have brought up many concerns that certainly relate to others. I'd like to spend the rest of the session discussing some of those issues. Let's take the one you mentioned first. (Mentioning Carol by name and using some of the content she has been discussing increases the likelihood that she will not feel cut off.)
- Julio, your thoughts are interesting. However, I am aware that we are running out of time, and we still have one more major item to discuss. Why don't you summarize your position, and then we will move on.

- I want to shift the discussion to the whole group since we really want to hear a number of ideas and views. What do the rest of you think?

As you can see in these examples, shifting the focus often involves cutting off. The next chapter covers that skill in detail.

Shift from a Person to an Exercise

As mentioned earlier, the leader can use a round as a very good way to shift the focus; that is, ask members to rate on a 1–10 scale or give a word or phrase about some subject. Also, the leader can simply ask the members to pair up and discuss what the member has been talking about, or to talk about any thoughts or feelings they had when the member was speaking. Many other group exercises can be used to shift the focus. The following are a couple of ways to introduce such exercises:

- I want to take what you are talking about and get the whole group to think about it. Everyone get out a piece of paper and something to write with. I want you to do the following. . . .
- Ruth, your energy and enthusiasm are appreciated. I want to see if I can get everyone as excited and interested as you are. Everyone stand up—I want you to move to this side of the room. Now, here's what I want you to do. . . .

Deepening the Focus

A leader must consider not only holding or shifting the focus, but also whether or not to deepen the focus. *The key to most groups is deepening the focus to a level that is productive and meaningful for the members.* In many groups, members have a tendency to get sidetracked or avoid delving too deeply into their issues. Therefore, it is the leader's responsibility to make sure the group "funnels" to a meaningful depth. Depth is measured differently for various groups—for education and discussion groups, depth is measured by assessing learning and the exchange of ideas. Task group depth is measured with regard to productivity and how well members are working together. Counseling, therapy, growth, and support groups are measured by new insights about living and belonging, and the level of sharing when doing personal work. A leader deepens the focus by:

- Asking very thought-provoking or challenging questions
- Asking members to share at a more personal level
- Working with a member in a more intense manner
- Conducting an intense exercise that gets in touch with some deep, personal issues
- Confronting members about certain dynamics that are interfering with the group

In later chapters on middle sessions and therapy, we discuss in detail many skills and techniques for deepening the focus.

Depth Chart

To discuss the depth of the group in a concrete way, we have devised the *depth chart*. (See figure at the bottom of this page.). The depth chart is a scale in which 10 represents surface-level talking or sharing, and 1 represents deep, intense, personal sharing. During the life of a group, the depth of discussion will vary. In the beginning, the depth is usually only a 10 or 9 because members are telling stories or talking superficially about some topic or issue. As a group moves to the middle phase, the depth should reach below 8 to at least a 7; for most groups, the leader will want the group to reach a depth of 6 or below. Too often, groups bounce from topic to topic and never go deep enough to derive any benefit, following a pattern of 10, 9, 8; new topic, 10, 9, 8; new topic, 10, 9, 8.

By using a depth chart, a leader can better visualize and understand what is happening in her group. In most groups, the desired depth during the working phase is 7 or deeper, with some groups going to an intense level of 3, 2, or even 1. If the group is staying at the 10, 9, or 8 level, the leader will want to intensify the discussion. The leader may want to move to a deeper level by using an exercise that encourages members to explore an issue in greater depth. Processing the exercise can lead to discussion or individual work at a level of 6 or lower. In some groups, the leader may draw or explain the depth chart and periodically ask the members how they would chart the discussions and interactions within the group.

When to Deepen the Focus

There are two considerations when thinking of deepening the focus. The first is the phase of the session, because deepening the focus should only be done during the middle phase of a group and not during the warm-up or the ending phase. When there is an opportunity to deepen the focus during the middle phase, the

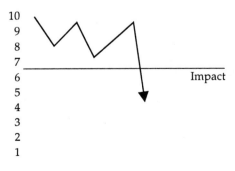

leader should also consider if there is enough time to adequately cover the issue or topic. Beginning leaders often will deepen the focus and then run out of time and leave members hanging—this is not good leadership.

How to Deepen the Focus

There are a number of considerations regarding how deep to focus a group. The most important is the purpose of the group. Too often in education, discussion, and task groups, leaders deepen the focus on individuals to a level far below what the purpose is. This makes members uncomfortable and can be harmful because members did not expect nor even agree to a therapy group; and all of a sudden that is what is happening. *Always consider the purpose of the group before deepening the focus to a very personal, intense level.*

Even if the members are open to going to a deeper level, it is always advisable for a leader to think about the members and what depth is appropriate. For most school groups—especially elementary groups—leaders would not want personal sharing to be below a 4. The leader always should consider whether a member can handle sharing personal concerns or receiving feedback in the group. Members differ in the degree to which they are ready and comfortable to share and receive feedback, and can be harmed if they are not able to deal with what is being said. Too often, beginning leaders get so involved in the process that they forget to consider if certain members are ready and able to deal with the depth toward which the group is heading.

There are two other considerations regarding how deep to focus: multicultural issues and expertise. Leaders must consider the cultural background before delving too deeply too quickly with a group member, since some members may be very uncomfortable. It is very important to make a contract with the member before pushing him or her to deeper work.

Sometimes in groups, issues come up that the leader may know little about. It is unethical to push a member into deeper work when the leader does not have the experience, knowledge, and understanding to deal with the problem. Too often, we hear of unqualified leaders dealing with some very intense therapy issues.

Concluding Comments

A good leader understands that paying attention to the focus is one of the most important skills of group leading. There are many different techniques for establishing, holding, shifting, and deepening the focus. The focus of a group is always on either a person, topic, or activity. Being aware of where the focus is and whether it needs to be shifted or held enables the leader to maintain control over what is happening in the group. The leader also is aware of how deep the session is, and may use a depth chart to monitor the development of a session. Before deepening the focus, the leader should consider the purpose of the group, the stage of the group, the phase of the session, the amount of time left, and how deep to focus the group.

In Chapters Two and Three, we introduced concepts that, along with the focus, serve as "maps" for understanding the interactions and development of your group. Because these maps are so useful when leading groups, we have summarized them here to help you see how the four go together.

- *Purpose:* Why the group is meeting
- *Stage:* Where the group is in its development
- *Phase:* Where the session is
- *Focus:* The content of the group
    Establishing the focus
    Holding the focus
    Shifting the focus
    Deepening the focus

CHAPTER EIGHT

Cutting Off
and Drawing Out

Cutting Off

To lead an effective group, a leader must be willing and able to cut off members when necessary. Of all the skills we present in this book, cutting off is probably the hardest to use because leaders often fear that they will hurt a member's feelings or that members will become angry. In addition, the skill is difficult because when growing up, we do not learn to stop others from talking when their remarks are boring, long-winded, or inappropriate. However, a group leader is responsible for ensuring positive group outcomes; when group members' comments are counterproductive, the leader should intervene.

Cutting off is the term we use to describe a leader's stopping a member from talking (Harvill, Masson, & Jacobs, 1983; Masson & Jacobs, 1980). Other terms used to describe this skill are *blocking* (Trotzer, 1989) and *intervening* (Dyer & Vriend, 1980). While cutting off may sound like we are advocating that the leader be rude or authoritarian in the group, we are not. We merely mean that there are instances when the leader must interrupt a member in order to protect other members or to move the group in a better direction.

There are two broad situations when the leader will want to use cutting-off skills: (1) when a member has the "floor" but is either rambling, storytelling, or avoiding going deeper; and (2) when a member is saying something inappropriate. Before discussing these, we want to mention a number of important points regarding cutting off.

Timing

Perhaps the most important thing to understand about cutting off is that it has to be timed properly. The leader should stop members before they ramble too long, argue for an extended period, or offer unhelpful advice. On the other hand, leaders will want to make sure they are not interrupting a legitimate and worthwhile comment; this can anger and frustrate members. Unfortunately, there is no way to spell out exactly when the leader should cut off someone since each situation is different. Experience and feedback from members will probably be the leader's best teacher.

Use of Voice

Voice tone, pitch, and inflection have a lot to do with how effective a leader will be in using cutting-off skills. If the leader seems critical, gruff, or angry, members are likely to react in a negative way. When cutting off, the goal is not to criticize but rather to stop something that is not helpful. It is important to remember that members are usually not consciously giving the leader or other members a hard time; rather, they don't understand or have not yet learned how to be productive group members.

Clarifying

It is important in the first session to explain to the members that you will at times cut off certain discussions for various reasons (see Chapter Five). Often, the leader will also explain at the time of cutting off why he is doing it. Explaining is a good practice because confusion and anger can result if someone feels cut off for no apparent reason. Some may think it is because the leader does not like them or that their opinions don't matter. Others may assume that they should not speak unless asked to do so. Of course, there will be many instances when the leader will choose not to offer an immediate explanation for cutting someone off—for example, if the leader feels it is important to move on immediately.

Nonverbal Signals

Sometimes the leader's avoiding eye contact can serve as a signal to let a member know that he wants the member to stop. Some members will "wrap up" once they notice the leader not looking at them.

Another technique the leader can use is to signal the member with his hand that he would like the member to stop. Just a slight gesture, such as would be used by a traffic officer, is sometimes enough to cue the member to "wind down."

Cutting Off a Member Who Has the Focus of the Group

In any group, there will be times when the group will focus on a member who is either rambling, not getting to the point, or avoiding exploring an issue at a deeper level. Some members drone on and on, totally oblivious to the negative effect that their rambling is having on others. If left unchecked, these members will often drain the energy and enthusiasm present in other members. Therefore, the leader has to use some kind of cutting-off technique.

The leader has three possible decisions regarding cutting off in a situation where a member has the attention of the group. The leader can (1) cut and stay with the person, (2) cut and stay with the topic, or (3) cut and leave the person and topic.

Cutting and Staying with the Person

Many times, the leader sees value in interrupting and keeping the focus on a member. There are a number of techniques that can be used.

1. *Ask a question.* The leader, using a kind voice, can cut off a member by asking a focusing type question, such as any of the following:

> How can the group help you with this?
> If we give you 10 more minutes to talk about this, what would be helpful?
> You seem to be rambling. What is your point? Where are you going with this?
> Are you wanting to just tell us about this, or are you asking the group for some help?

2. *Ask the person clarifying questions.* The leader may interrupt and either ask or have the members ask some questions to break up the monologue of the rambler. The leader will want to be sure that the questions are not ones that allow for more storytelling.

◆ E X A M P L E S

Danie: *(Who has been telling stories for a couple of minutes about her alcoholic father and is not expressing her feelings)* And another thing he did was—

Leader: Just a second here. Let us ask you some questions about you and your dad. I want each of you to think of something you can ask Danie that will get her to explore more deeply her feelings about her situation. One question I want to ask is, "How much do you blame yourself for his drinking?"

Danie: And another thing he did was—

Leader: Just a second here. Let us ask you some questions about you and your dad. I want each of you to think of something you can ask Danie that will get her to explore more deeply her feelings about her situation. Who has a question they want to ask?

Malik: I do. How can we help you? All you do is come here and tell us stories. Do you really want help?

Danie: I think I do. But what I was going to say—

Leader: Hold on, Danie. Who else has a question?

Lee: Is there anything we can do to get you to quit denying that your father is an alcoholic?

Danie: *(Tearing up)* I don't want him to be. I really need help.

3. *Have the person do some focused activity (perhaps using chairs, drama, or some experiential activity).* Using the example of Danie, the leader could put a chair in front of Danie and ask her to pretend that her father is sitting there and ask her to have a conversation with him. Or the leader could ask Danie to act out one of the scenes she has been describing, using members of the group to play her father and other family members. (Often reenactment of scenes triggers emotional reactions.) Many other activities could also be tried. The point is that the leader has stopped Danie's storytelling, kept the focus on her, and tried to deepen the focus.

4. *Have the person comment to each member (from her seat, or have the person sit in front of each of the members).*

◆ EXAMPLE

Leader: Danie, let me get you to do this. I want you to turn to Lilly and complete the following sentence: "When Dad drinks, I . . ."

Danie: *(Looks at Lilly, who is sitting next to her)* When Dad drinks, I feel that it is my fault.

Leader: Now look at Amos, and start with the same phrase.

Danie: When Dad drinks, I feel I should do something.

Leader: Turn to Tomika, and start with the same phrase.

Danie: When Dad drinks, I get scared that someone will get hurt. I feel I have to protect my little sister. *(Begins to cry)*

Leader: Stay with those feelings.

5. *Have the members give the person feedback.* If the member is not benefiting from talking, the leader can interrupt by asking the members to give feedback.

◆ EXAMPLES

Leader: Danie, I want to stop you for a second, and I am going to ask the group for some feedback. What do you think Danie is trying to say?

Harvey: I think she is trying to say that she doesn't know what to do, but she thinks she should. She is doing what I used to do, which is take responsibility for the family and the drinking because no one else was trying to fix the problem.

Leader: What do you think Danie needs to explore but is avoiding?

Sonya: She seems to feel bad about herself, but she won't talk about it. Danie, you are blaming yourself, and it is not your fault!

Danie: *(Head down, softly crying)* But why does it feel like it is?

6. *Have the members role-play the person.*

◆ E X A M P L E

Leader: I want you to become Danie. Try with your voice and body to be her. Start with, "I'm Danie, and here's what I am trying to say." Who can do this?

Monica: I think I can. *(With head hanging and in a weak voice)* My dad came home last night and started in on us.

Danie: Is that how I really look and sound? No wonder I feel so bad.

The leader could even ask the member who is playing Danie a number of deepening questions. If a member can role play Danie well, this can prove to be very enlightening to her. This activity and the previous one in which feedback was given can be valuable because the focus stays on the member, but the member stops talking and listens and watches. *Some members actually can benefit more by listening to themselves being discussed than by talking.*

These are just some of the techniques that can be used to cut off and stay with the person. With experience, leaders develop a number of ways to interrupt and stay focused on a member who is rambling or making nonproductive comments.

Cutting and Staying with the Topic

There will be times when the leader will want to shift the focus away from the member who is talking but stay with the topic. When the leader makes the decision to intervene in this manner, the member often does not feel so cut off. Using the example of Danie, the leader might say:

Leader: Danie, let me get other members' comments about their relationship with their parents. Can any of you relate to what Danie is saying?

Cutting and Leaving the Person and the Topic

Inevitably, there will be times when the leader will need to cut off and redirect the group because it is off on a tangent or it is time to start closing the group. In such instances, the leader might say something like:

Leader: I think we need to move on. I want to shift our attention to an exercise that I think you will find interesting.

The important thing to understand is that you have choices when you are thinking about cutting off.

Other Situations That Call for Cutting-Off Skills

There are a number of situations when a leader may want to use the skill of cutting off. We discuss seven of them:

1. When a member's comments conflict with the group's purpose
2. When a member is saying something hurtful
3. When a member is saying something inaccurate
4. When the leader wants to shift the focus
5. When it is near the end of the session
6. When members are arguing
7. When members are rescuing other members

When a Member's Comments Conflict with the Group's Purpose

One of the main uses of cutting off is to ensure that the group's content fits with its purpose. Whenever a member's comments are not in line with the group's purpose or when the group is discussing a nonproductive or unrelated topic, the leader should use cutting off to re-focus the group on a more relevant issue. Too often, a member will get going on some irrelevant topic, and the leader will let that person continue indefinitely. Instead, the leader should say something like:

Leader: Let me interrupt. I think we have gotten away from the purpose of the group. I'd like us to get back to our task, which is . . .

When a Member Is Saying Something Hurtful

There will be times in support, counseling, and therapy groups when a member will begin to make very critical comments to another member. These must be cut off by the leader.

◆ E X A M P L E

Kirk: . . . and I just feel that it is important that I share this. I have not been completely honest here. You see, my lover is not a she, but actually is a he—that is, I am gay.

Bob: That's disgusting! I think—

Leader: Wait a second. Bob, that is your issue. I want to stay with Kirk and his feelings.

The leader should block Bob's comments because they were going to be hurtful. Some beginning leaders let a member like Bob continue because they are not comfortable cutting off. This could be potentially harmful to a disclosing member and the group in general.

Extreme, value-laden comments about certain issues also need to be cut off. Members may attempt to lecture others about such things as the evils of having an affair or an abortion. A member may want to comment at length about how organized religion is a harmful institution and should be banned or about how divorce is the ultimate failure and all marriages can be saved. These types of comments usually represent one particular member's point of view and have the potential of being hurtful. To let that member go on and on would be a mistake on the part of the leader, especially since other group members could be greatly offended.

When a Member Is Saying Something Inaccurate

In discussion, education, and task groups, comments can be made that are inaccurate, misleading, or inappropriate. For example, in an education group about birth control, a member might say, "The pill should never be used because it has been proven to cause cancer. I have two friends now who are suffering from its side effects. Let me tell you about them." The leader would want to use cutting-off skills to correct this member's exaggerated statements. Whenever something is being said that is not accurate, the leader should not feel that he has to wait until the person is finished before he can comment. In fact, it is best to cut off "speeches" that are not beneficial to the group as soon as you identify them as such.

In counseling, therapy, and growth groups, it is especially important to listen for inappropriate comments or advice since members can say things harmful to others. For instance, a member might say to another, "I think you should divorce her immediately. Any woman who won't go to church with her husband is not a good woman." In this situation, the leader needs to cut off the member for giving inappropriate advice.

A common phenomenon in many groups is the guaranteeing of someone's behavior. That is, a member will say to another, "If you do X, then your wife (son, boss, parents) will do *Y*." It is important that the leader not let anyone make promises about how another person will think, feel, or behave. Here are some examples of such promises:

- If you get mad a couple of times, she'll change. You just need to let her know who's boss.
- Go home and tell your mom you're sorry for what you did. She'll understand, and everything will be fine.

In these examples, members are promising some behavior over which they have no control. The leader should cut off any comments similar to this. One cardinal rule for leaders to follow and one to teach members to follow is *Do not guarantee anyone's behavior other than your own. Human behavior is highly unpredictable.*

◆ E X A M P L E

This group is composed of stepparents who are sharing feelings and experiences about their particular situations in the hope of discovering new ways of coping.

Jim: My stepson, Jeff, seems to prevent himself from getting emotionally close to me because of his loyalty to his biological father.

Edgar: *(Dogmatically)* You should spend more time with him, Jim. If you'll limit his time with his father and use it for the two of you, he'll grow to love you more. That's what I did with my stepson, and it's working out OK. I guarantee you that Jeff will respect you if you take a little control over the situation. Besides—

Leader: Edgar, let me stop you here to say a couple of things. First, I appreciate your attempt to help. I'm glad that it is working out well between you and your stepson. I'm not so sure that your particular method will work for Jim and Jeff. What Jeff is experiencing is actually a very common and normal thing. Many stepchildren experience divided loyalty between their absent parent and the new stepparent. Each of you may want to think about this issue as it applies to your children. . . .

In this example, the leader was aware that Edgar was making guarantees to Jim based on his own experience and that his advice was not appropriate.

When the Leader Wants to Shift the Focus

Frequently, when a topic has been thoroughly covered or the focus has been held on one member too long, the leader's task is to shift the focus. Sometimes, a natural break occurs in the interaction, and the shift is easy. At other times, the leader will need to use cutting-off skills to accomplish the shift.

◆ E X A M P L E S

This is a growth group for high school girls. The issue being discussed is love relationships. While Amy is telling a story about her sister, the leader notices that Sherry seems to want to speak.

Amy: I just don't understand. Tom and Cindy got along so well in the beginning. They were so happy together. They could talk to each other about anything. I thought it was for keeps, but after a couple of months, things were not so rosy. I think they maintained the relationship for several months because they kept hoping they could regain what they once had. Let me give you an example. They were— (*The leader notices that Sherry is listening intently and nodding her head in agreement.*)

Leader: Amy, let me stop you before you really get into the story, unless there is a personal note to your comments. (*Amy shakes her head, indicating that it is not personal*) It seems that Sherry is reacting to what you are saying, and I want to give her a chance to comment. Sherry, would you like to offer some comments?

Sherry: Oh, yes. What Amy was saying about the relationship being so good at first and then changing also happened to me. My boyfriend and I ended our relationship a week ago. It just seemed that we suddenly had nothing in common anymore. I. . . .

In this example, the leader decides to cut off Amy and shift to Sherry for two reasons. First, although Amy was telling an interesting story, she appeared to have no personal investment in the topic. Second, Sherry appeared interested in the discussion and seemed to relate to it personally.

The members have been discussing their families of origin. The discussion has been going on for about 10 minutes, and the members still seem to be on the surface. The leader decides that the "Family Sculpture" exercise would be a way to get members to really focus on their home environments. The members are currently discussing vacations they had with their parents when they were young.

Leader: Let me jump in here. I'd like to make this discussion about families more meaningful. An exercise that I have used before and one that is quite helpful in getting you to look at how you were affected by your early family experiences is called "Family Sculpture." This involves having you pick members of the group to represent your family as it was when you were growing up. . . .

In this example, the leader used cutting off to move to a structured activity to funnel the group from merely conversational to more insightful reflections.

When the Session Is Nearly Over

There are two situations when cutting off is necessary near the end of a session. When leading a group with a designated ending time, the leader will sometimes have to cut off members to allow time to summarize and end the group promptly. It is very important to have enough time to close the group, and sometimes the only way to do this is by cutting off what is going on.

The second situation is when a member brings up an emotional issue with little time remaining in the session. A skilled leader will quickly cut off the member before he gets too far into his issue. Obviously, this is a difficult situation to handle, but there are times when there is not enough time for dealing with the concern.

◆ E X A M P L E

There are approximately 10 minutes left in the first session of a group made up of adults who were adopted when they were very young and who are now trying to find their biological mothers. Tracy starts to talk about her fears and the problems her search has already caused.

Tracy: *(In a distressed voice)* I am so afraid that my search is going to end in nothing. I have so much anxiety and worry. I have three choices now and I—

Leader: *(Using an understanding voice)* Tracy, could I ask you to hold that until we meet next week? I don't think we have enough time now to really deal with your issue, and we need to stop in about 10 minutes. Now, in the last few minutes left, I'd like us to summarize tonight and get different reactions to this first session. I think we are off to a good start.

In this example, Tracy's concern is obviously a sensitive and personal one, and the leader is wise to hold off on it until the next session. The leader also does the right thing by cutting her off quickly, before the momentum of the group shifts to Tracy's anxiety and worry.

When Members Are Arguing

Any time people come together to form a group, there is the potential for arguments. Members usually leave it to the leader to stop arguments; if left on their own, some members would spend the entire session arguing. Therefore, the leader has to intervene and come up with better ways of discussing or resolving issues. Ordinarily, it is best to cut off arguments quickly because they are usually not productive and are often detrimental to the group. Arguments do nothing to build cohesion, and can erode trust. Arguments can also set a negative tone for the group and use up time that can be spent in a much more productive manner.

In a few situations, a leader might allow an argument to continue for a short period. For example, the leader may want to observe the argument and then focus on process instead of content to help the members learn about their style of interacting and arguing. A good rule to follow is *Don't let members argue unless it is productive in some way for them or the group.*

When members are arguing, the leader can use the following techniques:

- Cut off and focus on process by discussing what is happening in the group.
- Cut off and focus on content by getting some of the nonvolatile members to discuss the issue.
- Cut off and focus on content by asking the volatile members to continue the discussion but tone down their remarks.
- Cut off and focus on content by discussing the issue calmly herself.
- Cut off and shift the focus to a new issue.

◆ E X A M P L E

This group is composed of clients at a mental-health center. Members are discussing their different living arrangements; it is the third session.

Rita: I live in a communal-type situation with three men and four women.

Sam: *(Sits bolt upright)* I think that's disgusting!

Rita: What do you mean by that?

Sam: I mean I think that's wrong—God didn't put us on this earth to live in sin!

Rita: Who says it's a sin?

Sam: God does! In the Bible—

Leader: *(Calmly)* Hold on. Let me say something to everyone. Maybe I haven't touched enough on the subject of attacking one another. Our purpose here is not to judge whether others are right or wrong in their actions or beliefs but rather to listen to the variety of ideas expressed and learn about differences in the way people live. Human relationships require listening without judging. I hope in this group you will learn to get along with people who are different from you. Rita, you were saying. . . .

In this example, the leader recognizes that the exchange is not productive. The leader decides to make a brief comment on the purpose of the group, which serves both to cut off the rapidly escalating argument and to inform the members that making moral judgments about the actions of others is inappropriate. By speaking in a calm way, the leader is able to defuse the hostile tone being created.

When Members Are Rescuing Other Members

Some members on occasion present a helpless, "poor me" self-portrait in which they paint themselves as victims of their environment. When this happens, other members will often want to rescue them by saying certain soothing things or by offering all kinds of advice. This usually sounds something like, "It'll be okay; everything is going to work out," or "Don't cry; things will get better." This kind of member behavior is usually not productive because it tends to reinforce the "working" member's belief that he is helpless.

◆ E X A M P L E

A group of recently divorced women is meeting for the purpose of support.

Alice: *(Crying)* I'm just no good to anyone. I'm not pretty and obviously not interesting. The divorce was all my fault. I'm sure no one will ever ask me out.

Terri: *(Patronizingly)* There, there, Alice. *(Patting her on the arm)* Everything will be OK. There are lots of men out there who are just waiting for someone like you to come along. There's no need to cry. I'll bet your husband—

Leader: Wait a minute, Terri. *(To the entire group)* Helping someone doesn't always involve making them feel better immediately. Alice, I'm not sure if you are asking for help or just telling us your current feelings.

The leader quickly stepped in to prevent Terri from rescuing Alice because Alice is not making any attempt to improve her situation but rather is wallowing in self-pity. In essence, there is no indication from Alice that she really wants to work on her issues. The leader would want to get such an agreement from her; otherwise, Alice might simply manipulate the group with her "poor me" routine.

Certainly it is desirable for members to help each other, but there is a difference between helping and rescuing. Leaders often mistakenly let rescuing go on when such behavior should be cut off. A similar mistake is to allow members to hug or touch another who is crying because of a "poor me" attitude. This kind of physical support can serve to reinforce the "I'm weak" position taken by that member. With experience, the leader will come to recognize when it is appropriate to stop rescuing behavior and when it is appropriate to offer support and caring touch.

Practice

In this section, you will have the opportunity to practice what you've learned. Four examples follow, which you may respond to in your own words. Read each one and think about what you would say and why; you may want to write out your responses. Each example is discussed after it is presented.

◆ E X A M P L E S

This group is composed of prisoners, all of whom have committed violent acts against others. The purpose of the group is to help members overcome their inability to control their anger. The members are talking about events during the past month that have triggered their anger. Don has been talking for the past 90 seconds, and as he ruminates about an event, he becomes angrier and angrier.

Don: And then that @!*#!* just looked at me and grinned, and I knew I couldn't do a thing about it. If he'd been out on the street, I would have fixed him. The next time that @*#!* pulls that on me I'm . . .

Think about what you would say if you were the leader. Your goal would be to stop Don from continuing to speak, since he seems to be escalating his anger. Take some time here to formulate one or two different ways to handle this situation. Here are some possible cutting-off responses:

Leader: Don, let me break in here if I may. (*Looks at all members*) I want to talk about something I am sensing in the group. I think many of you have short fuses like Don's; when the fuse goes, there is an explosion, and that explosion gets you into trouble—namely, prison. I hope we can lengthen those fuses so that you can stay out of trouble and not hurt anyone unnecessarily. How could Don have stayed calmer in that situation?

Leader: Don, do you want help with this and if so, how can we be of help?

Leader: Don, you obviously lost it in this situation. I want you to turn to Bill and tell him one thing you could have done so that you would not have gotten so angry.

These are some possible responses. Yours may have been different but equally as effective. The important thing to note in this example is that the member was getting more and more agitated, and Don's comments were not helpful to himself or to other members. This would be a definite signal that some form of cutting off was needed.

This group is composed of middle school students whose parents are divorced. The leader has been encouraging members to share any feelings they have about their family situation.

Sarah: I've just been hoping that Mom and Dad will get back together. Mom is seeing another guy named Dave, and I just can't stand him. He always kisses me, and it just makes me sick. Sometimes when Dave is there, I sit in my room and cry, wishing that my dad would come back.

Mike: Your dad was a drunk! Why would you think about him? Anyone would be better than him. I remember when he took us to the zoo. He. . . .

What would you say if you were the leader? Stop and think of a couple of different options. Here are some possible responses:

Leader: Mike, stop. Let's stay with Sarah and her feelings.

Leader: Mike, let me stop you because I don't think you are tuned into Sarah very well. Sarah, say some more about how you are feeling.

Leader: Mike, hang on for a second. We need to work with Sarah and then maybe even talk about how everyone in the group can learn to be more sensitive to others. I do want you, Mike, to think about whether you were coming from Sarah's viewpoint or yours. Sarah, let's get back to you, and then we can come back to this other topic.

Leader: Mike, rather than focus on Sarah's dad, I'd like to work with you on your comments since you often tend to say things that are not sensitive to the member who is sharing. Have others of you noticed that Mike tends to do this? Sarah, we will come back to you, but I do think it is important for Mike to get some feedback.

The leader would certainly want to cut Mike off and then decide whether to focus on Sarah or Mike. Probably the best person to focus on is Sarah. The leader could also use the incident as a way to talk about being more sensitive to others when commenting. Some leaders might mistakenly get angry at Mike and hold the focus on him and his behavior, thus leaving Sarah, who is in pain. The last response is one in which the focus is held on Mike.

This is a weekend growth group composed of married couples whose goal is to discuss and eliminate problem areas in their marriages. Couples have been sharing about their hobbies and vacations. One couple, Mary and Tom, are now arguing about how they take their vacations.

Tom: Why do we have this insurmountable difference over where to go on vacations? You always demand that we see your parents.

Mary: That's because we see my parents only once a year, but we practically live with yours. Besides, all you want to do on vacation is fish or camp, and you know I hate that! You are so uncaring and unfair! Why don't you care about *me*?

Tom: Don't start that again. You always do this!

What would you do if you were leading this group? Take a moment and think of a couple of different responses. Some leaders might make the mistake of allowing the argument to continue. It is apparent that the couple has fought over this issue a number of times. There are several things the leader could say:

Leader: Let me stop you, because I don't think you are hearing each other. *(To the group)* What do some of you think is going on with Tom and Mary?

(This holds the focus on Tom and Mary but gets others involved and stops the useless arguing.)

Leader: I want you to stop since it doesn't seem that you are getting anywhere. I want the two of you to listen to others who have probably had similar problems. Have any of you had problems like this? (The leader is second-guessing that other couples have had problems over vacations.)

Leader: I want to ask you something. Why do the two of you get nowhere with this argument? Think about it. What is happening to each of you as you talk? (This holds the focus on them and will probably involve other members because the focus has shifted to communication patterns.)

Leader: I want to try something here that I think may help you see what you do to each other. I need someone to play Tom and someone to play Mary, and I want you to act out this argument. Tom, you and Mary just watch. I think you'll learn something. Who can play either Tom or Mary? (This cutting off stops the arguing and shifts to a role play that should generate more involvement for all members. Tom and Mary should especially benefit.)

This group is composed of high school seniors. Its purpose is to discuss various situations that young adults face once they leave high school.

Leader: *(To start the session)* What did you find out about loans and credit? Did any of you ask your parents or friends about this?

Larry: I did. I found out a lot about loans and interest and how that all works. *(Larry goes on for a couple of minutes.)*

Leader: How about others of you? What did you find out about the different places to borrow money?

Larry: Oh, I found out that there were a number of places. They are. . . .

Leader: *(Notices that there is silence when Larry finishes)* Let's talk about buying a house. From talking to some of you before we started this afternoon, I know you found out some interesting things regarding home buying. Who would like to share what they learned?

Larry: I would.

It is a good bet that Larry's constant replies are affecting the other members. Any time a leader allows a member to dominate a group, the other members usually share less and feel less involved. This is especially true when the dominant member is not saying particularly interesting things, but rather seems to be talking due to anxiety or a need for attention. How would you respond if you were the leader? Take a minute and think of a couple of responses. Listed are some of the options available to the leader.

Leader: Larry, let me cut in and stop you in order to give other members a chance to speak. Others of you, what reactions do you have?

Leader: Larry, I want you to hold off on your comments until others have shared.

Leader: Larry, I notice that you are always ready to speak first. I'm wondering if that has any significance, and I'm also wondering if you'd like some feedback from the group on how they feel about your always commenting. (This shifts the focus to Larry, and the leader would only want to do this if she thought Larry would benefit from feedback. Often, the leader can tell by the members' nonverbal reactions how they are feeling about the "talker.")

Drawing Out

If cutting off is the most essential skill a leader needs to know, then drawing out is probably the second most important skill. A skilled group leader understands when and how to draw out members. *Drawing out* is the term we use to refer to the skill of eliciting group members' comments. Throughout this section, we discuss various reasons for drawing members out and how to accomplish this effectively.

Reasons for Drawing Members Out

One of the main reasons for drawing out is to get greater involvement from the group members since one of the benefits of being in a group is to hear different ideas from the members. Another major reason for drawing out is to help members who have a difficult time sharing in a group. In most groups, there is usually a member who has trouble talking in front of others. If at all possible, a leader should try to draw out *all* the members during the early stage of the group—ideally, during the first session. Getting members to talk early in the life of the group can ease some of the anxiety about speaking in the group. The longer a shy or silent person waits to make his first contribution, the harder it will be. In addition, involving members during the beginning stage reduces tension in another way—if a member remains quiet for an extended period, the other members usually begin to wonder why. They sometimes imagine that the quiet member doesn't like the group or that he feels superior. By drawing out all members, the leader can often prevent members from making up what others are thinking and feeling.

Getting a member to go deeper is a form of drawing out that is very helpful to members in support, growth, counseling, and therapy groups. Some members will share but not really explore a problem in depth; that is, they stay on the surface. People usually gain more when they explore "uncharted waters."

Reasons for Members' Silence

Most leaders consider using drawing-out skills when members are silent. Understanding the reasons for silence is necessary because drawing out is not warranted for all types of silence. A leader often has to decide if drawing out is needed. The following is a list of reasons why members may be silent.

Fear	Not prepared
Thinking or processing	Confusion
Quiet by nature	Lack of trust or commitment to the group
Not mentally present	Intimidation by a dominant member or leader

Fear

Even when members desperately want to speak, they sometimes do not because they are afraid of what other members might think. They conjure up images of people laughing at them, turning away in disgust, or thinking "What a stupid fool." Drawing out these individuals is very important because they need to realize they are, in fact, imagining how the group will respond. Drawing out is difficult because the members may feel "picked on" unless the leader is careful.

◆ E X A M P L E

In this example, the leader of an ongoing therapy group knows why Frank is in the group (from the intake interview) and knows that he is afraid to speak.

Leader: Frank, you have not shared why you are here. My hunch is that you are afraid of what others are going to think of you. All I can say is that we are not here to judge you or anyone else; rather, we are here to help. Would all of you agree? *(Members nod)* Also, Frank, the way you are going to help yourself is by talking about it.

Frank: It's hard to face anyone. I don't know why I did it.

Leader: I know you don't, and I hope that by sharing here and in individual counseling, you will come to understand yourself better.

Frank: *(Looking at the floor)* Well, I'll try. I know that all of you will think this is horrible, but I exposed myself to these teenage girls last month.

Leader: *(After glancing at the members' faces and seeing that they are concerned for Frank)* Frank, if you will look up you will see that no one here is thinking you are the scum of the earth like you seem to think.

In this example, the leader felt confident about how the members would react because he had been meeting with the group for several weeks. However, the leader cannot absolutely guarantee how the members will react and should be prepared for a negative reaction. If this leader felt Frank could not handle negative feedback, he would have wanted to avoid drawing him out—or at least have been fully prepared to deal with the various comments.

Thinking or Processing

A second reason for silence is that members are thinking about or processing the group interaction. This occurs most frequently immediately after an exercise or some intense work on the part of a member. By scanning the room, the leader can usually pick up on the facial expressions of members who seem to be really thinking or experiencing something. This kind of silence is productive because the members need time to reflect and think. However, such silences can become prolonged, and sometimes a member who is ready to speak is a little hesitant to do so. Usually, the leader can sense when members are on the verge of speaking and can often elicit their comments through a simple head nod or hand gesture. The leader also has a number of possible drawing-out statements that could be used:

- ◆ Go ahead.
- ◆ It looks as though you are thinking. Would you like to share your thoughts?
- ◆ You seem to be reacting to something. Is there anything you would like to share?
- ◆ It seems that you were relating to our discussion on _____.

Quiet by Nature

A third reason for silence is that some members are naturally quiet people. They grew up listening more than speaking and are not in the habit of saying much even to family and friends. It is important for the leader to assess this and not attempt drawing out if it is going to make the member uncomfortable. However, it is important to realize that, if it is done with caution and forethought, drawing out may help this type of member say more in the group.

◆ E X A M P L E

In this example, the leader decides to try to draw out Lucinda, who has contributed very little during the first three sessions of an education group on improving communications.

Leader: I'd like to get a number of you to share your reactions to the model, and then we will practice some. Speaking up does seem to be difficult, and knowing these different categories can be helpful. *(In a gentle, caring voice)* Lucinda, I realize that you are a rather quiet person. Did the model give you any additional understanding of yourself?

Lucinda: It is true that I am rather quiet. I am the quietest in my family. It was interesting to hear about a model that allowed for people to be quiet. I do think I will say things when I think I have something to say. In this group I have been a little quieter than usual, but I really have not wanted to say more. I. . . .

Not Mentally Present

Some members are silent because they are not mentally present. Their thoughts are on things outside the group, such as their term paper, financial worries, or children. Allowing these members a couple of minutes to talk about what is on their minds can help them get focused on the group.

◆ E X A M P L E

The leader has noticed that Phil has been silent for the first 20 minutes of the group. She decides to draw him out.

Leader: Phil, you have been quiet. Is there something on your mind?

Phil: Well, yes, I guess I am not with it today. My father is at the doctor's right now because he has a spot on his lung, and they are supposed to tell him what it is.

Leader: Even though this is not really in line with our purpose, if you would like to take 5 minutes or so to talk about that, we could. Obviously, it is a major concern.

Phil: But this group is about career planning and job interviewing.

Leader: I realize that, but I think we can spare 5 minutes. Also, if we allow you some time, then you may be able to focus a little more on what we are talking about here.

Not Prepared

In certain groups, members may not be prepared, and thus they will be silent. In discussion, education, and task groups in particular, there are often out-of-group assignments to complete before the next session. A member who has not completed the assignment will probably not be as involved. Drawing out these members in an effort to combat their silence will be largely unsuccessful. What is needed instead is a way to motivate the members to do the assigned work.

Confusion

Members may also be silent because they are confused. Rather than speaking up or asking for clarification when they are unsure about what is going on in the group, some members will remain silent. It is good for the leader to be aware of this kind of silence because when members are confused, they often withdraw or get annoyed with the leader. If the leader thinks the members are being silent for this reason, the following might be an appropriate comment:

Leader: I have noticed that some of you have been quieter than usual. I was wondering—is it because you might be confused, since things have kind of jumped around?

Lack of Trust or Commitment to the Group

Members are often silent if they don't want to be in the group and have no commitment to what is happening. This lack of commitment is common in nonvolunteer groups—such as groups for drunk drivers, prisoners, or youth in group homes. Another reason for silence is that members don't trust the leader or some of the other members in the group. When there is little trust, members will tend to be relatively silent.

Intimidation by a Dominant Member or Leader

A final reason for members' silence is that the leader or one of the members tends to dominate, causing others to sit back and listen rather than contribute. Also, in situations where one person dominates, members may have found that when they have tried to speak, they were interrupted by the dominating person, and the leader did nothing.

There will be some instances in which a member is silent, and the leader has no idea why. In these situations, the leader may choose to ask the member directly, put himself in a dyad with the silent member and then ask, or wait until the end of the session to ask.

Direct Method of Drawing Out Members

The most direct method of drawing out members is to ask them if they would like to comment, or if they have any reactions to what is taking place.

◆ EXAMPLES

This group is composed of high school teachers who are discussing the current guidelines for handling behavior problems in the classroom. Ron, who is usually very verbal, has not spoken.

Leader: Ron, we've discussed many new procedures, and several ideas have been offered. Is there anything that you would like to offer at this time?

Ron: Well, yes, I have one idea that I think could work. It deals with. . . .

❖❖❖

This group is composed of officers of the junior and senior classes who are planning the spring prom. Donna, the junior class president, has been nodding in agreement with some of the decisions being made.

Leader: Donna, you seem to have been reacting positively to some of the decisions today. Would you like to comment?

Donna: I like the ideas! I do have one suggestion. I think we. . . .

This group is composed of members who have AIDS. One member has died recently; and John, his close friend, has been very quiet.

Leader: *(Very calmly and supportively)* John, you have been very quiet this session. I can only guess that it may have to do with Ted's death. Is there any way we can help?

John: Well, yeah, I really do think about Ted a lot—especially on group night. I. . . .

Drawing Out Delicately

Sometimes drawing out is a real art. The skilled leader is able to get a member to talk, share, or express herself without feeling forced or pressured. The challenge is to be able to invite members to share but at the same time give them a number of ways to decline. The idea is to give the member *permission* to speak— possibly even gently encouraging her to do so—without alienating her. Beginning leaders often make the mistake of putting people on the spot when they are trying to get them to speak. For example, such a leader might say, "Marvin, what do you think?" or "Cheryl, you have been quiet—why don't you share your ideas?" In certain situations, this type of probe would be totally acceptable, but if Marvin and Cheryl were not ready to speak, they would certainly feel uncomfortable.

The art of drawing out is evident when one is able to allow "outs" for the members while getting most of them to join in and share. One way to provide an out is to call on two or three members instead of just one. Then the leader may use her eyes to see if one of those members seems willing to speak. Focusing one's eyes for too long on a member can make him feel as though he were under a spotlight, so the leader will not want to gaze at just one member for any length of time. By looking at the member for a brief moment, the leader can let her eyes invite the member to speak. By shifting her eyes, the leader gives the member an out and relieves him of any pressure beyond that caused by having his name mentioned. (This slight pressure would be intentional since the leader would be trying to draw the member out.)

Two other components of drawing out are the leader's voice and attitude. At no time should the leader use a tone of voice that could be interpreted as condescending. The leader should never ridicule or embarrass a member for not being an active participant but rather should try to understand that member and then, if it seems appropriate, try to draw him out.

Two examples follow. The first one illustrates how *not* to draw out; the leader puts a member on the spot and does not give her an easy way out. The second example illustrates a more effective way to use the skill.

◆ EXAMPLES

This group is composed of high school seniors who are about to graduate. They have been discussing plans for after graduation. It is near the end of the session, and one of the members, Jackie, has not spoken.

Leader: *(In a demanding tone)* Jackie, why haven't you said anything? Would you like to tell us about your plans? *(The leader maintains eye contact with Jackie. All members of the group have their eyes on her.)*

This is the same group and situation as in the preceding example.

Leader: *(Tentatively)* Jackie, I've noticed that you have been silent this session. I am not sure if you would like to comment or not. Certainly we'd like to hear from you if you feel comfortable. *(Shifts his eyes to scan the group)* Who would like to comment on anything that they are thinking about? *(The leader watches to see whether Jackie seems to want to talk.)*

In the first example, the leader comes on too strong. Also, the leader puts Jackie on the spot by maintaining eye contact and directing the group's attention to her. If Jackie is quiet because of discomfort, the leader's behavior can only increase that discomfort. Another error lies in not giving Jackie a choice whether to participate.

The second example is quite different. The leader is tentative in his approach and does not focus the group on Jackie. In fact, the leader acknowledges that Jackie has not spoken, invites her to do so if she wishes, and then moves on. Because of this, Jackie feels no unnecessary pressure to speak. Assume that Jackie is unmarried, has recently found out she is pregnant, and is considering whether to share this in the group—the leader in the second example has a much better chance of drawing her out than the leader in the first example.

Use of Dyads for Drawing Out Members

Dyads can be used to draw out members. When members are paired and given directions to discuss something of interest, the inevitable result is that the two individuals will talk to each other. The energy generated is often sufficient to stimulate comments in the large group from members who might otherwise have been silent. When the dyad is completed, the leader may use any of the following to draw out members:

- Who would like to comment on what you discussed?
- What are your reactions to discussing _____?
- What did you learn by discussing _____ with your partner?
- Please comment on any thoughts or feelings you may be having.
- Joe, what did the two of you discuss?
- Chandra, what did you learn from doing the dyad?

These questions are usually nonthreatening because the members are warmed up as a result of the dyads. Also, the members will usually have something to say, since they were just discussing the issue.

Another way the dyad can be used to draw out a member is for the leader to pair himself with the member he wants to draw out. By talking with this member, the leader can often encourage him to share in the larger group, or at least the leader can find out why the member has been silent. It is appropriate for the leader to ask a member why he does not talk much. However, it is usually best to do so privately.

Use of Rounds for Drawing Out Members

Rounds are another very useful technique for getting silent members to say something because in a round, the leader is asking everyone to comment without singling out any one member. Most members are willing to share a word, phrase, number, or brief comment. (Rounds and dyads are discussed in great detail in the next chapter.)

Another way to draw out a member through a round is to end the round on the person to be drawn out. In this way, the leader can more easily ask the member questions because she is the last to comment in the round, and the focus must shift from the round since it is complete.

◆ E X A M P L E

This group is composed of women who are single parents. All group members have been actively involved in the discussion except Beth. Interest in the current topic is beginning to wane, so the leader decides to shift the focus to a new topic that may add energy and get Beth involved.

Leader: OK, if we're finished with this issue, I'd like to shift the focus. In a word or a phrase, what is the hardest thing about being a single parent? Think about that for a moment; then I'm going to get everyone to comment. (After about 15 seconds) Jamie, in a word or a short phrase, what is toughest for you? (*Jamie is seated next to Beth.*)

Jamie: It's finding time for myself.

Sally: *(Seated next to Jamie)* Being both parents!

Jane: Money—making ends meet.

Molly: Dating and not feeling guilty.

Beth: Not feeling appreciated by anyone.

Leader: What exactly do you mean by not being appreciated?

Beth: My teenage daughter doesn't appreciate any of my sacrifices or efforts. She blames me for the divorce.

Leader: I believe others here struggle with that. Could you elaborate on your feelings and your daughter's feelings?

Beth: Well, my daughter. . . .

In this example, the leader chooses to focus on Beth and purposely has the round end on her. He then draws her out by asking some questions.

Use of Written Exercises for Drawing Out Members

Another method of drawing out is to have members complete a writing task. Writing tasks can be making lists, answering some questions, or completing sentences. Drawing out in this manner is nonthreatening because the leader merely asks members what they wrote. With the answers in front of them, members usually do not mind being asked to share their responses. Also, when the leader calls on members, it does not seem like the spotlight is on them but simply that the leader wants them to share their written answers.

Use of Eyes to Draw Out

Another component of drawing out that we have alluded to in the earlier examples is the use of the leader's eyes. It is often possible to elicit comments from members by establishing eye contact with them and holding that contact for a few seconds. The leader's eyes are especially useful in drawing out members who are waiting to talk. By acknowledging people with his eyes and possibly a slight nod, the leader can often get them to comment. Or, if someone else is talking, the leader can cue others with his eyes and a slight nod indicating that they will be next to speak. One way to draw out a member while giving her an out is by maintaining a lot of eye contact with that member while speaking to the entire group.

◆ EXAMPLE

Leader: *(Looking mainly at Carol)* Is there anyone else who wants to comment on his or her relationship? *(Scans the group, then looks again to*

Carol. If Carol does not seem to be ready to respond, the leader shifts his eyes to other group members.)

If done skillfully, Carol would feel gentle pressure to speak, but the leader's broad request for comments allows Carol to refrain if she chooses. The leader has to believe in Carol's right not to speak. That is, if the leader is really trying to force Carol to talk, staring at her will cause her to feel singled out, and she will not hear the leader's words but rather the intent, which would sound to her like, "Carol, SPEAK!"

Additional Comments Regarding Drawing Out

It is important to assess how much a particular individual needs to talk. Sometimes leaders mistakenly believe that it is important for all members to speak up equally. Some members find it comfortable and beneficial to participate verbally at only a minimal level, yet they learn a great deal. The rule is *Don't draw out unless it seems needed.* Also, before drawing out a reluctant or scared member, it is important to think about the kind of response the member will get from other members. If the tone of the group is such that the leader feels a negative response is possible, drawing out has to be done carefully or not at all since the member may be too uncomfortable.

There are some members you may not want to draw out. Beginning leaders think they should always draw out uncommitted members, and this often is not the best option. When drawn out, uncommitted members will frequently resist the efforts of the leader and the other members and try to create a negative tone. Our suggestion is to be careful with uncommitted members. The same is true for members who do not seem focused at the beginning of the session. You may choose to run the group as planned—that is, choose *not* to draw out members who don't seem focused. Frequently, the interaction and comments of the other members will help get those members "aboard," which means that no drawing out is necessary.

Practice

As in the previous section on cutting off, you now have an opportunity to practice. Think of various drawing-out responses to the following three examples. You may want to write down your responses and then compare them to ours, which follow each example.

◆ E X A M P L E S

This group is composed of seven women who are patients in the mental-health unit of a community hospital. The group meets daily. All the members have been there for at least a week except for Ambuja, who has been in the hospital only 3 days. Ambuja has only commented when asked, and each time she has said very little. She is in the hospital because she attempted suicide. How would you try to draw her out if you were the leader? Take a minute to think of different ways to draw out and then check our suggestions that follow. Jot down a couple of different responses.

Leader: Ambuja, you have not said too much yet in the group. I think you would probably find it helpful to share some of your thoughts, feelings, and reactions to being here in the hospital. I think we can be of help to you if you will just open up to us.

In this method, the leader asks Ambuja directly if she wants to share. It is important to note that the leader keeps commenting after he initially urges Ambuja to talk. These additional comments let him observe Ambuja's reaction; if she seems resistant or afraid, the leader may move on by saying something like, "Well, Ambuja, what do you think about sharing? Right now, it seems like that would be too uncomfortable."

A second way to draw Ambuja out would be to use a round that ends on her. The leader could ask the members to comment in a word or phrase on how they are feeling now about whatever it was that brought them to the hospital.

Mary: I'm doing better. My family was here yesterday.

Dot: I understand why I am so depressed. Being here has really helped.

Ambuja: I am doing OK.

Leader: What do you mean when you say you are doing OK?

Ambuja: Things don't seem as bad as they did.

Leader: Maybe you can tell us a little about how it was.

Ambuja: I think I would like to. The reason I am here is because. . . .

Still another way the leader might get Ambuja to participate would be to focus on the topic of suicide, since Ambuja has attempted suicide.

Leader: A number of you have mentioned that you were depressed or lonely. I'd like to talk about how you have chosen to handle those feelings. I know for some of you suicide may have been considered or even attempted.

Mary: I have never thought of suicide, but I sometimes feel that life really stinks. I didn't know how to deal with my feelings, but things are getting better.

Leader: Ambuja, what about you? I know a little about your history, although I do not know many of the details.

Ambuja: Well, uh, I tried suicide because I have been so lonely since my husband left me. The feelings are. . . .

❖❖❖

This group is composed of six ministers who are on a weekend retreat to discuss the stresses and strains of being a minister. During a discussion about the effects that being a minister has on families, both Mike and Jake have been exceptionally quiet and look troubled. How would you, as the leader, try to draw these people out? Take a minute to think of at least two different ways to draw them out.

In this situation, the leader may guess that the ministers who are quiet are having problems at home. He will need to decide whether to draw both out at the same time or just one of them. To draw both out, the leader could say something like this:

Leader: Mike, I can't help but notice that both you and Jake have been quiet since we started the discussion about families. (*Looking at both of them*) Would either of you like to comment?

If the leader wanted to draw out only one of them, he could address that person directly:

Leader: Jake, you seem to be thinking about what we are saying. My guess is you are thinking about your family situation.

The leader would choose to draw out only one member if it appeared that one was in greater need or if the other did not seem ready to share. By focusing on the one member, the leader could later draw out the other when he seemed more open to sharing. The leader could also use an exercise that would get at the ministers' feelings about their families.

Leader: On a 1 to 10 scale, with 10 being very stressful and 1 being not stressful, how would each of you rate the stress that the ministry has caused your family?

This group is composed of five college women who are discussing values as part of Mental Health Week. The discussion is about premarital sex. Helen has been quiet the entire session. Carolyn has shared with the group that she is not a virgin and now has her head down as April talks about how she plans to save herself for her husband because it is God's way. Susan and Janice have shared some of their thoughts but have not commented personally on their feelings about premarital sex. They seem to be uncomfortable as they listen to April. How would you continue the discussion if you were the leader? Take a moment and think of a couple of ways to draw out the other members.

The leader probably would want to stop April from talking, since other members seem to be reacting to what she is saying. The leader would then need to decide whether to draw out Carolyn, who is obviously feeling bad. If the leader decides to do so, she could say something like this:

Leader: Carolyn, it is important for you to realize that what April is saying is her opinion. Other members feel differently. When she was talking, I could not help but notice your reaction. What were you thinking or feeling?

The leader could also choose to draw out Janice and Susan, since their opinions might differ from April's. Drawing them out first could make it easier to later draw out Helen and Carolyn. If the leader senses that Carolyn is feeling quite bad, she would probably shift the focus to Carolyn.

Since the leader could see that the other members differed with April, he could use a brief exercise to elicit comments from others. This would also serve as a way to cut off April.

Leader: I want each of you to complete this sentence: "For me, sex is _____."

This exercise would enable the leader to hear from Helen, Janice, Susan, and Carolyn, and would make it easier to draw out those members since the leader can simply ask them about their responses.

Concluding Comments

Cutting off and drawing out are absolutely essential skills for good group leading. Knowing how and when to draw out and cut off members improves the quality of the group because the leader is able to get more involvement from the members. Cutting off allows the leader to make sure that the content of the group fits with the purpose. Cutting-off skills are needed to hold, shift, and deepen the focus. It is important to understand when cutting off a member, the leader can choose to cut and stay with the member, cut and stay with the topic but not the member, or cut and leave the topic and the member. Many situations require that the leader use cutting-off skills, including when a member's comments are hurtful, off track, or inaccurate; when the focus needs to shift; when members are arguing or rescuing; or when the time is nearly out and the leader does not want to start on a new topic.

Members are silent for a number of reasons, including being afraid, not mentally present, not prepared, confused, bored, not committed, or intimidated. By understanding why members are silent, the leader can better choose how and when to draw out certain members. Rounds, dyads, and written responses are three excellent ways to draw out members.

CHAPTER NINE

Rounds and Dyads

Rounds

The round is an activity in which each member is asked to respond to some stimulus posed by the leader. *The value of rounds cannot be overemphasized—no skill, technique, or exercise mentioned in this book is more valuable than the use of rounds.* In all groups, rounds are extremely helpful in gathering information and involving members. Rounds also help in controlling overly verbal members.

There are three kinds of rounds: (1) the designated word/phrase or number round, (2) the word or phrase round, and (3) the comment round.

Designated Word or Phrase Round

These rounds can be completed quickly since the members respond with either a designated word or phrase. By designated word or phrase, we mean that the leader asks the members to use one, two, or three possible choices when responding to a question or issue, such as "yes" or "no," or "very helpful," "helpful," or "not helpful."

◆ EXAMPLES

Leader: I want you to think about the film you just saw and give your reaction using one of three descriptions: "very valuable," "valuable," or "not valuable." *(The leader gives members a moment to decide, then goes around the group, hearing from everyone.)*

The round helps keep one member from commenting for a long period of time before the others have had a chance to give some reaction. Also, by hearing the members' reaction, the leader can lead a better discussion

Leader: *(Near the beginning of the session)* Who has something they would like to talk about tonight? We'll do a simple yes-or-no round. If you have something you'd like to discuss, just say "yes"; if not, say "no." *(pause)* Frank, we'll start with you.

Frank: No.

Eric: No.

Fred: Yes.

Aba: Yes.

Tracy: Maybe, not sure. If we have time, check back.

Martin: Yes.

Hero: Yes.

Leader: Since there are a number of *yeses*, briefly, what is your *yes* about?

Fred: Mine is about fighting with Mom about playing football.

Aba: I want some help on how to handle it when I see my dad for the first time since he left 3 years ago. It is going to happen in 3 weeks.

Martin: I want to talk some more about getting along with my stepdad.

In this round, the leader quickly found out that there were a number of people wanting to work on some issue. The follow-up for the *yeses* was helpful to determine who was in need now and who could wait if need be. This kind of round is an especially useful one in support, counseling, and therapy groups since the leader has no way of knowing who has concerns they want to bring up. Also, members like knowing that they can state at the very beginning that they want some "air time."

Another designated phrase round is "here/getting here/not here." This round is usually done at the beginning of a session as a way of assessing if the members' attention is on the group or something else. This round serves two purposes: It helps the leader know who is mentally present, and it serves as a signal to the members to turn their attention to the group. The following example of a weight-loss group illustrates this round.

◆ E X A M P L E

Leader: Let's start with a round of "here/getting here/not here"—that is, are you focused on what we are trying to do and what you can contribute and learn from the group, or are your thoughts somewhere else? If you are focused on the group, say "here"; if you are somewhere else, say "not here." And don't be afraid to say "not here." If you feel you are getting here, you can say that.

Rudy: Here.

Julie: Here.

Alice: Getting here.

Merv: Not here.

Carol: Here.

Kelly: Here.

Mel: Not here.

Leader: Is there anything we can do to get you more here?

Merv: I'm getting here—I've got a job interview at 4:00 today, and I am nervous.

Mel: I'm tired. Also, I didn't eat lunch. I'll get here.

Leader: OK, then we'll begin. Merv, would you want to take 5 minutes to discuss your job interview before we get into the topics for today, which are what to do when you slip from your diet and how to handle holiday feasts?

In this situation, the leader chooses to invite Merv to talk about his interview, even though it is not related to the purpose of the group, in order to help him reduce his anxiety enough to refocus on the topic of the day.

Designated Number Round

The 1–10 round can serve many purposes. For example, it can encourage members to think more specifically about the topic. A 1–10 round usually generates interest because members are curious about how their rating compares to that of other members. The round can also serve as a quick way for the leader to gather information. Here are some examples.

- On a 1–10 scale, how comfortable are you being in the group?—10 is very comfortable.
- On a 1–10 scale, with 10 being "very much," how much did you like the article you read for this week?
- On a 1–10 scale, with 10 being "very valuable," how would you rate tonight's group?
- On a 1–10 scale, with 10 being a lot, how would you rate the amount of fighting, arguing, and tension in your early home environment?
- On a 1–10 scale, with 10 being great, how would you rate your current love relationship?

Word or Phrase Round

Another kind of round a leader can use is the word or phrase round. For this round, the members are asked to respond with only a word or a short phrase to keep comments brief. Here are some examples of word or phrase rounds:

- In a word or phrase, how are you feeling about being in this group?
- In a word or phrase, how would you describe your feelings about school?
- In a word or phrase, how would you describe our task as you see it?
- How often would you like to make love in a week—think of the number, and we'll do a round.
- I'd like to hear from everyone, so I want you to think of a word or phrase that describes you reaction to the proposal.
- How would you describe your current exercise habits? Answer in a word or phrase. You may say "none" or "daily" or "don't like to exercise" or whatever.

As you can see, there are an infinite number of word or phrase rounds that a leader can use; as you start to use rounds, you will learn how valuable they really are for quickly gathering information and focusing the members. By using a word or phrase round, the leader gets members to talk, which in turn makes it easier to draw people into discussion.

Comment Round

For this kind of round, the leader asks an open-ended question and gives the members the option to comment. The comment round is used when the leader wants members to say more than just a few words, either because the leader thinks they will benefit from hearing comments or because the question does not lend itself to a word or phrase answer. The following examples are taken from different types of groups and should give you some idea of this kind of round.

- Let's do a round of progress reports—how has the week been? What have you tried?
- I'd like to get a brief reaction from each of you regarding how you think we should approach the task.
- What stood out to you about the group today? We'll do a round and hear from everyone.
- When you think of remarriage, what feelings or thoughts do you have? Take a moment and think about this, and then we'll do a round.
- When you think of parenting, what is hardest for you?

The difference between this round and the other two kinds of rounds is that, in the other two, the leader controlled the content and length much more than in the comment round. In comment rounds, members may talk for 1 or 2 minutes. As each member comments, other members are able to gather their thoughts so they too can comment effectively. By using a round instead of just asking the question, everyone will get a chance to speak, instead of just one or two eager members.

Use of Rounds

In this section, we discuss eight different uses of rounds.

1. Build comfort, trust, and cohesion
2. Get members focused
3. Gather information and locate energy
4. Shift the focus to involve all members
5. Draw out quiet members
6. Deepen the intensity
7. Process exercises
8. Summarize

Use of Rounds to Build Comfort, Trust, and Cohesion

Rounds provide an easy way for members to talk and, thus, often help members feel more comfortable. Simple and specific information rounds during the first and second sessions, when members are still getting to know each other, can be useful in building comfort and trust. Members are curious about each other, and rounds can satisfy some of that curiosity. The skilled leader is always thinking of possible rounds that will ease members' discomfort and help them get to know more about each other. Also, information rounds help members feel linked to each other when they hear that their situations are similar.

Use of Rounds to Get Members Focused

The round gets members to focus on an issue or topic in two ways: first, members have to think of what they are going to say; and second, members listen to others comment on the subject at hand. Any of the three kinds of rounds can be used to focus the group.

◆ E X A M P L E S

This group is made up of first-year college students who are having difficulty adjusting to college. To get the group focused, the leader might say one of the following:

Leader: On a 1–10 scale, with 10 being very well, how well did the week go for you?

Leader: In a word or phrase, how would you describe your week?

Leader: Let's do a quick round. I want you to think of the best thing and worst thing that happened to you this week. I'd like to hear from everyone.

This group is a task group in a human-resources agency discussing a new program. The members are having difficulty focusing on one issue. The leader might say:

Leader: I want us to talk just about the staffing of the program. Think of how many staff members we'll need. In a minute, we'll go around, and I'll get each of you to state the number you think we need. Then we'll discuss your rationale and so forth.

Use of Rounds to Gather Information and Locate Energy

At various times, the leader will want to know how members are thinking and feeling about some issue, topic, or assignment. The round is an excellent way to do this in a quick, controlled manner. By asking members to rate something on a 1–10 scale or to express their feelings in a word or phrase, the leader can quickly assess who is most interested in working on or engaging in that particular discussion. It is much easier to lead when you have some idea of how the members view a topic or issue. The next two examples further illustrate the value of rounds with respect to focusing, gathering information, building interest, and locating the energy in members.

◆ **EXAMPLES**

This group consists of four students who are doing a placement at the mental-health center. The leader is conducting an education group, and the topic for the session is therapeutic drugs. The leader decides to start with a round because he has no idea how much the students know about medications.

Leader: I want to get some idea of what you know about therapeutic drugs. On a 1–10 scale, with 10 being quite a bit and 1 being very little, how would you rate your current knowledge?

Jan: Uh, about a 2.

Deepa: 1.

Eddie: 4.

Art: 8 or 9.

Leader: Art, why an 8 or 9?

Art: I did a 3-hour independent study course on medications and wrote a 25-page paper on the subject. I'm glad to be here, though—I want to learn more!

Leader: Good, and certainly feel free to comment. Let's do another round; then we'll get started. How do you feel about using drugs as a form of therapy? Respond with "believe in them," "don't believe in them," or "not sure."

Jan: Not sure.

Deepa: Believe in them.

Eddie: Don't believe in them. My brother has had all kinds of medications, and he is still not any better after 3 years.

Art: I started out as a nonbeliever, but after doing the paper and talking to different therapists, I see some value in medications in certain situations.

This group is a discussion and education group for parents. The members have been assigned a reading in a book that the leader plans to discuss.

Leader: Let's do a word or phrase round on your reaction to the chapters on mealtimes and fighting.

Sandy: I liked them very much.

Pat: Helpful but hard.

Melina: I don't know if I agree with the idea of letting kids settle their own fights. My kids differ in age by 4 years, and . . .

Leader: Can you hold that?

Melina: Oh, sure.

Leader: Bill, what about you?

Bill: Mealtimes still have been bad—I've got some questions.

Dania: I tried to get my husband to read it so he'd understand, but he wouldn't. *(She starts to tear up a little.)*

Leader: *(To the whole group)* Not getting cooperation from a partner can be very frustrating. Dania, let's talk after the group about your situation, OK? *(The leader purposely chooses not to go into Dania's pain.)*

Dania: Yeah, I do need to talk to someone.

Leader: *(Decides to do a second round to focus the group)* What is hardest for you at mealtimes? I'd like each of you to briefly comment on mealtime problems.

Pat: Getting them to eat what I fix!

Bill: Getting them to the table, to not fight at the table—you name it!

Leader: Sandy, what about you?

Sandy: Dealing with the baby while trying to give my 3-year-old some attention.

Leader: Looks like tonight should be interesting and helpful. We'll start with mealtimes. Your comments and questions are helpful to me in knowing where to start. Let's begin by . . .

Use of Rounds to Shift the Focus to Involve All Members

Rounds can be used to shift the focus from a person to a topic. If one person has been talking for a while, the leader may use a round to get other members involved. Members who have been drifting away during the session often will get reinvolved when asked to participate in a round.

◆ E X A M P L E

This group is a support and therapy group for teenage boys; it is the second meeting. Andre has been talking for a couple of minutes about how bad his home life is.

Andre: . . . and it really is unbelievable how strict it is.

Leader: Andre, I want to get everyone in on this. Each of you think for a minute of a word or phrase that describes your home life; then we'll do a round where all of you will comment. *(The leader waits a few seconds and scans the room to see when people seem ready)* OK, let's start here on my left, with Gary.

Gary: Well, you see they are divorced and, uh, it all started.

Leader: Gary, let's do this for now—tell with whom you live—like mom, brother, sister—and then add the word or phrase that best describes your home life. *(The leader changes the round a little, realizing that the group would benefit by hearing each person's living situation.)*

Gary: OK, my mom, my grandmother, and my two older sisters. As for a description—lousy—everyone is always bossing me around.

Leader: Tim?

Tim: My mom, my stepdad, my little sister, who is 2. My other brother lives with my dad on the farm. As for how it is at home—bad. My stepdad and I hate each other! Just last week . . .

Leader: Hang on, Tim. Let's get everyone to comment, then we'll come back to you and others.

Asid: I live with my mom and dad. They are real old, though—in their fifties. They just don't understand how things have changed.

Rick: I live with my grandparents—my mom can't handle me along with her three other kids. My real dad—well, I don't know where he is; I think he's in Georgia—he left when I was 2. As for things with my grandparents, well they are OK, I guess. Boring, but my grandparents let me do what I want. *(The leader lets Rick speak a little longer than the others because up to now he has not said very much in the group.)*

Joe: I live with my uncle—my dad was killed in a car accident, and my mom is in the, uh, well, the hospital. Nerves and stuff. It's bad—my uncle really doesn't want me there. *(Joe is the last person.)*

Leader: Let's talk about how your home life affects your behavior; that is, how the environment you live in may be contributing to some of your problems in school and on the streets.

After the above round, the leader has much more information and a much clearer idea of the kinds of home conditions members are experiencing. The leader knows that some members are missing parents, some are fighting at home, and that Joe may have some strong feelings about his mom being in a mental hospital. The round opens up options and aides the leader in deciding where to focus. Also, the members are now more involved in the topic.

In the preceding example, the leader, wanting to focus the entire group on the topic of home environment, spun off from what Andre was saying. There will be other instances when the leader will want to involve all the members because the member talking needs to be cut off.

◆ E X A M P L E

In this group, business executives are discussing how to bring more enjoyment to their lives. One member has been talking on and on about his summer vacation plans, and the leader interrupts him.

Leader: Jamil, let me jump in and pick up on what you were saying about summer plans not being fun oriented. Think about your summer; I want to get each of you to briefly say what your plans are and if they are fun oriented. I'll give you a few seconds, and then we'll do a round.

In this example, the leader used a round to stay with the topic and expand it to include the entire group.

Use of Rounds to Draw Out Quiet Members

In Chapter Eight, we discussed a number of ways rounds can be used to draw out members. By definition, a round gets everyone to respond, thus giving the leader greater opportunity to encourage or draw out any member. If a leader wishes to encourage a certain member to share more, she can end the round with that member. When the round ends, the leader can naturally focus on the last person who talked—the one the leader wants to draw out. (See Chapter Eight for more on drawing out quiet members.)

Use of Rounds to Deepen the Focus

In support, growth, counseling, and therapy groups, rounds can be used to get members to delve deeper into their thoughts and feelings. For instance, if the topic being discussed deals with personal worth and the members are sharing their beliefs about how they "get" their worth, the leader might suggest the following word or phrase round:

Leader: I want each of you to think for a minute—what do you believe affects your feelings of personal worth the most? Now really think about this—

think of a person or situation in your daily life that would describe this. It may be "Mom," "work," "my weight," or something else. What would it be? We'll go around and get each of you to comment.

Such a round encourages most members to think more deeply about the issues. They know they are going to share their comments out loud, and they want to find a term that reflects their feelings accurately.

In the next example, the leader uses a comment round to deepen the focus for members in a group for widows.

Leader: Now that we have shared how each of you came to be a widow, let's go a step further and talk about your feelings and fears. In a couple of sentences, how would you describe what you have been feeling since your husband's death?

Use of Rounds to Process Exercises

"Processing" an exercise means to get members to share their reactions or feelings. A good way to do this is by using a round. Sometimes a quick word or phrase round will provide a lot of information.

◆ E X A M P L E

This group has just completed an exercise on their fears about being in the group.

Leader: Now that you've done the exercise, how do you feel? In a word or phrase, how would you describe your feelings now?

Wayne: Better!

Akira: A little more comfortable, but still scared.

Sarah: Much better.

Tom: I still have my fears of being laughed at.

Tandy: It was helpful to hear that others were afraid. I still am hesitant to share a couple of things. I guess I want someone else to go first as far as sharing "heavy" stuff.

In this example, a quick round was used, but there will be times when the leader will want to use comment rounds to process an exercise. Keep in mind that, often after an exercise, members have thoughts they want to share with the group. The round allows people to make some comments, which may be all they need; that is, they may not have a lot to say, yet they do want to say something. The round also gives the leader a chance to hear what is on their minds and who may want to explore further some reaction or feeling.

Another benefit of processing an exercise with a round is that it keeps a dominating member from taking over since the leader is only calling for a word or a phrase. Very often beginning leaders let the first person who speaks continue for a long time without hearing from the others. Frequently, the first person to speak is not the one who really wants or needs to work on something.

Use of Rounds to Summarize

At times, the leader may want to use some kind of round as a way to summarize reactions to the session. A round gives the leader a chance to hear the important things that members experienced. The leader can then close the group, addressing the important comments heard during the round.

Additional Comments about Rounds

In this section, we discuss six additional aspects of rounds.

1. How to set up a round
2. Where to start a round
3. Stopping in the middle of a round
4. Handling members who refuse to talk
5. How to process a round
6. Overusing rounds

How to Set Up a Round

Rounds, like any other group activity, have to be set up properly. The leader has to think about when a round would be useful and then introduce it in such a way that the members understand what is being asked for. When introducing the round, the leader wants to be sure to specify the kind of round: a word or phrase round, a 1–10 scale only, a scale with comments to follow, or a comment round. The leader also needs to allow enough time for members to formulate their answers and not let an eager member start before the others are ready.

Where to Start a Round

The leader chooses where to start a round. Many times, where the round starts does not matter, but the leader will not want to always start with the same member; for instance, always with the member on his left. It is a good practice to vary the starting point so that different members get to speak first and last.

It is important to think about where you start and end your rounds. In some groups, there will be members who always tend to be negative. One way to keep those members from setting a negative tone is to not start with them. The leader would also not want to end the round on the negative person because the focus of the group could easily shift to that person's negative comments. By arranging the round so the negative members are neither the first nor the last to speak, the leader gains some control over the tone.

It is not a good idea to start the round with a member who is long-winded or confused about what you are trying to do. If a member tends to ramble, it is easier to cut her off if she is not the first or last person in the round. If a member is confused, hearing other members' responses usually helps clear up the confusion before it is that member's turn to speak. As we have mentioned earlier, the leader may want to end a round with a certain member in order to draw out that member.

Stopping in the Middle of a Round

Normally, it is best to finish any round, especially a serious round where members have had to give much thought to their answers. If the leader does not complete the round, the members could feel "stranded." However, the leader must be flexible; if she is conducting an information round that is not of a personal nature, stopping in the middle of the round can be fine. During an information round, a good topic may be raised, and the leader can spin off from it into a group exercise or mini-lecture that is more beneficial than completing the round. If the leader does stop a round in the middle, it is best for her to acknowledge that she is aware of doing so. She can then quickly scan the group to see if any member seems upset at stopping.

When doing a serious, personal round, there will be times when a member will begin to cry or in some other way indicate the need for immediate attention. The leader will then have to decide whether to continue the round or work with the member. The leader has several options:

- The leader can work with the member, acknowledging that she will try to get back to the round.
- The leader can explain to the member that she will come back to him but that she feels it is important to let everyone share first.
- The leader can ask the members how they feel about stopping the round so the group can help the troubled member.

You can see from these options that there is no one rule to follow. With experience, you will learn which option is appropriate.

Handling Members Who Refuse to Talk

When doing rounds, there will be times when a member refuses to comment or can't comment because of fear, confusion, or lack of anything to say. If the refusal is based on fear, skipping that member is usually the best policy. Some beginning leaders make the mistake of focusing on that member, which often makes the individual feel even more uncomfortable. If the refusal is based on a negative attitude, the best policy would again be to move on to the next person, making a mental note about the problem with that member. Although the purpose of rounds is to hear from everyone, the leader should rarely push someone into commenting. If a member is not ready to comment when her turn comes, simply tell her you will come back to her at the end. And be sure to do so! If the member still does not want to comment, simply move on to something else.

How to Process a Round

Most rounds need to be "processed." Processing involves discussing the responses in a focused, conscious manner. If a leader does a 1–10 or a word or phrase round, he has many options for following up:

- He can ask different members questions about their word or rating—why it was low or high, for example.
- He can pair up the members according to their answers or ratings and have them discuss the topic further.
- He can focus on one member specifically.
- He can use the different answers to introduce a topic.
- He can do a follow-up round for further information

◆ E X A M P L E S

The leader has just completed a round that asked, "Is there someone in your life right now with whom you are angry?" Everyone responded "Yes." The leader then does a follow-up round.

Leader: We'll do a second round—I want you to state who this person is; that is, mom, friend, boss, or whomever—then in a sentence or two, state what your anger is about.

Doing both of these rounds gives the leader a lot of information to work with and gets the members focused on the topic. The leader would then ask questions based on what was said, or focus on one member.

The leader has just done a round asking how each member sees her present love relationship. The round has just ended, and the leader processes the round by focusing on one member.

Leader: I want to go back to what Melba said. Melba, what exactly did you mean by "distant"? Do you mean you feel distant or he feels distant?

The leader has just completed a word or phrase round on the members' reactions to three chapters in a book and decides to focus on a topic.

Leader: It seems like many of you got something out of the three chapters. Let's start with the first chapter—some of you said this was the best reading for you so far. Nelly, you mentioned that the chapter made you think about how change *is* possible. Let's talk about change. What do you think about changing?

The leader has just completed a round on adjusting to the group home. Members have had a variety of comments and reactions to being at the home. The leader decides that there is a lot of energy for the topic and that members are still trying to get comfortable with being in the group. Based on this information, the leader follows up the round.

Leader: All of you have heard the different reactions to being here at the home. Now, I'd like you to pair up with someone you feel you don't know very well and continue talking about how you feel.

It is important to understand that the leader used the round to get members focused, and then used the answers to develop the next part of the session.

Overusing Rounds

Even though rounds are very valuable, beware of overusing them. Some beginning leaders conduct one round right after the other. This misuse of rounds can cause members to become bored, confused, or resentful of what they may view as a gimmick. Also, the overuse of rounds can prevent the group from going deeper. Leaders should use rounds to get members focused and thinking, not just to fill time. Remember, rounds can help you get the group focused on its purpose—however, they should not *be* the purpose!

Dyads

A dyad is an activity in which members are paired to discuss issues or to complete a task. Dyads are immensely valuable because they can be used for many different reasons. Group leaders need to know when to use dyads, how to pair up the members, and the length of time dyads should last.

Uses of Dyads

In this section, we discuss eight uses of dyads.

1. Developing comfort
2. Warming up members and building energy
3. Processing information and group exercises
4. Finishing a topic
5. Getting certain members together
6. Providing leader/member interaction
7. Changing the format
8. Providing time for the leader to think

Developing Comfort

In any group, there will be occasions when the leader will want to focus on building the comfort level among the members. A dyad can be a helpful exercise because people are often more comfortable talking to one other person than to an entire group. Two occasions when it is particularly important to use dyads to build comfort are during the beginning stage of the group, and when members are exploring a new topic or issue that is personal.

In the first or second session of a group, members are often uncomfortable at the prospect of talking in front of other people. Placing members in dyads gives them a chance to talk to just one person. Also, dyads provide better contact between members—they experience each other as individuals rather than as faces in the group. For these reasons, a leader should consider using dyads during the first session. Following are examples that could occur almost any time during the first session.

◆ E X A M P L E S

Leader: So that you can get a little more comfortable with some of the other members, I would like each of you to pair up with someone whom you don't know very well and share why you decided to be in this group.

Leader: We are going to do something a little different now. I am going to ask you to get into pairs and talk for a few minutes. This way you'll get to know one other member a little better, and you'll get a chance to share your ideas. I'd like you to share your ideas about _____. Then we'll come back to the group and share your various thoughts.

Leader: I would like you to get into pairs and discuss how you are feeling about being here. Discuss your excitement and fears.

Warming Up Members and Building Energy

Warming up and energizing are often needed when a group begins or when a new topic is introduced. One option is to begin a session by having the members form dyads: The leader asks the members to pair up and talk about such things as their week, the assignment, their hopes for the session, or their progress on a project.

◆ E X A M P L E S

This career-awareness group for 11th-graders is beginning its third session.

Leader: Let's get started. *(Pauses until members become quiet)* To get warmed up, I am going to pair you up and have you discuss some of the things you may have thought about as a result of our last meeting. As you recall, we spent a lot of time talking about the pros and cons of college and technical school. What have you thought about? We'll take just a couple of minutes to do this. Joe, you and Hector pair up. . . .

In this example, dyads are used to warm up a group of parents regarding their feelings about having a child with disabilities.

Leader: During the next few minutes, you are going to get a chance to share your feelings about your child. To start with, I'm going to ask you to pair up with a person next to you and share for about 3 minutes two or three of the hardest things you have dealt with as a parent of a child with disabilities; then we'll come back to the large group and continue that sharing.

Dyads can also be used to develop comfort when the topic is very sensitive or personal. Topics such as sex, marital problems, or fears often can be shared more easily in a dyad than in a large group. When members have a chance to share in pairs, they often begin to feel more comfortable and are more willing to share when the large group reconvenes. By starting the topic with a dyad, the leader can get members focused and ready to share their thoughts and feelings.

◆ E X A M P L E

Leader: We've agreed that sex is an important issue to discuss. Let's begin by pairing up and talking about some of the things you'd like to explore. Talk about any topics you think would be good to bring up and any concerns you have about discussing sex.

Processing Information and Group Exercises

Members can also benefit from talking in dyads when they have just learned some new material or have just completed a group exercise. The advantage of using the dyad is that it provides each member with the opportunity to give reactions, share ideas, or raise questions. If the leader processed the exercise or information in the large group, more time would be needed, and considerable time would elapse before the last few members could speak. The dyad allows for everyone to share immediately.

◆ E X A M P L E

The leader of this assertiveness-training group has just presented information about the differences between being assertive, nonassertive, and aggressive.

Leader: To give you a chance to process what I have been saying, I want you to pair up with someone you have never been paired with before and discuss what we have just been talking about. Try to relate the information to yourself; that is, how you are assertive, nonassertive, or aggressive. We'll do this for about 5 minutes.

Finishing a Topic

Dyads can be helpful in ending a discussion about a topic. If the group has been discussing an issue or topic for a long time, the leader may feel that it has triggered some thoughts in most of the members, and may choose to close off the discussion by using dyads. This gives all members a chance to share their final thoughts but not necessarily with the entire group.

◆ E X A M P L E

This group had been discussing ways of improving their relationships with their parents; the leader feels that things are winding down and that the group needs to stop.

Leader: I think this discussion has given each of you food for thought. Before taking a break, I'd like you to get into pairs and talk about what the last 30 minutes have stirred up in you and what, if anything, you are going to do differently. Be sure to focus on your relationship with your parents. We'll go for about 5 minutes and then close for today.

Getting Certain Members Together

In some group situations, the leader may want to get certain members talking to each other. This may be because they have something in common—such as both being single parents or recently having had a parent die—or because they don't feel comfortable with each other, and the leader thinks that if they get a few minutes together, some of the discomfort might dissipate. Another reason for wanting certain members to pair up could be because they have differing views on an issue. The point here is that, as the leader gets to know the members and as issues come up in the group, he may see the usefulness of dividing the group into pairs to give certain members a chance to interact with one another.

Providing Leader/Member Interaction

Whenever a leader wants to spend more time with a particular member—helping him finish something, encouraging him, or helping him get clearer on something—she can use dyads. That is, she can put all the members into dyads and pair herself with that member. The leader can also use the leader/member dyad to get to know individual members better.

Changing the Format

Dyads also can be used to provide a refreshing change from sitting in the group, and are useful whenever the leader senses that members are restless and in need of a change. Members often value the opportunity to talk to just one member.

Providing Time for the Leader to Think

Because groups are so unpredictable, there may be times when the leader needs some time just to think. This may be necessary if the leader finds that the energy for a topic has waned sooner than expected or if the interests of the group have moved in an unexpected direction. Another such time may be when a group activity has not worked well and a new focus is needed. By placing members into dyads, the leader obtains a "time-out" period without the group actually taking a break. The leader gives the members something to talk about in their dyads while he is busy thinking about what to do next.

Pairing Members for Dyads

In the examples given so far, we have, for the most part, implied that members choose each other without any specific instructions from the leader. Often this system works fine. However, on many occasions, the leader will choose to facilitate the pairing, either to make the process go more smoothly or because the leader has a particular goal in mind. In this section, we discuss techniques for pairing members and the rationale for using each technique.

Members' Choice

One approach to pairing is allowing members to choose whomever they wish to be with in a dyad. As demonstrated in many examples in this chapter, the leader can merely say, "Pair up with someone" or "Choose a partner." The members then make a choice. Friends may choose each other, or a member may identify with another member based on something that was said in the group. If there is an age spread in the group, older members may pair with each other, as might members of a similar racial background or members who are married or divorced or who have children. Usually members will pair in the most comfortable way possible. For this reason, allowing members to make their own independent choices usually is a less threatening experience. A word of caution here: While this method usually goes smoothly, the leader should be on the lookout for any negative reactions. There may be some who feel uncomfortable with this method, such as those who find it reminiscent of feeling left out when not chosen for a team. In groups where there is great diversity, letting the members choose may work well or it may be a disaster, depending on the members and their backgrounds. The leader also needs to pay attention to make sure everyone is in a dyad.

A disadvantage of allowing members to choose on their own is that they will often continue to choose the same people and therefore will not get acquainted with other members of the group. Since the purpose of the dyad may be for members to have contact with those they don't know, the leader might say any of the following:

Leader: Pair up with someone you would like to know better.

Leader: Pair up with someone who seems to be different from you.

Leader: Pair up with someone with whom you don't feel comfortable.

A variation on having members choose at random is for the leader to choose a member who in turn picks a partner.

◆ EXAMPLE

Leader: Tim, pick a partner to be with.

Tim: James.

Leader: OK, Carol, you pick someone.

Carol: Ralph.

Of course, this method may bring up members' fear of not being chosen, as mentioned earlier.

Leader's Choice

By seating Of all the ways the leader can assign dyad partners, the easiest is by seating arrangement. The leader says, while pointing at two members sitting next to each other and then moving to the next pair, "The two of you pair up; the two of you, and the two of you." Even in this situation, the leader may want to exercise some control over who pairs up with whom. This can be done by starting the pairs at any point in the circle. Suppose a group of six are sitting in a circle in this order: Joe, Bill, Bob, Sam, Roy, and Ed. If the leader starts the pairing with Joe and Bill, the other two pairs would be Bob with Sam and Roy with Ed.

But if the leader wanted to split up Bob and Sam, he could start pairing with Bill and Bob, thus leaving Sam with Roy and Ed with Joe.

One common mistake that beginning leaders make is to say to the group, "Turn to the person on your left and talk about . . ." This seems as if it would work; however, if everyone tried to talk to the person on her left, no one would, in fact, talk to anyone!

By leader's discretion   Sometimes, the leader will think that a particular member would benefit by being in a dyad with some other member. In this case, the leader can assign the dyads by saying, "We are going to spend the next few minutes processing what has happened here. Tom, you and Carl pair up; Jana, you and Phil; Isao, you and Sharon. Take about 5 minutes to talk about what you have experienced during this last half-hour."

The leader may pair people on the basis of similarities or differences. For example, the leader may decide to pair those who feel religion is very important if their lives with either those who feel similarly or those who feel differently. The pairing would depend on the leader's purpose. In addition, the leader may want to avoid pairing certain people, such as those who do not like each other or those who have a strong relationship outside the group.

Another point to keep in mind is that the leader can choose whether or not to be in a dyad. At times, the leader will want to talk with one member in particular; when setting up the dyads, the leader pairs up with that person. If there are two members the leader wants to be with, the two of them can be put together and the leader can join them.

Additional Thoughts about Dyads

How Much Time to Allow

Dyads can last anywhere from 2 to 10 minutes, depending on their purpose. If the time is too short, members may get frustrated; but if it is too long, they may get bored and wander from the topic. For instance, in a group to help clients at a rehabilitation center learn how to get a job, dyads to discuss techniques for greeting a receptionist may need only a couple of minutes. By contrast, dyads to discuss feelings about applying for a job could take 5 to 7 minutes.

When leaders are using dyads to build energy, they will want to end the dyads before the discussion has peaked so that the members bring some energy back to the group. However, if the members are working on a task, the leader will want to give them ample time to finish. Keep in mind that some pairs may move at a very slow pace, and the leader would not often want to wait until the very last pair finished since the others' focus and/or energy would be lost.

Leaders should always tell the members in advance the approximate amount of time that the dyad will last. Sometimes, once the members have been talking for a while, the leader will see that either more or less time is needed. In that case, the leader can ask the members how much more time they need. It is also helpful to give members some warning before bringing the dyad to a close. For example, the leader might loudly say one of the following:

Leader: We'll go for another 2 minutes.

Leader: Please wind down in the next 30 seconds or so and then come back to the large group.

Time warnings are very helpful when there are a number of subjects the leader wants the members to cover in dyads, such as the answers to five questions or feelings about school, work, and friends. Often people will get stuck on one topic or one person; the time warnings help keep them moving. Also, time warning and the proper allotment of time bring dyads to a smooth end. Abrupt endings can cause members to become frustrated and angry with the leader.

Giving Clear, Simple Instructions

Make sure the instructions are easy to understand and that everyone does understand them. Usually, directions are given before the members pair up. However, if the instructions are somewhat complex, it is often better to have members get into pairs first and then tell them what to do. If the leader gives lengthy or confusing instructions for the dyad, members may misunderstand and fail to do what is asked.

Making Sure Members Stay on Task

Often, members may be slow getting to the task or may stray from the intended purpose of the dyad. The leader may want to remind members of the purpose about 30 seconds or a minute after the dyad has started. Another way to ensure that the dyads are on target is to listen in on each of them for half a minute or so to hear if they are in fact doing what was asked. If not, the leader can urge the members back to the topic. (Another advantage to listening in for brief moments is that the leader gets some ideas for discussion in the large group.)

The Leader's Role during Dyads

The leader has many options when members are in dyads. It is up to the leader to decide whether or not to participate. In any case, the leader should first make sure that everyone understands the dyad's purpose. If the leader decides not to be involved in the dyads, the time can be used to plan the remainder of the group. A leader who is participating may pair up with a member, "float" from dyad to dyad, or join one dyad for the entire time. It is important to remember that while participating in a dyad, the leader still needs to be aware of the time, give time warnings, and end the dyad at an appropriate point.

Some reasons why the leader may want to participate include getting to know the members better, allowing the members to get to know her better, having a chance to work with one or two members, or making up an even number if the group has an odd number of members. If the leader does not want to be in a dyad even though the group has an odd number of members, she can simply make one of the dyads a triad instead.

The Physical Arrangement for Dyads

Usually the dyads take place in the area where the group is meeting. However, at times, the leader may want them to meet in other parts of the room or even in other parts of the building. This would be appropriate when the dyads are going to last for a relatively long time (8 to 10 minutes) or when the leader feels that the members can benefit from being in a more private, less noisy situation.

Using Triads Instead of Dyads

Although this section is about the use of dyads, there are times when grouping members in threes instead of twos can be valuable. With three people, more ideas or points of view are presented. For this reason, triads are often used in educational, discussion, and task groups. Another advantage is that even if one person is not involved, the other two people can interact. A disadvantage is that quiet members may be able to "hide" more easily while the other two members carry the conversation. Also, more time is usually needed for a triad than for a dyad since people need more time to take turns expressing themselves.

Concluding Comments

Learning to use rounds and dyads effectively is important for any group leader since they can be used in so many different ways and situations. There are three kinds of rounds: a designated word, number, or phrase round; a word or phrase round; and a comment round. Rounds are useful because they allow the leader to gather information quickly and they help with drawing out and cutting off members. Rounds also can be used for deepening the focus, shifting the focus, and processing an exercise or discussion. A leader should give thought to where to start and end a round, and how to handle a hesitant member. A mistake of beginning leaders is to overuse rounds.

Dyads are important for developing comfort, warming up members, processing exercises, and providing time for the leader to think. The leader has many choices as to when and how to use dyads. Members can be paired up by seating arrangement, by their own choice of partners, or by the leader's choice of partners. It is important to pay attention to the selection process.

CHAPTER TEN

Exercises

The term *exercise* is used among group leaders to refer to an activity that the group does for a specific purpose. An exercise can be as simple as having members get into dyads to discuss a topic or as involved as the "Blind Trust Walk," in which one member leads around a blindfolded member. Other examples of exercises include reading and discussing a poem, completing sentence stems, and drawing pictures of situations or feelings. In other words, *when the leader directs the behaviors, discussion, or attention of the group members by using a specific activity, it is an exercise.* In this chapter, we discuss the reasons for using exercises and the kinds of exercises available for use in groups. In Chapter 11, we discuss introducing, conducting, and processing exercises of all types.

According to Yalom (1995), structured exercises were first described for group work in the T-groups of the 1950s. Since then, the use of exercises in groups has been described in great detail by a number of authors. In fact, a number of books that contain nothing but group exercises have been written (Lewis & Streitfeld, 1972; Morganett, 1990; Pfeiffer & Jones, 1972–1980; Simon, Howe, & Kirschenbaum, 1978; Stevens, 1972). Most experts now agree that group exercises can play an important role in making a group meaningful and interesting (Corey, 1995; Gladding, 1995; Yalom, 1995). Exercises that are well thought out and used properly can be of great benefit in almost all groups.

The exercises described in this and the following chapter come from a variety of sources. Some appeared initially in the excellent resource volumes of Pfeiffer and Jones (1972–1980). Others originated in the work of Stevens (1972) and Simon, Howe, and Kirschenbaum (1978). Many of these exercises have been modified over time and passed along through workshops or by word of mouth. *It is important for the beginning leader to adapt exercises both to the needs of the group and to the age level, cultural background, and sophistication of the members.*

Why Use Exercises?

There are at least seven reasons for using exercises in a group.

1. To increase the comfort level
2. To provide the leader with useful information
3. To generate discussion and focus the group
4. To shift the focus
5. To deepen the focus
6. To provide an opportunity for experiential learning
7. To provide fun and relaxation

Exercises Help Increase the Comfort Level

Exercises may be used to increase the comfort level of the members. Many members experience some degree of anxiety during the first couple of group sessions; getting-acquainted exercises often increase comfort among members. The use of dyads can be helpful in increasing comfort during the early sessions, as well as when a very personal topic is about to be discussed. Written exercises help with comfort because members usually do not mind sharing what they have written.

Exercises Provide the Leader with Useful Information

Exercises may be used to get information from the members. Rounds are often used in this way. For instance, the leader might ask members to use a single word to describe their home environment when they were growing up. In describing their home environment, members might use such words as "playful," "warm," "hostile," "cold," "competitive," "abusive," or "healthy." By hearing how each member describes his or her early environment, the leader obtains information that can help him to focus the group. Another way to gather information about the home environment is to have members draw a family scene. An exercise in which members talk about what kind of animal they would like to be can be very informative for the leader. Throughout this chapter, we discuss many more exercises that are very useful in gaining information about the members.

Exercises Help Generate Discussion and Focus the Group

Using group exercises often increases member participation by providing a common experience. Also, exercises serve as a way to stimulate members' interest and energy. Some exercises can be helpful when dealing with members from different cultures because exercises can make concepts more visual and concrete. An exercise can be used to get members focused on a common issue or topic. For example, if the leader wanted to focus the group on the benefits of good study skills, she could say:

Leader: On a piece of paper, I'd like each of you to list three benefits of planning your study time.

Or if the leader wanted to focus the group on the topic of anger, he could use different lengths of cord to represent one's "anger fuse" and could say:

Leader: I want you to think about your anger and the length of your fuse. *(Points to all different lengths of cord from 1 inch to 12 inches)* Pick the length of fuse that best represents you—a short, medium, or long fuse.

Exercises Can Shift the Focus

A leader may want to use an exercise to shift the focus when she feels a new topic is needed. For example, if the leader wanted to shift from discussing anger at parents to feelings about themselves, she could say:

Leader: It seems like each of you has a wide variety of feelings of anger toward your parents. Hopefully, our discussion here has given you some new ways to look at your relationship with them. Now, I would like us to shift to a different topic—how you feel about yourself. I want you to think of three things that you like about yourself and three things you don't like about yourself.

Exercises Can Deepen the Focus

Exercises can be quite powerful and cause members to gain insights into themselves. Certain exercises can help members to get more in touch with who they are and how they interact. Many feedback, trust, creative, fantasy, and movement exercises are designed to deepen the focus because members are asked to share or experience something at a more intense level. We discuss these kinds of exercises later in this chapter and give many examples of how an exercise can be used to deepen the focus.

Exercises Provide an Opportunity for Experiential Learning

Another reason for using exercises is to provide an alternative approach to exploring issues other than through discussion. Sometimes, it helps to get members to act out themes rather than just talk about them. For instance, let's say the discussion centers on not being accepted by peers. To focus on this theme through nonverbal sharing, the leader could have all members except one stand and gather in a circle with arms interlocked. The member outside the circle would then be instructed to try to break into the circle by whatever means possible while the members tried to prevent the person from entering. This exercise usually gets at feelings of loneliness and members' methods of attempting to gain others' acceptance.

Another experiential exercise is have members pair up and experience the "pulls" on them as they try to reach their goals.

◆ E X A M P L E

Leader: This is an exercise about trying to reach your goals and feeling what keeps you from getting there. I want each of you to think about your goals for the next 2–5 years. *(Pause)* Now, I want you to pair up and then number off either 1 or 2. *(Members get into pairs and determine who is 1 and who is 2.)* Number 1, you will go first—face away from your partner and extend your right arm back. Number 2, you take your partner's arm by the wrist with both your hands. On the count of three, Number 1, while thinking about your goals, you try to make progress and Number 2, you offer some resistance. The resistance may help you to get in touch with what is holding you back. Be sure to do this without laughter since some of you will really get some insights. Ready. . . .

Exercises Provide Fun and Relaxation

Certain exercises can loosen up the group through laughter or relaxation. Using these kinds of exercises may be quite helpful when the group seems to need a change of pace, and it is the kind of group where it would be appropriate. One fun exercise is called "Pass the Mask," in which one member makes a face at the next member and that member tries to make the same face back. Then, the second member turns to the next member and makes a new face. The third member copies the mask and then creates a new one for the fourth member. This takes place rapidly and usually results in fun and laughter.

There are a number of relaxation exercises. A popular one calls for the leader to take a few minutes to go through a series of relaxation steps. The leader asks members to close their eyes and, starting with their heads, try to relax their muscles. They proceed to the neck, shoulders, and so on, until the entire body is relaxed. Another relaxation exercise is a group massage. In this exercise, one person lies on the floor and is massaged gently by all the other members. In our later discussion on touching exercises, we discuss the value of this exercise and offer caution about using such an exercise.

One common mistake of school counselors is that they spend too much time making the group fun and relaxing and not enough time making the experience meaningful. As one elementary school counselor said, "I realize I have too much fluff in my groups."

When to Use Exercises

An opening name and information round is often helpful when beginning a new group. Exercises may also be used when opening any of the subsequent group sessions. During the first several minutes of a group session, members often are not focused on the task at hand. They may be nervous and unsure of what will take place, or they may be thinking about something that happened just before coming to the group or something that concerns them at work or at home. Using an exercise to structure the first several minutes often helps members get focused on being in the group.

As the leader develops a plan for a particular group session, it will be helpful if he considers what exercises might be useful. For example, if he plans to focus on members' relationships with their parents, he could consider using a checklist of parent-child relationships, a sentence completion exercise, a 1–10 round, or word or phrase round to begin the discussion. Then he would want to consider other exercises, such as having members role play communication problems with parents, or exercises that involve TA since it is an excellent theory for under-standing interpersonal relationships. *It is important to remember that exercises are usually not in and of themselves helpful; rather, it is the time spent personalizing and processing the exercise that is the helpful component.* Many beginning leaders mis-takenly conduct one exercise after another and do not spend enough time discussing the material that comes up as a result of the exercise. We discuss processing of exercises in great detail in the next chapter.

Kinds of Exercises

There are many kinds of exercises. Certain kinds will be more useful and relevant than others, depending on the kind of group you are leading, the issues to be dealt with, and the age, cultural background, and needs of the members. In some instances, these exercises are interchangeable in terms of their purpose and utility, but sometimes one kind of exercise is better than another. We will discuss the following kinds in some detail:

Written	Common reading
Movement	Feedback
Dyads and triads	Trust
Rounds	Experiential
Creative props	Moral dilemma
Arts and crafts	Group decision
Fantasy	Touching

Written Exercises

Written exercises are one of the most versatile and useful of all the exercise types. Written exercises are structured activities in which members write lists, answer questions, fill in sentence-completion items, write down their reactions, or mark checklists relating to an issue or topic. The major advantages of written exercises are that members become focused while completing the writing task, and that members have their ideas or responses in front of them when they are finished. Writing out responses eliminates the pressure of having to create responses on the spot. Drawing out members tends to be easier when they have answers or reactions readily available.

Sentence-Completion Exercises

One of the most useful types of written exercise is the sentence completion. A sentence completion is a written statement with a portion left blank for the member to fill in. Sentence completions generate interest and energy among members because members are usually curious about how other members have responded to the same sentence stems. Sentence completions can be devised for any topic or issue. For example, if the topic of discussion is divorce, the following sentence-completion exercise could be developed to help generate discussion:

Being divorced means _____.

The hardest thing about being divorced is _____.

When I think of future relationships, I _____.

The thing I would most like help with from the group is _____.

There are only four sentence stems here, but a leader can develop as many as she likes. The length and kind of sentence completion should depend on the kind of group, the purpose of the group, and the depth of answers desired. Usually a leader will not want more than 5 or 6 sentence stems, although there may be times when as many as 10 or 15 are used. Also, the leader may use only one sentence stem to generate discussion for an entire session.

The following are three additional examples of helpful sentence-completion questionnaires. The first example is an excellent one to use in the beginning of many kinds of counseling, therapy, growth, and support groups. It could be used right after an introduction exercise or later on in the first session. The questions give members a chance to share many thoughts and feelings about being in the group and about themselves. Also, the questions are worded so the leader can use the responses to comment on how the group will be conducted and what will happen in the group.

When I enter a new group, I feel _____.

When people first meet me, they_____.

When I am in a new group, I feel most comfortable when _____.

When people remain silent, I feel _____.

I feel annoyed when the leader _____.

In a group, I am most afraid of _____.

Those who really know me think I am _____.

I trust those who _____.

I feel closest to others when _____.

This next sentence-completion form is intended to generate discussion about how individuals view themselves.

My greatest asset is _____.

I need to improve _____.

I regret _____.

My best accomplishment is _____.

Compared to others, I think I am _____.

I want most out of life to _____.

My biggest fear is _____.

I am _____.

This sentence-completion would be used to focus discussion on members' thoughts and feelings about sex.

I think sex is _____.

Many of my feelings about sex come from _____.

Discussing sex in this group is _____.

I would like to have sex _____ times a week.

The sexual topic I would most like us to discuss would be _____.

Devising sentence completions that are consistent is very important. If you are devising your own sentence-completion forms, be sure that the sentences focus the members in the areas that you desire. For instance, in the third example, the leader wants to focus on issues pertaining to sexual activity. An inappropriate sentence stem would be "I enjoy being the sex I am because _____." It would be inappropriate because it would generate discussion about gender and sex roles rather than sex and sexual behavior.

Listing Exercises

Having members make a list is another very useful written exercise. Lists can be done quickly and can easily be geared to the level and needs of the group members. Some examples of lists include: characteristics of friendship, hobbies and other recreational activities, important people, positive personal qualities, traits desired in a love partner, or characteristics inherent in the ideal job. Making a list is useful to members because it allows them to summarize their thoughts in a succinct fashion; it also helps them to focus. Once the list is complete, it can be used in a variety of ways. The leader can ask members to share a portion or the entire list, or have members share lists in dyads or triads. For example, in an education/growth group about stress, the leader may ask members to list things that are stressful to them. Once the members have done so, the leader could ask them to get into triads and discuss their lists, starting first with work stressors, then home stressors, then other stressors.

Written-Response Exercises

The third type of written exercise we call the "response" exercise since the leader asks members to respond in various ways to problems or questions posed by the leader. For example:

- Members write their own epitaph or obituary.
- Members write short responses to questions such as "What is the role of a school counselor?" or "How does having children change one's life?"
- Members complete multiple-choice, preferences, or one-word answers to different questions.
- Members write reaction papers after viewing movies or TV shows, or reading books or poems. For example, the leader, knowing that a certain movie will be on TV, might ask the members to watch it and afterward write a personal reaction reflecting what the movie meant to them. The members would bring their reactions to the group.

In each case, members would have their reactions or answers in front of them when the leader asks them to share their responses.

Diaries

A fourth type of written exercise uses diaries either during the session or at home. Within the session, members write personal reactions to what has taken place in the particular session. Often, this is done at the end of the session; the leader allots the last 5 or 10 minutes for members to write.

◆ E X A M P L E

Leader: We're now finished except for writing in your diary. As I explained last week, this is time for you to write any thoughts, feelings, or reactions

EXERCISES **205**

that you have had during the session. Take as much time as you'd like to write. Also, remember that your diary will be a good summary of the group and something you may want to read years later.

The diaries are usually left for the leader to read; this gives her both immediate feedback about the session and the opportunity to write comments in the diaries. The leader gets an idea of what the members are gaining from the group and what might need to be addressed in future sessions. We have found that some members will write things that they would not say in the group. Also, by leaving the diaries, the leader has a chance to write back to the members. (The members usually read the leader's comments at the beginning of the next session.) Written comments can be encouraging statements, clarifying comments, or suggestions regarding how the member may use the group experience. Riordan and White (1996) found that 9 out of 10 members report feeling favorable toward the practice of writing in a diary.

Even though leaving the diaries for the leader is helpful, if the leader feels that members will not respond honestly or deeply because they know she will read the diaries, she may choose not to have members turn them in. The obvious disadvantage to this is that the leader does not get to read what the members are saying about the group experience.

Diaries can also be used at home. Members take their diaries home and write their reactions to the group and/or to anything that happens to them during the week that is relevant. These journals or diaries would periodically be given to the leader. Reading the diaries helps the leader know what is helpful in the group and also how members are reacting and feeling about things that happen to them during the week. An advantage of jotting down thoughts or events throughout the week is that members focus on themselves at different times during the week and not just during the hour or two each week that the group meets. Writing also helps members remember what happened to them so that they can report these happenings to the group. With the member's permission, comments from a diary may also be shared with other members if the leader feels something has been mentioned that would be helpful to the whole group.

Movement Exercises

Movement exercises require members to do something physical; that is, the members move around. The movements can be as simple as standing up and moving about in order to stretch or as complex as "Breaking In" (an exercise in which members, standing and holding hands, try to keep a member who is circling the group from breaking in). Descriptions of several movement exercises follow.

Changing Seats

This involves members standing and then finding a different seat in which to sit. The purpose is to allow members to stretch and move around and also to sit next to and face different members by virtue of changing location. The leader might introduce this exercise by saying:

Leader: I'd like you to stand up and take a minute to stretch, then find a seat other than the one you had. Try to seat yourselves next to members whom you have not sat next to.

Milling Around

This involves having the members walk around. There are a number of activities that the members may be doing while milling, such as experiencing or avoiding eye contact, or touching another member gently on the shoulder or elbow. The specifics of what to do while milling will depend on the purpose of the exercise. The milling would last for no more than 3 minutes. To begin, the leader might say the following:

Leader: I want you to stand up. *(Members stand)* We are going to do a nonverbal milling exercise. The first thing I want you to do is to move about the room with your head down, avoiding eye contact with anyone. *(Members do this for about 1 minute)* Now, I want you to mill around making eye contact for as long as you desire.

This exercise gets members in touch with their comfort level with others. It can be used in groups that are exploring their feelings about interacting with others.

Values Continuum

With this exercise, members position themselves according to how they think and feel about an issue. The leader designates certain locations in the room as symbolic of a viewpoint. One side of the room represents one point of view and the other side the opposite point of view. The members are asked to stand in the middle of the room and then move to the position on the continuum between the two designated spots.

Leader: I want everyone to stand and line up here in the middle of the room behind Jim. OK, now on the count of 3, I am going to ask you to position yourself where you feel you are on the continuum that I am about to mention. The continuum is from the wall on your right, which will be "high risk taker," to the wall on your left, which will be "play it very safe." *(Pause)* Everyone understand? OK—on 3, position yourselves. Ready? 1, 2, 3.

Possible continuums include saver/spender, happy/unhappy, winner/loser—the list is endless. The benefit of having members walk to a designated area is that all the members have to declare their position at the same time, and everyone can visually see how others feel about a given issue. It also offers a change in the format; instead of stating their position, this exercise gives members the opportunity to move and to view others' "positions."

Goals Walk

In this exercise, the members line up across from each other. Each member will take a turn walking through the area between the members. The members act as obstacles in the walker's path toward his or her goals, which are at the other end.

Leader: I want everyone to stand up and make two lines with three on one side and four on the other. Stand a few feet apart, making sort of a road. What we are going to do is have each of you walk down the road. Let me have a volunteer. *(Hilda volunteers and steps to the front of the group where the leader is standing.)* Hilda, in a minute, you're going to walk through the group. I'd like you to look down the road and envision reaching your goals and life being fairly smooth as being at the other end. OK, now I want you to think of your goals and then tell us how difficult you perceive it will be to reach those goals. If you see it as hard at first, then, Jane, you and Sandy will want to sort of block her and make it hard since you are in front here. If it is going to be hard in the middle, then Kevin and Karen will make it hard. I know some of you have some pretty tough things ahead of you. What we want to do is give each person a chance to experience physically some of the bumps in the road toward his or her goals. You'll make it hard by blocking, holding, or whatever, but it is important not to make it impossible and also not to laugh since that will take away from the person's experience. OK, Hilda, tell us how you see the road ahead.

If done right, this exercise can be very thought provoking. If members know each other well, certain members in the line can play certain characters in the person's life, such as drinking buddies, old lover, ex-spouse, mother, or "the bottle." The leader has to pay close attention to make sure it does not get too physical or turn into a joking kind of activity. We have used this in many different ways and found it to have great impact.

How Far Have You Come?

In this exercise, the leader has the members stand side by side and think about how far they have come during the group in terms of reaching their goals.

Leader: I think this exercise can be of help in getting you to see where you are in the group. Everyone stand and line up next to each other. *(The leader stands about 8 feet away)* If the imaginary line that I'm drawing represents your reaching the goals that we talked about in our first session, how far have you come toward reaching them? Some of you have come pretty far; others, not so far, but I want each of you to position yourself in terms of your progress. On 3—*(Pause)* 1, 2, 3.

After people position themselves, there can be much discussion. The leader can also have them put one foot forward, symbolizing a step toward their goal and have each person talk about what their next step could be.

Sculpt Your Feelings about the Group

This is an exercise in which the leader has the members stand in a circle and "sculpt" how they feel about the group, using their body and hands.

Leader: I want everyone to stand and make a large circle. In a minute, I am going to ask you to indicate how you are feeling about this group by using your body language and position. If you are really into the group and open for it, you would come to the center and have you arms open. If you are against the group, you would turn your back to the group and have your arms closed around you. Everyone understand? *(Pause)* OK, on 3—1, 2, 3.

This is an excellent exercise if the group is not going well and the leader believes it has some potential. The exercise should lead to a discussion about the group.

Family Sculpture

In this exercise, the leader has members sculpt their families as they see them now or when they were growing up. This exercise is usually very revealing. Members find it interesting to sculpt their own family and to see how other members sculpt theirs. The exercise is used to generate discussion about past and present family relationships.

◆ E X A M P L E

This group is composed of male teenagers.

Leader: Today, we are going to focus on our families. To do this, we are going to do an exercise called "Family Sculpture." What this entails is that each of you will "sculpt" your family by picking other members to play your parents or the adults you live with, your siblings, and any other significant person in your family, and positioning them to show how they relate to one another. For example, the parents may be holding hands or they may be far apart with their fists raised. The kids may be close together or very far apart. Some may be close to Dad but not Mom, or they may even have their backs to their parents. Who will volunteer to go first? I'll explain more as you go along.

Tony: I will. What do I do?

Leader: Stand here in the center. Who lives at home with you?

Tony: My mom, my dad, and my little sister.

Leader: Pick a member to be each one of these, and pick someone to be you.

Tony: Bob, you be my dad. Sam, you be me. Don, I guess you will have to be my mom, and Bill, you be my sister.

Leader: Now position these people as you see them. Are your mom and dad close?

Tony: No, they hardly speak. They would be at opposite ends of the room. Can I put them there?

Leader: Sure. Where would you put you and your sister?

Tony: My sister is real close to my mom, so I would put her over there with her. I am not close to anyone, so I would be way over in the other corner away from everyone. Gee, this is heavy!

The leader will usually spend 2 or 3 minutes discussing the sculpture as each member designs it. When everyone has had a turn, a long discussion usually takes place on family issues.

Group Sculpture

Similar to family sculpture, group sculpture is an exercise that has the members sculpt how they see the group. That is, members position people in the group according to how they see the different relationships and roles of the members. This can be a good exercise for groups in which members know each other well, such as in a residential group or a long term counseling or therapy group. It serves as a feedback exercise in that members show how they see the different members of the group.

Home Spot

Members stand in a circle holding hands. Each one picks a spot in the room to try to maneuver the group toward. Since most members will have a different spot in mind and all are holding hands, many different dynamics occur.

Leader: Let's try something different. We've been discussing how many of you do not always go after what you want and need. There is an exercise that I think you'll find interesting. I want you to stand and move your chairs all the way against the wall. (*Members do this*) Now come to the center and form a circle, holding hands. Not too tight of a circle. Now, I'd like each of you to look around and pick a spot in the room. In a minute, I am going to ask you, while still holding hands, to try to move to that spot. This is to be done without any talking or laughter. Your main goal is to get to your spot without letting go of the other members' hands. Get ready. OK, try to move to your spot.

Members will pull, push, give up, kneel on the floor, and so on. The leader will stop the exercise after a minute or so and then process the various reactions. The purpose of the exercise is to get members to focus on how hard they try to get what they want.

Personal Space

This exercise begins with members standing in a circle not too close to each other—almost at arms' distance. The leader then instructs them to close their eyes and to feel the space around them, exploring around their head and in front, to the sides, and in back of them. The leader will then instruct them to venture out of "their space" by using their arms, which usually results in members touching each other. Discussion often centers around the comfort level of their own space and feelings about venturing out. Eventually, the leader will want the discussion to move to members' feelings about their "space" as they live their daily lives.

Become a Statue

This exercise requires members to stand at some distance from each other; on the count of three, they all become "statues" of how they see themselves, either in the group or in their lives outside the group (depending on the purpose of the exercise). This exercise is good for giving members the chance to visually represent themselves. Discussion and questions that follow center on their self-images and how they see others.

Opening Up

In this exercise, members get into pairs. One person sits on the floor and curls up in a ball; the other then takes hold of the partner's arms and gently but somewhat firmly tries to "open him or her up." The exercise usually arouses feelings of control, resistance, fear of being open, or liking being opened up by another.

Trust

There are a number of trust exercises that involve movement. These will be discussed later, in the section titled "Trust Exercises."

Reasons for Using Movement Exercises

1. Movement exercises give group members a chance to *experience* something rather than discuss it.

2. The drama of movement exercises may cause members to remember what took place in the group more readily in the days or weeks following than might otherwise occur if only discussion is used.

3. Movement exercises usually involve all the members. That is, all members are up and doing something, whereas in discussion exercises some members may not be involved.

4. Movement exercises give members a chance to stretch and move around. This can be good for young people and for members who have been sitting for a long while. It is important to remember that members can become bored and fatigued if seated too long or if the format remains unchanged for extended periods.

Cautions for Using Movement Exercises

Various situations and client populations may not be conducive to using movement activities. Leaders should not attempt strenuous movement activities with the elderly or persons who have significant health problems. Any time the exercise calls for vigorous movement, make sure objects such as chairs, desks, or tables are well out of the way. Also, make sure that members remove eyeglasses or any other items that may be damaged or that may injure others. Some movement exercises involve touching, and some members do not want to be touched by other members.

Dyads and Triads

Dyads give members a chance to (1) interact with one other individual, (2) practice some skill, or (3) do an activity that calls for two people to interact in some prescribed manner. We discussed the use of dyads extensively in Chapter Nine, but we did not discuss the use of dyads as a specific exercise, as in the following examples.

One exercise is called "I Have To—I Choose To." In this exercise, members pair up and take turns saying aloud their list of things that they feel they "have to" do. Then they go back and change the recitation from "I have to" to "I choose to." A variation of this would be starting with the phrase "I need to," which would change to "I want to." These kinds of exercises give members a chance to hear how they can change some of their demands or needs. Saying statements out loud to another person makes more of an impact than saying them only to oneself.

Another dyad exercise is one in which a member says to the partner, "I should . . ." and the partner firmly responds, "No, you shouldn't!" Each partner would go through his or her list of "shoulds" and experience being told "no." This exercise helps members think through what really are "shoulds" in their lives.

Another dyad or triad exercise that can prove to be very enlightening is to have members pair up and each assume the role of one of their parents. Then the "parents" talk about their son or daughter. This exercise can help members experience how they perceive their parents' opinions of them, and is a valuable exercise for all age groups. Stevens (1972) calls this exercise "Parents' Chat."

Rounds

As we said in Chapter Nine, rounds are probably the most valuable exercises available to the leader. One kind of round not mentioned in Chapter Nine is the forced-choice round. This consists of the leader reading a statement and the members stating how they feel about the statement. The members would usually respond with "strongly agree," "agree," "disagree," or "strongly disagree." The following are some examples of statements that could be used:

- ◆ Blacks and whites should never marry each other.
- ◆ Extramarital affairs are always harmful.
- ◆ Divorce means failure.
- ◆ A person's personal worth is always changing.
- ◆ Physical attractiveness is very important.
- ◆ One should love one's parents no matter what.
- ◆ Having children is essential for happiness.

As you can see, responses to these kinds of sentences have the potential to generate a lot of discussion. The leader's skill comes in choosing appropriate statements. Forced-choice sentences can be an effective way to stimulate interaction in a group.

Exercises Using Creative Props

Impact Therapy (Jacobs, 1994) emphasizes making counseling multisensory and concrete. The use of different counseling props is a way to make group counseling more multisensory, interesting, and engaging. Items such as rubber bands, styrofoam cups, a small child's chair, and an empty beer bottle all can be used in groups. The following group exercises show how leaders can use props effectively.* (For a full discussion of these and other creative techniques, see *Creative Counseling Techniques: An Illustrated Guide* (Jacobs, 1992).)

Rubber Bands

◆ **E X A M P L E S**

Leader: I want each of you to take one of these thick rubber bands and stretch it until you feel the tension. Hold your hands out and experience the stress. Given our focus on stress management, I thought that rubber bands may help you to see how you are doing. Since our meeting last week, is the stress in your life greater or worse? I want you to either increase the tension or loosen it. Also, think about ways you can reduce your stress and note that for the tension on the rubber band to decrease, you have to do something! Think about this for a minute, and then I'll ask you to share your feelings and thoughts.

Leader: This is now the third meeting of our couples group, so I thought we would take a look at the tension you have in your relationship. I want each of you to get with your partner and take a rubber band. *(Some playfully act as though they are going to "pop" their partner.)* I see some of you already are kind of acting out parts of your marriage. I want you to think about how you can use the rubber band in various ways to symbolize your relationship and interactions. I'll give you about 3 minutes to work with your partner and the rubber band. *(Members work together for a few minutes.)*

Jane: We pulled until it nearly broke and then we sort of looked at each other. Neither one of us gave in, though, so here we sit with the tension at its maximum.

Eto: Ours was very different. We played with it, and then we each popped each other sort of hard. It made us realize that we do hurt each other sometimes.

Styrofoam Cups

◆ EXAMPLES

Leader: I want each of you to take a cup and a pencil. I want you to think of the cup as representing your personal worth, and then I want you to punch holes in the cup as you think about the things that cause you not to like yourself. A hole may represent your appearance, not having friends, your parents' reactions to you, your intelligence, or anything else you can think of. When you are done, each of you will get a chance to share your cup. Some of you may have some holes that you don't want to share yet with the group, and you can just say something like, "There are two more big ones that I am not ready to share yet." The point of the holes is to help you see what you may want to work on in the group.

Leader: I want everyone to look at this cup I am holding and think of it as your own self-worth. *(The leader now stands on a chair.)* As I start to squeeze the cup, I want you to think of whom you give your worth to—whom you have on the chair that you allow to hurt or squeeze you. *(Everyone looks up and seems to be in deep thought.)* Any comments or reactions?

Small Chair

◆ EXAMPLE

Leader: We have been talking about having fun, so I want you to focus on the idea of having fun. To help you, I want you to look at this small chair and think about the fun little boy or girl inside you. I want you to think about what happened to him or her as you have grown up. Since many of you said you don't have fun, we need to hear from the child part of you. *(All stare intensely at the chair. A couple of members start to cry.)*

Cathy: This is very powerful for me. I stopped having fun when I was 14 because of something that happened. *(Cries)*

Matt: I used to have fun, but when my mom died, I felt that I had to help out, and I have been doing that ever since.

Leader: What about others of you? Our goal is to get you to have fun—to listen to that part of you that wants to enjoy life.

Beer Bottle

◆ E X A M P L E

Leader: I want each of you to look at this beer bottle and this string. I want you to let the string represent either your life, your ability to control your mood, or your tolerance for not getting angry. Now watch what happens to the long string as I put it into the bottle. What do you see?

Carlos: It gets shorter.

Dottie: It gets gobbled up. Disappears.

Leader: Now, what do you take this to mean for you? *(The leader places the bottle in the center of the group. Everyone stares at it.)*

These are just some of the props a leader can use to focus the group on a topic. Some other useful props are shields, old cassette tapes, playing cards, and furnace filters (Jacobs, 1992).

Arts and Crafts Exercises

Arts and crafts exercises require that members draw, cut, paste, paint, or create something with a variety of materials. These exercises can generate interest, focus the group, create energy, and trigger discussion. Arts and crafts exercises allow members to express themselves in a different way. That is, members can put their thoughts and feelings into a project before they share verbally with others. This is especially helpful for members who have difficulty identifying or expressing feelings directly. For this reason, arts and crafts exercises are useful with younger children—but they are also useful for all ages. Having members draw their dream house or their imaginary coat of arms can stimulate very interesting discussions.

One example of an arts and crafts exercise involves the use of paper bags, magazines, scissors, and tape or glue. All these materials are passed out to each member. Members are then told to look through their magazines and cut out any word, phrase, or picture that describes them right now. Those aspects they are willing to share with the group are to be pasted on the outside of the bag. Those they are not willing to share are placed inside the bag. When it comes time for discussion, members hold up their bags and tell the group about themselves. This exercise is particularly useful in helping members become acquainted with each other, and it makes sharing easier. The leader can also choose to focus on what is in the bag by discussing why people tend not to want to share parts of themselves.

A second reason for using arts and crafts exercises is they can serve as projective devices for the members' thoughts, feelings, and experiences. That is, current problems may be represented in a creative project. For example, the leader might ask members to draw a picture of themselves and their family engaging in a typical interaction. Often, much is revealed by such drawings.

A third benefit is that members seem to enjoy seeing what other members have drawn, painted, or built. Thus, sharing oneself and listening to others becomes more interesting when members can see what is being talked about.

Another reason for using arts and crafts exercises is that they are nonverbal and may be helpful in groups where language is a problem. We encourage leaders who have members from many different cultures to consider these kinds of exercises if they are finding they are having trouble getting members involved in other kinds of exercises.

Fantasy Exercises

Fantasy exercises are most often used in growth and therapy groups. Fantasies help members become more aware of their feelings, wishes, doubts, and fears. An example of a fantasy exercise is the "common object." The leader directs the members to imagine themselves as an object that is in the room (a book, wastebasket, cup, purse, window, pencil, chair, and so forth). The leader guides the members through the fantasy by asking what it feels like to be the object, what life is like being that object, their role in life, and so forth.

◆ **E X A M P L E S**

Leader: *(Very slowly and softly)* I want you to look at this briefcase, and I want you to become this briefcase. Think about what your life is like as a briefcase. How does it feel? *(Pause)* What happens to you as a briefcase? *(Pause)* What is it like being a briefcase? *(Pause)* In a few seconds, I am going to ask you to share your experience of being a briefcase. I would like you to start by saying, "I am a briefcase, and as a briefcase, . . ."

❖❖❖

Leader: I want each of you to close your eyes and get comfortable. *(Pause, then using a soothing voice with a slow pace)* Now I want you to imagine that you are a tree. *(Pause)* What kind of tree are you? *(Pause)* What are your surroundings? *(Pause)* What is life like as a tree? *(Pause)* How does it feel being the tree that you are? *(Pause)* OK, who wants to go first and share what you experienced?

Other examples of fantasy exercises include the "stump/cabin/stream" fantasy (members imagine themselves as each of these objects, describing their relationship with each other as well as their differences); the "rosebush" fantasy (members imagine themselves as a rosebush); the "wise man" fantasy (members imagine taking a trip up a mountain to visit an old wise man to get an answer to a most important question); and the "funeral" fantasy (members imagine their own funeral and the reactions of people attending it).

When members discuss their fantasy, the leader encourages them to determine if the feelings attributed to the object or fantasy do, in fact, apply to their daily lives. Because certain kinds of fantasy exercises may cause members to explore thoughts and feelings that have been denied to their conscious awareness, leaders who use fantasy exercises should be prepared for members to get in touch with some painful material.

Common Reading Exercises

Common reading exercises require that members read a short passage, poem, or story. Such readings often serve the purpose of triggering ideas and thoughts and of deepening the focus on some topic or issue. For example, in growth groups, the "Gestalt Prayer" (Perls, 1969) may serve as a stimulating common reading:

> I do my thing, and you do your thing.
> I am not in this world to live up to your expectations
> And you are not in this world to live up to mine.
> You are you and I am I,
> And if by chance we find each other, it's beautiful.
> If not, it can't be helped.

Although members have a variety of reactions to this passage, it usually triggers discussion about demands and expectations placed on others as well as the need for approval and acceptance. Other passages and poems that have proven effective have come from *The Prophet* by Kahlil Gibran (1923) or poems by T. S. Eliot. The following example comes from Robert Frost's poem, "The Road Not Taken."

> Two roads diverged in a wood, and I—
> I took the one less traveled by,
> And that has made all the difference.

This is a very inspiring passage and often gives members permission to be different and not follow the crowd. As members read the passage, they are reminded of incidents in their own lives concerning choices they have made. Some may have taken the less-traveled road, while others did not. Usually, a good discussion follows the reading of this passage.

The key factor to keep in mind when using common reading exercises is the purpose of the group. Make sure that the material will trigger thoughts related to the purpose. Another consideration is the intellectual capabilities of the members when asking them to read and react to a poem or written verse. Obviously, the preceding examples would not be appropriate for elementary school children. There are interesting materials written for all educational levels.

Feedback Exercises

One potential benefit of being in a group is the opportunity to hear what others think of you. Diana Hulse-Killacky, a leading counselor educator, has spent the last few years studying "corrective feedback" in group settings, especially counselor training groups (Hulse-Killacky & Page, 1994). Several feedback exercises that follow may be valuable to members. Feedback exercises allow the members and the leader to share their feelings and thoughts about each other. Leaders should not conduct a feedback exercise unless they feel the members have enough goodwill to try to be helpful rather than cruel or insensitive. It would be a major mistake to conduct a feedback exercise with members who have no desire to be helpful or to listen to feedback from others.

First Impressions

This is an exercise in which members share their first impressions of other members. This can be done in the first session or can be used in later sessions when the members have had a chance to revise their first impressions. If used in a later session, members get a chance to hear how they are perceived now and how they were perceived when others first met them.

Adjective Checklist

Members take turns being the focus of the group. Members are given a written list of 15 to 20 adjectives that describe people and are instructed to pick 3 to 5 adjectives that describe the member who is receiving feedback. Using the adjectives gives members a structured way to describe each other.

Talk about the Members

There will be times when the leader will decide to focus on a member for the purpose of giving him feedback. The leader would have members talk about the member, focusing on whatever the leader thinks would be helpful, such as how he presents himself, issues he is avoiding, or positive qualities. When doing this, the leader may have the member being discussed sit quietly, or close his eyes, or turn around so as not to face the group. This will depend on the member receiving feedback, the members giving the feedback, and the kind of feedback that is about to be given. If the leader feels the members will speak more openly if the member who is receiving feedback is not watching, the leader may have that member turn around. Also, the member may be able to listen better when he is not looking at others while they are talking about him.

Strength Bombardment

This is similar to the preceding exercise in that the members talk about each other; but in this exercise, the feedback is done in a more organized fashion. That is, the leader directs the group to describe the strengths of the designated member. The leader appoints one member to keep a list of all the strengths so that the member can have the list when the exercise is over. A variation would be to also list weaknesses or areas needing improvement.

Wishes

A nonthreatening way to give feedback is by using wishes. The leader sets this exercise up by asking members to verbalize any wishes that they have for a given member. The leader would say something like:

Leader: What I would like you to do is think of wishes that you have for various members. We'll focus on one person at a time, and anyone who has a wish for that person will say, "My wish for you is. . . ."

This is a good exercise for members who are concerned for each other and who have various things to say to each other. It is a good exercise for support groups and some growth, counseling, and therapy groups.

Metaphorical Feedback

The leader asks members to think of an animal, a character in the movies or on television, or an inanimate object—such as a sunset or a babbling brook—that reminds them of a designated member. Each member gets to hear how others see him, but the feedback comes in metaphorical fashion.

Written Feedback

In this exercise, members are asked to write out feedback for each member of the group. This is usually done between sessions since it takes quite a bit of time. The value of this kind of feedback is that members experience reading about themselves from the point of view of a number of other people. Most people have not received written feedback from six or eight people at one time. This kind of feedback activity can only be used with members who are basically stable and who have been meeting for quite a while. The leader would provide members with instructions on what kind of feedback to write. The leader may decide to read the responses before giving them to the members.

Most/Least Feedback

This kind of feedback involves members sharing how they feel about other members by using a "most" and "least" designation. For example, the leader may ask members to designate the following:

- With whom they feel most similar and least similar
- With whom they feel most comfortable and least comfortable
- Whom they trust most and whom they trust least
- Who they feel is working hardest in the group and who they feel is working the least

This kind of exercise can create much interaction and must be used with care. The leader can ask for just one category such as "most comfortable" instead of both categories. Members will not only give feedback but will receive feedback by being named by others. After the initial round of members offering their views, they should be allowed to ask questions as to why they were named by another member.

These are just some of the feedback exercises that are possible. Different kinds of feedback exercises will elicit different kinds of responses. The important things to remember when deciding to focus the group on feedback are the level of trust and goodwill of the members and the purpose of the group.

Trust Exercises

Because groups involve sharing, *the amount of trust that members have in each other is a group dynamic the leader must access.* If the leader finds that members do not trust one another or that more trust seems to be needed in the group, he may choose to have the members participate in trust exercises. Each of the following exercises is intended to focus members on the issue of trust.

Rounds

Following are some examples of rounds that can be used to initiate a discussion of trust.

- On a 1–10 scale, with 10 being a person who can trust others easily and 1 being someone for whom it is difficult to trust, how would you rate yourself?
- In this group, do you feel that there is a lot of trust, moderate trust, or little trust? I want each of you to think how you would respond to that question, and we will go around the group and hear from each of you.

♦ When you were growing up, would you say your environment was very trusting, moderately trusting, or not trusting at all?

In each of these rounds, the issue of trust would be the focus. The first two could relate directly to the group, whereas the last one would reflect what members learned about trusting at an early age. Certainly, some of what they learned is probably affecting them in the group.

Trust Lift

In this exercise, members stand in a tight circle with one person in the center. The members gently move that person around by the shoulders for about a minute. During this time, the member's eyes are closed, his feet are stationary if possible, and everyone is silent. Then, gently, the members take the person by the feet, waist, shoulders, and head and gradually lift him over their heads. Then they slowly rock the person while bringing him gently to the floor. A member willing to do this would be trusting the group not to drop him. The leader should focus discussion both on being lifted and on being responsible for lifting.

The obvious caution for this exercise is that the members must be capable of lifting the person. Also, the leader should be prepared for one or two members to choose not to participate due to their fear of being dropped or perhaps even of being touched. During this exercise, the leader must make sure that someone holds the person's head and neck; otherwise, it would be uncomfortable.

Trust Fall

This exercise is done in pairs or threes. It consists of one person standing, with one or two members right behind her. The person in front falls backward, and the others catch her at a safe distance above the floor. The cautions mentioned in the "Trust Lift" would also apply to this exercise.

Blind Trust Walk

This exercise is done in pairs, with one person blindfolded and the other serving as a guide. During the exercise, there should be no talking except for directions, such as "step down." The purpose of the exercise is for members to experience trusting another person to lead them. When doing this exercise, the leader would want to be in a setting that would accommodate members walking around without interference. It probably would not work in an agency or school unless there was a very large room or if it were after hours. Each member should be led around for about 5 minutes to get the effect; ideally, the walk should be such that the blindfolded member experiences more than walking around in a circle. That is, it is good to have members walk where there are doors, chairs, steps, tables, and so on to maneuver around. In addition, most of the time should be spent discussing trust, although some time will be spent on discussing the experience of the walk.

Experiential Exercises

Several group exercises can be classified as experiential because the members are involved in some kind of individual or group experience that is active and often challenging. Some experiential exercises can also be used to build trust. Probably the most well known set of experiential exercises is the "Ropes Course," which is "a blend of activities designed to take individuals and groups beyond their own expectations, or perceived willingness to try" (Project Adventure, 1992). The activities are done outdoors on a carefully designed course made up of ropes. Some of the activities are very challenging and seem dangerous, forcing individuals to come face to face with themselves (Project Adventure, 1992). Other activities on the ropes course depend on members cooperating with each other; thus, it is good for team building. Some group leaders use the ropes course as one part of their group, whereas other leaders just lead groups through the ropes course or some other kind of experiential activity.

When thinking about experiential exercises, you will want to make sure that the exercise fits the purpose. There are many outdoor activities that are fun and interesting, but they may not be appropriate for the group you are leading. If they fit with your purpose, it is a good idea to consider using experiential activities because they are interesting and give your members a very different experience.

Moral Dilemma Exercises

Several group exercises can be considered "moral dilemmas"; that is, a story is read or passed out to the members, and each member has to decide how she would handle the situation. Some of these stories involve stealing food to sustain life, deciding whom to let stay in a lifeboat, or deciding whether to tell the authorities about a crime. Simon, Howe, and Kirschenbaum (1978) describe one involving a fallout shelter and whom to let in. Probably the most popular moral dilemma exercise is called "Alligator/River." It is a story about a woman needing to cross a river to obtain a lifesaving medicine. She must decide whether to give in to the demands of the riverboat captain in order to get across. You may wish to use these exercises or invent your own. Moral dilemma exercises have been found to be very helpful in facilitating discussion among adolescents.

◆ E X A M P L E

Leader: You are on a ship when it wrecks. Seven people want to get into the life raft, but it only holds five. The people are you, a 12-year-old hoodlum-type kid, a 69-year-old retired teacher, a 35-year-old star baseball player, a 22-year-old auto mechanic, a 52-year-old preacher, and a pregnant, 39-year-old homemaker. Who would you think should *not* be allowed on the life raft?

❖❖❖

These exercises usually generate a discussion about values, justice, and fairness. They can be used at the beginning of a session and become the focus of the entire session, or they may be used as an exercise that takes about 30 minutes to discuss and process.

Group Decision Exercises

Other kinds of exercises that can be used in groups are group decision activities. These involve members working together to solve some sort of problem, such as being stranded on the moon with only certain supplies. The group would be asked to determine the best way to use the supplies. Depending on the size of the group, the entire group may work together as one unit or be divided into two or three groups of four members each. Another activity calls for sharing resources such as rulers, scissors, tape, paper, string, and pencils to complete a project. This one would usually be done nonverbally. Members would be given different resources and a task to complete; they would be told that they can share or do anything they like except talk in order to complete the task. It would either be stated or would quickly become apparent that they do not have all the resources themselves, and that other members of the group have different resources than they do. This kind of activity is interesting and, depending on how it is used, can generate discussion about competition, sharing, and cooperation.

Johnson and Johnson (1997) describe a number of different kinds of group decision activities. Two examples are (1) having members try to figure out the right supplies to take ("Winter Survival") and (2) having members try to complete a complicated puzzle through cooperation ("Hollow Squares Exercise").

Touching Exercises

A number of exercises can involve touching. Some are done with the entire group—such as a group massage or milling and touching; others are done in pairs—such as members lightly touching each other's hands or faces. The value of these exercises is that touching can be a very comforting and supportive activity if done properly. Many of the trust exercises involve touching in some manner. Also, some people are "touch deprived"; therefore, experiencing being touched can be a very helpful and freeing experience.

We cover touching exercises as a separate category because there are some cautions to consider when doing them. *Any leader using any exercise in which touching is going to be involved must consider the appropriateness and comfort of the members.* First, be aware that some members may not be comfortable with physical contact. If an exercise involves any form of touching, be sure members understand what will happen and then allow anyone who so wishes to opt out of the exercise. Second, in almost all situations, it is best to avoid touching exercises that may have a sexual connotation. Some massage exercises, for example, may be interpreted as sexual unless properly conducted. With this exercise or any other that may be misinterpreted, you would want to be *very* careful to explain the exercise and its purpose, and to allow members to choose not to participate. Exercises that tend to arouse sexual feelings usually serve no useful purpose, may frighten members, and may inappropriately arouse feelings between two members.

Concluding Comments

Using exercises can be very beneficial, especially when the proper ones are chosen. There are several reasons that leaders should use exercises, including: generating interest and energy, shifting the focus, deepening the focus, providing valuable information, providing an opportunity for experiential learning, increasing comfort, and providing fun and relaxation. A skilled leader understands why and when to use exercises. There are many kinds of group exercises, including: written, movement, dyads and triads, rounds, creative props, arts and crafts, fantasy, common readings, feedback, trust, experiential, moral dilemmas, group decision, and touching. There are many good books on exercises for all kinds of groups. You will most likely want to explore various sources that pertain to the population you are working with.

CHAPTER ELEVEN

Introducing, Conducting, and Processing Exercises

For exercises to be productive and useful, they must be introduced properly, conducted properly, and processed in a way that is helpful for the members. In this chapter, we address each of these important skills.

Introducing an Exercise

Proper introduction means, among other things, giving clear instructions to members on how to carry out an exercise. Introducing an exercise properly is as important as the exercise itself. Leaders often give ample thought to the exercise, but if their instructions are not clearly presented or if certain cautions are not expressed, the likely result will be confusion and the exercise will be almost meaningless.

During the introduction of an exercise, it is important to set the right tone. To accomplish this, the leader should pay careful attention to the use of his voice. If the exercise is to be a serious or thought-provoking one, the leader will want to slow down his delivery, using pauses and a quieter voice. If it is to be an energizing, fun exercise, the leader would probably want to speed up the delivery, using a very enthusiastic voice. Too often, leaders fail to use their voices effectively, and the exercise in turn does not produce the kind of responses that are desired.

When a leader introduces an exercise, it is also important that the leader gain the cooperation and goodwill of the members. Therefore, members should not be made to feel that the leader is doing something to them or that the members are being forced to participate. *The leader should make it clear that members have the right not to participate if they so desire.* There is greater likelihood that the exercise will be beneficial if the members are participating of their own free will.

General Considerations

Inform Members of the Purpose and Procedure

When introducing most exercises, the leader will want to inform the members of the purpose and how the exercise will be carried out. A straightforward introduction will enable members to have a clearer understanding of the exercise and to be more cooperative.

EXAMPLES

Effective Introduction

Leader: Today, I am going to show you some pictures I cut out of a magazine. I am going to ask you to make up a story about one scene. One purpose of this exercise is to help you realize that each of us has our own way of seeing things. There are no right answers, and I think you will find this really interesting.

In this example, the leader tells the members what the purpose is and that there are no right or wrong answers in the hope of relieving any uncomfortable feelings that members might have about sharing their stories.

In the following example, the leader is less effective because he does not tell the members why they are being asked to make up stories about the various pictures.

Ineffective Introduction

Leader: I want you to look at the picture and tell me what you see. Who wants to go first?

In some exercises, it will not be desirable to inform the members fully of the purpose because telling them could interfere with the effect. When introducing such exercises, it is a good idea to tell the members that the purpose will be explained following the exercise. Again, the leader's attitude—as reflected in tone of voice, gestures, and related cues—will be a major factor in ensuring cooperation.

Avoid Confusing Directions

When introducing an exercise, the leader must clearly present what the members are to do. If the instructions on how to complete the exercise are not clearly presented, members will become confused and will not fully participate. If the group consists of members from different cultures, the leader will want to make sure the members understand the directions. The directions should be as simple as possible. If the exercise is a complex one in which members are going to be asked to do a number of things, we suggest that leaders practice giving the directions to colleagues or friends before doing so in the group. In the following ineffective example, the leader would have seen that the directions were too vague had he practiced them with someone first.

◆ E X A M P L E S

Ineffective Introduction

Leader: Each of you will receive an envelope that has a task described in it and some materials. You are to try to complete the task without talking to others. The tasks are different. The goal is to try to finish before anyone else.

The exercise involves members cooperating with each other; they may actually share materials and work together to complete the task, but the leader fails to point this out. By failing to tell them that they may share, this leader causes some members to become frustrated and think that materials were omitted from their envelopes or that others were given more items and that the exercise is unfair.

Effective Introduction

Leader: Each of you will receive an envelope that has a number of things in it, such as a tape, a pencil, or a ruler. Also included is the description of a task to complete. The task will be something like making a 3-by-6-inch red rectangle and taping it on a white circle. In order to complete the task, you will need to share with others since your envelope will not include all the materials necessary for completing the task. You can negotiate with other members, but you can do this only nonverbally—that is, no talking. The goal is to try to finish before anyone else.

When giving directions for an exercise, the leader should be watching members' reactions. Nonverbal cues will often tell him if the members understand the directions. If the directions are not clarified at the beginning, members will interpret how to do the exercise in many different ways, causing the leader to have a difficult time processing it effectively. Also, members find it very frustrating when they do not understand directions.

Another mistake occurs when the leader comments on how the exercise will help the members focus on some topic when, in fact, it does not do so. Members start thinking in one direction and then, when the actual directions are given, they experience confusion.

◆ E X A M P L E S

Ineffective Introduction

Leader: Today, we are going to focus on how you have fun in your life. I think more thought needs to be given to this topic of fun. I want you to pair up and, with your partner, discuss how you and your family spent weekends, vacations, and summers when you were young.

Here, the leader makes two mistakes. The leader implies that the discussion about fun will relate to the present, but then focuses the members on the past. Second, the leader assumes that "fun" takes place on weekends and vacations. This may be the leader's frame of reference, but she overlooks the fact that people can have fun completing a difficult task, playing with children, cooking dinner, and so forth.

Effective Introduction

Leader: I want you to pair up and, with your partner, discuss the different ways you have fun by yourself and with others. Think about during the week and weekends and vacations. All the different ways you have fun.

Ineffective Introduction

Leader: In a minute, I'm going to ask you to do an exercise that should get you in touch with your thoughts about the difficulties of having a deaf child. There are many difficulties, and I think this exercise will help you get in touch with them. Get out a sheet of paper and a pencil. *(Pause)* I want you to write down the first things that come to mind when I say these key words: *anger, guilt, failure.*

Again, the leader is operating from his own frame of reference. Of the many difficulties that parents of a deaf child may encounter, feelings of guilt or anger may be one, but others have to do with financial problems, baby-sitting and day care, obtaining public services for their child, handling their own fatigue, and so on. This leader may anger the group members by his insensitivity to the range of issues. The leader should have used a different exercise, such as a sentence-completion form with three or four sentences.

Ineffective Introduction

Leader: Today, we are going to talk about your family of origin and what life was like in your home. I want you to think of the different feelings you had growing up: how you felt about your mom, dad, and any siblings. Maybe there were other significant people in your life such as a grand-parent, neighbor, or teacher. On the paper in front of you, I'd like you to draw a rough sketch of the house you grew up in. You can fill in the area around the house—really, anything you want.

As you can see, the leader switched the focus from feelings about family members to a visualization of the house in which members grew up. The two may be related, but they also may be totally unrelated.

In each of the ineffective examples, the leader gets the members thinking one way and then does an exercise that is only slightly related or not related at all. Time and time again, it seems that beginning leaders introduce a topic and then do an exercise that does not relate to that topic. This causes the members to be quite confused. Beginning leaders make this mistake primarily because they have not thought through the issue sufficiently. For instance, in the third example, the leader apparently jumped to the conclusion that focusing on the houses members grew up in would stimulate them to think of their families. After considering this more thoroughly, the leader would have realized that the drawing exercise would probably get members in touch with feelings about themselves or events that occurred rather than with feelings about family members. Obviously, there is a major difference in these two topics. A leader should make sure that the introduction fits the exercise *and* that the exercise is relevant to the topic being discussed.

Avoid Lengthy Directions

A common mistake group leaders make when introducing exercises is giving directions that are too long or complex. If the instructions are necessarily long or complicated, it may be best to give them in stages. For example, if the leader wants members to form triads and each play a certain role for the exercise, he should have them form triads and determine who is playing which role before proceeding to the next stage of the instructions.

◆ E X A M P L E S

Ineffective Introduction

Leader: I want you to get into threes; one of you will be the mother, one will be the child, and one will be the father who is returning the child from a visit with him on the weekend. Each of you should be upset about something—the mom can be upset about how the dad is always late in bringing the child back. The child is upset about a number of things—he wanted to stay with the dad longer and wanted to go with his dad next weekend, but the dad had to say "no." The dad is upset about not being able to keep his son longer and because he could not have his son next weekend for a special occasion.

Effective Introduction

Leader: I want you to get into threes. *(Pause while they do this)* Now, I want you to decide who will be the mother, the dad, and the child. *(Pause— leader checks to make sure everyone is doing this)* OK, now all those who are playing Mom, here's the role I want you to play. . . . All those playing Dad, here's the role I want you to play. . . . And all those who are playing the child, here's the role. . . .

By presenting the instructions in stages, this leader minimizes the confusion.

Other Common Errors

Leaders sometimes assume that the members are prepared to discuss some magazine article, movie, or task assigned from the last session. Instead, the leader should first ask the members if they have completed the assignment. At times, the leader may want to go ahead with the exercise even if one or two members are not prepared, telling them to observe or participate as best they can. An alternative plan is always needed, however, in case the majority are unprepared.

Failure to tell members how long an exercise will last is another mistake typical of beginning leaders. Without guidelines concerning time, members may either rush in order to finish or procrastinate and be halfway through when it is time to stop. Something direct, like "We'll spend 5 minutes on this exercise," is sufficient.

Exercise-Specific Considerations

Written Exercises

When introducing a written exercise, the leader should distribute or ask members to get the necessary materials (usually paper and pencil), let them get settled back into the group, and then give the instructions. If the leader fails to do this and the members have to search for materials, one or more members will forget the instructions.

A leader should always be prepared to provide the necessary writing materials, such as pens, pencils, and paper. Even if the leader is certain that members will bring materials with them, it is a good idea to have extra materials on hand in case pencil points get broken or ink runs out. When passing out any forms that are going to be completed, it is best to turn them face down and ask members not to look at them until the instructions have been given completely.

Movement Exercises

When introducing movement exercises, it is often best to have members stand and move to the designated starting position before giving the instructions. It is also important that the leader not give the instructions while the members are moving around since they will not be paying attention.

◆ E X A M P L E S

Ineffective Introduction

Leader: We are going to do a movement exercise involving milling. Each of you is to start out in a spot in the room that is far from the center. I am going to ask you to walk around, moving to different parts of the room with your eyes looking downward; then I am going to have you mill around while glancing at each other. Then you will make steady eye contact. OK, move to a spot that is away from the center. *(Members move to various spots; a couple have to find new spots because another member is there already.)*

James: Now, what do we do first? I forgot. Do we glance at each other?

Effective Introduction

Leader: We are going to do a movement exercise involving milling. First, I want each of you to find a spot in the room that is far from the center. *(Pause while members do this)* I want you to look down. *(Checks to see that this is happening)* In a minute, I am going to ask you to mill around while looking down, then I will have you do some additional things. OK, please start milling around, but continue to keep your heads down.

Arts and Crafts Exercises

Introducing arts and crafts exercises is very similar to introducing written exercises, in that materials should be in front of the members before directions are given. Of course, arts and crafts exercises may require many more materials, such as paste, scissors, paint, crayons, and rulers. It is important to provide the space necessary for members to participate in the exercise in a comfortable manner.

Common Reading Exercises

When introducing common readings, the leader may choose to give the instructions before handing out the reading, or he might want to hand out the reading first, face down. Usually, it is a good idea to tell members to mark the sentences or paragraphs that stand out to them as they read—this helps when processing the exercise in that the leader can ask which sentence or paragraph they marked. Also, the leader will often want to give a very brief introduction to the reading to help the members get a sense of what they will be reading.

Fantasy Exercises

When conducting a fantasy exercise, leaders should speak slowly to evoke the feelings and images necessary. It is also important to suggest that members close their eyes during the exercise, but also give them the option to leave their eyes open. Giving members such a choice can help them feel more comfortable with the fantasy exercise.

Some leaders make the mistake of closing their eyes. It is important for leaders to keep their eyes open and observe the reactions of the members. Observing the members helps the leader pace the exercise. Also, some members may not "get into" the fantasy. If the leader observes this, she can anticipate different reactions from those members than from the others.

Feedback Exercises

When introducing a feedback exercise, the leader should allow members enough time to think about what they are going to say before they give feedback to other members. The leader will also want to take a minute or two to explain the value of giving helpful feedback. He may want to give examples of what would be helpful and what would not. If a leader is not careful in the instructions, the members may give only superficial and meaningless feedback.

Conducting an Exercise

There are several considerations that the leader needs to be aware of when conducting an exercise:

- Making sure members are following instructions
- Allowing members to not share
- Handling emotional reactions
- Changing or stopping the exercise
- Keeping members informed of the time
- Deciding whether the leader will participate

Making Sure Members Are Following Instructions

Once members begin the exercise, the leader should observe whether they are following through as expected. For example, when members are talking in pairs, they may discuss an issue unrelated to the purpose of the exercise. If the leader observes this, she may move quietly to those members and clarify what they should be doing. If the leader sees that members are laughing or talking when they were instructed not to, the leader will want to intervene, especially when the exercise is meant to be a serious, thought-provoking experience. If several members seem confused, the leader may want to go through the instructions again.

Allowing Members to Not Share

In many exercises—such as in rounds or sentence completions—members are asked to respond with a number, a word, or a short answer. The leader needs to be prepared for a member wanting to pass, either because the member feels uncomfortable sharing or because she has not formed a response. When this situation arises, the leader should be sure not to cause the member discomfort by focusing attention on her. When everyone has commented, the leader may or may not want to bring the focus back to that member. This will depend on how uncomfortable the member seems, and what the purpose of the group and exercise is. Some leaders make the mistake of waiting for a member to respond; this usually causes that member to become more uncomfortable.

◆ E X A M P L E S

This leader is doing a round in which members describe in a word or phrase their early home environment.

Mike: Loving, but strict.

Carlos: Confusing.

Marty: Good, steady.

Rosa: Can you skip me?—I just don't want to say.

Leader: Fine. Bill?

Bill: Happy.

Sam: Good with my mom, hell when Dad was home.

Leader: Rosa, is it hard to share because it hurts too much?

Rosa: Yes, and I would rather not discuss it right now. Maybe later.

Leader: Sure. Let's come back to what all of you said. I want you to think about how your upbringing affects you today.

This leader has asked members to get into pairs to discuss their feelings about their marriages. The dyads have been in progress for about 45 seconds when one member gets up and walks toward the leader.

Peggy: I don't feel like talking about this; can I be excused?

Leader: *(To Peggy's partner)* Dan, why don't you join Jim and Gloria? Peggy, let's you and me talk for a minute so that I know what is going on.

If a member chooses not to participate at all in an exercise, the leader will want to do everything he can to make that member and the others as comfortable as possible with that decision. Depending on the exercise, the member may sit and observe or leave the room temporarily. If possible, the leader will want to determine why the member does not want to participate and, if appropriate, the members should know why. In most instances, the leader would not want to take too much time at that moment determining the reason if it was going to detract from the exercise. As a general rule, unless a member is experiencing a major psychological crisis, it is best not to let one member's needs stop an exercise.

Handling Emotional Reactions

When doing an exercise that focuses members on personal issues, the leader must be prepared for one or more members to react emotionally. Fantasy exercises, feedback exercises, and some movement exercises tend to do this more than others, but any exercise can stir up intense feelings. If the leader sees that a member is experiencing a strong emotional reaction, he has several options. Which option he uses will depend on the intensity of the situation, the kind of exercise, and the purpose of the group. The leader can stop the exercise and focus on the member; form dyads, pairing up with the member to discuss his or her reaction; or acknowledge the member's discomfort and continue the exercise, allowing the member to listen and learn from the discussion among the other members. If the leader feels the member's reaction is too intense to be handled then, he might choose to have the member take a break until the exercise is over or to have another member take a break with that member.

◆ E X A M P L E S

This group has completed giving feedback to two of five members in a group.

Leader: OK, let's move to Kathy next. Each of you look over the list of 25 adjectives and think of those that best describe Kathy.

Joe: Quiet, reserved, caring.

Miguel: Quiet, warm, sensitive.

Betty: Caring, quiet, nice.

Leader: *(Noticing that Kathy is starting to tear up)* Kathy, would you like to talk about what you are feeling?

Kathy: I don't like it that I am quiet. I wanted so much for someone to say "intelligent" or "strong." All I have ever been seen as is *quiet!* I hate it!

Leader: Would you like to discuss this some more? *(Kathy nods)* OK. Let's talk about how you can change that. Before we start, because our time is limited, I'd like to ask Joe and Yoshe if we can postpone their feedback till next week. *(They nod)* Kathy, tell us how you would like to be different.

❖❖❖

This group is discussing a sentence-completion form. The questions pertain to attitudes about sex. The sentence they are discussing is "I feel _____ about my early sexual experiences."

Leader: This question is one that may get you in touch with some guilt or pain. I hope you will be willing to share what you wrote, and perhaps more.

Diane: I said mostly OK.

Don: Guilty about one thing—good about the rest.

Leader: Sharon, what did you answer?

Sharon: *(Starting to cry)* I don't want to talk about this right now.

Leader: OK, we'll skip you. *(Looking around the group as he talks)* I do want to say that no matter what any of you did, you do not have to feel guilty about it. Hopefully, we can focus on how to let go of guilt. Sharon, if it gets too uncomfortable, let me know; otherwise, I hope that you will listen and maybe later join in. Carol, what did you answer?

Carol: I said that I feel I learned a lot from those early sexual experiences.

Changing or Stopping the Exercise

When doing an exercise, the leader sometimes decides to change it or to stop. He might do this either because he feels that it is not producing the kinds of responses he had anticipated or because a good topic for discussion has emerged.

◆ EXAMPLE

The members of a growth group were asked to list three significant people in their lives. Two of the five members have already shared their lists.

Bobbi: My dad is the most significant person in my life. Last week he went into the hospital with cancer.

Jud: *(Abruptly)* My mom has cancer, too. I didn't put her down as one of my most significant people, but I'm really scared she might die.

Leader: What we might do for a few minutes, if Bobbi and Jud would find it helpful, is to talk about this.

Bobbi: I think it would help me.

Jud: It would definitely help me.

Leader: OK, let's focus on Bobbi and Jud now, and then we may come back to your lists a little later.

In this example, it seems appropriate to stop the exercise and focus on Bobbi and Jud, who both have immediate needs in common. The topics of illness and worry are ones that most members can relate to.

❖❖❖

Keeping Members Informed of the Time

Leaders should keep members informed about how much time is left to complete the exercise. A statement such as "Take about 2 more minutes to complete the exercise" is usually a sufficient cue to let members know the amount of time left. Informing members of the time remaining gives them some idea of how to pace themselves so they can complete the exercise or wind down the discussion. Members are then better prepared to return to the large group to process or discuss material from the exercise. Also, by observing members' reactions to an exercise, the leader may want to lengthen or shorten the amount of time that was originally allotted to it. For instance, if the leader sees that members are actively sharing in their dyads, he may choose to let them continue for a couple of minutes longer than originally planned.

Deciding Whether the Leader Will Participate

A leader has the option of participating or not participating in an exercise. As a nonparticipant, the leader can closely monitor group members' activities. For example, if members are talking in dyads and their discussion is not on task, the leader can intervene and help them focus by reiterating the purpose. Another benefit of listening and watching rather than joining in is that the leader can hear what members are saying and see what they are doing. During the processing of the exercise, he may even use what he heard by saying something like, "I was listening to John and Eileen, and Eileen brought up a very important point about . . ."

Another reason for the leader not to participate is that the members may focus too much on the leader's opinions or comments. In most rounds or sentence-completion exercises, the leader usually should choose not to participate to avoid emphasis on his answers unless the answers can be very useful for the members to hear; in other words, the leader should only participate when his participation can be of value to the members.

Another argument for nonparticipation is that the leader can more easily get a sense of when the energy for the exercise is waning, or when members have neared completion of the task. In certain kinds of exercises, the participating leader can get so involved that he loses track of time, forgets to pay attention to the energy of the group, or both.

As a rule, the leader should not participate in an exercise that could cause him to focus on his own thoughts, feelings, or "unfinished business." A leader should not do personal work in a group he is leading. It is a good idea, however, for him to have previously done or given considerable thought to any exercise that he uses in a group.

Participating in the activity also has benefits. For example, it can help members get to know the leader. Members are usually very interested in the leader's opinions, ideas, reactions, and feedback. If members see the leader as distant and non-disclosing, they may be less likely to share personally relevant material in the group.

The leader may also wish to participate to create a certain effect. For example, in certain kinds of groups, the leader may want to play devil's advocate to get the members to see both sides of a dilemma. Participation may also be helpful in a dyad exercise if the leader sees the need to give feedback or to help out a particular member.

The leader may also participate in an exercise when there is an odd number of participants and an even number is needed.

Processing an Exercise

Exercises merely act as catalysts for initiating interaction among members by triggering thoughts and feelings. *Understanding the processing of exercises is essential since it is by far the most important phase of any exercise.* By processing, we mean spending time discussing thoughts, feelings, and ideas that result from doing the exercise. Many books on exercises tell the potential leader what materials to use and how to conduct the exercise, but spend very little time discussing how to process the exercise. In this section, we address not only how to process an exercise but also a number of considerations regarding the processing of exercises.

Although some exercises do not need processing because they are used for warm up or for fun, most exercises will be of little value unless they are processed. For many exercises, the processing and the conducting of the exercise overlap in that the discussion is a part of the exercise. This would be true for some feedback, sentence-completion, and experiential exercises in which the leader asks processing questions while conducting the exercise. For other exercises, such as a trust walk or completing the ropes courses, the processing comes when the exercise is completed.

The leader will want to keep in mind several questions regarding the processing:

- What is the goal of the processing?
- How much time is needed for adequate processing?
- What methods of processing should be used?
- What kinds of processing questions should be used?
- How much time should be spent discussing the actual exercise?
- Should the focus be on the entire group or on one individual?
- When should the focus be held, and when should it be shifted?
- Is the exercise present-centered or past-centered? Should the focus be on the past or present?

Goals of Processing

The first consideration regarding the processing of an exercise is the goal or purpose. There are three possible goals when processing an exercise, each having a slightly different focus.

1. *To stimulate sharing and discussion about topics or issues.* This is the goal of most exercises. Sentence completions and other written exercises are used to get members talking about different subjects. Often movement, experiential, common reading, and moral dilemma exercises lead to beneficial discussions.

2. *To stimulate members to delve deeper into thoughts and feelings.* Leaders often use fantasy exercises, certain common readings, creative exercises, and many other kinds of exercises to get members in touch with their feelings. The goal is to get members sharing at a deep, personal level.

3. *To stimulate sharing and discussion related to the group dynamics and group process.* For example, a trust walk exercise can lead to a discussion about trust and then specifically about trust within the group. An exercise in which members rate how they feel about the group will usually lead to a discussion about the group dynamics and group process. Group decision exercises and experiential exercises often lead to processing that focuses on what is happening within the group.

Time Needed for Adequate Processing

A leader should always make sure there is enough time to process the exercise to the depth desired. Many exercises are designed to take members to a very deep, personal level. Unfortunately, a number of group leaders fail to allow enough time for processing. They either begin the exercise when there is not adequate time to discuss members' reactions, or they move on to another activity too soon. Both of these mistakes can lead to frustration, confusion, and a shallow, meaningless experience.

◆ E X A M P L E

Ineffective Processing

Leader: I want you to think of an animal that you would like to be if you could be any animal in the world. What would it be? *(Pause)* Who wants to go first?

Frank: A cat.

Dannie: A tiger.

Mel: A big black bear.

Sharon: A bird.

Dave: An alligator.

Leader: Any comments?

Sharon: Dave reminds me of an alligator.

Dannie: I agree, he does. He sort of sits and waits.

Leader: Any other comments? *(Pause)* Now, what I'd like you to do is think of where you would like to live if you could live anywhere you wanted.

In this example, the leader does not spend time discussing the members' choices before going on to a second exercise. Therefore, very little, if anything, is gained from the exercise. The skilled leader would have a purpose for doing the animal-fantasy exercise. The leader would spend a few minutes having members share why they chose their particular animal and then get into a discussion of how what they have attributed to an animal may relate to their own lives. This exercise usually can lead to discussion that can last an entire session if the leader understands its purpose.

Another way leaders make a mistake regarding time is by letting the exercise take up too much time, leaving only a few minutes for processing. For example, an elementary school counselor could mistakenly give members 15 minutes to draw their family and then have only 5–7 minutes to talk about the drawings. *In most cases, the majority of time allotted to an exercise should be for processing the exercise and not for conducting it.*

Methods of Processing

When an exercise has been conducted and completed, it can be processed in several ways:

- Through rounds
- In dyads or triads
- Through writing
- In the entire group
- In any combination of the preceding four ways

The round is a good way to start the processing. The leader can say something like, "In a sentence or two, what stood out to you about the exercise?" or "Let's go around the group and hear from each of you as to what you thought of the reading."

A leader may want to use dyads or triads when there seems to be a lot of energy and members could benefit from sharing their thoughts and feelings. The use of dyads or triads gives everyone a chance to talk. Writing can be used after exercises when members have many thoughts and feelings they might want to express but do not want to say to anyone else. Exercises that are very thought provoking and emotional, such as family sculpture or certain fantasy exercises, may lend themselves to this kind of processing along with other kinds of processing.

Even if the first three methods are used, most often the majority of the processing will occur among the entire group. The first three ways listed often serve as a way to start the processing. Once the group is warmed up, the leader will use certain questions to stimulate the discussion, such as, "Does anyone want to share thoughts or feelings?" or "What was triggered for you?" or "Let's talk about your reactions." The leader can also use these questions at the beginning of the processing if she feels that no warm up is necessary.

◆ **E X A M P L E S**

Members have just completed an exercise in which they drew their egograms (a transactional analysis diagram) of themselves at home, at work, and with their family of origin.

Leader: This activity usually stirs up a lot of thoughts and feelings. First, I am going to get you to pair up and share your egograms and any thoughts that you have. Let's see, the two of you pair up, and the two of you, and the two of you. . . .

Leader: *(After allowing 5 minutes for sharing)* Let's come back to the large group. What have you learned from doing this exercise? Do you see some changes that you want to make?

In this example, the leader uses dyads and then the whole group for processing the exercise.

In this example, the leader uses a round and then opens the discussion to the entire group with questions that will deepen the focus.

Leader: Let's do a quick round on your reaction to the exercise on a 1–10 scale, with 10 being "has you really thinking" and 1 being "the exercise had no impact." Who wants to start?

Ramos: 10.

Clyde: 8.

Marlene: 9.

Paulette: 8.

Tray: 8.

Leader: So everyone is really thinking. We should be able to have a very interesting session. What hit you? What are you thinking about?

Kinds of Processing Questions

The skilled leader will always consider the kind of processing questions to be asked because the questions will direct the focus of the processing (Kees & Jacobs, 1990). The questions can cause members to focus on the exercise, the group, issues or topics, or individuals. Questions such as "What happened?" "What did you draw?" and "What part of the reading stood out?" are the kinds of questions that will get the members to talk about the exercise. These questions often are used at the beginning of the processing phase, but some leaders make the mistake of using only these questions, which can lead to a shallow group.

If the leader wants the members to go deeper, she should use other kinds of questions, such as the following:

- ◆ What insights did you get from doing this?
- ◆ What feelings were stirred up for you?
- ◆ How can you use this exercise to help you in your life?

Leaders will always want to make sure that their questions are congruent with the goal of the exercise. The biggest mistake leaders make is asking questions that do not foster any in-depth exploration—questions that generate discussion at the 10 or 9 level instead of at the deeper 8, 7, or 6 levels. The processing questions should help funnel the group to a deeper level.

Amount of Time Spent Discussing the Actual Exercise

Often, the leader will have to decide how long to discuss the actual exercise. For instance, if the group has just engaged in a fantasy exercise, the leader would want to let members tell their fantasy; but the main purpose of processing would be to get them to talk about what feelings they got in touch with. The same would be true of a movement exercise in which people struggled to reach their goals. The processing would initially be on what it felt like when they had to struggle, but the leader would want to rather quickly get the discussion to center on the struggles they are having in their lives, not the struggle in the exercise. It is very easy to allow members to share at a superficial level about the exercise itself and thus not maximize the benefit of the exercise. Too many leaders make the mistake of having members merely talk about the exercise and do not try to take the discussion to a deeper, more meaningful level. Good, thought-provoking questions that tap into the emotions and feelings of the members can eliminate this mistake.

◆ EXAMPLES

This leader has just completed a movement exercise in which the members were told to form a circle, hold hands, and then silently pick a spot in the room toward which they were to try to pull the rest of the group. The purpose of this exercise is to see how determined and persistent members are, and to see how they attempt to get what they want.

Leader: What was that like? What happened?

José: Boy, that was tough. I really got into that exercise. Sandy, you should have seen the look on your face as you tried to pull away from the group!

Sandy: Yeah, I was surprised at how strong you were, José. All I could think to do was to free myself from your grip.

Donald: I had no idea that you girls could pull as strongly as you did. . . .

It is evident here that the discussion is conversational. No real learning is taking place, since the members are merely discussing their actions during the exercise itself. This is fine for the first couple of minutes, but to effectively process the exercise so that they learn from it and apply this learning to their lives, the leader would need to ask some additional questions such as, "Think for just a moment not so much about what happened during the exercise but about what this exercise meant to you. What did you learn that you can apply to your current life situations?" The leader could also say, "Did the exercise we just finished have any meaning for you in terms of your lives outside this group?" Group discussion following such leader prompts might sound something like the following:

Angie: Yes, I think I learned something. The thing that stood out to me about this exercise is that I tend to fear competition. I've always shunned opportunities to compete and, as a result, I think I've been missing out on some potentially rewarding experiences.

Donald: That's interesting, Angie. I feel almost the opposite, in that I always compete and have a difficult time just enjoying life without always comparing myself to others. I often come up short when I play the comparing game.

In this dialogue, the group members are applying their reactions to their lives, and the exercise acts to trigger thoughts. Keep in mind that the exercise usually only stimulates members' reactions. It is the leader's guiding statements that will often enable members to personalize the experience.

This group has just completed a fantasy exercise that involved having the members visualize themselves on a journey to see an old wise man.

Ineffective Processing

Leader: What was it like seeing the wise man?

Jerry: My wise man had a long, gray beard.

Ted: Mine was dressed in a long, white robe, and carried a cane.

Cristina: When we met each other, I gave him a hug.

Janet: "He" was a "she," and she never said a word to me, but I know that she was glad to see me because she smiled.

Leader: What else happened when you saw the wise man or woman?

Joey: I was frightened. I thought he had too much on his mind to see me.

Tammy: It felt good. He was glad to see me, and I wanted to stay longer.

Leader: Did the wise man or woman give any of you an answer to your question?

Ted: Yes.

Janet: She just smiled when I asked her my question.

Leader: What about when you left? How did you feel?

The discussion could continue like this for the entire session, with members recounting what they thought and imagined during the exercise. The discussion would remain on a surface level, with no significant learning taking place. The members are not applying the exercise to their lives.

Effective Processing

Leader: Did any of the thoughts, feelings, and images you had as you went to see the wise person relate, in any way, to your own personal life?

Cristina: It did for me. Seeing the wise man was just like going to see my grandfather. I'm always glad to see him, and we always hug.

Joey: I was really scared as I walked up that mountain. I was afraid that he wouldn't be glad to see me or wouldn't have time for me. I sometimes feel that way when I'm at home. I have four brothers and sisters, and sometimes I feel like Mom and Dad don't have time for me.

Leader: Maybe that's something we can talk about in a minute. It seems important.

Ted: It felt like the wise man was telling me not to worry about school and home so much. I worry a lot about those things sometimes, and it makes me sad.

Leader: I never thought of you as worrying about your home life. Would you like to talk about that?

Ted: Yes, I think I would.

Leader: OK, we'll do that sometime before the session is over. I want to get a few more comments about the experience of seeing the wise person. Janet?

Janet: When I asked the wise woman my question, she just smiled. Then I realized that I have the answer inside me, and I don't always have to rely on other people to make decisions for me.

Leader: Any significance or importance that you changed the person to be a woman?

Here, the members are relating in a personal manner. The exercise opens avenues for discussion and allows members to share their thoughts and feelings as well as to hear the reactions of others. Because the processing of the exercise has caused members to share personal information, several concerns have emerged. The leader may now choose to focus more intensely on Ted or Joey's concerns.

Focusing on One Member or on the Entire Group

When processing exercises for personal growth, support, and therapy groups, the leader will sometimes have to decide whether to focus on one person or on the group. *It is usually best at the beginning of the processing phase to hear from all the members who feel like sharing in order to get a sense of what is going on with the members.* This can be done by using rounds or by just asking for some brief comments about their reactions to an exercise. If there are members who would like to work on something, the leader will have to make a decision whether individual work is better than continuing the discussion with the entire group. (We discuss working with individuals in Chapter Thirteen.) The last scenario in the preceding example is a good illustration of the leader having to decide whether to go with a group discussion or an individual focus on either Ted or Joey.

It is difficult to give specific guidelines as to when the leader should focus on individuals. If the group is a growth group, you may not want to hold the focus too long on one individual. If the group is a support or therapy group, it often is very beneficial to let the focus be on one person for 10 to 20 minutes, especially if that person is willing to work at a deep personal level (6 or below on the depth chart).

Holding and Shifting the Focus

An error commonly made by inexperienced group leaders when processing an exercise is to focus the group for too long on the first person who talks. It is usually best to give all or most of the members a chance to talk before holding the focus on any one person or issue. Exercises should create energy and stimulate interest among all the members. Focusing prematurely on one member may result in losing the interest and attention of others who have not had a chance to react to the exercise.

Also, be aware that the first person who speaks may be speaking out of anxiety or a need for attention or a desire to please the leader. This member's response may therefore be a function of those needs rather than a reflection of genuine feelings about the issue.

◆ E X A M P L E S

Ineffective Processing

Leader: *(Following a sentence-completion exercise)* Who would like to share an answer with the group?

Tod: *(Appearing anxious to respond)* I would. On that question concerning my thoughts on divorce, I thought about what different reactions people have. My one uncle was depressed for months and hardly left his house except to go to work. My other uncle, however, seemed to be happier as a result and went on about his life as though nothing had happened. What do you suppose was the difference?

Leader: I don't know. What do you think the difference could have been?

Tod: *(In a storytelling voice)* Well, one difference could have been the length of time that they were married or the fact that one uncle had been divorced once before. He told me. . . .

In this example, Tod is the first to speak, and his response is not relevant to the group. His voice indicates he is not speaking introspectively but rather with a storytelling intent. The leader makes an error in continuing to focus on him instead of tapping into the energy generated from the sentence-completion exercise.

Effective Processing

Leader: Who would like to share an answer with the group?

Tod: *(Appearing anxious to respond)* I would. On that question concerning my thoughts on divorce, I thought about what different reactions people have. My one uncle was depressed for months and hardly left his house except to go to work. My other uncle, however, seemed to be happier as a result and went on about his life as though nothing had happened. What do you suppose was the difference?

Leader: I'm not too sure in their particular cases, Tod. If you are interested in exploring this, you and I can do it after the group adjourns. Right now, however, I would like others to share their specific answers with the group.

Tim: For number 1, I said divorce does not always mean failure.

Leader: What did others answer for number 1?

In this example, the leader chooses not to focus on Tod even though there seems to be some energy. Also, the leader realizes that it would be a mistake to hold the focus on Tod because the purpose of the exercise is to get members talking more personally about divorce. Many novice leaders are so relieved that someone is speaking that they will focus on the first person to speak rather than give others a chance to comment briefly.

Present-Centered or Past-Centered Exercises

Although most exercises focus on the present, many are designed to get members to reflect on their past. Members may be asked to draw the house they lived in when they were young or to describe how they felt when they were 10 years old.

A very potentially powerful exercise that focuses on the past is to have members bring in pictures from childhood.

There is no right or wrong about where exercises should focus although we feel that, in most cases, focusing in the present about the past is usually more productive than just focusing on the past. The reason for this is that group members cannot change their past, but they can change how they are affected by it. It is good to focus on the past to get at various hidden and possibly painful material, but then it is usually important to bring the discussion to the present. This can be done by asking such questions as these:

- How do you think your past affects you today?
- What can you learn from looking at those past relationships?
- It is important to take a look at how our past experiences affect us today. What did you learn?
- Does this stir up some unfinished business that you may want to work on?
- What feelings from your childhood do you need to sort out?

The leader should almost always be considering how to help members in the present, even when conducting a past-centered exercise. We stress this point about past-centered exercises because we have seen too many group leaders focus on the past, and not have members consider what they need to do in the present to change their feelings or thoughts. Too often, leaders process a past-centered exercise by just having the members describe past experiences. By failing to explore the connections between past experiences and present behavior, members become "unzipped" and are left "opened up."

Concluding Comments

The last two chapters discussed the kinds of exercises, when to use them, how to introduce them, and how to conduct and process them. Throughout this chapter, we have pointed out a number of common mistakes made by leaders when using exercises. The following is a review of some of the main points to consider when using an exercise in your group.

- Choose the kind of exercise that is best for what you are trying to accomplish.
- Make sure the exercise is relevant to members' needs and the group's purpose.
- Make sure directions are clearly stated.
- Try to clear up any confusion before the exercise actually begins.
- Keep directions short and simple.
- Make sure all necessary materials are present and in front of members before introducing the exercise.
- To avoid distraction, place handouts or sentence completions face down before starting.

- Generally, have members stand and get situated before giving directions for movement exercises.
- Give directions that include enough information for completing the exercise successfully.
- Allow members to refrain from participating.
- Explain the purpose of an exercise before beginning it.
- Explain how long the exercise will last.
- Remember that exercises are means, not ends. Learning comes through processing.
- Open processing discussions with thought-provoking, open-ended questions.
- When processing an exercise, make it relevant to group members' lives.
- Do not use exercises one right after another without processing sufficiently in between.

CHAPTER TWELVE

Leading the Middle Stage of a Group

The most important stage of a group is the middle stage because this is when the members should be working, learning, and deriving maximum benefit from being in a group. The middle stage encompasses discussing, sharing, and working on problems or tasks. The emphasis in this chapter will be on groups that meet for a number of sessions; however, the information will also be useful for groups that meet only once or twice since they, too, will have a middle stage. In this chapter, we discuss the planning and assessment tasks that leaders face during the working stage, as well as some essential leadership techniques and activities that can be helpful. Also, we offer outlines for covering common topics, discuss the mistakes that leaders often make during the middle sessions, and present strategies useful to certain types of groups. In the next chapter, we continue the discussion of leading middle sessions, focusing on conducting counseling and therapy in groups.

Planning and Assessment

During the middle stage, the leader has to decide how much planning is needed based on the purpose of the group, the personalities and needs of the members, and the levels of trust, interest, and commitment. Some leaders plan the entire series of sessions before the group begins and make the mistake of failing to modify those plans according to the evolution of the group. *It is important to realize that session plans that were conceived well in advance or that were used for a previous group may not work for the current situation.* To plan the middle sessions, the leader must take into consideration how the members are feeling about the group.

Assessing the Benefits

Periodically during the middle stage, the leader will want to assess the group's value to its members. This is essential in planning because if the group is not beneficial, he will want to make adjustments. To assess the benefits to the group, the leader can use any of the following activities:

- Conduct a 1–10 round on how valuable the group has been. The leader would follow up with a discussion of the ratings.
- Conduct a comment round in which the leader asks each member to comment on the value of the group.
- Initiate a discussion of the value of the group by saying something like, "For the next half-hour or so, I'd like people to comment on how this group is being helpful." This differs from a round in that not everyone necessarily comments, and the discussion will be more extensive.
- Have members review each topic discussed. Getting members to comment on what has stood out to them can help the leader evaluate the effectiveness of the group experience. If the members are not remembering the main points or if they have little to say, there is a good chance the group is not as beneficial as it could be.
- Ask members to write for 5 to 10 minutes on what they have gained from the group up to this point. Good stimulus questions include the following:

  How is this group helping you?
  What activities are most beneficial to you?
  How do you feel about the group?
  What things do you dislike about the group?
  What would make the group better for you?

  Writing can be done at the end of the session and the members would leave what they wrote, or it could be given as an out-of-group assignment to be brought in at the next meeting or mailed in.

By engaging in one of the preceding activities, the leader should have a better understanding of how the members feel the group is benefiting them, which in turn will help improve future sessions. Although it is the leader's responsibility to try to make the group a meaningful experience for everyone, it is important to remember that this is not always possible. Some individuals may lack the personal resources—such as attention span or communication skills—to benefit from certain kinds of groups. Likewise, the leader should not be overwhelmed or feel defensive if members have various criticisms. It is important that leaders remember that not everyone will always like everything that takes place in the group.

Assessing Members' Interest and Commitment

Another important assessment for the leader to make during the middle stage is that of the members' interest and commitment levels. To make this assessment, the leader observes the frequency of absences and late arrivals, which is often one indication. Also, the leader observes the energy throughout the session. The leader will want to look for patterns of disinterest over a period of two or three sessions rather than in a single session since outside stresses and concerns can easily affect a member's level of commitment for any given session.

When the members' interest seems to be declining, the leader first has to assess whether the loss of interest applies to everyone or just a few of the members. When only a few of the members have lost interest, the leader will want to try to understand why. It may be that their interest was low from the very beginning due to being forced to be in the group. Other reasons that members may not be committed to the group include not finding the content interesting, not feeling their needs are being met, and not being ready to make changes in their lives. No matter what the reason, the leader will want to try to remedy the situation, possibly by using one of the following options.

If most members have lost interest, the leader can:

- Decide that the group has served its purpose and end the group
- Plan the group differently with the belief that a change of format will generate new interest and commitment
- Bring up the issue for discussion in the group

If a few members have lost interest, the leader can:

- *Bring up the issue with the entire group,* keeping in mind that there will be differences of opinion. The discussion may prove helpful in clarifying the purpose of the group and in revealing why certain members are not interested. Depending on what is said, the leader may or may not be able to make changes that will increase some members' interest.
- *Meet with those whose interest seems low* and talk to them about how they could be more involved. If they are no longer committed to the group, the leader may choose to ask them not to return. This option should not be used often, but it should be considered since no group can go well when a number of members lack commitment to its purpose.
- *Give members permission to drop out of the group.* This can be done in two ways: (1) mention that some may want to drop out and this would be a good time; or (2) have a closing session for the current group, letting members know they have the option of requesting to be in a second group that will be starting immediately.

Assessing Each Member's Participation

During the middle sessions of any group, the leader will want to consider each member's frequency and style of participation. While there is no "correct" way to participate in the group, active, verbal participation is usually better for most members than merely observing or occasionally commenting. The leader may feel the need to get members to participate more. As a rule, it is desirable to try to get quiet members to share their thoughts and feelings in the hope that they will become more comfortable sharing in the group. There will be times when getting members to share more is either not possible or not desirable. However, for some members, observing with little verbal participation may be the best way for them to experience the group.

A related member-participation problem arises when the leader feels that members are only making superficial comments. To change the level of participation, the leader can use a variety of skills and techniques:

- ◆ He can change his voice so that it reflects the tone he desires—a quiet, deliberate voice usually indicates a more serious tone, and members tend to respond more seriously.
- ◆ She can mention her observation of what is happening and suggest that the level of participation change. She can use the depth chart as a visual tool, showing that the group is not going below 7 with any discussion.
- ◆ He can shift to an exercise or activity that has the potential for generating more serious discussion.
- ◆ She can shift to a topic that will generate more personal discussion.

Assessing Members' Level of Trust and the Group's Cohesion

During the working stage, the leader needs to be aware of the level of trust that the members are feeling. Trust develops best when there is a positive environment, which the leader provides by encouraging members to express support and concern for others in the group and by stopping members from attacking or criticizing others. When the leader does not pay enough attention to the continued development of trust, it may deteriorate and lead to members feeling uncomfortable in the group.

If a leader finds herself in a situation in which the group's trust level is low, she will want to focus on the issue of trust, either by bringing it up for discussion or by using one of the several trust exercises, such as the Trust Walk (see Chapter Ten).

Assessing How Much to Focus on Content and How Much to Focus on Process

During the working stage, the leader should pay attention to both group content and group process and should constantly decide on the proper balance between the two. It is important to mention this because no matter what the purpose, there will be times when focusing on process is very important and necessary. A common mistake made by both beginning and experienced leaders is to ignore the process and just focus on content. Not focusing on process can lead to a very superficial group when dynamics exist such as members dominating the group; members not trusting each other; or members feeling attacked, judged, or inferior. If the leader wants the group to be maximally beneficial, he has to monitor and deal with group dynamics, especially if they are negative.

Screening Out Members

As a group moves to the middle stage, one situation that occurs occasionally is the consideration of screening out a member. We mentioned this in an earlier chapter, but it bears repeating—there will be times when the best way to handle a difficult member is to ask him or her to leave the group. We know of too many situations in which a group has been "sacrificed" because the leader was afraid to ask a member to leave the group. This is something that should be done only after many attempts to "reach" the member and after much thought, but it should be done when one member is causing such disruption that nothing can be accomplished by the other members.

Some leaders want the group to decide whether another member should be asked to leave, and in some situations, this may be a good idea. However, most of the time, the leader should make the decision because the leader is in the best position to decide whether the member is interfering with the development of the group. *Always keep in mind that it is your responsibility to try to make sure that a group has the proper membership composition so it can be maximally beneficial.*

Dealing with Breach of Confidentiality

There will be times when there is a breach of confidentiality by one or more members in the group. This obviously is a situation that must be given much thought. Before anything is done, the leader should talk to the member who breached confidentiality to get some idea as to what happened and why. If the leader finds that the occurrence was accidental and innocent, then she may consider letting the member remain in the group. Before making the decision, the leader would definitely want to get a sense of how the other members feel about having the member in future sessions. This can be done at the start of the next session with either the member present or not present. Having the member stay depends on the situation, the other members, and the member who breached confidentiality. If the member stays, he could be attacked by some or all of the other members (especially in groups of teenagers) and not be able to handle it, or he may benefit greatly from the feedback and comments of the other members. The leader has to gauge what she thinks is the best approach for helping the group and the member. There are no set guidelines for this type of situation except to give it much thought and, if possible, consult with colleagues to get their input and suggestions.

If the breach of confidentiality occurred out of anger, revenge, or idle gossip, then the leader may feel the member should not be allowed to remain in the group. In this case, the leader would need to tell the member he cannot return to the group and then process with him any feelings he has. The leader would, if possible, want to turn the situation into a learning experience for the member and for the group when it meets the next time.

One of the most difficult situations that can occur around breach of confidentiality is when the leader, due to agency policy, does not have the option to ask a member to leave the group. The leader must then decide the best way to minimize the effects of having the member remain in the group. Needless to say, this is not a good situation, but it does occur in certain settings.

Leadership Skills and Techniques for the Middle Sessions

Several skills and techniques are especially appropriate for the middle sessions. To make the group a valuable and worthwhile experience, the most important skills to remember are cutting off, drawing out, and holding, shifting, and deepening the focus—all of which have been discussed thoroughly in earlier chapters. In this section, we elaborate on some additional skills that are valuable when leading middle sessions. Because we have already mentioned these in previous chapters, our descriptions are brief.

- Stimulating members' thoughts
- Introducing topics for discussion
- Using progress reports
- Varying the format
- Changing leadership style, if warranted
- Changing the structure of the group, if warranted
- Using outside materials and assignments
- Meeting with members individually
- Informing members in advance when the group is ending

Stimulating Members' Thoughts

Leaders must be prepared to stimulate discussion since members cannot always be counted on to be ready to share their ideas. To stimulate the group, leaders may use exercises and various activities. The leader may also use some general questions or comments that encourage and facilitate sharing and discussion. Sometimes, all the leader needs to do is ask a general question. At other times, the leader will want to make a brief statement and then ask a question. Many leaders use questions only and do not realize the value of sometimes prefacing their question with a brief comment. Following are a few examples of ways to stimulate thought:

- Many of you seem to be deep in thought. What are the one or two points that stood out to you?

- The feelings that Zeda is sharing are quite common, and often people don't express these feelings. I appreciate Zeda's honesty. We'll come back to you in a minute; but first, let me ask, does anyone else have similar feelings?
- I think some of you would disagree with what has been said, and it is important that you share your thoughts. Would anyone like to react or comment?
- In listening to the comments, I felt that many of you were holding back your true feelings. For this group to be truly helpful, I urge you to share how you really feel. *(Pause)* Any comments on what I just said?

Introducing Topics for Discussion

To keep interest high, the leader must continually be listening for new slants or themes as members discuss various subjects. When the leader sees that the energy is starting to wane, he will want to introduce new topics for discussion. The leader can accomplish this by spinning off what has been said; that is, by shifting the focus to a topic that has emerged from the ongoing discussion.

◆ E X A M P L E

The members have been discussing communication with their spouses and how to handle trouble areas, such as children, in-laws, and money.

Jane: We do OK in most of these areas. Money problems we now seem to have under control. We still have problems over sex and religion. We cannot discuss those at all. I really do feel at a loss. Last Easter was really a bad scene. He refused to go to church! But I guess all couples have some areas of conflict. I know my parents fought about many different things.

Leader: Let's take a look at communication with regard to religion. For some couples, this is a major source of friction. Anyone want to comment?

In this example, the leader took a topic that one of the members mentioned and introduced it to the group by making a brief comment.

The leader can always choose to introduce a new topic as the need arises.

◆ E X A M P L E S

Leader: Another topic that's important to talk about in regard to communication with your spouse is sex. Let's spend the rest of the time discussing how you and your partner communicate about sex.

Leader: We have covered a variety of issues, but no one has mentioned _____, which is probably the most important one. It also may be the hardest one to talk about, yet I think it is essential that we do so. What are your thoughts on _____?

❖❖❖

Using Progress Reports

In groups, members often will share aspects of their lives that need to be followed up on during the next session. An excellent way to do this is by starting each session with progress reports from various members. Not only is this helpful to the members who share their progress, but this kind of sharing also helps build cohesion in the group. However, leaders should not make the mistake of letting progress reports take up too much time. Five to 10 minutes should be sufficient.

◆ **E X A M P L E**

Leader: Why don't we start. I think it would be good to get updates on what has happened since last session. I recall that a number of you said you were working on some significant issues. How was the week? Let's spend 5 or so minutes catching up on what happened.

Varying the Format

The leader should always give thought to the format of the group and whether it needs to change. In some groups, members seem to like and benefit from the same format. The leader will want to vary the format only when she sees that the group members are bored with the same agenda. If the leader senses that changing the format would be beneficial, she can decide or have the group decide on how to spend time so that the sessions are more interesting and helpful.

◆ **E X A M P L E**

Leader: It seems to me that we may want to change how we have been doing group. There are many excellent topics that we could cover, but we mostly spend time with different people's issues. It does seem that members are getting help, but my question to you is, Do you want to devote the whole time to members' issues that sometimes seem to be repetitious, or do you want me to think of some group exercises that would trigger other issues?

Dax: I like it the way it is.

Millie: I think the group could use some new things. I am kind of bored.

Tray: Can we do both? I would like to know that I can come here and talk about my problems, but group exercises sound good to me.

Dax: I guess if we did both that would be better for me.

Changing Leadership Style If Warranted

Sometimes, during the middle stage of the group, the leader may feel there is a need to change the style of leadership. Often, this takes the form of doing less leading and encouraging the members to take more responsibility. The leader gets members to do most of the cutting off, drawing out, and generating topics for discussion. Other situations may dictate that the leader take a more active role, especially if the group has evolved into a therapy group.

Changing the Structure of the Group If Warranted

There may be times during the middle stage of the group that the leader will see the need for a change in structure. Changes may take the form of adding new members, meeting less often, or having an extended meeting, perhaps over a weekend. Before deciding on any of these changes, the leader would want to introduce the idea for discussion.

In certain kinds of groups, some members will want the purpose of the group to be one thing, while others will want the group to serve an entirely different purpose. When members want two or more different structures or purposes, a difficult situation exists. Each situation is unique, so the solution is not always the same. There are a number of options for dealing with such a situation.

- The leader can divide the group into two subgroups. (This often is not possible due to size, or time considerations, but it is an option to be considered.)
- The leader can divide the time in half—that is, half the time the group will do one thing, and half the time it will do another. (This will work only if the members can be cooperative when the group is doing the half in which they are not as interested.)
- The leader can let the members decide how to handle their differences of opinion about what the group should be doing.
- The leader can inform the group that there are no options since the group has a specific purpose to which they must adhere.

If you find yourself in this situation and you take some action, it is important to realize that some members may be upset with you or with the group, creating a dynamic that will need to be monitored.

Using Outside Materials and Assignments

Some groups lend themselves to homework assignments. Homework can be in the form of reading assignments, writing assignments, or *doing* assignments. By *doing*, we mean such things as calling someone, talking to a certain number of people, signing up for some kind of lessons, varying the morning routine, and so forth. For many groups, assigned outside reading, TV shows, and other forms of homework can keep members involved in the group between sessions and serve as a stimulus for discussion during the group meeting.

One assignment that has been used is to have the members write an encouraging letter to themselves that they bring to the group with a self-addressed, stamped envelope. They leave the letter, and the leader mails it so that each member gets a letter from himself or herself during the period between sessions. The leader may choose to read the letters and make some additional comments or just mail the letters, depending on what seems most beneficial.

Meeting with Members Individually

In certain kinds of groups, during the middle stage, the leader may want to meet with some or all of the members individually to discuss feelings about the group. Such a meeting gives the member a chance to share his opinions and reactions to the group with the leader. It also gives the leader a chance to discuss with the member various issues without the time constraints and dynamics that exist during a group session. Some experts feel that meetings of this nature can detract from the group. We have found the opposite to be true in that some members may need the opportunity for some private time which, in turn, frees them up to share more in the group. Simply stated, counselors are in the business to be helpful, and we encourage you to do whatever you can, within ethical guidelines, to be as helpful as possible.

Informing Members in Advance When the Group Is Ending

Members should have at least 3 to 5 weeks' advance notice that the group is going to end. Usually the ending of a group is determined during the beginning stage, although there will be occasions when no ending time has been set. Even when the ending time is set, it is a good idea for the leader to remind the members that the group will be ending in a few weeks.

◆ E X A M P L E

Leader: Our last meeting will be in 4 weeks, so you may want to think about how to maximize your time in these last three sessions. The last session will be primarily for ending the group, so be sure to not save important, major issues until the last session. I would encourage you to bring up things this week or next week.

Middle-Session Topic Outlines

Too often, an important topic is brought up in the group but wasted because the leader has not given thought to the various key issues regarding that topic, nor to exercises that might facilitate discussion and sharing. *One of the most important things a leader can do during the middle stage of a group is to think through the different issues that are relevant so that she is prepared to focus on the issues in a meaningful, effective way when they come up.*

To further help you, we have taken a number of topics common to many kinds of groups and outlined the key issues, introductory exercises, and other exercises that might be covered. We have outlined four topics: the need for approval, self-esteem, religion, and sex. These were selected from a list of common topics that emerge as focal points during the life of a group. (We could have chosen several other topics, such as worry, anger, love relationships, divorce, death, or parents—all are major topics.) The outlines give some possible ways to focus on the topic and ways to deepen the focus so that the discussion would be meaningful. We suggest you use this structure for any major topic that may arise in groups that you are leading. It is important that you realize much thought must be given to the appropriateness of any of the exercises described in these outlines.

Topic 1: The Need for Approval

KEY ISSUES
1. Sources of approval: parents, lover, boss, children, friends.
2. Where does need for approval come from?
3. How people seek approval.
4. How strong is the need for approval?
5. Positive and negative ways that people seek approval.
6. Trusting oneself.
7. Dependence/independence.
8. Difference between needing and wanting approval.
9. How to reduce approval-seeking behavior.
10. Use of REBT, TA, and attachment theory to understand need for approval.

POSSIBLE INTRODUCTORY EXERCISES
- Round: How important to you is the approval of others? (1 to 10)
- Dyads: Discuss early experiences in your family. Did you feel you were approved of? How does that affect your current functioning?

- ◆ Rounds or dyads: Whose approval do you seek, and how do you seek it?
- ◆ Written exercise: List people whose approval is important to you. Arrange in order of importance. Then discuss in dyads, triads, or in the group.
- ◆ Sentence completion or rounds:

If my parents did not approve of me, I would _____ .

If my supervisor/teacher did not approve of me, I would _____ .

If my spouse/lover did not approve of me, I would _____ .

I approve of myself _____ percent of the time.

If I sense disapproval, I _____ .

DEEPENING ROUNDS, DYADS, AND EXERCISES

- ◆ Round: The need for approval is a desire, a necessity, or a burden. (Choose one.)
- ◆ Written exercise: Make a list of gains and losses resulting from your approval-seeking behavior.
- ◆ Dyads: Discuss ways you attempt to gain approval from others and classify each as effective or ineffective.
- ◆ Round or movement exercise: Respond with "strongly agree," "agree," "neutral," "disagree," or "strongly disagree" to this statement: "Approval from others is more important to me than my own self-approval."
- ◆ Set up some role play in which members experience disapproval.
- ◆ Give feedback to each other (make sure it isn't all positive). Discuss reactions.
- ◆ Have members pair up. One stands while shaking finger, looking very disgustingly at the other, who sits in a small chair. Discuss the different reactions, memories, etc.
- ◆ Set up situations; then get members to react using REBT and TA.

Topic 2: Self-Esteem

KEY ISSUES

1. What is self-esteem?
2. Where does it come from?
3. How to raise self-esteem.
4. Can a person change his or her feelings of self-esteem?
5. Parents' roles.
6. Siblings' and friends' roles.
7. Spouse's or lover's role.
8. School, grades, intelligence, and self-esteem.
9. Appearance and self-esteem.

10. Sports and self-esteem.
11. Work and self-esteem.
12. TA and the Child ego state.
13. REBT, self-talk, and self-esteem.
14. What is a winner, and what is a loser?
15. Guilt, shame, and self-esteem.

It is important for anyone who is leading a group on self-esteem to have a theoretical understanding of self-esteem. We mentioned TA and REBT, but certainly there are other theories that are useful when working with self-esteem. We have had very good results with school-age children using these theories.

INTRODUCTORY EXERCISES
- Round: If 10 is liking yourself a whole lot and 1 is hating yourself, what rating would you give yourself?
- Round: What one or two things affect your self-esteem—that is, affect how you feel about yourself?
- Written: Using a 1–10 scale, with 10 being very good, list how you feel about yourself on the following: appearance, intelligence, personality.
- Written: In a sentence or two, define self-esteem. Then write down your ideas regarding it: Can I change, and if so, how? If not, why not?
- Dyads: Pair up and discuss how you feel about yourself and why.
- Sentence completion: My self-esteem goes up when_____.
  My self-esteem goes down when_____.

DEEPENING ROUNDS, DYADS, AND OTHER EXERCISES
- Round: What is the one thing you need to do to improve how you feel about yourself?
- Round: What negative sentences do you tell yourself that cause you to feel "less than" others?
- Dyads: Pair up and discuss what you were told about yourself by significant others when you were growing up.
- Creative-prop exercise: I want each of you to take a Styrofoam cup and think of it as your self-esteem, or self-worth cup. Now, I want you to take a pencil and punch holes in the cup, with the holes representing the holes you have in your self-esteem. Many of you have big holes from childhood, parents, school, and various other relationships and incidents. Take a minute or so to think, and then punch your holes.
- Movement: I want everyone to stand and line up side by side, facing me (about 8 feet away). I am going to draw an imaginary line here in front of me that represents your feeling really good about yourself. In a minute, I am going to have you move toward the line to where you see yourself. Where you are standing now is feeling very "not OK" about yourself. . . . On 3, move—ready, 1, 2, 3. (*Everyone moves*) What can you do today to help you move closer to this line?

Topic 3: Religion

KEY ISSUES
1. Early messages/parental messages
2. Religious history of members
3. Benefits in your life
4. Restrictions in your life
5. Religion as a personal choice versus a "should"
6. Effects of religion on
   a. guilt
   b. sexual issues
   c. marriage and divorce
   d. abortion/birth control
7. Determinism versus free will
8. Life after death
9. Degree of importance of religion in your life
10. Belief in God

With any discussion of religion, the leader needs to be aware the discussion can become very emotional and heated, which—in most instances—would not be to the purpose. Rather, the usual purpose of a discussion about religion is to help members feel comfortable with their beliefs and behavior and to be tolerant of others.

POSSIBLE INTRODUCTORY ROUNDS AND DYADS
- Round: What issues regarding religion would you like to discuss?
- Round: Briefly give your religious background and tell where you currently stand with regard to organized religion (church member? nonmember? nonbeliever?)
- Round: How much influence does religion have in your life? (1 to 10)
- Round: Does religion cause any problems in your life? (yes/no)
- Dyads: Are you bothered by any current issues concerning religion? If not, what were some past issues that bothered you?
- Dyads: Do you profess a particular religion? How do you practice your religion?

These introductory rounds and dyads would be useful to the leader in gathering information about how the members feel about religion. The introductory activities would also get the members focused on the topic. The following exercises would be used only when appropriate and usually would not be used as beginning rounds to introduce the topic of religion.

DEEPENING ROUNDS, DYADS, AND EXERCISES
- Round: If you are currently in a relationship, do you and your partner agree or disagree about religion?
- Dyads or triads: Discuss briefly what is the most disturbing aspect of religion in your life.

- Dyads or round: What do you find the most helpful and the most difficult about your religious beliefs?
- Triads or round: What would you do differently with your children concerning religious training than your parents did with you?
- Written exercise: List early messages about religion.
- Set up some relevant role-play situations in which religion in some way is causing a problem.
- Respond to the following statements with "strongly agree," "agree," "neutral," "disagree," or "strongly disagree":

Religion is the opiate of the masses.
We all have free will.
There is life after death.

Topic 4: Sex

KEY ISSUES
1. How you learned about sex
2. Satisfaction with sex life
3. Guilt
4. Early experiences
5. Difficulties and inhibitions regarding sex
6. Preferences, frequency
7. Sex without love
8. Sex and religious beliefs and early messages about sex
9. Communication with partner
10. Orgasm
11. Masturbation, fantasy
12. Extramarital sex
13. Homosexuality

It is important for any leader discussing sex to be clear about the many different issues since the members, more than likely, will not be. Any leader choosing to discuss this topic should not be judgmental and should be tolerant of various sexual attitudes, beliefs, and behaviors. The leader would also want to be prepared to deal with members' negative reactions to such issues as homosexuality, affairs, or unorthodox sexual practices.

INTRODUCTORY EXERCISES
- Round: If 10 is very comfortable, how comfortable are you with discussing sex in this group? (1 to 10)
- Round: If 10 is very important, how much importance do you place on sex in your love relationship? (1 to 10)
- Dyads: What are some issues related to sex that might be discussed in the group? (Have pairs report back to the entire group some topics they discussed.)

- Round: Complete the following sentences:

  I think sex is _____.

  Discussing sex in this group is _____.

  Many of my current feelings about sex come from _____.

- Round: In a word or phrase, how would you describe your present sex life?

DEEPENING ROUNDS, DYADS, AND OTHER EXERCISES

- Reaction sentences: Have members give their reaction to any of the following sentences. Reactions could be given in writing, in a round, or by having members locate their opinion along a continuum (by moving) from "strongly agree" to "strongly disagree."

  Masturbation is a bad thing.
  It is my obligation to make sure that my partner has a satisfying experience.
  If either partner fails to have an orgasm, the encounter is a failure.
  Everyone should have sex before marriage.
  To have a good sexual relationship, you must be in love.
  Sex is fun.

- Round: I would like to have sex _____ times a week.
- Triads: What is your greatest concern or fear regarding sex?
- Round: Do you have any "leftover" or current guilt regarding sex? (yes/no) (If there are yesses, the leader could ask if the members want to work on their guilt, or the leader could introduce a helpful discussion about sex and guilt.)
- Round: In a word or phrase, how would you describe your comfort communicating with a partner when having sex?
- Written exercise: List your expectations in a sexual relationship.
- Round: If my partner had an affair, I would _____.
- Written exercise: Write on a 3-by-5-inch card anything pertaining to sex that you would like to talk about. (The exercise is anonymous so that members can write such things as "having been sexually abused," "having an affair," "having certain sexual fantasies.") The leader would then collect the cards and lead a discussion about the various written comments. (This can be a very powerful and helpful exercise if conducted properly.)

As we stated in the beginning of this section, the preceding examples are just some of the key issues and possible exercises for the chosen topics. There are many more exercises that could be outlined. Our intent is to encourage you to thoroughly think through a topic before you lead a group on it.

Middle-Session Leadership Tactics for Specific Groups

In addition to the skills and techniques already discussed, specific kinds of groups call for particular leadership tactics. In this section, we briefly discuss some additional techniques for education and task groups. In the next chapter, we discuss skills that are useful for the working stage of growth, support, counseling, and therapy groups.

The Education Group

Leading the middle stage of an education group requires paying much attention to shifting from giving information to facilitating discussion and back again to giving more information. This sequencing keeps the group flowing and increases the chances of achieving the goals of helping members learn and apply their new knowledge to their lives. The key is to provide enough information and enough sharing and discussing time. Often, beginning leaders lose sight of the experience of being in a group and focus too much on providing information, or spend too much time on sharing, and not enough information is covered. A true education group will have a good balance of information and interaction.

The Task Group

The task group leader's role during the middle stage is to help members generate options and help them move toward a decision or resolution. Since the task group involves a group goal rather than individual goals, members may take strong stands on issues. The leader will always want to keep in mind how the members feel about each other and about the task they are working on. The leader needs to be aware of who are the more influential members of the group and what type of pressure they exert on other members. Also, the leader should be aware of any hidden agendas of the members. In other words, when leading a task group, the leader must look out for many different group dynamics and must be willing to focus on the dynamics if they are interfering with the progress of the group.

Helping Members Generate Ideas and Options

The discussion of various options during a task group is sometimes difficult because members become emotionally identified with their own ideas and find it hard to discuss others. The leader must be able to get members to discuss and exchange ideas in a productive manner. The leader's choice of any of the following strategies listed will depend on the number of members in the group, the kind of goals the group is working toward, the level of agreement among members, and their overall attitude of cooperation. Brainstorming, the fishbowl, working in small groups, and guided fantasy often prove to be valuable tools for generating options and moving the group to some resolution.

Brainstorming Brainstorming is the technique of having members generate as many ideas as possible without regard to practical limitations. The theory behind brainstorming is that people often impose unnecessary limitations on their creativity by assuming constraints that may not exist or that may be possible to change. Once ideas are out in the open, members may come up with creative changes that eliminate the constraints. The basic rule for brainstorming is that no idea is too wild or crazy to be brought up. The fact that ideas are not evaluated or censured during brainstorming also reduces the members' feelings of defensiveness. Brainstorming may be done in the entire group or in small groups of three or four. A time limit helps the group stay focused.

Once ideas have been brainstormed, overlapping ideas should be eliminated or consolidated. Then the remaining ideas are listed, discussed, and ranked. Several of the better ideas can then be examined in greater detail and elaborated on as needed. If the leader uses the brainstorming technique effectively, every member should feel he or she has had the opportunity to provide some input.

The fishbowl The fishbowl is a technique that can be used with a variety of groups, but it works especially well with larger groups. The group is divided, with half the members forming an inner circle and the other half an outer circle. While the inner group discusses an issue or idea, the outer group listens. (People often can listen better when they know they are not going to speak.) After a given time period, the members switch places, with the new inner group sharing its reactions to the previous discussion. The new inner group may provide constructive criticism or build on the ideas already generated.

Small-group variations Small-group interaction can almost always be useful, in that members have the opportunity to discuss ideas in greater detail and more people get to talk since the group is smaller. Members in small groups may all work on the same task or on different phases of the task. The results of the small-group discussions are then shared in the larger group.

Guided fantasy In a task group, the guided fantasy provides a chance for members to picture, think about, or get a feeling for the outcome of various solutions generated by the group. Also, members may fantasize the outcome and then construct what must happen for that outcome to be realized, thus generating various solutions. Following is an example of how a guided fantasy could be used.

◆ E X A M P L E

A school counselor is leading a task group consisting of parents. The task is to develop a valuable summer program for school kids in the community. The leader introduces a guided fantasy by saying the following:

Leader: At this point, let's think about the outcome of the program you might envision. You might want to close your eyes to try this. Picture an ideal summer day when the program is in place. What are some of the things that are happening? What different things do you see happening, and where are they happening? *(Pause)* How many different programs do you see going on? *(Pause)* When you are ready with your ideas, write them down.

This technique helps establish goals, which in turn aids the leader in developing and maintaining the focus.

Helping Members Move toward Resolution

One of the primary functions of the task group leader is to make sure the group accomplishes what it is supposed to. Groups can easily discuss an issue "to death" but not resolve anything. The skilled leader is always thinking about when and how to help the group accomplish its purpose. If the group is not progressing, one good strategy is to focus the members on the process so they can become aware of what they are doing.

◆ E X A M P L E

Leader: I want to stop you and get you to focus on what is happening in the group—not the content, but the process. What is going on here that is keeping you from getting more accomplished? Think about what you are doing and what others are doing. I think some of you may even have some strong feelings about what is happening.

Common Mistakes Made during the Middle Sessions

There are many mistakes that leaders can easily make during the middle stage of a group. We discuss the following ones:

- ◆ Underleading or overleading
- ◆ Letting the warm-up phase last too long

- ◆ Letting the focus shift too often
- ◆ Focusing too long on a member
- ◆ Focusing on only one or two members
- ◆ Planning only one or two activities
- ◆ Failing to allow time to process an activity
- ◆ Choosing uninteresting speakers

Underleading or Overleading the Group

The leader is the pivotal person in the success of a group, seeing to it that interesting discussions and interactions happen. The skilled leader leads to the degree that members gain from his guidance; beginners often mistakenly lead too much or too little. It is possible to overlead; that is, not to let the members have enough input into the group. This is especially detrimental if the leader is focusing on boring, uninteresting, or irrelevant material. On the other hand, it is possible to underlead by turning the group over to the members when they do not understand how to make the group valuable.

Letting the Warm-Up Phase Last Too Long

In our workshops, we discuss how, for the inexperienced leader, the warm-up phase can end up lasting far too long. We ask participants for a show of hands of how many have let the warm-up phase get away from them. Almost everyone raises his or her hand, which indicates that this is a common occurrence. Workshop participants have shared that too often in the beginning of a session, they let members ramble or focus on irrelevant subjects. The purpose of the warm-up phase is to get the members focused on being in the group. The skilled leader pays close attention and makes sure that the opening does not drift along or head in a direction that is not useful or productive. Often, the leader will use a round to hear from the members since rounds keep members from telling long stories or giving little speeches. The leader may include in the warm-up progress reports by the members; that is, members give brief comments or updates on whatever may be relevant to the purpose. It is very important that the warm-up serves the purpose of getting members focused rather than allowing members to get off on tangents that end up using valuable group time. *Remember, the majority of the time should be spent in the working phase and not the warm-up phase.*

Letting the Focus Shift Too Often

Inexperienced leaders often make the mistake of not holding the focus long enough for there to be impact. Because many leaders are uncomfortable with cutting off, they let the focus shift too often, thus never allowing the interaction to go deep enough. In any group situation, it is very easy for the focus to move from topic to topic unless the leader holds and deepens the focus. We feel that the leader should always be aware of the focus and the depth of the focus. During the working stage, the leader should try to get the focus to a level that is meaningful for all or most of the members.

Focusing Too Long on a Member

It is a mistake to focus too long on a member who does not understand the content of the group. This occurs most frequently in education or discussion groups but may occur in any kind of group. For example, in a parent-education group in which a member is just not able to understand the difference between two methods of responding to a child seeking attention, the leader has a number of options for handling the situation. This is important to realize because many leaders think they have only one option: to spend as much time as necessary to get the member to understand. This option is often not best because too much time can be lost, and frequently, other members get very bored. Beginning leaders often cater their group to the confused or slow member, which results in only a marginally valuable group for the other members. Here are some of the options available if a member does not seem to understand the content:

- Take time to explain, if it can be done in a relatively short time.
- Have members try to explain or clarify the issue.
- Tell the member you will explain after the session or at a break.
- Tell the member you will meet with him at another time to go over the material.
- Arrange for another member to meet with that member to go over the material.
- Ask another member to go to another part of the room with that member and explain the material. You would not want to do this often because the helpful member would be missing the group.

If a member repeatedly has difficulty understanding material in the group, the leader may ask that person not to remain in the group. This is an option that you would probably not use very often, but it is an option. In the next chapter, we discuss the common mistake of focusing too long on a member who has a counseling concern.

Focusing on Only One or Two Members

It is a mistake to devote an inordinate amount of time trying to help any one member. If a group has a member who is very talkative or very needy, some beginning leaders will devote week after week focusing on the same member. This practice is very easy to fall into because the member seems to need help, and the members all want to be helpful. Another type of member that leaders tend to focus on is the resistant member. Too often, beginning leaders devote a considerable amount of time trying to get this member to want to get some help while the member rigidly resists. This often does little good, and much valuable time is wasted. We discuss the resistant client in Chapter Fifteen.

One way to avoid focusing on just one or two members is to use a member assessment technique. The leader can answer the following questions about each member.

- How does "X" feel about coming to the group?
- What does "X" need to learn from the group?
- What does "X" need to talk about but is afraid to bring up?
- How much "air time" has "X" had in the last few weeks?

By answering these questions for each member, the leader should be able to get some sense of what each member wants or needs from the group. The answers help a great deal in planning the session and also enable the leader to go into a session with a number of possible options and topics.

Planning Only One or Two Exercises or Activities

Another mistake is to plan only one exercise or topic. There will be times when a topic or an exercise does not generate discussion or interest. In such a situation, if the leader has mistakenly planned just one or two exercises for the entire session, the leader and the group will flounder. It is always wise to have backup plans because there are times when your plans don't generate much energy.

Failing to Allow Time to Process an Activity

It is important to allow enough time to discuss and process any film, guest lecture, or group exercise. Films that last the entire session should not be used. Speakers should be told in advance how long they have to speak and should be interrupted when the leader sees there is not going to be sufficient time to discuss the presentation. Usually, the majority of the time should be for sharing and processing rather than for viewing the film, listening to the speaker, or doing the exercise.

Choosing Uninteresting Speakers

When using a guest speaker, the leader should make every effort to ensure that the presentation is interesting and stimulating. It is helpful to meet with the speaker in advance to get a preview of the talk and to make sure the speaker is clear as to the purpose of the group and her presentation.

Concluding Comments

In this chapter, we have outlined skills, techniques, and roles that the leader will want to use during the middle sessions. When planning the group, the leader will want to assess the benefit of the group and the members' interest, commitment, and trust levels. When leading the middle sessions, the leader should stimulate thought, introduce new topics, use her voice effectively, and vary the format when necessary. The leader will always be thinking about the leadership styles and the structure of the group, and will change either of them if necessary. The leader will also want to keep in mind the kind of group she is leading because different strategies are needed for the various kinds of groups. Planning for different topics is very important during the middle sessions. By outlining the key issues, introductory exercises, and deepening exercises, you will be prepared to lead your group on the various topics that you plan or that come up during the session.

There are several mistakes that leaders might make during the working stage. These include: underleading or overleading, letting the focus shift too often, focusing too long on a member, focusing on only one or two members, planning only one or two activities, choosing uninteresting speakers, and failing to allow time to process an activity.

CHAPTER THIRTEEN

Counseling and Therapy in Groups

For most counselors, leading counseling and therapy groups is the most difficult, most rewarding, and the most exciting of all the groups that we have discussed in this book. Counseling and therapy groups are conducted in many different settings, such as schools, child guidance centers, psychiatric units, mental-health centers, hospitals, college counseling centers, rehabilitation centers, youth crisis centers, child abuse centers, women's shelters, and juvenile training schools. Counseling and therapy groups may focus on personal problems in general or on specific topics, such as anxiety, depression, cancer, AIDS, panic attacks, recovery, shyness, divorce, or relapse. For ease in reading, we use the terms *therapy group* and *counseling group* interchangeably. School counselors are often not allowed to conduct "therapy" groups, but they certainly do conduct counseling groups in which they try to help youngsters with many different personal concerns. Throughout the chapter, we use the terms *therapy* and *counseling* interchangeably, with both defined as "the process of helping clients with insight into their behavior." We are not saying necessarily that the counseling and therapy groups are the same but rather that the skills and techniques discussed apply to both. Many of the techniques that are valuable for therapy groups are also useful for support, growth, and experiential groups.

Goals of Therapy Groups

Behavioral researchers have identified two types of therapeutic goals for groups: *process goals* and *outcome goals*. Outcome goals are goals that pertain to behavior changes in the member's life, such as obtaining employment, improving an interpersonal relationship, maintaining sobriety, or feeling greater self-esteem. Therapy groups that primarily focus on the concerns of the members are usually much more beneficial than groups that focus primarily on the interactions among the members. Leaders who emphasize outcome goals get members to focus on their issues at a depth level of 6 or below on the depth chart. (For review of the depth chart, see Chapter Seven.)

The term *process goals* refers to goals that are related to the group process. For example, process goals can be to help members improve their comfort level in the group, to increase their openness in group, and to learn to confront members in a more productive manner. Some educators teach that the focus of the group should mainly relate to what is happening in the "here and now" and that outside concerns are less important. With this approach, much time is spent on interactions, member feedback, and confrontation. Although focusing on process goals can be a valuable aspect of therapy groups, we feel this should not be the main focus for any therapy group. Focus usually should be on individual concerns and outcome goals.

Establishing Therapy Groups
Size and Membership of Therapy Groups

The "ideal" therapy group is composed of five to eight members with the membership remaining constant once the group has begun. In the ideal group, the members attend voluntarily and share at a very personal level. In private practice, college counseling centers, schools, mental-health centers, and various other settings, groups can be like this. Unfortunately, in many other settings, groups are not at all like this. We describe the less-than-ideal group to prepare you for what may happen once you start working in the helping field. Groups with such limitations are often found in youth crisis centers, drug and alcohol agencies, residential treatment centers, prisons, and psychiatric hospitals. In these settings, leaders may be asked to lead groups with anywhere from 15 to 20 members, with an ever-changing membership consisting of members who are forced to attend. The leader regularly has to devote group time to introducing a new member or saying good-bye to a member who is leaving. In such large groups, it is difficult to involve all the members in any discussion or give individual attention to one member. Sharing will be less personal because members do not feel the sense of cohesion and trust that exists in groups in which there are 5 to 8 members who want to be in the group.

Large, nonvoluntary groups are much more difficult to lead and are usually only minimally effective. In a situation in which the members are *very* negative, resistant, or mentally disturbed, or in settings where a large group (12 or more members) is mandated by agency policy, the leader may want to try leading an education/discussion group for all the members and then a smaller therapy group for those who seem to have some commitment to personal change.

Screening Members

When establishing a therapy group, the leader should screen the members, if possible, since screening can eliminate having members who do not belong in the group because they are in too much pain or are too emotionally unbalanced.

Groups are usually easier to conduct when there is a common problem, such as drug abuse, child abuse, depression, divorce adjustment, shyness, or agoraphobia. In such groups, the purpose of the group is usually clarified more quickly, and it is easier for the members to focus on the issues. Screening the members gives the leader a chance to include members at various stages of the problem, which often helps in the development of the group.

In many situations, the leader will be selecting members from a caseload, or the agency may require all patients to be in groups. Either of these situations leads to the formation of a group composed of members with very different problems. In such a group, one member may express concerns about keeping employment because of aggressive behavior; another, about her marital troubles; another, about his lack of assertiveness; and another, about anxiety that prevents her from going places more than three miles from home. Screening can be helpful in trying to get the right mix of members. With experience, the skilled leader gets more adept at selecting members for groups. If the option is possible, it is good strategy to verbalize to the members that the groups are not permanent and that, during the first few weeks, members may be switched to other groups.

When to Meet

There really is no specific number of times that a therapy group should meet. Some groups meet on a daily basis for 1 or more hours, while others meet once or twice a week for 1 to 3 hours. For different populations and settings, the leader should try various meeting schedules to determine the optimal number of meetings per week or month. In schools, counseling groups usually meet once every week or every other week.

The Leader's Role and Responsibilities in Therapy Groups

The leader is the primary orchestrator of change within the group. The members are very important, but it is the leader who creates the therapeutic climate and is responsible for focusing the group. This does not mean that she does all the talking or counseling, but it means the leader is in charge, thus having many different responsibilities. We discuss six.

1. Knowing the subject or topic
2. Providing the right atmosphere
3. Directing the focus
4. Being aware of individual members
5. Watching the clock
6. Apportioning the "air time"

Knowing the Subject or Topic

It is the leader's ethical responsibility to have a good grasp of the issues that may arise in a therapy group. For instance, in an Adult Children of Alcoholics (ACOA) group, the leader would need to know about trust, intimacy, and relationships. Too often, we hear of therapy groups being led by someone who does not know the issues, nor what to do when important topics are brought up. In groups for depression, anxiety, sex addiction, or anger management, knowing the issues would enable the leader to introduce topics that are relevant and use exercises that are designed to get members to explore their inner thoughts and feelings.

Providing the Right Atmosphere

It is the leader's responsibility to create an atmosphere for the group in which members feel safe to share their thoughts and feelings. The members should feel that they will be listened to if they choose to speak. The leader provides the right atmosphere by creating a positive environment in which trust and respect are communicated and modeled. This requires cutting off comments that are negative, hostile, or insensitive. The leader uses certain phrases that serve to remind members they are there to help each other. Some good phrases to use are the following:

- What ideas do you have that might be helpful?
- What is something you can say that may help?
- I appreciate the sharing and caring that you are exhibiting. With this attitude, I know we can have a good group experience, and people can be helped.
- We are here to help and support each other. Does anyone have a suggestion, thought, or reaction that they think may be helpful?

Directing the Focus

The therapy group leader should always be aware of the focus and whether it should be held or shifted. If the group is focused on helping a member with a concern, the leader must assess whether the concern being discussed has relevance for the other members, and whether the members can get involved in helping the member with her problem. For example, in a group for recently divorced women, it would be quite appropriate to discuss such issues as fears about dating or anger at the ex-spouse. If, however, a member wanted to discuss the problems she was having with her neighbor over a new fence, the leader would probably want to shift the focus to something more relevant. She would offer to discuss the fence issue with the member after the session or some other time.

Being Aware of Individual Members

Another responsibility of the leader is to pay close attention to each person in the group, because at any moment a member may react strongly to something being discussed. By watching all the members—not just the one who is speaking—the leader will observe different reactions and draw out certain members who seem ready to share.

Given that more and more groups are made up of members with very diverse cultural backgrounds, the skilled leader is continuously monitoring the reactions to the different topics and problems. There may be times when the leader, for his understanding or for the group's understanding, will need to ask a member how his or her culture deals with the situation being discussed. This discussion can be valuable in expanding members' cultural awareness and in understanding the specific member's reactions. It would be unethical to work intensely with an individual in the group if the leader did not understand the member's cultural frame of reference.

Watching the Clock

Another responsibility is making sure that enough time remains in the session to cover an issue adequately. Sometimes, leaders make the mistake of introducing a topic or allowing a member to begin discussing a very personal issue with only a few minutes left. Examples would be the topic of death, or a client sharing that she was raped when she was young. Much time would be needed to cover these topics adequately.

Apportioning "Air Time"

It is the leader's responsibility to be aware of the amount of time that each member has had to bring up problems. Members should not necessarily have equal time, but it is important not to devote an inordinate amount of time to one or two members. If a member seems to need much of the group's time, it may be best to see that member individually or, in extreme cases, request that the member not remain in the group. The leader must realize that the group should not be dominated by one person's therapy needs.

To avoid spending too much time on one person, the leader should reflect on the following questions:

- How long has the group been focused on the member?
- Is the discussion relevant for most of the other members?
- Do members seem annoyed at the amount of time being spent on the person?
- How much time in past sessions has been spent on this person?

The Process of Therapy in a Group
Getting, Holding, and Deepening the Focus

The difference between a therapy group and the other groups we have talked about is the therapy group is supposed to move to a deeper level—this is the purpose. The skilled leader understands the value of focusing the group and trying to deepen the focus. Following are a number of examples that illustrate how the leader can be very instrumental in deepening the focus, which in turn makes the group more personal, more interesting, and more therapeutic.

◆ E X A M P L E S

Leader: On a 1–10 scale, with 10 being very satisfied, how satisfied are you
with your present love relationship? (Your life? Your family?
Yourself as a student? Yourself as a parent? Your job?) *(Pause)* What
would it take for you to raise your number?

When asked questions like these, members usually will get more focused and often will want to share their answers.

This group consists of patients at a mental-health center. The leader has introduced for discussion the topic of guilt. One member has described how she felt guilty about leaving her dog at home by itself all day; another, how he felt guilty about not going to visit his grandfather more often. Neither of these members seemed too bothered by their guilt, but the leader senses that many of the members are, in fact, very much bothered by their guilt feelings. The leader decides to deepen the focus.

Leader: I guess I am wondering if some of you have some guilt feelings that
are hard to live with. That is, you feel bad about something you did or
are doing, and those actions cause you to think less of yourself. Guilt is
often associated with doing something that runs counter to some value or
expectation we hold for ourselves. Religion and sex are often involved in
guilt. Let me ask this—is there something that you feel guilty about that
would be hard to share? I'll ask you to say "yes" or "no," but you do not
have to share what it is.

Troy: No.
Maria: Yes.
Bob: Yes.
Beth: No.
Cindy: Yes.
Ted: Yes.

Leader: What makes it hard to tell?

Cindy: I am afraid of what people would think of me.

Leader: I think that is true for many people. More important, though, is how you feel about what you did or what you are doing. How many of you answered "yes" because of things that you are doing currently? *(Maria, Ted, and Cindy indicate that they did.)* How can a person quit feeling guilty?

Ted: I don't see how I cannot feel guilty—it is wrong. I never thought it would go this far. *(Looks down)*

Leader: Ted, perhaps if you talk about it, you will see it differently. I urge each of you to talk about what you are feeling guilty about because there are solutions to guilt. You do not have to continually beat up on yourself. How much longer do you want to punish yourself?

Ted: You're right about the punishment. I hate it, but I feel so rotten.

Leader: From what you said earlier, Ted, my hunch is that it has to do with your marriage and possibly an affair. Others of you may have guilt over something in your marriage or your past that pertains to sexual issues.

Ted: That's it—you see, at work. . . .

In this example, the leader asked members to be more specific. The leader also made some comments and asked thought-provoking questions to get members to personalize the discussion. The leader kept exploring the topic until one person was moved enough to want to work on his issue.

Members of an eating-disorder group are talking about their problems with food.

Sally: When I am bored or upset I eat, and when I start eating I can't stop.

Lenny: That's true for me. I like all kinds of food, but cookies and candy are my real downfall.

Sara: My downfall is ice cream. My favorite is chocolate chip.

Najwa: Ice cream is one of my downfalls. Let's list our favorite downfalls. *(Everyone laughs.)*

Leader: *(In a slow, deliberate voice)* Rather than focusing on what your downfall is, I'd like each of you to think of how you lose control over your food intake. When does it occur, and how do you cause it to occur? Think about that for a minute. *(Pause)* Any thoughts?

In this example, the leader shifted the focus to a new, more personal topic because she saw that the group could get focused on a "surface" topic. As a result of the leader's question, each member has to think about him or herself. Too often, leaders will get caught up in the flow of the discussion and not direct the members to more personal and meaningful dialogue.

This group consists of members who all experience frequent panic attacks when they are out in public (agoraphobia). Three different members have been sharing about their intense fear.

Joe: . . . and as a result of those attacks, I have not been out of the house for longer than 4 hours in the last 5 years. I get out maybe once every 2 months. It's hell!

Leader: I think Joe is right. It *is* hell, and since you are all here for the same reason, I know that most of you feel the same way. One purpose of this group is to help you realize that you are not alone. The other purpose is to get you over your fears. To do this, we have to look at the causes of panic attacks, and what can be done about them. I want each of you to think about your panic attacks and the events and thoughts that occur right before they happen. Please comment on your understanding of what happens to you right before the attacks and during the attacks.

In this example, the leader is introducing a meaningful topic rather than just letting the members relate incidents from their lives. By focusing on what happens right before an attack, the members are more likely to share personal information and to get to pertinent issues.

The members are sharing events of the week without giving much thought to what they are saying.

Leader: I'd like to say something that I think will be helpful to each of you. *(Using a soft, encouraging voice)* We have three sessions left, so I want to urge you to really give some thought to what you want to talk about tonight. In the past few weeks, we have discussed a number of personal issues, and I want to encourage you to look into yourself and see if there are other issues that you may need to talk about. What obstacles are in the way of having your life go the way you want it to? Are there some fears or unfinished business from the past that you need to talk about? Really stretch yourself in these last sessions. Are there some things that you would like to bring up in this session?

Sandi: *(After about 20 seconds)* There is something I would like to bring up. It has to do with me and my appearance. . . .

Obtaining a Contract

The leader always needs to get a "contract" from an individual when the focus is going to be held on her for any length of time. By a *contract*, we simply mean that the member agrees to be the focus of the group's attention. When a leader senses that a member may benefit from being the focus, she might ask:

- Would you like to work on that?
- Would you like to discuss that for a few minutes?
- Would you like to understand that better?
- How can the group be of help to you?
- If we work with you on this issue for 20 minutes, what would be helpful?

The leader needs to be sure that there is a contract, because on many occasions leaders make the mistake of focusing on a person who is not ready or willing to work on the issue. Many times, a member will describe a problem or concern that appears to be severe enough to warrant help from the group. The severity of the problem or the emotional state of a member is not necessarily an indication of a desire to receive help. We have observed leaders who forego getting a contract and dive right into trying to help. As a result, suggestions are often met with a "Yes, but" response. Often, this becomes frustrating for the other group members.

There are several reasons why members share their problems but do not really want to work on them. First, some members have a history of blaming or externalizing their problems. These individuals have little desire to take charge of their own lives. Second, some members are frightened by the possibility of committing themselves to a plan of action in front of others. Third, some members tell a story to gain the sympathy of the group or to have others reinforce their position on some issue. The point is that there are many instances in which seemingly needy members do not want to receive the help of the group.

Use of Theories in Therapy Groups

When working with one member, the leader directs the personal work by using theories and other techniques to help the member gain insight and understanding about his problem. *No leader should lead counseling groups without an in-depth knowledge of counseling theories.* Unfortunately, many people who lead therapy groups do not have much experience in individual counseling or a background in counseling theories. They think the members will be the agent of change, and all they need to know is information about group process and group dynamics. This is not true. For instance, in groups for sexual abuse victims, agoraphobics, suicide patients, sex offenders, drug abusers, children of alcoholics, and codependents, members need a leader who has a complex understanding of their pain since they have no theoretical understanding of their problems. We encourage leaders to teach group members the basic tenets of one of the major counseling theories. We usually teach REBT and TA because these theories are very valuable in understanding human behavior and can be learned rather quickly by members regardless of age.

Very often in therapy groups, the focus is held on one member for 10 to 20 minutes (sometimes longer). During the time when the group is focusing on a member, there may be times when the leader chooses to conduct a few minutes of individual counseling. To do this, the leader needs to have the theoretical knowledge and skills to take the session deep enough so that the members are very much involved even though they may just be watching. (For leaders who do not yet have the ability to conduct interesting and engaging counseling, we suggest using the members' input rather than conducting slow-moving individual counseling while members just watch and listen.) Following are examples of theories being used.

◆ E X A M P L E S

This is a counseling group for eighth-grade girls talking about self-esteem. The leader has taught the members both REBT and TA. It is the fourth session.

Loretta: *(crying)* . . . I don't see how I can ever get over the fact that my mom left me and ran off with this man. If I am not enough to keep my mom, I know I can't keep a boyfriend! If I don't have a boyfriend, I am worthless.

Leader: Let's use that REBT model we learned a couple of weeks ago. Is Loretta telling herself things that are true, or is she using not true self-talk?

Jeanna: It's not true at all what she is saying. She thinks something is wrong with her because her mother met some guy and ran off with him. There's nothing wrong with you, Loretta.

Enid: Jeanna's right. You are telling yourself things that are not true, and that is what is upsetting you. It is not your mom or your not having a boyfriend, but rather it is your self-talk. Can we put it on the board like we did last time? Loretta, I don't have a boyfriend right now, and I don't feel worthless at all, so I know that sentence is not true.

Leader: Go ahead—you can use the board.

Iona: Can I say something?

Leader: Sure.

Iona: I used to feel the way you did because my father left home. Learning this self-talk model has really straightened me out. I used to beat myself up inside my head with all kinds of negative self-talk. Loretta, I am afraid you still believe the tapes in your head. *(Picks up a tape that is there as a prop to be used)* Will you try to edit your tape? We can help you. The group sure has helped me. *(Loretta has stopped crying and is listening. She also is staring at the tape.)*

Enid: I want to do the board thing. The first thing I want to write down on the true side is "I am smart, attractive, and fun" because that is true about you. *(Loretta is paying close attention and is obviously thinking.)*

Leader: Wait. Don't write that since the model is really for disputing her self-talk and not getting at positive characteristics. Enid, what you said is true about Loretta, but she is going to have to be able to dispute the sentences about being worthless because her mom left and she does not have a boyfriend.

Enid: *(Excited)* Oh, that's right. Having a boyfriend has nothing to do with my worth. How do we get that as a sentence?

Angie: On the true side it is something like, "I would like to have a boyfriend, but if I don't, I still am worthwhile." That's true as I see it.

In this example, the members know and are able to use the REBT model to help the member. The leader lets the members do the work unless they get stuck. The benefit of having the members know this theory is that they have a common language to use and a framework for understanding different problems that are presented.

This therapy group consists of members who have not yet adjusted to their divorce. The leader has decided to focus on one member. It is the third session, and the leader had taught TA during the last two sessions.

Mona: I am so afraid to go on a date. I am afraid I won't know what to say or do, and God forbid if he ever tried to kiss me. I had a guy ask me out after church, but I told him I was busy, and I just ran off to my car. This guy is a nice guy, and that scares me.

Leader: *(Pulling up the small child's chair that was used last week to represent the not-OK child ego-state)* Mona, you have to decide if you want to live your life from this seat, or from this one. *(Pulls up a regular size chair, glances around and sees everyone is staring at the two chairs)*

Mona: But I haven't dated another man in over 15 years.

Leader: Sit in the little chair. *(She does this.)* How does that feel?

Mona: Small and like I am a little girl.

Leader: You are not a little girl. You are a 33-year-old woman who has a full life ahead of her. Sit in the big chair.

Mona: I don't think I know how to act from that chair.

Leader: Can anyone sit in the big chair and play Mona who is afraid but not crippled by her fear?

Cassie: I think I can. *(Moves to the chair)* Boy, it's scary thinking about dating, but it is also exciting. I sure know more now than I knew when I was 18. I don't have to worry if he is going to like me—I just want to be myself and find a guy that I like. One who likes sports, doesn't drink or smoke, and someone who understands that I have a career that I love. *(Cassie knows Mona really well.)*

Leader: Anyone want to play the child part so Mona can watch this dialogue?

Shania: I can because this is me. I am also afraid. I don't think I can play the other part.

In this example, the leader used TA and the chairs to make the counseling concrete not only for Mona but also for the other members. Having the TA theory as a common language helps the counseling go better, and members can get involved with either Mona or themselves.

Ivan: I can't stand the way my parents fight, and I feel like I'm in the middle. I thought when they divorced, it would get better, but now I have to work that much harder to keep the peace. It's awful! I hate it! Why can't they stop?

Leader: Let's try to help. What were your reactions to what Ivan said?

Chris: Why do you feel you have to stop them? Why not stay out of it? I know my parents still fight, but I have learned, mostly from the group, that it is not my problem. I don't like their fighting, but now I walk away.

Ivan: But they drag me into it and then claim I am taking sides! The other day, Dad pumped me for 30 minutes about what Mom has been doing and what she has been saying about him.

Carla: I used to get that all the time until I finally said to each of them, "I will not tolerate your talking about the other one." This worked pretty well. They still do it some, but not nearly as much.

Ivan: I can't do that. I just think I should be able to help them.

Chris: Heck, you're just 15 years old! You're not a shrink.

Ivan: Yes, but I just feel—

Leader: Let me jump in here. *(In a kind, caring voice)* Ivan, do you really want help from us, or do you just want to talk about it and play sort of the "yes, but" game?

Ivan: I think so, but—

Leader: *(In a kind voice)* Do you hear Ivan's "yes, but"? Often, when faced with a problem, many people play the "yes, but" game. Each of you can think about this for yourself. Many of you are playing the "yes, but" game with yourselves. Ivan, let me ask you again, do you want help?

Ivan: *(With tears in his eyes)* Yes, I do. I don't know what to do.

Leader: I'm glad you want help. What do you think Ivan can do to feel better about his situation?

Andra: I would think he has to let go of the idea that he should be the one to fix his parents. They are grown-ups.

Ivan: But they are my parents. I can't stand to see them crying.

Leader: *(Realizing that to take Ivan deeper, she will need to take charge and use some counseling theory because the members don't know how to help)* Ivan, I think you can really benefit from hearing what everyone here is saying. It is not your job to fix your parents' situation, nor does it seem possible, given how you describe their behavior. Remember the TA model about the Parent, Adult, and Child? What we want to do is help you get an

Adult perspective on the situation. Right now I think most of what is happening to you is coming from your Child, the little boy who wants to please. *(Turning to the group)* I think most of you can see how Ivan's Adult ego state is contaminated by his Child ego state. You may want to think about yourself and see where your Child gives you trouble.

Carla: My Child is in the way big time when it comes to my brother. Can I tell you what happened?

Leader: Let's stay with Ivan for now, and then, Carla, you and others can comment on your insights. Let me use two chairs to represent the Adult and the Child.

The leader would then do some work with Ivan. She would continue using the TA theory and have the other members join in when appropriate, commenting from a TA perspective in reference either to Ivan or to themselves.

We could give many more examples of how theory is vital when focusing on an individual. Hopefully, these three examples underscore the value of theories and how much more effective groups are when the members know a theory. If you know the theories well, it is fairly easy to incorporate their use in groups. If you are looking for a specific book on the use of the different theories in groups, Corey (1995) has written an excellent one.

Techniques for Conducting Therapy in Groups
Techniques for Engaging the Members

In most situations when the focus is being held on one member, the skilled leader usually involves the other members in an active way. The leader does this because it keeps the members interested, it is therapeutic for members to be helpful to a fellow member, and members often have excellent ideas for the working member. Following are a number of techniques that can be used when the group is focused on one member.

Members ask questions Once a member has talked for a few minutes about the specific concern, the leader can use the technique of having the members ask the working member questions.

Leader: I want you to think of a question that would be helpful for Ralph to answer. Who has one?

Judy: I do. If your wife lost weight, would you feel more attracted to her? *(Ralph answers.)*

Carlos: Why do you think you can't develop a long-term relationship with the other woman? *(Ralph answers.)*

Sarah: If you rid yourself of the notion that divorce is wrong, would that help you make a decision? *(Ralph answers.)*

Members make guesses about what the problem is Another way to involve members and enable the working member to stop and think is to have the members guess what the problem is. The leader would use this technique when the member is being vague or confused.

Leader: I want you each to try to guess what Ralph's problem is. I am not sure, and I don't think Ralph is, so perhaps our guessing will help.

Judy: I think Ralph would really like to be divorced but is afraid of his parents' disapproval.

Carlos: I sense that Ralph is afraid to get divorced because he fears he will be left with nothing.

Sarah: I think Ralph is feeling guilty about the thought of leaving his kids and wife of 15 years.

There are a number of benefits from having members ask questions or guess what the specific concern might be.

- It gets the members involved and prevents them from becoming bored or disinterested.
- It breaks up the member's storytelling. (Many times, members will ramble without really concentrating on what the specific problem might be.)
- It enables the member to think about what she is saying.
- Good questions may be asked.
- The working member gets to hear how he might be feeling. This is especially true if some of the members are very good at pinpointing what the working member is feeling.
- The working member gets to feel understood if the other members are on target.
- While the members ask questions or make statements, the leader has time to think about the direction he believes the therapy needs to go.

It is important that the leader closely monitor the questions and guesses to make sure they are relevant and useful. Sometimes, the guesses are projections of how members would feel, based on their own values and past experiences.

Members role-play the working member A technique that is effective and also enables the members to be involved is to have the members role-play the working member. By this, we mean that another member acts as the working member. Here is how this may occur:

Leader: I would like someone to role play Ralph, using his body language and voice pattern so Ralph can see how he presents himself in the group. Be sure to speak in the first person singular, just as if you were Ralph. Try to feel what he is feeling based on what you have heard him say. *(After* *giving the members about a minute to think, the leader begins.)* Sarah, would you like to go first?

Sarah: I think that Ralph—

Leader: *(Cuts in)* Sarah, see if you can speak as if you were Ralph.

Sarah: *(Drops her head, slumps down in her chair, using a weak voice)* OK. I'm Ralph, and I'm real confused about what to do. I feel torn. Also, I feel guilty when I think about leaving my family. I'm not sure if this desire for a divorce will pass or not.

Leader: Are you tired of being so stuck? This has gone on for 2 years.

Sarah: *(In a weak voice with head still down)* I just don't know what to do. I really fear my father's wrath.

Ralph: Do I really look that pathetic?

Members: Yes!

Ralph: I had no idea that I was acting that way.

Creative use of members Members can be used in many creative ways that help to make the counseling more concrete and effective. The following techniques are for specific kinds of problems and would be used only if the timing was right and the activity fit the problem being presented.

- Members are asked to stand in front of the working member, who sits on the floor and looks up at the standing members. This activity would be used when a member expresses feelings of "less than" or insignificance in comparison with others. By seeing the other members standing, the seated member experiences visually what he is expressing. This often stimulates further discussion.

- Members can play various ego states of the working member. This technique assumes that the members have been taught the theory of TA. For example, if the working member appears afraid to take risks, the leader might appoint another member to play the working member's not-OK child ego state. In essence, the other members act as different ego states of the member.

- Members are asked to talk about the working member in a kind, caring way while the member listens. (If the leader feels it would be helpful, the member may be told to close his or her eyes or face away from the group to facilitate listening.) This gives the member a chance to hear how others see him or her or the problem. To facilitate this, the leader would say, "Jeff, I want you to close your eyes and just listen as we talk about your situation. *(To the others)* What do you think of Jeff's situation and how he is handling it?"

- If a member does not feel part of the group, the leader may have the group stand in a circle holding hands and have the member walk around the outside of the circle with the option of asking or "fighting" to break into the circle. This can be very effective if the issue is feeling left out or not knowing how to be a productive member of the group.

- An experiential technique could also be used with a member who feels held down by all of his obligations and responsibilities. To help the member experience this, the leader might have the member sit on the floor, with four or five other members holding him down. The leader instructs the member to experience the feeling and then decide on a course of action. Some members do nothing; others fight very hard to break free. The experience usually proves valuable to the member and often to other members as well. This exercise should only be used by an experienced therapist and must be used with great caution since it often evokes the emotional release of some deep-seated pain from childhood or former relationships.

   ♦ Another effective way for experientially helping a member is to use drama to act out a scene that the member is worried about, such as a job interview or a conversation with her parents. (Members would play the supervisors or parents.) The person can get feedback and then try the scene again. In some cases, the leader may get another member to play the working member's role to give the individual a chance to view how the conversation could be handled more effectively.

   ♦ Psychodramatic enactments are conducted using other group members to portray the different people in the protagonist's (working member's) life. Psychodrama involves exploring in action not only historical events but, more importantly, dimensions of psychological events. Psychodramatic enactments are usually quite intense since they often involve reworking traumatic experiences, memories, or unpleasant or puzzling events. Psychodrama is a valuable tool for therapy groups, but a detailed discussion is beyond the scope of this book. We encourage you to read any of the many excellent books on psychodrama (Blatner, 1988a; Blatner, 1988b; Moreno, 1964).

   ♦ Members are asked to pull on the working member's arms to symbolize feelings of being pulled in two directions. The following dialogue illustrates this example.

Dan: I just feel pulled, you know? A part of me wants to get married because . . . *(States the reasons)* Another part of me doesn't. *(States the reasons)* I just can't seem to make up my mind.

Leader: Bill, you and Tom stand up. Dan, you stand too. Bill, I want you to stand on one side of Dan and take his arm, and in a minute I want you to tug on his arm, saying all the reasons why Dan wants to marry. Do this as if you were Dan—that is, in the first person. Tom, you get on the other side and pull on the other arm, saying all the reasons why Dan does not want to marry. OK, begin.

What happens is that Bill and Tom talk and pull Dan's arms simultaneously. Thus, Dan feels pulled in both directions. Dan is merely instructed to listen to each side and pay attention to the sensation of feeling pulled. He is also instructed to pay particular attention to whether one side of the issue emerges as more powerful or persuasive than the other side. Note that using techniques such as the one just described requires that the leader make sure that everyone knows his or her part. The working member must not experience merely two people pulling on his arms but rather the mental struggle between two sides of an issue.

This technique may seem like a gimmick or a slapstick routine if the leader does not set the tone properly. The leader must explain the purpose of the technique and remain serious about carrying it out, even if the members laugh or snicker.

The Use of Therapeutic Rounds

A therapeutic round differs from the rounds described in Chapter Nine in that, in a therapeutic round, the working member is the one completing the round. The following descriptions of therapeutic rounds should make this clear to you.

The in-depth, stationary round   This is a round in which the working member says something to each member of the group while remaining in his seat.

The first type of in-depth, stationary round is one in which the working member makes the same statement to each member. The members serve as a sounding board for the working member by listening as the member repeats a belief that he has.

◆ E X A M P L E

Ralph has been talking for about 10 minutes, and one of his concerns is his parents' reaction to a divorce.

Leader: Ralph, I would like you to turn to each member, starting with Sarah on your immediate left, and say, "I'm afraid to get a divorce because of what my parents will think."

Ralph: *(To Sarah)* I'm afraid to get a divorce because of what my parents will think.

Leader: Now, look at Carl and say the same thing. And then repeat it to Judy, Liz, and Asel.

Ralph: *(To Carl)* I'm afraid to get a divorce because of what my parents will think.

Ralph: *(Looks at Judy, obviously thinking)* I'm afraid to get a divorce because of what my parents will think.

Ralph: *(To Liz)* I'm afraid to get a divorce because of well, uh, this is nuts! I have got to live my life for me. My parents are not unhappily married—I am!

By saying the same thing over and over, Ralph gets a chance to listen to himself. It is important to note that in this type of round the members do not say anything. They merely act as listeners. By repeating something out loud to others, a working member is usually able to gain some insight about his thoughts and feelings.

The second type of in-depth, stationary round is one in which the working member turns to each member and completes the same sentence stem.

◆ E X A M P L E

Kara has been talking about how she is not good enough.

Leader: Kara, let's clarify what you mean. So far, you are being kind of vague. Here's what I want you to do. I want you to look at each member and start with, "I am not good enough because," and then complete the phrase. Start with Marj.

Kara: *(Looking at Marj)* I am not good enough because I am not pretty.

Leader: Now, look at Nan and start the same way.

Kara: *(Looking at Nan)* I am not good enough because I am not smart.

Kara: *(Looking at Dee)* I am not good enough because, uh, *(looks down)* my family does not have as much money as most of my friends *(tears up)*.

Leader: Is that what bothers you the most?

By having the member do this type of in-depth, stationary round, she can be more specific about what she is concerned about. It helps the group understand her, and it usually helps the member to better understand how she is thinking and feeling. Using the members is more powerful than having her just talk to the group, and also the members feel more involved.

The third type of in-depth, stationary round is one in which the working member responds to a repeated question from the other members.

◆ E X A M P L E

Leader: I want each of you to ask Charlie the following question: "Charlie, does being gay make you less of a person?" *(Pauses and sees that Bonita is ready.)* Bonita, you go first and ask Charlie that question. Charlie, you look at Bonita and respond to the question. Then look at the next person.

Bonita: Charlie, does being gay make you less of a person?

Charlie: Everybody in my family thinks it does.

Leader: Look at Meg. Meg, you ask Charlie the exact same question.

Meg: Charlie, does being gay make you less of a person?

Charlie: I don't want to think that I am less.

Leader: Turn to Jenny.

Jenny: Charlie, does being gay make you less of a person?

Charlie: *(In a very thoughtful voice)* I thought I had resolved this, but it is clear to me that I haven't. I need to get clear as to what I believe.

❖❖❖

A fourth type of in-depth, stationary round is one in which each member asks a different question of the working member, using the round format.

◆ E X A M P L E

Leader: I want each of you to think of one question that you want to ask Jesse in terms of what he is saying about his guilt. Try to make the question one that will cause him to really think about what he is saying and feeling. Who wants to start with a question? Jesse, make your answers brief. Faith, we'll start with you, and we'll go around the group, and each person will ask Jesse a question about his guilt.

Faith: Jesse, do you think you can ever be forgiven for the accident?

Jesse: No, I don't ever deserve to be happy given that I killed three people when I was drunk.

Wayne: Do you think your guilt is helping anyone?

Jesse: Well, no, but I am not sure what you mean.

Wayne: What I was . . .

Leader: Wayne, hold off. Let's go on.

Justin: If you don't think you can ever get over this, then why are you here, and why do you continue to go to church?

Jesse: *(Pauses, head drops)* I so much want to get over this pain.

Justin: You can if you will let yourself be helped by us and by God.

Anne: *(With a caring but irritated voice)* Why do you think you are the only one who has done a bad thing? In our own way, each of us here has plenty to feel guilty about, so why do you think you are so special?

Jesse: *(Somewhat taken aback. With a shaky voice)* I just haven't thought of it the way you are getting me to. I sure don't feel special, and I do want help. *(Tears up)*

Often members will ask good questions that enable the working member to explore the concern in greater depth. In addition, this allows the other members to be more involved.

The in-depth, movement round   In contrast to the in-depth, stationary round in which the working member remains in a stationary position, the in-depth, movement round involves the member moving in front of each of the other members, thus intensifying the experience. This kind of round is one of the most powerful techniques for producing intense, in-depth exploration. Moving in front of the other members creates a potent atmosphere that often enables the working member to gain insight. During these rounds, there will be times when the leader will ask the members to sit silently as the person makes the round. Other times, the leader will instruct the members to ask a certain question or to respond in a specific way, such as "No, it doesn't mean that." The role of the members will depend on the content of the specific round and the purpose that it is serving.

◆ E X A M P L E S

Sherry has been talking about not liking herself but has been vague.

Leader: Sherry, I want you to sit in front of each member and say, "I don't like myself because _____."

Sherry: *(Moves in front of Pam)* I don't like myself because I am fat.

Sherry: *(Moves in front of Kate)* I don't like myself because my teeth are ugly.

Sherry: *(Moves in front of Beth)* I don't like myself because my parents never liked me. *(Starts to cry. Beth starts to reach out and take her hand, but the leader shakes his head "no" because he believes Beth would be trying to "rescue" Sherry from her pain.)*

Sherry: *(Moves in front of Patty)* I don't like myself, oh, I don't know if I can say it. *(Cries more and looks down.)* I don't like myself because of what my father did to me when I was growing up.

Leader: Was it sexual?

Sherry: *(Sobbing, looking down)* Yes!

Leader: *(In a calm, firm voice)* Sherry, I want you to look up and see the others' faces. No one here thinks less of you. Look up—don't watch that movie that says "Sherry's a horrible person." *(Sherry slowly looks up.)*

In this example, the round serves as a way to get the member into her feelings. The leader also used a couple of other skills. First, he continued to push the member even though she had begun to cry. Often, in groups when a member cries, the other members and leader make the mistake of rushing to support the member, causing the work to cease. There are times when a person in pain needs to struggle with her pain.

The second skill was having Sherry look up right after she disclosed the sexual abuse. By doing this, the leader did not allow Sherry to reinforce her negative feelings by watching negative images in her mind. Also, by seeing the faces of concerned, caring members, Sherry could experience that they did not think less of her. This latter technique obviously requires that members in the group be empathic and sensitive.

Vicente has been talking about how he feels worthless because he was put up for adoption when he was 4. The leader has been challenging Vicente's irrational, self-defeating belief and thinks that Vicente may be about to give up this belief.

Leader: Vicente, I want you to sit in front of each member and answer the question "How does being adopted make you worthless?" Each of you ask Vicente that question. Vicente, start with Bonnie.

Bonnie: Vicente, how does being adopted make you worthless?

Vicente: Well, if they loved me, they would have kept me.

Leader: Vicente, move to Donna. Donna, ask him the same question, and if he does not answer the question, try to get him to be more specific.

Donna: Vicente, how does being adopted make you worthless?

Vicente: If your parents give you away, you are worthless.

Donna: You said that they gave you away because they just could not handle their own lives and they had no money! Now, how does that make you worthless?

Vicente: I don't know. I feel it.

Leader: Go the next person. Calvin, try to ask something that will challenge Vicente's thinking.

Calvin: I don't believe being adopted makes you less of a person. My closest friend is adopted, and he certainly doesn't feel worthless, and I don't think he's worthless.

Vicente: Well, uh, maybe I've been seeing this all wrong. I think I'm getting the point.

To reiterate, the use of in-depth, movement rounds can be very beneficial when they are used at the right time and with the right kind of problem. A leader should only use the in-depth, movement round when she is trying to get a member in touch with some intense feelings or thoughts.

Spinning Off

When the focus is being held on one member, the leader should constantly be thinking about ways to get others involved in either the member's work or in their own work. To get members involved in their own work, the leader will periodically seek comments from them while putting the working member "on hold." We call this *spinning off*. To do this, the leader might say the following:

Leader: David, I want you to think about what you have said in the last few minutes while I hear from others. *(Looking at the other members)* What has this made you think about in reference to yourself?

This question serves a number of purposes: (1) members get to share what is on their minds (at this time, the leader would not focus on a new person because he has the other member on hold), (2) the leader gains information about how many others are ready or almost ready to work, (3) the sharing can be helpful to the working member, and (4) the working member gets some time to collect his thoughts before the leader comes back to him.

Another way that the leader spins off is by making a few comments to the group about what the working member is saying:

Leader: Let me comment on what you are saying, Joe. Joe is talking about his part in weekly fights over household chores. Each of you may want to think about any routine fights that you have and the part that you play in those fights. It is really important that you understand your part in a fight. If you can see how you contribute to any fight, then I think many of you will choose to change. Joe, let's get back to you.

Spinning off to the members is *essential*. By making thought-provoking comments to the members and eliciting their comments about themselves, the leader can cause more members to be thinking about themselves and thus be ready to share when the current person's work is completed.

In the preceding sections, we discussed many ways the leader can involve the members when the focus is being held on an individual. *Too often, leaders just conduct individual counseling and do not take advantage of all the possible ways to involve the members.* It is very important to realize that much of the help that members receive in a counseling group comes from the sharing, caring, supporting, and challenging that takes place. Also, the leader has a much greater chance of helping and keeping the members' interest when he involves the other group members.

Techniques for Helping More Than One Member at the Same Time

There will be occasions in therapy groups—or even growth and support groups—when two members will be in need of help at the same time, often concerning the same issue. For example, let's say the members of a therapy group are sharing about guilt. One of the members, Susan, gets in touch with some old feelings of guilt about an abortion. As she begins to talk about her abortion and her sense of guilt, another member, Donna, begins to cry and says that her tears are about an abortion she had 2 years ago. At this point the leader has several options:

- ◆ Ask Donna if she can wait until the work is completed with Susan.
- ◆ Ask Susan if it is OK to shift to Donna, since her pain seems greater.
- ◆ Work with both of them at the same time.
- ◆ Ask a co-leader or another member to go to another area of the room with one of the two members.

The first and second options require that the leader hold the focus on one member until her concerns have been alleviated enough to switch the focus to the other. In the preceding example, there may be no need to do this since their problems are similar, but in an instance in which one person is talking about guilt over an abortion and another brings up guilt over her husband's suicide, the leader may find it extremely difficult to deal with these issues simultaneously. The leadership skill required in this situation is knowing how to put one member on hold. This is done by being straightforward with the two members and asking if one can wait. If the leader feels both members need immediate attention, she may use the last option, which is to get help from a co-leader or another member.

In many instances, the concerns are so similar that it would save time and benefit the two members for the leader to work with both of them simultaneously. Instead of only one member being the main focus of the group, there are two. Sometimes, the leader will have one or both of the working members complete an in-depth round and then have them talk about each other's round. Or the leader may have the two members give advice or suggestions to one another. The leader could have the working members complete a sentence stem, such as "Because I had an abortion, it means I am _____." The leader could have the members answer to each other or to the other members. At other times, the leader will do an in-depth, stationary round by having the members ask each working member the same question, such as "Why does having an abortion make you less of a person?" The benefit of working with two members simultaneously is that each member sees another person in the same situation and will most likely identify with the therapy being done or will recognize her own faulty thinking by seeing the faulty thinking of the other.

Techniques for Working with Individuals Indirectly

At times in therapy groups, the leader will do therapy in an indirect manner with one or more members. Indirect counseling may be helpful for a member who does not feel comfortable being the focus of the group. Let's assume that one of a group's members, Rita, had a friend who died tragically 2 years ago. Although Rita has never mentioned this in the group, she did write about it briefly one time in the journal that she leaves at the end of each session. Rita has not participated much verbally and has never been the focus of the group. If the leader does not think Rita wants to work on the issue in the group, he has a couple of options for working with her indirectly.

- He can bring up the issue of death and grieving to get a discussion going, and hope that this will be therapeutic and may even prompt Rita to share.
- He can work with another member who has a grief issue, knowing that the work will probably be beneficial to Rita.

If the leader chooses the second option, the group will focus on a member's pain over a death. While working with that member, the leader would observe any reactions from Rita in the hope that the work being done will trigger Rita to open up and request help. Or, using dyads, the leader could pair the working member with Rita. Both of these methods may be successful in getting the silently working member to share.

If these methods are not successful in drawing out comments from the targeted silent member, the leader should keep in mind that members benefit from hearing others, whether or not they actively discuss their own personal concerns. Hearing the concerns and coping strategies of the other members can indirectly help the working member.

Therapy That Focuses on Process

Throughout this chapter, we have emphasized the focus on individual problems when conducting counseling groups. We do want to mention that there will be many times during a therapy group when focusing on group process will be therapeutic. By focusing on process, we mean focusing on what members are doing or feeling in the group. For instance, a member may constantly try to one-up everything that is said. Feedback from the members can be very therapeutic. Or a member may ramble, and the leader or another member may point this out to the rambler in hopes that he may get some insight on how he comes across to people. In some groups, some members are afraid of what others will think, so the leader may want to focus on this as a topic. Feelings of being one down, not being a part of the group, or fear of rejection are all potential material that is therapeutic to discuss. Conflict or tension among the members can be turned into therapeutic gains if the leader handles the subject well. The skilled leader is always paying attention to process as well as content and will focus on group process when it seems necessary and valuable to do so.

◆ E X A M P L E

This leader has noticed that there has been little energy in the group during the session, and no one is sharing anything very personal. She has been aware that the last couple of times when someone did share, a couple of members—Sheena and Gerta—were quick to offer some judgmental comments. These two members have been the kind of members who bring up problems but then resist help from the group.

Leader: What do you think is happening here in the group? *(Silence)* It is clear to me that no one is saying much of importance, and I am going to guess that it has to do with something that is going on in here.

Gerta: Maybe no one has any problems. That is possible you know. I can always talk about my dad, but he's always going to make me mad.

Leader: *(Ignoring the issue with the dad)* I know that some of you have issues that we could talk about, but I think it is more important that we discuss what is happening here and why. I want each of you to think about how it feels being in group.

Sheena: *(Responds very quickly)* It feels fine. I like it here. It's a little boring today, but I think we—

Leader: *(Cutting off Sheena with a thought-provoking voice)* Wait just a second. Take some time to think about your feelings.

Suzie: I don't like coming here as much as I did at first. I don't know why.
(Evelyn and Barb nod in agreement.)

Leader: Let's explore that. What is different now than 3 weeks ago? Evelyn, you were agreeing with Suzie.

Evelyn: I am not as comfortable.

Leader: Everyone, think about your feelings and why you are having them. Very often, the feelings you have in the group are similar to feelings you have at home or here at school.

Barb: I feel a tightness in my chest that I often feel when I visit my dad and stepmom.

Leader: Did you feel that when the group first began?

Barb: I did, but after the first couple of sessions, I didn't feel the tightness; but it is back.

Leader: Could it have to do with fear of approval or fear of being judged? *(Barb looks down, with a scared look.)*

Millie: I think it has to do with what happened last session and how some of us are feeling judged. I personally don't like it when some members judge others.

Leader: Why don't you say that specifically to the members you think did that. I don't want people to feel attacked, but I do think that some feedback and discussion can be beneficial for everyone here in the group.

Millie: Well, uh, okay, what the heck. Gerta, you and Sheena last week. . . .

The leader would get others to comment on how they were feeling. Also, the leader would focus on what happened last week, what is happening this week, and relate it to how the feelings are probably similar to feelings they have in other places. The leader would focus on both the feeling of being judged and the judgmental behaviors of Sheena and Gerta. The focus on process is essential for rebuilding trust and also is valuable therapeutically in that members are saying how they feel and confronting each other in a safe environment.

Intense Therapy

In this chapter, we have discussed therapy in many ways—from helpful insight to deep therapy. Many counseling groups, such as those in schools, are not aimed at intense therapy. However, many therapy groups have as their goal deep, personal work; that is, the leader funnels the group to individual work at a level of 4 or below on the depth chart. In these groups, the leader usually directs much of the therapy because the members are limited in their ability to be helpful. They can share and offer good suggestions or insights, but if the therapeutic process goes deep enough, the members will not know how to be helpful. For instance, in groups of recovery from incest, rape, or abuse, we use a variety of techniques, including Gestalt, psychodrama, or in-depth rounds, to get at the deep-seated emotions. We then use REBT, TA, Gestalt, and other theories along with some creative techniques to help the client work through the pain. Any leader who is getting members to look at their buried emotions has to know how to help the members get through their pain. Stated another way: *Do not unzip members unless you know how to zip them back up!*

If you plan to work in settings where you will be doing some intensive group therapy, we strongly suggest that you become knowledgeable and skilled as an individual therapist. *Intense group therapy requires that you have good individual counseling skills.* We also suggest that you read some of the literature on psychodrama since it includes many skills and techniques that can be used to help members get in touch with some deep-seated issues. It is these skills, coupled with the ideas in this book, that will make you a good group therapist.

Providing Therapy in a Nontherapy Group

At the beginning of this chapter, we mentioned that therapy may take place in nontherapy groups. Quite often in groups in which the purpose is something other than counseling, the opportunity will arise to focus on one member's concern. Topics discussed in a support group or even a discussion or education group can enable members to get in touch with unfinished and/or painful issues.

The first thing that a leader must do when the opportunity for counseling arises in a nontherapy group is to decide whether therapy would be appropriate. If the leader decides it is appropriate to focus on one member's concern—that is, the topic is relevant to the other members—and if there is enough time, she should ask the member if he desires immediate help. She would also want to ask the other members if they are willing to spend some time focusing on one member's problem. Once the leader has consent from the members, she will use many of the skills and techniques outlined in this chapter. The following are examples of when it might be appropriate to hold the focus on one member and do some brief therapeutic work in a nontherapy group.

- If a member of an education group for pregnant teenagers starts crying about how she hates being pregnant, the leader might choose to work with her for a few minutes because, more than likely, others are having similar feelings.
- If a member of an experiential group that is doing the ropes course shares how bad he felt about himself when he was growing up, the leader might decide to funnel the group to a deeper level by focusing on this member.
- If a member of a parenting group discloses that she feels guilty because her baby was the result of an affair that her husband does not know about, the leader might want to take a few minutes and try to be helpful since the topic is guilt, which is something that most people can relate to. Working with the member from a theoretical base could prove to be valuable for all the members.

The benefits of conducting therapy in nontherapy groups are very much the same as for therapy groups. The main difference is that the therapy portion of the group is short-term. The focus is then brought back to the main purpose of the group.

Common Mistakes Made When Leading Therapy Groups

Several errors are common among leaders of therapy groups. These errors have been discussed earlier in the chapter or in other chapters, but because they are so important, we want to review them briefly.

Attempting to Conduct Therapy without a Contract

Many leaders attempt to focus on a member of the group without first getting agreement from that person. The result is that the member resists the leader's attempt to be helpful, time is wasted, and members become frustrated and even resentful.

Not Involving the Other Members

One of the most common mistakes made by beginning leaders is to conduct individual counseling with a member without involving the other members. It is a mistake to have members sit and listen while the counselor tries to be helpful to one member unless the leader is very skilled at taking the counseling to a deep level, using theory and a multisensory approach. By using these, the other members will be able to relate to their own problems or become very involved in the intense work. Whenever possible, it is best to involve members in some way rather than have them be totally passive.

Spending Too Much Time on One Person

Some leaders make the mistake of spending week after week trying to help one member who is in pain, or spending too much of the session on one member. It is important for the leader to realize that some members seek and/or need inordinate attention from the group. The natural tendency of the leader is to focus on those individuals, especially if other members are not as talkative. The skilled leader keeps a mental record of how much time is being spent with the various members.

Spending Too Little Time on One Person

Many beginning leaders will be hesitant to hold the focus on one member when others also want to share. When this happens, one member shares for a minute or so, then another member, then another member. Sometimes this is helpful and valuable, but at other times this type of sharing is not as personal as when the focus is held on one member. Holding the focus on one member causes him to delve more deeply into his problem, which in turn often causes other members to look more closely at their own concerns.

Focusing on an Irrelevant Topic

Too often, the leader will let a member ramble on about a personal experience, even if the story has no relevance to the group. The leader might even ask the member questions about the story or have other members ask questions. A similar mistake occurs when two or three members are focused on some irrelevant topic, and the leader fails to shift the focus. It is important to realize that if the leader does not cut off certain topics and individuals, the session is likely to be much less meaningful for the majority of the members.

Letting Members Rescue Each Other

Earlier, we gave an example of "rescuing behavior." If a member begins to cry, it is often a mistake for another member or the entire group to immediately rush to the member's side, take his hand, and try to comfort him. The leader should discourage this type of behavior when it is antitherapeutic. Many times, the member needs to be with his pain instead of being "rescued" from it. The members should show support, care, and concern, but should not rescue. The leader prevents rescuing by saying something like, "Let Mike be with his pain—I think he knows that we care. Mike, do realize that we care and want to help." As we also discussed earlier, there are times when supportive touching is quite appropriate and very therapeutic—leaders need to know the difference.

Letting the Session Become an Advice-Giving Session

Very often in groups, leaders make the mistake of turning the session into an advice-giving session. That is, a member will bring up a problem, and then all the other members will try to solve it by giving advice. This is *not* what a therapy group is supposed to be. Sometimes advice is given and is helpful, but by and large each member should work on his or her own concerns with the help of the other members. Advice-giving sessions often occur when the leader does not know theories and thus relies on the members' advice to be the agent of change.

Concluding Comments

Counseling and therapy groups are different from support and growth groups in that the leader focuses on the members in an in-depth manner. The main purpose of counseling and therapy groups is to help members alleviate personal concerns that interfere with quality living. Many of the techniques discussed for therapy may also be used in nontherapy groups.

The approach we have described for leading counseling groups emphasizes the leader as being responsible for the therapy. The leader of a counseling group should be in charge because she is more knowledgeable about counseling and therapeutic techniques.

When one member is exploring a problem in depth, the leader can use a variety of skills and techniques. He can use his individual counseling skills to help the member clarify and work through the problem. He can also use the other members to play various roles, or he can use himself to help dramatize the problem. It is the leader's responsibility to establish a positive tone for the members and to get a contract from a member before focusing intensely on him or her.

Once there is an agreement to work on a concern, the leader may need to help the member clarify the problem, using any of a number of techniques, such as having the member engage in a clarifying round or having the other members ask the working member questions. A very valuable technique when working with an individual on a concern is the in-depth, therapeutic stationary or movement round. When conducting individual therapy in a group, it is important to spin off to the group and hear members' personal reactions and get them involved in trying to help the working member. By spinning off and pointing out the themes, the leader keeps members more interested, and this usually enables them to be ready to share when the focus shifts from the working member. We view the leader as the conductor of the group who orchestrates the focus on different members and topics.

CHAPTER FOURTEEN

Closing a Session
or Group

Two kinds of closings are discussed in this chapter: the closing of a session and the closing of the entire series of sessions. The *closing phase* is the period of a session when the leader wraps things up until the next meeting. The *closing stage* may be the last session of the group or the last few sessions, depending on the kind of group and the total number of sessions involved.

The Closing Phase

Every session should have a closing phase. The length of the closing phase will depend on both the length of the session and the kind of group being led. Usually, the longer the session, the more time is required. For a 1-hour session, the leader may find 3 to 5 minutes is enough; a 2- to 3-hour session may require 5 to 10 minutes for the closing phase. The closing phase of a discussion or task group may simply be summarizing the main ideas or decisions made. Since this is fairly straightforward, less time is required. In a support or therapy group in which members share a range of thoughts and feelings, more time is required to pull together key points, clarify goals, check for unfinished business, and encourage reactions. With experience, the leader learns to judge the amount of time needed to bring closure to the session.

During the closing phase, the leader has the opportunity to encourage members to share their thoughts and feelings about the session. In general, sharing during the closing phase can contribute to a greater sense of involvement with the group and cohesiveness among members. Members may share how they benefited from activities or discussion that took place during the session or from comments made by other members. It is especially important for the leader to hear from those members who were less verbal in the session. The leader can benefit from hearing how they feel about what is taking place and whether they are feeling comfortable. Also, because less active members may be perceived negatively, their sharing can help link them to the group and enable other members to gain some better understanding of who they are and how they are experiencing the group.

It is important to inform the members that the session is entering the closing phase. This can be done by saying any of the following:

- We need to start winding down, so I want you to think about the session today and what it has meant to you.
- Since there are only a few minutes left in today's session, let's review what we have gone over.
- I think we are at a good stopping point, so let's spend the next few minutes summarizing the session today, and then we'll talk briefly about next week's session.
- Let's begin the closing phase of the session because we need to stop in about 10 minutes.

Purposes and Goals of the Closing Phase

The closing phase may serve one or more of the following purposes: (1) summarizing and highlighting the main points, (2) reinforcing commitments made by individual members, and (3) checking for unfinished business from the session.

Summarizing and Highlighting the Main Points

One purpose of the closing phase is to pull the session together by highlighting and summarizing important points. For example, in discussion or task groups, key ideas or decisions can be highlighted. In education groups, members may focus on what they learned and what impact this new information may have on their lives. Members of support, growth, counseling, or therapy groups can look back on what helped them. Pulling together salient points or experiences helps members remember them after the session has ended; the impact of the session can thus be increased. Having the group focus on key points also gives members a chance to hear what was important to others. This sharing often tends to build greater trust and cohesiveness among members.

Reinforcing Commitments

In many groups, members may make commitments to some task or change in their behavior. Reviewing such commitments in the closing phase is valuable. The following two examples show how a leader might clarify goals and strengthen commitments.

◆ E X A M P L E S

It is the end of the second session of a task group made up of members who work at a mental-health agency. Their task is to develop a new residential program for adolescents.

Leader: Let's review who is to do what. Joe, what are you going to do before the next meeting?

Joe: I am going to call those two agencies that have residential programs and find out what problems they have had.

Leader: Good. See if they'll send you any material, too.

Pablo: I am going to draw up a tentative list of rules for the unit that the residents would have to live by.

Leader: Be sure to get input from us, especially from Cindy since she worked in a residential program.

Cindy: I am going to devise a list of personnel who would be needed to staff such a unit.

Bill: I'm going to try to get funding for the unit.

Leader: Bill, I think what we decided was that you were to look into possible sources for funding and that you would bring that list to the group. Then we, as a group, would decide the best route to take to get the unit funded.

It is the third session of a therapy group. Members have shared a variety of concerns during the session, and the leader wishes to clarify members' goals and reinforce their commitments to those goals.

Leader: Each of you in today's session has expressed a desire to change an aspect of your life. Three or four of you worked on specific goals you want to follow through on before our next meeting. As we close today, let's take a few minutes and briefly hear from each of you about your goals.

Chang: I want to go home this weekend and not fight with my mother. And I now think I've got some ways to avoid fighting.

Leader: You sound pretty committed to that, Chang. I'd like to suggest you keep notes and report back to us on how that works. *(Chang nods)* Who else feels they might try something different this week? *(Pause)*

John: *(Looks around at the group)* Well, I know I've got to do something about staying out so late.

Leader: What did you decide as a result of discussing it here today?

John: I am going to discuss with my wife which days are better for her to have me stay out late.

Leader: Didn't you also say that first you have to see if she will agree to your staying out at least two nights, and that you are going to ask her if she would like to come with you?

John: That's right! I forgot that part, and it's important.

Leader: You bet it is. You have it now, so what are you going to do?

John: I'll talk to her and really try to be open with her.

Leader: Fine; we'll look forward to hearing at our next session how it went.

In both of these examples the leader increases the likelihood that the members will follow through on their commitments. A good closing phase is necessary to review and clarify decisions made during the working phase of the session. Sometimes members make commitments and plans that are unrealistic. Reviewing various members' commitments and plans during the closing phase allows such unrealistic goals to be clarified. The following are two examples of a leader helping a member modify an unrealistic goal.

◆ EXAMPLES

It is the third session of a personal growth group in a college counseling center. During the closing phase of the session, the leader asks various members about their goals.

Leader: I think we've summarized what we covered today pretty well. In the next few minutes, it might be helpful if people share specific goals that they are shooting for this week. Betty, I know you decided to try a different approach with your boyfriend when he's late.

Betty: Today I learned that yelling only gets us into a fight. When he is late, I'm going to calmly tell him that I'm disappointed and that I'm only willing to wait for 20 minutes. I feel better knowing I can be in control.

Leader: Frieda, how about you? You said you wanted to set up a study schedule. Have you come up with any thoughts about how you might do that?

Frieda: I decided I'm going to study 6 hours every night. That should really help me catch up.

Leader: *(Turning to the other members)* What do you think about Frieda's plan?

Will: That seems like a lot. I'd get burned out in one day. *(Other members nod in agreement)*

Leader: What do you think, Frieda?

Frieda: Well, maybe that is a lot. I guess I'll start with 2 hours and see how that goes. Anything will be an improvement.

By helping the member develop a realistic goal, the leader has increased the likelihood of her success.

During the session, Al discussed his desire for a salary increase. With the help of the group, he role played strategies for talking with his employer about the raise. Although he made progress, Al needed further assistance in increasing his assertiveness and in exploring ways to handle potential rebuffs and excuses from his boss. The group is now in the closing phase.

Leader: Who else learned something from today's session?

Al: Boy, I did. That role playing about asking for a raise really helped. Even though you think I am not ready, I do. I think I'll go in tomorrow and ask for the raise!

Leader: Al, if he says no, what are you going to say? We didn't get a chance to practice that.

Al: Oh, I didn't even think of that. All I was thinking about was how I now know what to say. You're right. I'm not prepared for a negative answer. I'll wait till we talk about it next week in group.

If the leader had not clarified the member's goal during the closing phase, Al would probably have asked for a raise even though he had not developed the resources to cope with the situation. By reviewing Al's reaction to the session, the leader was able to discover his unrealistic plan and caution him about moving ahead prematurely.

Checking for Unresolved Issues (Unfinished Business)

The closing phase is also the time to check with members for any issues that are not fully resolved during the session. That is, issues are brought up that may need some additional closure as the session comes to an end. The leader may have found it unproductive to focus for too long a time on a particular member or issue and thus brought temporary closure to the discussion. The closing phase may be used to refocus on that previous issue or concern, providing an opportunity for the member to express new thoughts or for the leader to help the member agree to continue to work on the issue in the next session. Occasionally, a member may have unfinished business that cannot wait until the following session, either because a decision is imminent or because the issue is causing considerable discomfort for the member. The leader could ask the members if they would be willing to extend the session to work on the issue. If this cannot be done, the leader may see the member individually as soon after the session as possible.

To find out if members have unfinished business from the session, the leader could say something like:

- Does anyone have something that got "stirred up" during the session that they want to mention? We'll either deal with it now if it won't take too long, or we will deal with it at the next session.
- Is there any unfinished business from the session that you think needs to be discussed for a few minutes?

Because there are time constraints during the closing phase, the leader may need to carry unfinished business into the next session. However, by having members mention their unfinished business, the leader can either help them finish the issue or assure them that they will be able to discuss the matter at the next session.

◆ EXAMPLES

During a counseling group at a rehabilitation center, John expressed some angry feelings regarding his parents' not visiting him often enough, but he was not able to see how he was making himself upset by blaming his parents. After working with John for about 20 minutes, the leader chose to focus on another member. Now, during the closing phase, the leader wants to see if John has had any additional thoughts about his anger toward his parents.

Leader: We'll spend the next few minutes bringing things to a close for today. I'd like each of you to think about what stood out for you. *(Pauses and scans the group. After a short silence, the leader makes eye contact with John.)* John, I felt there were more feelings you had to express about your parents. While we don't have time to work a lot more with those feelings today, do you have additional thoughts you would like to share with the group?

John: I feel better after talking about it, but I still think they should visit more. I don't feel as angry.

Leader: I'd like you to keep thinking about this between now and our next session. We'll bring it up next week and see if we can help you work on it more. *(John nods in agreement.)*

Here, the leader contracts with the member to work on the issue during the next session. He wants to make it clear to the member and the entire group that he is not forgetting the issue and plans to come back to it. He also wants to make sure that if there are any pressing feelings, they are handled before the session ends.

A group of divorced men and women are meeting for the fourth session in a support/therapy group. One member, Ann, worked on guilt feelings about giving the custody of her two children to her husband. During the session, Ann came to the conclusion that she did not have to feel guilty about her actions. However, when the focus of the group shifted to another topic, Ann continued to think about her decision. Now, the leader is bringing the group to a close.

Leader: Several of you worked on some pretty important issues today. It might be useful to review our session and see if you have additional thoughts about anything you discussed.

Sue: It was really helpful for me to see that, even though my parents don't believe in divorce, that's their value and it's OK for me to have a different value.

Leader: I'm glad that helped, Sue. What about other people?

Ann: *(Looking down and speaking in a weak voice)* I've been sitting here thinking about my kids. I know being without them right now is best for me. Yet, to be a good mother, I still feel I should be with them. I guess I'm confused all over again.

Leader: Ann, it's apparent there is more we need to do to help clear up your concerns. It sometimes happens that after we work on something, the old feelings can surface again. If you feel this can wait till our next session, we will work on it then.

Ann: I think it can wait, and I really want to work on it.

Had the leader not checked for unfinished business, Ann might have left the group feeling stranded with those feelings. Also, the leader could have finished the session thinking that Ann had worked through a personal issue when, in fact, she was still struggling with it.

Formats for Closing a Session

There are several formats that can be used for closing a session. The choice of format for a particular session should depend on the kind of group, the purpose of the particular session, and what went on during the session. Formats for closing a session include using rounds, dyads followed by comments to the group, having the members or leader summarize, or written reactions. The leader may want to vary the closings of different sessions. In a discussion, education, or task group, it may not be important for each member to speak during the closing phase since members have shared ideas and thoughts rather than personal feelings. In support, personal growth, counseling, and therapy groups, it is usually valuable for members to share their reactions and feelings about the session.

Rounds

Eliciting brief comments from members about what they learned or what stood out as they think back on the session is an excellent way to close a session. The format we use most frequently is the round or series of rounds. The round provides a chance for every member to comment and encourages those who have talked less during the session to share their reactions. A round also allows the leader to respond to certain comments if it would be helpful. When setting up a round, the leader should instruct the members to limit their comments to a sentence or two. Longer responses defeat the purpose of the closing round, which is to highlight important points for each member.

◆ E X A M P L E

Leader: In a sentence or two, what will you take away from the session today? *(Pause)* Tim, let's start with you.

Tim: I learned that I am more nonassertive than assertive.

Guillermo: I learned that it is hard for me to be assertive. I guess I'm chicken.

Leader: I wouldn't say chicken. You simply have not learned to be assertive.

Bill: I learned that my parents are the cause of my being so aggressive.

Leader: Bill, let me clarify that for you and everyone here. We learn things from what our parents do and say. Often, we tend to act like them unless we pay attention to our behavior. *(Turns to Bill)* In your case, from what you described, your parents are very aggressive. However, this does not mean you have to be aggressive, but you probably will be unless you monitor yourself. I hope the group will be a big help to you.

Dyads Followed by Comments to the Group

Starting the closing phase with dyads is a good way to involve all the members. Dyads are beneficial during the closing phase when much has happened in the group, and the leader wants members to get a chance to share but does not have the time to hear all that each member has to say. Dyads allow for members to get to say out loud to another many of their thoughts and feelings. Also, dyads can be used to energize members, especially if the energy level is low toward the end of a session.

◆ EXAMPLES

Leader: Let's take the next few minutes to close. I'd like to form pairs composed of Phil and Pat, Roger and Paula, Ted and Ramón, Mike and Kay. What I'd like you to do is share with your partner one or two things that were particularly important to you about today's session. Then we'll come back to the large group and share any thoughts and feelings.

In this example, the leader decided to pair the members, but he could have allowed the members to select partners. If the leader decides to do the pairing, he should give special thought to anything that occurred during the session that might make it especially valuable for certain members to be together; for example, two members who expressed similar concerns or worked on similar problems could be paired.

In this example, the leader decides to participate in a dyad to encourage a member to share during the closing phase. It is the second session of a support group made up of spouses of alcoholics. One member, Sally, has spoken only a couple of times during these first two sessions.

Leader: As we're closing tonight, I'd like to take a few minutes to see how each of you is feeling about the group so far, what you think has been helpful, and what other topics or issues you'd like to discuss. To do this, I'd like people to pair up for about 2 minutes and then come back to share your thoughts. *(The leader pairs up the members, pairing herself with Sally. She learns that Sally is worried about how other members might view her because she has continued to live with her abusive, alcoholic husband. The leader reassures Sally that she will not let the members attack her and that it might be helpful if Sally shared some of her concerns before the session ended. Sally agrees. The leader ends the dyads and brings the group together again.)* I'd like each of us to share our thoughts about the group.

Carme: The group has been good for me to just get things off my mind. I feel better knowing there is a place I can come to unload.

Bill: Jack and I talked about what it was like to have alcoholic wives. I feel relieved just knowing other people are in the same boat.

Leader: Sally shared some of her fear about talking about her family situation in the group. We both agreed it would be helpful for her to talk a little about that before we stop.

Sally: It's real scary for me to be here. I feel I contributed to my husband's drinking by trying to cover it up.

Carme: I didn't know you'd been thinking that all this time. I feel the same way—I hope we can talk about this at the next meeting.

The leader knew it was important for this quiet member to "break the ice" with the group before the end of this session so that she and the other members would begin to feel comfortable with one another.

The Members Summarize

A simple yet useful way to close the session is to have one or more members summarize what has transpired. The leader can ask for a volunteer to summarize or may select a member who would do a good job. If one member summarizes, other members may also be given the opportunity to add what they feel is important. The leader may also want to add any important events that were overlooked by the members. It is important that a summary during the closing phase not be long or boring. The purpose is to give the members a brief review. Following the summary, members may wish to comment on particular points that were especially important to them.

The Leader Summarizes

The leader may choose to summarize the session. The advantage of this method is that the leader can emphasize certain points and focus on certain members' comments. The disadvantage is that the leader may forget something that was important to one or two members; this may result in those members feeling hurt or resentful. To prevent this, the leader may find it helpful to let members contribute additional summaries following the leader's.

Written Reactions

There are several ways the leader can use written reactions during the closing phase (Riordan & White, 1996). The leader can begin the closing phase of a session by asking members to write their reactions to the session.

◆ E X A M P L E

Leader: It's about 8:40. Let's summarize and close the group. First, I'd like you to spend 5 minutes jotting down any reactions, thoughts, or feelings regarding the session tonight. We'll then share some of those thoughts and stop by 9:00.

Writing can be helpful for those members who respond more comfortably after having had a chance to put their ideas on paper. A different use of writing during the closing phase is to have the members write for 5 to 10 minutes at the very end, when the group has completed the closing. The writing is usually done in a journal that the members leave with the leader, who then has an opportunity to read their reactions. The leader may choose to write encouraging or clarifying comments in the journals and then return them to the members at the next session. A second benefit of the journal is that it provides for each member a lasting chronicle of the entire group experience from the first to the final session.

Helpful Closing Skills and Techniques

Clarity of Purpose

The leader needs to be very clear as to the purpose of the closing phase. A variety of issues and concerns may be raised by members during the closing phase that can take the group in unproductive or new directions. When members bring up new topics, the leader will want to explain to them the purpose of the closing phase and offer the option of bringing the topics up at the beginning of the next session. The important thing to remember during the closing phase of a group session is that the session is ending.

Cutting Off

To maintain the necessary focus on closing, the leader must be ready to use cutting-off skills. Members will not only bring up new material during the closing phase, but often will get into rehashing the session rather than highlighting or summarizing.

◆ E X A M P L E S

Leader: What else did you learn from the session today?

Linda: I'd like to know from the other girls if they have to go to church every Sunday. I do, and I hate it!

Leader: *(In a warm, caring voice)* Linda, that seems like an important issue for you, but we really do not have time to get into a new topic right now. If you will bring that up at the next session, we'll certainly talk about it.

In this example, the leader stops other members from answering by speaking first. She does so to make sure that a new topic does not get started during the closing phase.

This example is similar, but the leader has to cut off a member who is rambling.

Leader: We seem to have a good list started. What else did we talk about that we are going to observe this week?

Frank: The thing we don't have there that we really need to talk about is getting some improvements in visiting hours. I'm so tired of visiting hours always getting changed around. My family can never get here—

Leader: Frank, I'm going to jump in here. Visiting hours may be an important area to look at, but it will have to wait till next week. We want to summarize for the next few minutes the things we talked through today so we don't lose anything.

Tying Together

The skill of tying together is especially beneficial during the closing phase of a session. By using this skill, the leader can create a sense of interrelatedness of themes, issues, and personal experiences. It is important for the leader to identify those points that relate to one another and then share them in such a way that the members see how patterns, issues, and people are connected. This is something the members are often unable to do themselves.

Drawing Out

Drawing out is also an important skill to use during the closing phase of a session because the leader usually likes to hear from as many members as possible. Several of the techniques for closing mentioned earlier—especially the use of dyads and rounds—will facilitate the drawing-out process. It is especially important for the leader to draw out members who are less active during the session, both to help them feel involved and to get their reactions to the session.

Wishes

A useful technique for closing certain kinds of growth, support, and therapy sessions is the use of "wishes." This activity helps build positive and supportive feelings among members.

◆ E X A M P L E

Leader: I think that pretty much summarizes the session. Any comments? *(Pause—no one seems ready to comment)* Let's do this. *(Speaking slowly)* Look around the room and see if there is anyone you have a wish for. If there is someone, identify the person and then say "My wish for you is . . ." For example, Joe, my wish for you is that you will call your parents and say those things that you want to say.

Max: Don, my wish for you is that you get out at least twice this week.

Joe: Cherry, my wish for you is that you will stop blaming yourself.

Acknowledging a New Member

The leader may want to vary the closing slightly when a member is present for the first time. The leader might want to allow some extra time during the closing phase to focus on the new member if the member seems to feel comfortable enough but has been relatively quiet. Focusing on the new member gives that member a chance to share, which can help her feel even more comfortable. It also gives members a chance to know a little more about her. By hearing from the new member, the leader also has a better idea of how that person is feeling about being in the group.

◆ E X A M P L E

Two members have finished summarizing the session, and others have commented.

Leader: Connie, I hope this has been interesting and maybe even helpful.

Connie: Well, I was really nervous for the first 10 minutes, but I did relax. I am sorry that I didn't say more, but I really don't like talking in front of groups. I hope it will get easier for me.

Leader: Was the session helpful?

Connie: Oh, yes. I already realize that others have feelings similar to mine. I really identified with what Patty was saying.

Leader: I hope that during the next session you will feel free to share. Anyone else have any closing thoughts before we stop?

Acknowledging a Member Who Is Leaving

There are occasions when a member leaves a group even though the group continues. In a closed group, members may drop out for any variety of reasons. More often, the departure of one member occurs in an ongoing, open-membership group, such as residential treatment programs in substance abuse or physical rehabilitation centers. Members leave the group because they are going home.

When a member is leaving, it is important that the leader allow some time during the closing to focus on that member. The leader may get the member to review his goals upon entrance to the group and the progress he has made, and have the members provide encouragement, give feedback, and say good-bye. Although the exiting member will be the major focal point, the leader may wish to use this experience to help other members think about when they will be leaving the group and what they still need to do to get themselves ready for leaving.

The amount of time that should be given to a member who is exiting will depend on the length of time of the session, the purpose of the group, and the kind of member he has been. In open-ended groups, members may be exiting fairly often, so the time devoted to a leaving member will need to be monitored. It is important not to devote most of the session to the departing member because this could mean that every session or two would be focused on departing members rather than those who are in the group. Five to 10 minutes is usually sufficient for saying good-bye to the exiting member.

◆ E X A M P L E S

Leader: We have about 20 minutes left in the session, so what I would like to do is begin to summarize the session. Also, I want to leave the last few minutes free to focus on Walt, who will be leaving the group after today. I want each of you to think of the one thing that stood out for you today. *(Pause)* Mike, you seem ready.

Mike: The discussion about the importance of not keeping our feelings inside was really helpful.

Andy: The thing that stood out for me was . . .

Leader: *(After spending time completing the round and processing the session)* OK, let's spend a few minutes saying good-bye to Walt. Most of you have known Walt for awhile now. I want you to think of how you see Walt as different than when he first entered the group. We'll share that, and then we'll share any wishes that we have for him. How is Walt different?

Mario: He is really different. *(To Walt)* When you first came into the group, you didn't talk or even look up. I really do think the program has helped you.

Leader: I agree. You really have changed. I see you as a lot more open, and that chip on your shoulder seems to be gone.

Carl: That's right! You did have a chip on your shoulder those first two meetings. It's gone.

Leader: *(After others have shared)* If you had a wish for Walt, what would that be?

Jeff: My wish is that you have that conversation with your wife that you practiced in here.

Bruno: My wish is that you don't let that chip come back. The soft, gentle side is much nicer.

Leader: *(After two other members have shared wishes)* Walt, what thoughts or reaction or closing comments do you have for the group?

Walt: Well, I appreciate all your support. I also want to say. . . .

In this example, the exiting member got a chance to hear some good and encouraging feedback.

There will be times when a departing member has not really used the group or the treatment program that much. In this case, the leader may want to focus on feedback and wishes, in the hope that something might be said that will help.

Leader: In saying good-bye to Sharon, I want each of you to think of what you think will be the roughest thing for Sharon to handle when she goes home.

Paul: I really think that Sharon is going to have trouble.

Leader: Instead of talking to me, could you address Sharon?

Paul: Sure. Sharon, I think you are going to have trouble with a lot of things, because you still seem angry at your parents.

Biff: Sharon, I think you are fooling yourself when you say that you can make it without going to AA meetings. I hope your pride will not keep you from calling someone for help.

In this example, the leader wants to make sure that the member is not attacked since she is leaving that afternoon, but at the same time, he is hoping that something someone says will be helpful because Sharon really does not seem ready to leave the program.

Warning Members

While the group experience can generate strong feelings among members, the leader should explain to the members that they will probably not experience the same kind of sharing at home and that it is OK. During the session, members often share at a very personal level, take risks, and experience warm, caring acceptance. They may go home and want to experience the same thing with their spouse, parents, friends, or coworkers, and when this does not occur, some members become angry, frustrated, or resentful at the people in their lives and/or the leader of the group. Leaders should be aware that members may actually feel closer to other members of the group than to a spouse, children, or long-term friends. We do not believe that this is the purpose of the group.

◆ E X A M P L E

Leader: I want to say something now, and I will probably say it again in
our last session. Many of you are really opening up and sharing with
the group, and I think it is great. Also, the way you are responding to
what is being said is terrific. I think nearly everyone is experiencing good
feelings as a result of being here. For many of you, these feelings are
unique, and I want to caution you about going home and trying to share
like this with your spouse and friends. Remember, they have not been in
this group and have not had this experience. If you want this kind of
sharing, give them time. Don't expect them to be able to do this immediately.
Also, realize that they may never be able to do exactly what we are doing
here.

Handling Criticism of the Session

The leader should be prepared for criticism about the session or the group
during the closing of the session. It is important that the leader not be
defensive. In most cases, the leader will not want the closing to be spent
entirely on criticism unless he senses that the majority of the members are
having the same feelings. The way the leader handles the criticism will
depend on the kind of criticism, the merit of the criticism, and the amount of
time needed for the actual closing. The following are several ways the leader can
handle criticism during the closing phase.

◆ E X A M P L E S

Melvin is a member who has tried to dominate the group, and the leader has had
to cut him off on numerous occasions. The leader has a strong sense from the
members' nonverbal responses that they appreciate the fact that Melvin is not
allowed to dominate.

Melvin: *(In a hostile voice)* I have something I want to say. I feel you lead too
much. In other groups, the leader hardly said anything—this is more your
group than our group!

Leader: *(To Melvin and the entire group)* I do hope you feel that this is your
group. There are times when I direct what is happening simply because I
am trained as a counselor and a group leader. And, as I said earlier, there
will be times when I may cut you off in order to hold the focus on another
issue or when it seems like you have gotten a little long winded. Certainly,
I do not want you to feel that I am dominating the group. Does anyone
else feel that way? *(No one responds)* Let's go back to summarizing the
session. Other thoughts or reactions?

In this example, the leader briefly responded, got support from the members, and then went back to closing the group.

Leader: Who else wants to comment on what stood out to them?

James: I feel like the group gets too personal. When Troy was talking, I felt you really pushed him too hard!

Leader: James, let me answer that. *(Looking at the entire group)* The group is personal, and I do push members hard because all of you have problems that need to be dealt with on more than a superficial level. Certainly, I try not to push you *too* hard, but do realize that not dealing with your problems is what got you into the hospital.

Troy: I'm glad you pushed. I think I understand why I get so angry.

The leader has been feeling that the group has not gone well the last couple of sessions.

José: I don't mean to be critical, but the group has not been very valuable for me lately.

Leader: How do others of you feel? I, too, think something is missing.

Rusty: I would like us to be more personal rather than just discussing things. Does anyone else feel that way?

Pam: I do. The discussions about legal issues, custody, and so on are all good, but there are personal things that I think I am ready to share.

Paul: I would like that better.

Leader: So what you are saying is that you would like this to be more of a sharing group than a discussion/education group. How about the rest of you, how do you feel?

In this example, the leader decided to focus on the criticism because he felt that the group did perhaps need a new emphasis.

Final Thoughts on Closing a Session

The leader who does a good job bringing a group session to a close enhances the value of the session considerably. Without an effective closing, many important issues discussed during the session may become blurred or lost. The closing phase requires thought and planning. If done well, members come away with a sense of completeness. Effective closing of a session also helps build cohesiveness since members get to hear others' reactions.

The Closing Stage

Probably the most important point to remember when preparing for the closing stage of a group is that the group is not an entity in itself, but a collection of individuals. When the group is over, it is the individuals who go away, taking with them new information, decisions, or beliefs that make everyday living happier and more productive. The leader's task during the closing stage is to focus on these benefits.

Time Allowed for the Closing Stage

The amount of time allowed to complete the closing stage of a group will depend on the kind of group, its purpose, the number of sessions, and the needs of the members. As a general rule, the greater the number of sessions and the more personal the sharing, the longer the closing stage will be. For example, in a therapy group meeting for 2 hours weekly for 15 sessions, the leader might begin the closing stage toward the middle of the 14th session since there will be a considerable amount to cover. In contrast, a task group working on improving a residential treatment program for drug abusers, meeting an hour each week for four sessions, may require only 15 minutes of the last session for the closing stage. The closing stage of education and discussion groups would usually not take more than 10 to 20 minutes of the last session. Similarly, a children's self-concept group meeting for 40 minutes a week for five sessions may take only 10 to 15 minutes of the last session for closing. Although it is possible that the closing stage could take two or more sessions, the last session is usually enough time for closing.

Purpose and Goals of the Closing Stage

The purpose of the closing stage is to pull together the significant ideas, decisions, and personal changes experienced by the members during the group. This is a time for members to look at their progress in the group and to compare their goals at the start of the group with their accomplishments at the end. While the leader may focus to some extent on the dynamics of the group itself—such as how the members have interacted or how they have helped each other—the main focus for most groups will be on each member's growth and development. Following are the tasks of the closing stage.

- Reviewing and summarizing the group experience
- Assessing members' growth and change
- Finishing business
- Providing feedback
- Handling good-byes
- Planning for follow-up care

Reviewing and Summarizing the Group Experience

One of the first tasks during the closing stage of most groups is to review and summarize the significant developments of the group. The leader can accomplish the task of review and summary by (1) summarizing the entire group, (2) getting members to summarize their experience, or (3) facilitating interaction that focuses on summarizing and reviewing. The first option can be used if there have not been many sessions and the leader remembers most of the significant events. If the group has met for a number of sessions, this might not be the best option because the leader may not remember some important topics or discussions. The second option, having the members summarize their experiences, can be valuable if the group is small and the summaries can be kept to 2 to 3 minutes each. If the group is large (10 or more), this is not usually a good option because it would probably take too much time and become repetitive. Most often the third option, which allows members to share what has stood out to them, is best.

◆ E X A M P L E

It is the final session of a high school growth group.

Leader: Since this is the last session, I want to spend the remainder of our time reviewing the group experience and how it has affected you. First, I want you to think of three things that stood out to you during the sessions. What discussions, exercises, or comments do you remember the most? *(Pause)* Sandi, you seem ready.

Sandi: The discussion about my mom and how I can deal with her better than I do. Focusing on the difference between being assertive and being aggressive. A third thing would be the discussion about taking risks in order to get more out of life.

Phillipe: The discussion concerning risk taking was the highlight for me. I think about that every day.

Leader: Let me just ask—was that a major insight for some others of you?

Armand: It was number one on my list, too. Whenever I am bored or afraid, I think over what risks I can take or remember that it is OK to be afraid when I am trying something new.

In this example, the leader had members share things on their lists and then held the focus on risk taking, and got members to share their reactions. Having members share what was important and periodically holding the focus on various topics is an excellent way to bring the group to a close.

Assessing Members' Growth and Change

This task applies to groups such as therapy groups, in which the primary purpose is personal growth or change. By the time the closing stage rolls around, members should have experienced the implementation of some changes in their lives. One problem that members face when the group meetings stop is returning to their former, less effective ways of living. It is important for the leader to highlight this potential problem for members and to reinforce their efforts to maintain positive change. This can be done in part by getting members to evaluate their success in making changes. This assessment reinforces the changes and encourages members to pursue further growth and development.

◆ E X A M P L E

This group is in the closing stage of a personal growth experience in a university counseling center.

Leader: Since this is our last session, I think it might be helpful if each of you spent a few minutes looking at the changes you have brought about in your lives during these past 10 weeks. Some of you are more aware of your values and what you want to get from life; others of you brought problems or concerns that you resolved through the group, and so forth. Take a minute and think about the important changes you've experienced in the group. When you are ready, I'm going to ask you to share those thoughts with the group.

This sharing can lead to feedback from other members, encouragement, and plans for continued work on issues following the end of the group.

Finishing Business

During the closing stage, it is common to have a few loose ends that still need to be tied up before the members can comfortably leave the group. It is important for the leader to allow time for this because unfinished business can interfere with the sense of closure and may leave one or more members with unresolved issues. Following are some examples of unfinished business that might come up during the closing stage:

- An issue or question that was brought up in a previous session but never dealt with
- Negative feelings about how the leader handled a particular situation during a session
- A question a member has for another member or for the leader
- A member needing to work on some unresolved personal issue

While it is important to assess and handle unfinished business, the leader must be careful not to generate new business. For example, if a member expresses some dissatisfaction with how the leader handled a particular situation during an earlier session, the leader may simply want to accept the statement rather than get into a lengthy explanation or discussion. If a member wants or needs therapy on an unresolved issue, the leader may choose to refer the member for counseling or see the member after the session. Delving into new issues is seldom appropriate for the closing stage.

The following is an example of how a leader might introduce the topic of unfinished business.

Leader: One thing that is important to do during this closing is to allow some time for any unfinished group business that needs to be dealt with. I am not asking for personal work issues since we are trying to close the group, but rather questions you want to ask or reactions that you feel the need to share. If there is something that you want to say or ask, please do so. I urge you not to leave thinking, "I wish I had said this or that."

Providing Feedback

During the closing stage, some final feedback to members is often helpful. Members should be given a chance to comment to one another about the changes each has made. Such reinforcement should be sincere and as specific as possible. The leader should monitor the type of feedback given to make sure it is on target.

◆ E X A M P L E S

Leader: Let's spend a few minutes thinking of positive changes that you have seen in other members. I'd like you to pick three people who you feel have made some positive changes. I'll ask you to tell each person what the change is and how you think the change is helpful for the person. For example, Alan, I feel that you are much friendlier, and it is much easier to talk with you.

Leader: I want you to think about feedback that you feel would be helpful to give other members. You may want to think about changes that you have seen in members or thank them for something they said or did during a session.

Feedback can also be given to confront members who are still denying problems or who have not taken responsibility for their behavior. Such feedback, when given honestly and without anger or disappointment, can have an impact on a member who seems unwilling to face certain unresolved issues. Feedback may be given by the leader, the members, or both.

◆ E X A M P L E

In a drug treatment group, a member who is still denying that his continued use of drugs is having a negative effect on his family life may benefit greatly from feedback sincerely given by the other members of the group.

Sam: Dave, even though you are fooling your family, your therapist, and even yourself by your continued use of drugs, you are not fooling us because we've been there.

Ann: I agree. Dave, you really have to stop thinking that you don't have a problem. Face it, you have a drug problem! Even though this group is ending, I do hope you will decide to really get help.

In this example, the members can probably have more impact than the leader since they are seen as peers who have struggled and dealt with a similar problem. In other situations, the leader is better able to give confrontive or negative feedback because he sees aspects of a member's behavior that the members do not see or because he knows the member better from having worked with him on an individual basis.

Handling Good-byes

It is important for the leader to remember that for many members the ending of the group is the end of a very special event in their lives. The relationships formed in the group may be the closest relationships some members have ever experienced. These members will have especially strong feelings about the ending of the group. The leader should provide some time for those feelings to be expressed and for members to make final comments to each other. Members sometimes wish to exchange telephone numbers and addresses if they have not done so already.

Planning for Follow-Up Care

During the closing stage, it is the leader's responsibility to provide guidance, information, and the names and phone numbers of referral sources for any member who needs to continue working on personal concerns. For some, the best solution is involvement in another group experience. For others, individual, marital, or family counseling will be most helpful. Certain members may benefit most from joining a support group such as Alcoholics Anonymous.

Exercises to Use during the Closing Stage
Rounds

Rounds can be especially helpful during the closing stage. The round can be used to summarize key points, get overall reactions to the group or a particular experience, or check the degree to which members feel they accomplished personal goals. The leader might introduce closing rounds with one of the following questions:

- On a 1–10 scale, with 10 being very satisfied, how satisfied are you with your progress during this group?

- If you had to capture how you feel about your group experience in a sentence or two, what would you say? We'll do a round and hear from everyone.
- Since this is the last session, what word or phrase expresses how you are feeling about the group ending?

Wishes

The wishes exercise provides a special type of feedback for members during the closing stage. We gave an example of this earlier for the closing phase, but it is also an excellent activity for the closing stage.

◆ E X A M P L E

It is the last session of a support group for recently divorced persons.

Leader: Let's take the next few minutes and see if there are any wishes you might have for one another. You may or may not have a wish. It's OK either way. I have a wish for Darlene. My wish for you is that you will be able to let go of your angry feelings toward your husband and get on with your life.

Darlene: Thank you.

Bill: My wish for you, Jane, is that you realize your teenagers are old enough to help out around the house and that you can stop being their slave.

Josefa: I have a wish for you too, Jane. My wish for you is that you take a chance. You won't know if you can build a new relationship if you don't try.

Reunion Fantasy

An excellent exercise to use in closing certain personal growth, support, counseling, and therapy groups is the Reunion Fantasy. The purpose of this exercise is to get members to project their lives into the future. Many members are startled to find that in their fantasies they have the power to bring about significant changes. They are encouraged by this imagining process and gain confidence that their lives can change for the better. Conversely, members are also surprised to find that they are unable to imagine some of the changes they have worked for in the group. They realize the need for a greater commitment to change and that they must take more responsibility for their lives if change is to come about.

◆ E X A M P L E

Leader: I'd like you to relax. Close your eyes if that is comfortable for you. I want you to imagine that the time is 5 years from now; you have just gone to the mailbox and have received a letter from me inviting you back for a group reunion. In the letter, I explain that I have received a grant to cover all expenses. Now that you have decided to attend, I want you to think of what you will tell the other members about your life and any changes. Think about where you are living, with whom you are living, what you are doing, and any significant events that have occurred. *(The leader pauses to allow the members to experience the fantasy.)* What do you most want to say to the other members about your life now? In a minute, I am going to ask you to stand up and act like you are just seeing these people for the first time in 5 years, unless you will have remained in contact with some of them. Try to get into the role of having been apart for 5 years. *(Pause)* OK, everyone stand and start milling and sharing.

This exercise can be very thought provoking for groups in which the members have come to know each other very well. As with all exercises, this one must be tailored to the kind of group, its purpose, and the needs of the members as they experience the group coming to an end. This exercise would be good to use during the beginning part of the closing stage, since it would get members to think about the group ending and the issues and changes they have talked about in the group. (It also can be used during the middle stage of a group if the leader wants to get members to focus on the future and possible changes.)

Members Writing about Their Experience

The leader may provide an opportunity for members to write about some aspect of the group, either in their journals (if journals were used) or on paper provided. The members may write on a variety of topics: four or five things they learned, the most helpful experience for them during the group, personal goals at the beginning of the group and the extent to which each was achieved, or how decisions they made in the group will be applied outside the group. The leader may then have members share their written thoughts in pairs, small groups, or with the entire group. If the topic the members write about is lengthy or complex, the leader may ask each member to underline two or three key passages to share with the entire group in order to save time and maintain the focus. When using journals, members may also review their journal entries from all the previous sessions and write a summary paragraph that pulls together the key points of the group for them.

Using the Flipchart or Handouts

An excellent tool for reviewing, summarizing, and consolidating information is a flipchart/chalkboard. The flipchart can be used to list points during the review and can be referred to as those points are discussed. It also serves as an excellent focal point for the members in that they continually gaze at the flipchart and thus stay focused on the review. Writing on the flipchart also gives members a chance to have direct input into the review and summarizing process.

Handouts are a variation on the flipchart technique. They differ primarily in that the leader has already summarized the key points. The advantage of the handout is that it saves time and gets the members focused on the discussion immediately. A handout may be particularly useful with discussion, education, and task groups because the leader can often easily summarize the various key points.

Additional Considerations for the Closing Stage

As the leader plans the closing stage of the group, there are a number of points to think about. Not every kind of group will require consideration of all these factors. It is the leader's responsibility to determine which of these considerations are relevant.

- Dealing with feelings of separation
- Guarding against ending with strong emotions
- Helping members in their transition
- Conducting exit interviews
- Holding follow-up sessions
- Evaluating the group
- Ending with a party

Dealing with Feelings of Separation

We have already discussed the need for some members to say their good-byes as the group comes to a close. For most members, this will go smoothly. For some, however, the ending of the group will elicit anxiety over separating from the others. The positive effect of the group may be lessened if those feelings are not identified and dealt with by the leader. Clues to such feelings might be found in statements from members like these:

- I couldn't sleep last night because I knew today would be our last meeting.
- I feel like this is my second family, and I don't want to leave it.
- I don't think I can make it without this group.

When the leader hears such comments, the first task is to help members realize that these feelings are normal, and allow them to express their feelings of sadness or loss. Second, the leader might want to point out that although the positive sharing may have been a new experience, the kind of sharing and closeness members feel toward one another need not be unique. Such relationships can be developed outside the group with the awareness and skills members have developed. Also, if the leader knows that some members are going to have a tough time with the ending of the group, he may allow additional time during the closing stage to work with those members.

Guarding against Ending with Strong Emotions

When closing a group in which members have gotten very close, the leader will want to pay close attention to the emotional tone. The members may experience the ending as a very sad, intense, or extra special event. If possible, these kinds of feelings should be avoided. Members should ideally see the ending as a new beginning, feeling positive about the group experience and excited about their future. The first example that follows is of a leader talking about sad feelings regarding the ending of the group. The second is of a leader talking about the possibilities of ending on a "high."

◆ E X A M P L E S

Leader: When we stop today, I do not want you to feel really sad or feel that this is the end. I hope you will realize that it is a beginning for you to do the things you have learned in this group. I purposely will try to have us end with good feelings and not sadness because I feel the group really has been a good experience for all of us. It has served the purpose of members sharing and caring, and I hope you have already started to create the same kind of sharing with significant others in your life.

By presenting a positive yet calm attitude rather than one that focuses on sad or emotional good-byes, the leader can prevent the false high phenomenon. Rather than ending with the emphasis on the "high" with much hugging and joyous crying, you might try to end groups that have been very close and personal by saying something like this:

Leader: *(In a soft, rather neutral voice)* We are going to stop now. I do think the whole experience has been good, and the closing has been very good. I think you have had enough time to say what you wanted and to start a new beginning for yourselves. If I can ever be of help, please feel free to contact me. I certainly have found the experience to be a good one. Let's stop.

Helping Members in Their Transition

A third consideration during the closing stage is the importance of helping members make a transition back into the "real world." Members must learn to employ their new information and knowledge about themselves with people in their daily lives. This is especially important for group members who have been clients in a residential treatment program for a period of time. Some members, such as those who have had addiction problems, will need continued support and monitoring in the community. Many communities have a variety of support groups available either as independent organizations or through mental-health centers, hospitals, or rehabilitation programs. The leader should include a discussion of the value of these groups during the closing stage.

In some types of groups, members may form support networks of their own to ensure continued reinforcement of one another, or they may plan "booster" meetings periodically to report on their progress. The need for this type of follow up should be assessed by the leader in conjunction with the members. The entire group may be involved in the network, or members may choose one or more persons with whom to network. For members who ordinarily have difficulty developing and maintaining relationships, networking is very beneficial. Networking may also be a temporary measure for members who are new to a community or who have simply lost social contacts because of addictions or other problems. In some groups, time may be provided during the closing stage to develop individual plans for each member.

Conducting Exit Interviews

Earlier in this book, we discussed the value of interviewing potential group members before the group began to establish rapport and exchange expectations about the group experience. There is also value in conducting exit interviews with members as the group enters the closing stage. Exit interviews are not needed in all groups; the leader must consider the value of such interviews with regard to the kind of group and the needs of individual members. If exit interviews are conducted, they should last from 15 to 30 minutes. We suggest that they take place either before the final session of the group or very soon after the last session. By meeting before the last session, the leader can suggest how the member might use the closing stage to her benefit, such as requesting additional feedback from other members. The exit interview can also be a time for the leader to reinforce the gains a member has made, as well as to focus more individual attention on ways the member can apply those gains to everyday living. The interview further gives the leader a chance to ask for feedback about the group and various aspects of his leadership. Depending on the kind of group, some members may feel more comfortable giving the leader feedback on a one-to-one basis.

Holding Follow-Up Sessions

The leader may consider holding a follow-up session of the group several weeks or months after the final regular session. The decision to have one or more follow-up meetings will depend on the kind of group and the needs of the members. For example, members of a task group who work together in the same organization may wish to have a follow-up session to assess how things are going. With some support or counseling groups, follow-up sessions give members a chance to share how they are doing, and lessen the anxiety of separation. The leader may set up a formal follow-up program in which members are notified and encouraged to return for a meeting. Occasionally, members will decide they want to plan for a reunion in 6 months. This decision usually arises from the good feelings members have toward one another during the closing stage. Experience suggests that these reunions are usually not very successful because the feelings fade as time passes and members become involved in their own lives. If a reunion is planned, the leader should not feel disappointed by a small turnout, and members should be prepared for the experience to be very different from when they were meeting regularly.

One unique follow-up procedure that we use is to have members write themselves letters in which they assess their goals, give themselves feedback, and list plans for the future. The letters are given to the leader in a self-addressed, stamped envelope and are then mailed several weeks or months after the group has ended. Members have reported that this technique is powerful. They say that writing the letter is thought provoking, and knowing that it will come in the mail someday causes them to keep working even after the group has ended. Others have said that often their letter arrived at a good time, as they were needing a "booster shot." The letter exercise is designed for use in a personal growth, counseling, or therapy group, but could also be used with a task group as a way for members to check on the degree to which they have followed through on their decisions.

Evaluating the Group

When any group ends, the leader will need to decide how she will evaluate the experience. Groups can be evaluated formally with a questionnaire or informally with the leader asking specific questions during the closing stage. No matter how the evaluation is done, the leader should seek answers to the following questions:

- How valuable was the experience? (The leader could use a 1–10 scale.)
- What did members like about the group?
- What did members dislike about the group?
- What did members like about the way the leader led the group?
- What did members not like about the way the leader led the group?
- How could the group have been better?

These are just the basic questions that should be asked. Certainly, a more elaborate questionnaire could be devised that asked about specific topics, exercises, and events that occurred during the group. We encourage leaders—especially beginning leaders—to evaluate any group they lead. The responses and comments from their members can be very helpful in leading future groups.

Ending with a Party

A final consideration that comes up frequently is that members want to end the group with a party. They may suggest meeting at someone's house or meeting for pizza. The leader should give a good deal of thought to such a request because often when the group meets in another setting, a group session never really takes place and thus no real closing occurs. If the leader and the group decide to meet in a setting like this, the leader will want to tell members ahead of time that the first hour or so will be devoted to closing the group.

A variation of this is for the group to plan a party to be held after the group has officially ended. Sometimes, this type of party works fine; other times, it does not work out very well. We suggest that the leader at least prepare members for the possibility that the party may not go well.

Concluding Comments

The closing phase, a very important phase of a session, often is mishandled because the leader has not managed the time of the session very well. The closing phase serves the purpose of reviewing a session and ensuring that members leave feeling "finished." When a leader fails to plan for the closing phase, closing is either hurried or not done at all, leaving the members with no closure. It is very important to have a closing phase to each session.

The closing stage of a group is the last stage, when the group is winding down and is going to stop meeting. The closing stage is usually a portion of the last session, the entire last session, or perhaps the last two sessions. Its purpose is to maximize the impact of the group experience and to bring closure to the experience.

The closing phase and the closing stage are each very important aspects of a group because they allow members to review what has happened and to make commitments as to what they are going to do in the future. Also, closing is an important time for reflecting on the group and is a time for giving and receiving feedback. During the closing stage, it is important for the members to assess their progress, evaluate the experience, and discuss follow-up support.

There are several skills, techniques, and exercises that are useful during closing. Rounds are very helpful since they tend to get everyone to speak, and it is important to hear reactions from the quieter members. Writing as a part of closing has proved to be quite valuable for many different kinds of groups. Cutting off is essential since members will tend to tell stories or bring up new topics.

CHAPTER FIFTEEN

Dealing with Problem Situations

A group leader must be prepared to deal with many situations. In this chapter, we identify many of the most common problems that arise in the group setting and provide examples to illustrate some skills and techniques for handling these situations. The 13 common problems we have identified are as follows:

1. The chronic talker
2. The dominator
3. The distractor
4. The rescuing member
5. The negative member
6. The resistant member
7. The member who tries to "get the leader"
8. Dealing with silence
9. Dealing with sexual feelings
10. Dealing with crying
11. Dealing with mutually hostile members
12. Asking a member to leave
13. Dealing with prejudiced, narrow-minded, or insensitive members

The Chronic Talker

It is easy to spot the chronic talker by his persistent rambling and repetition. As a result of the talker's excessive chatter, other members who have concerns that they would like to discuss are prevented from doing so. Soon, the group members either tune out the chronic talker and lose interest in the proceedings or get frustrated and angry at both the talkative member and the leader, who they feel should cut him off. The chronic talker can be categorized into three different types, depending on the reason underlying his talkativeness: the nervous member, the rambler, and the show-off.

The nervous member talks to hide his feelings of nervousness or as a means of self-control. Easily recognized, the nervous member is often the first one to answer questions posed by the leader and the first to volunteer for some task. Because the nervous member is talking to alleviate anxiety, he will talk frequently and for as long as the leader lets him.

Ramblers dominate discussions because they are simply talkative people and are unaware of the effect their rambling has on others. They too are easily recognized because they tell long, drawn-out stories and often repeat themselves. The stories are often trivial and are not usually meaningful to others.

Show-offs are talkative because they are insecure and want to impress the group leader, other members, or both. The show-off seems to be attempting to show others what he knows. In doing so, he answers all questions, asks irrelevant questions in an effort to grab the leader's attention, and may offer unsolicited advice to other group members. The other members often resent this and grow to dislike this type of member. The problem with the show-off is that he can quickly sway the group from its intended purpose.

Handling the Talkative Member

To determine whether or not a member should be seen as a chronic talker, the leader should consider the following questions:

- For how long has the member been talking?
- How many comments has the member made compared with other group members? Are the member's comments in line with the intended purpose of the group?
- Is this member preventing others from talking?
- Are others becoming bored or irritated with the member's comments?
- Does the member seem to be talking because of nervousness or a desire to impress others?

There are several ways to handle a talkative member. For example, upon recognizing such a member, the leader could have members get into dyads, making sure she pairs herself with the talkative member. In the dyad, the leader could attempt to speak to the member about his "talkativeness." The advantage of this strategy is that the talkative member receives the message about his talkativeness from only one person, thus causing less embarrassment.

There are a couple of strategies that involve the whole group. One is to address the group with the hope that the talkative member hears the message. The other strategy involves seeking feedback from the members.

◆ EXAMPLES

It is early in the life of the group, and the leader wants to curb the rambler's talking without seeming critical of the member. Therefore, the leader decides to deliver the message to the entire group by looking at everyone as she speaks.

Leader: Keep in mind that the purpose of the group is for *everyone* to share thoughts and feelings. If any one member gets too long winded, the focus of the group changes from sharing to listening to one member. Please be aware of how much you are talking and whether or not you are dominating the discussion.

In this example, the leader introduces a feedback exercise since she believes members are wanting to confront the talkative member.

Leader: As I stated in the beginning of this group, one of the most potentially helpful aspects of a group such as this is for members to receive feedback about themselves from other members of the group. In effect, this feedback acts as a mirror, letting you know how others in the group see and react to you. Is there anyone here who would like to give another member some feedback?

The leader would use this kind of opening to a feedback exercise only if confident there were members who wanted to share their feelings about a member's excessive talking. If the leader felt that members would not speak up unless the leader did, a feedback exercise could be devised in which the leader also could give feedback to the rambling member. Sometimes, members will offer feedback without being prompted to do so. When this happens, the leader merely needs to make sure that the member receiving the feedback doesn't feel attacked.

If the leader is about to ask the group a question and is sure that a talkative member will again speak up and attempt to dominate the discussion, the leader might say something like, "I'm going to ask a question, and I would like to hear from some of you who haven't talked yet." The leader should say this while avoiding eye contact with the talkative member. These techniques may stop the dominating member as well as draw out comments from members who have been silent. At times, the leader unknowingly perpetuates a particular member's talking by maintaining eye contact with him and nodding her head as that member speaks. Maintaining eye contact reinforces the member's talking.

One direct way of intervening with the talkative member is to speak to the member immediately after the session or sometime before the next session.

◆ E X A M P L E

Leader: *(Talking to a member after the session has ended)* Wanda, tell me if I'm wrong, but you seemed a bit nervous during the group tonight. You were repeating yourself a lot as you talked, and you talked very rapidly.

Wanda: Yes, you're right. I was hoping that no one would notice. I just get uptight every time I'm around a new group of people. It is something that I definitely want to work on.

Another strategy that could be used if the leader were having the members turn in any kind of written reactions to the group would be to give the member feedback in writing. For example, the leader might write the following feedback at the bottom of the member's reaction:

> Tom, I sense that you are uncomfortable since you talked quite a bit and at a very rapid pace. I am hoping that you will be a little more comfortable and thus talk a little less. Let me know if there is anything that I can do to help you feel more comfortable.

Members usually receive this message very well and become more cognizant of their talkative behavior. In addition, a note such as this often helps members feel more comfortable about talking to the leader outside the group. This is a nonthreatening way to offer feedback; its disadvantage is that there is no guarantee that the member receiving the feedback will respond favorably to it, and if the member reads it somewhere other than in the group, no one will be there to help with processing the feedback.

The Dominator

The dominator is a member who tries to rule the group. This member is different from the chronic talker because this person wants to run things and be in control. This kind of member is fairly common in residential settings and in school groups. In education, discussion, or task groups, a dominator often is present. The leader should try some of the different techniques previously mentioned in dealing with the chronic talker, but quite often this kind of member needs to be met with privately to discuss his behavior in the group. Sometimes, he can be used as a helper or be given a role that makes him feel special. Other times, the behavior is such that he has to be asked to leave the group because he is not willing to give control to the leader.

The Distractor

The distractor is a member who is either seeking attention or is avoiding looking at herself. To accomplish this, she tries to get the group off task by bringing up unrelated subjects or asking questions that are not relevant. Some distractors make noises or move around as a way to distract members. This person is often found in school or residential groups and often in groups that are nonvoluntary. Sometimes, this member is very difficult to deal with because she is not intentionally trying to distract the group. Talking with the member privately and then ignoring her comments or behaviors during the session often will help to minimize the effects of the distractor.

The Rescuing Member

"Rescuing" is the attempt of a member to smooth over negative feelings experienced by another member of the group. When a member becomes upset, often other group members attempt to soothe the member with such statements as "Now, don't worry; it will be all right" or "Everything has a way of working itself out if you just give it time." This is usually not helpful, and such comments often sound patronizing. The negative effect of rescuing is that it prevents the member in pain from problem solving.

◆ E X A M P L E S

One of the members, Judy, cries as she tells the group about her upcoming divorce. As she does so, another member, Karen, attempts to rescue her.

Karen: Don't worry, Judy, everything will be OK. I went through a divorce myself, and you just have to make the best of it. I think—

Leader: *(Interrupting Karen in midsentence)* Judy, you are in a lot of pain right now, and if you would like, we can listen and try to be of help. By sharing, you will at least get some of your thoughts out, and I think that you will feel our support. *(Judy nods that she would like to. The leader allows her to share her pain while making sure members don't offer advice.)*

Leader: *(After Judy has discussed her divorce)* I'd like to say something to all of you here. Usually, when a member is struggling with some issue like a divorce, she doesn't need our sympathy or advice as much as she needs to be listened to and supported.

Members often think they are being supportive when in fact they are trying to rescue the member. Teaching members how helping and sharing is different than rescuing is important as the group progresses. In the early life of the group, the leader may need to intervene quite often because the group members are not aware of their rescuing behaviors. In the preceding example, the leader decided to convey the message about sympathy being unhelpful to the entire group so that they could observe her modeling being therapeutic in the group.

This group is a stress management group composed of first-year teachers. One of the members, Vivian, is expressing how upset she is with her husband. Another member hears this and gives her sympathy and pity.

Vivian: It is so stressful being a first-year teacher and juggling all the things with the kids and the house. My husband is always on me about the house and the kids, but it is hard to get it all done. I am trying, but sometimes I just can't get to the laundry or the cleaning, and then he doesn't have a shirt to wear. I feel so bad. I feel so lucky to have met such a good person who doesn't drink or yell that often. I just feel like a failure on all fronts—I am not pleasing him, and I am not being a good mom or a good teacher. *(Starts to tear up)*

Rose: Vivian, things will get better. The school year is nearly half over, and we all will know so much more about teaching next year. I think you're doing a good job. I like teaching with you when we have those joint classes. Don't the rest of you think Vivian is a good teacher?

Leader: *(With a kind voice)* Wait just a second. I don't think this is really about whether Vivian is a good teacher but more about the self-talk that is going on in her head. Vivian, would you like to understand more about where your stress is coming from?

The Negative Member

A negative member is one who constantly complains about the group or disagrees with other members of the group. Negative members are particularly troublesome because their attitude and behavior run counter to the leader's goal of maintaining a positive working tone. If one or two members are negative and begin to complain, other members will sometimes join in and also become negative. The result is that group sessions become gripe sessions, and very little is accomplished.

There are three possible strategies for dealing with the negative member:

- Talk to the person outside the group and attempt to establish why he is so negative. The leader can even ask for the member's cooperation and help in making the group productive. Sometimes, such members simply want the leader's attention or a role to play in the group and can be offered a positive role.
- Identify the allies (positive group members) in the group and direct questions and comments to them. Getting these members to talk more than the negative members can help to establish a more positive tone in the group.
- When asking the group a question, avoid eye contact with the negative person so as not to draw her out.

The biggest mistake is to confront the negative member in front of the other group members. This can turn into an argument between the leader and the negative member, which would not be productive for the other group members.

If the leader finds herself in any kind of argumentative situation, it is usually best to shift the focus to another person or topic and then talk to the negative member at the end of the group.

It is important to remember that groups will at times have one or two negative members. This is especially true at the beginning of a group—and particularly so if the group is a mandatory one. Many times, negativism diminishes as the group becomes more interesting. However, there will be times that no matter what the leader does, a member will remain negative. In extreme cases, it may be necessary to ask the member to leave the group or to sit quietly. Too often, leaders devote far too much time trying to work with the negative member, while ignoring those members who are interested in the group.

The Resistant Member

Some members are resistant because they are forced to be in the group. Sometimes, these members will work through their resistance if they are given a chance to express their anger. This situation is difficult for the leader because he does not know whether allowing the member to express anger will be beneficial, or if the member will merely complain and set a negative tone for the group. It is essential, however, for the leader to pay attention when a member is seemingly working through her resistance.

Following are four examples of resistant members:

- The member who, during the first meeting, says he does not know why he has to be at the meeting and does not see how the group can be helpful.
- The member who sits with her arms crossed and does not contribute unless forced to—and then says as little as possible.
- The member who always tries to get the group to focus on topics not relevant to the group, such as movies, sports, or the latest fashions.
- The member who is not resisting the group but is resistant to changing something about himself.

Some members have negative expectations about the effectiveness of the group. These members believe that the group will not be helpful, and they therefore refuse to participate cooperatively. If the leader is faced with a resistant member, her two primary strategies are to let the member share his feelings in the group, or to talk to him in a dyad or after the session and try to help him work through his resistance. If neither of these works and the member has to remain in the group due to the setting (such as a residential treatment center), the leader will want to be sure *not* to focus on that member. Often, beginning leaders will devote as much as half of each session trying to break down the resistance.

Sometimes a resistant member appears to be opposed to the leader's attempt to be helpful, but not to the members' attempts. If this seems to be the case, then another method of working with the resistant member might be to set up situations in which the member can share with other members of the group rather than be the direct focus of the leader. This can be done through the use of dyads, triads, and small-group discussions without the direct participation of the leader. Or if the member is the focus of the group, the leader can let the members do the majority of the helping.

Conversely, the resistant member may be opposed to the attempts of the group to be helpful, but not to the leader's. If this is the case, individual counseling within the group or privately may be the best way to help the member.

It is important that the leader distinguish between the member who is resisting the group process and the member who is resistant because she does not want to change something about herself or her situation.

◆ E X A M P L E

Angela has been discussing being a mother and having a career. She has stated that she wants to continue her career but doesn't know what to do with her children during the day.

Jackie: Could you leave them at a day care center?

Angela: Yes, but I'm not so sure that is good place for them.

Todd: Does your company have a program for taking care of employees' children?

Angela: Yes, but I don't like some of the children and workers there.

Frances: Do you have relatives nearby who would be willing to care for them?

Angela: Yes, but I hate to impose.

In a case like this, the leader should realize that the member is resistant or hesitant to hear suggestions. One way to deal with this resistance would be to say something like:

Leader: Angela, I think we understand the concern, but I am not sure how we can be of help here in the group. What would be helpful to you?

Another way to handle resistance in many groups is to focus on the resistant member in an indirect manner, as described in Chapter Thirteen. That is, the leader may work with a more willing member with the intent of helping the resistant member learn something by watching. Conducting therapy in this manner takes the direct focus off the resistant member. The important thing to remember is to not spend too much time with the resistant member if it takes away productive time from the other group members.

The Member Who Tries to "Get the Leader"

When leading a group, the leader should be prepared for what we call "get the leader." This can be defined as a member's attempt to sabotage what the leader is saying or doing in the group. Getting the leader can take the form of disagreeing with the leader, not following through with instructions given by the leader, asking unanswerable questions so as to make the leader look bad, or talking to others while the leader is talking. Get the leader is different from negativism in that the member is truly after the leader, whereas the negative member feels apathetic, disinterested, or angry in general.

There are a variety of possible causes for members to want to get the leader. Often, the reasons can be traced to something said or done by the leader that caused the member to become irritated or embarrassed. The following is a list of some leader behaviors that might cause members to want to get the leader.

- Putting a member on the spot in front of the other members
- Cutting off a member inappropriately (or even appropriately)
- Not giving a member the chance to talk or failing to recognize when a member wants to speak
- Telling a member that the group will come back to his issue or concern and then failing to do so
- Allowing the group members to offer too much negative feedback to a particular member
- Not being skilled enough to control the group
- Allowing the group to be boring due to the leader's lack of skill

Although the leader is often the cause of get-the-leader behavior in the group, there are other possible causes.

- Members who are not self-referred sometimes take out their frustrations and anger on the leader.
- Members sometimes project their fears about being in the group onto the leader.
- Members who have struggled in their relationships with authority figures might attempt to spoil the leader's efforts.
- Members sometimes want to be the leader's "favorite" and react angrily when they don't feel that they are.

Probably the first thing a leader should do when she realizes that a member is trying to get her is to shift the focus away from any power struggle between the member and herself.

◆ E X A M P L E S

Leader: I'd like us to begin today's session by talking about how drinking has affected your family life.

Joe: Why do you always have to start the group and pick the topics? I thought this was *our* group. Tell me!

Leader: *(Using a calm voice while making eye contact with all of the members, with no extra contact with Joe so as to try to discourage Joe from additional comments)*

Let me explain to all of you how I decide on the topics. Also, be aware that if there is a topic or something that you would like to discuss, you can let me know. There are a number of topics that I feel we should cover. . . .

Leader: I would like each of you to close your eyes and try to imagine that—

Lynn: *(Interrupting)* Are you going to do another one of those stupid fantasy exercises? What good are they!?

Leader: Lynn, feel free to sit quietly. *(To the other members)* I want you to close your eyes and imagine that you are an animal. . . .

Once the leader has sidestepped the member's attempt to get him, he should try to understand why the member has targeted him. Often, the leader will know why it happened, and if the problem is correctable by such techniques as paying more attention to the member, going back to the member's issue, or making sure not to put the member on the spot, then the leader should make the correction. If the leader does not understand why the member has targeted him, he might choose to pair up in a dyad with the member or talk to the member at the end of the session to see if he can gain some information. He might say something like, "Something seems to be going on between you and me. Is it anything I said or did that upset you?"

If the member does not want to share his thoughts, the leader might be able to gain some insight from talking to other members. Often a member will share disgruntled thoughts with a fellow member but not with the leader. If the leader seeks information from other members, he must be very careful to ensure that the members do not feel any pressure to share something they feel they should not share. This may happen in school or residential settings where the counselor interacts with the members on a regular basis.

If a member persists in trying to sabotage the leader, and the leader has talked to the member to no avail, the leader may get help from the group by asking for feedback about the member's complaints or behavior. The leader would do this only if he knew he had the support and understanding of all, or nearly all, the other members. The leader could ask the entire group, "Do you like the way the group is going and the activities I ask you to do?" Or he could be more specific: "I would like some feedback. Whenever I suggest anything, Cleve always wants to argue or question me. How do the rest of you feel about Cleve's doing that?" Assuming a favorable response was obtained from either of these feedback questions, the member should see that he is alone in his attacks or that the other members are annoyed with his behavior.

Too many beginning leaders fail to recognize "get the leader" and misread it as resistance or negativism when, in fact, it is something that they either caused or can change with a slight adjustment. Then again, there will be times when there is almost nothing the leader can do to stop the member other than removing that member from the group.

Dealing with Silence

There is both productive and nonproductive silence in a group. Productive silence occurs when members are internally processing something that was said or done in the group. Nonproductive silence occurs when members are quiet because they are confused about what to say, fearful of talking, or bored. Silence can sometimes serve as a signal to the leader. When the group is silent, the leader should ask himself "Is this silence productive?" The leader can usually tell by observing the members' reactions as they are sitting there and also by considering what has just occurred in the group. If the members seem deep in thought as a result of someone's intense work, the silence should be allowed. Sometimes, the leader may want to let the silence last for 2 or 3 minutes or for as long as it appears to be productive. The leader may choose to wait until someone else breaks the silence, or he may choose to break the silence by saying something like, "Many of you seem to really be thinking about what just happened. I'd like you to briefly share your thoughts." If, however, the members are silent because they are not interested, then the silence should be a signal to the leader to change the focus or to address the group about their lack of interest.

Sometimes members are silent at the beginning of a session because they are not yet warmed up to the session. It can be a mistake to let silence occur at the beginning of the session because what the members really need is some discussion or activity to get them started. This goes back to what we have said about the importance of leading the group rather than waiting for the members to take charge. Sometimes, the wait is very long and not productive.

If the members are sitting there with nervous looks on their faces wondering who will start or are sitting there with blank looks, we suggest that the leader break the silence after 15 or 20 seconds in order to get the group started. Although some experts feel very differently about this and will let the group sit in silence for 5 to 10 minutes in the belief that the members should be responsible for what happens in the group, we have found this, for the most part, to be counterproductive. In groups in which this has occurred, many members have reported that they were confused about what was going on and were bored sitting there waiting for something to happen. It can also promote verbal attacks among members. We feel that in situations where the members are not really thinking, the group time usually can be better spent when the leader breaks the silence with a question, a round, or an exercise that is relevant and productive.

When the leader feels the silence is being very productive and a member starts to speak, the leader can say to the member, "Let's wait just a few more seconds. People seem to really be thinking."

Dealing with Sexual Feelings

Sometimes group members will feel sexually attracted to other members, especially in therapy, growth, and support groups in which members share on a personal level. Certain group dynamics may emerge when this occurs. Members may try to impress each other; they may hold back sharing because of another; or they may become jealous, hurt, or angry at what another member is sharing. These kinds of dynamics can be detrimental to the group process, but a leader must keep in mind that sexual attraction can and will occur almost anywhere irrespective of the context. There is nothing the leader can do about it; in fact, leaders will not want to act as moral legislators. Some leaders set a ground rule that members cannot relate to one another outside the group. Our observation is that members are going to do this regardless of the rule, so the better strategy is to talk about how this can become a problem.

At times, members form relationships that do not interfere with the group; other times, outside relationships do cause problems. If a situation has arisen that is hindering the group (such as two people dating or one person being interested in another member who is not reciprocating), the leader may choose to talk privately to the person or persons involved about possible solutions to the problem. Other times, the issue can be brought up in the group, especially if other members feel that the relationship is disrupting the group in some way. This kind of situation is not easy to handle, but the leader should not ignore members' being attracted to or involved with one another. Sometimes, having one of the members drop out of the group is the best solution.

Dealing with Crying

Members may cry at any time during the group. They may cry when either they or someone else talks about topics such as low self-esteem, abuse, the death of a loved one, a divorce of their own or of their parents, the loss of a job, an illness, or moving from one place to another. The tears may range from moisture in the eyes (tearing up) to uncontrollable sobbing, and may indicate a range of emotions from sadness to fear, anger, depression, emptiness, confusion, anxiety, and even happiness.

Some leaders, when they notice that a member is starting to cry, will immediately start trying to help the member with the pain before getting a contract to do so. Often, members are not ready to discuss what they are feeling, so when the leader tries to help, the member feels pressure, which may lead to resentment. The leader should always be sure the member wants to work on the problem and that there is enough time. A common mistake that beginning leaders make when they notice a member tearing up is to focus on that member without considering how much time is left in the session. They then find themselves having to cut short the work with that person due to having to close the session. Naturally, if someone is in pain, the leader will want to be sensitive to that person, but he also needs to be aware of the time.

If time is not a factor, one strategy that the leader may use is to pair up with the member in pain to find out more about the pain. To occupy the other members, the leader would have them get into dyads and process what had just been discussed or some other topic that the leader thinks is relevant. Another strategy would be to acknowledge the pain and to suggest to the member that they talk after the group.

Another important consideration is whether the crying is a result of some struggle or painful event or is an attempt to gain sympathy. The natural reaction of most group members is to feel sorry for the person or to reach out and touch the person who is crying. Members are usually not aware of the difference between a member who is genuinely struggling with some painful issue and one who wants to be rescued. Often, it is appropriate to ask a member not to touch or hug another member who is feeling sorry for himself or playing a "poor me" game. Hugging or touching that member would not be therapeutic.

In some groups, such as educational or discussion groups or even some experiential groups, dealing for any length of time with a member in psychological pain would not be appropriate. If the leader observes that someone is beginning to cry, he may want to shift the focus away from that member and then seek her out after the group. Or the leader may want to say something like, "Martina, I can see that there is some pain going on. Let's talk after the group." Beginning leaders often make the mistake, when leading education, discussion, or task groups, of holding the focus on the person in pain, thus creating confusion in the members who are expecting a different kind of group.

◆ E X A M P L E S

This group is composed of cancer patients. One of the members, Wanda, has been discussing her failing health.

Wanda: Some days are better than others. I try to keep a positive attitude about the whole thing, and I succeed if I feel good that day. Today, I've felt bad. *(She begins to cry.)* It's on these days that I wonder if I'm gonna make it.

Jerry: *(Sitting next to her, he puts his arm around her shoulders and attempts to comfort her.)* Wanda, let it out if you need to. I don't think it helps to always try to keep up a positive image.

In this example, Wanda was genuinely struggling with a life-and-death issue. It was perfectly acceptable for Jerry to touch her.

Leslie: *(In a little-girl voice)* They just never let me grow up. Just like this past Christmas. I wanted to go to the mountains to ski, but my mother said that I should come home since my grandparents were going to be there. They make me so mad. *(Starts to cry)* And they also hurt my feelings. My dad said that I was selfish and that I only think of myself. I just wish they would learn to accept me and stop trying to make me a clone of them. *(Carey starts to put her arm around Leslie.)*

Leader: *(In a calm, soft voice)* Carey, don't do that. Leslie, I am wondering if we can get the thinking part of you to deal with this issue? Right now, I sense that you are coming more from the hurt, angry part.

One of the biggest mistakes that leaders make when a member begins to cry over some painful issue is to allow the other group members to ask a series of irrelevant questions. In the preceding example, some members might have responded to Leslie's statement in the following ways:

- Where do your parents live?
- How many grandchildren do your grandparents have?
- How often do you visit?

Group members can divert the central focus of the group by asking such irrelevant and untimely questions, often out of discomfort and a desire to stop the crying. When this occurs, the leader must step in and cut off the questions.

Another problem is a member's starting to cry during the first or second session, before the group is ready to deal with an intense emotional concern. Many times a member will be ready to delve into his concern. However, the leader needs to be careful in this situation because sometimes members become frightened by the emotional intensity and do not return. During the first and second sessions, you should be cautious about how much pain and emotion you let members express. If the majority of the group seems ready, then it can be valuable to let a member get into his intense pain.

Dealing with Mutually Hostile Members

In any kind of group, there is the possibility of one member disliking another member. This dislike may manifest itself in arguments, disagreements, and silence between members. Sometimes, members begin the group disliking each other because of something that happened before the group began. If possible, this should be checked out by the leader during the screening interview by asking, "Is there anyone whom you dislike and would not want to be in the group with you?" However, this is not a foolproof method for preventing members from disliking each other because even members who do not know each other at the beginning of the group can quickly grow to dislike each other as the group progresses. When this occurs, the leader may want to bring the issue up in the group if she feels that such a discussion would be beneficial. Often members' behavior within the group is indicative of their behavior outside the group, and focusing on the process of how members came to dislike each other can be one of the most beneficial discussions for them in terms of helping them become more accepting of others in their daily lives. Helping members come to terms with each other can also potentially be one of the most productive processes for solidifying the group and building group cohesion. The point here, however, is that there will be times when, no mater what happens in the group, members will not overcome their personal dislike for each other. In these cases, the goal is not to get members to like each other but rather to get the members to not let their dislike for another completely interfere with their benefiting from the group experience.

If the leader decides to focus on a major conflict between two members during a group session, we suggest that the leader discuss this with each member individually prior to the session to identify the issue clearly and explain the reason for wishing to deal with it in the group. This individual contact between the leader and each member should also be used to build additional rapport and enlist the cooperation of the members. Without getting a commitment from each member to work toward a resolution of the issue, the leader is setting the stage for a potential disaster. If the leader confronts the members unexpectedly, either or both members may use the group as a major battleground.

◆ E X A M P L E

Two members of a group in a residential treatment center for adolescents are in a power struggle over control issues in the center. The leader has the option of switching either member into another therapy group but decides to try to help them work on their issues. The leader meets with each member individually and then opens the session as follows:

Leader: Today, I'm hoping we can spend some time dealing with an issue that is important to all of us. As you know, Jack and Phillip have had some problems with each other since they've been here. I talked to each of them and got them to agree to try and work some things out in the group. *(The leader then turns to the two members to get confirmation.)*

Jack: Yeah, I agree to try.

Phillip: It's OK with me.

Leader: OK, I guess I'd like to start by asking the rest of you what you see as the cause of the problems between Jack and Phillip.

Moe: They each think they are right and can't stand it if the other is right.

Pete: They are always trying to one-up each other. Jack is a pretty good listener when anyone but Phillip is talking. When Phillip talks, Jack, you don't listen to him at all.

Jack: He doesn't listen to me. When I was talking about my dad, he said I was stupid!

Leader: So wait a minute. Some of your anger, Jack, is over the thing Phillip did when you were talking about your dad? How do others of you deal with someone who has upset you?

In this example, the leader chooses to allow the other members to provide feedback and will gradually involve these two members as the discussion continues. Instead of focusing on specific complaints, focusing on the general topic of conflict resolution and ways of dealing with anger may be the most productive direction. Later in the session, examples provided by the two members in conflict may be used to demonstrate how differences can be handled. The leader is not avoiding the conflict between these members by this approach. On the contrary, the leader is assuming they lack good techniques for resolving their power struggle and must be provided with such techniques before their efforts can be successful.

When members don't like each other, the leader may be able to prevent any further growth of animosity by paying attention to how he uses dyads and exercises. Placing members who dislike each other in pairs or having them complete an exercise with each other may only serve as a battleground for their dislike toward each other. On the other hand, forcing antagonistic members to work together may promote their coming to terms with their differences. Sometimes pairing the two members who dislike each other and then joining the dyad to help them talk through their dislikes is very effective.

If the dislike is so great that it is interfering with the group, one or both members should be removed from the group if possible and placed in a different group. In addition, if this type of behavior seems to be a pattern for a particular member, perhaps the member is not ready for a group and would benefit more from individual counseling before becoming a member of a group.

Asking a Member to Leave

Although asking a member to leave the group is not a regular occurrence, it is an option that leaders need to understand. There are several reasons a leader would ask a member to leave, such as being very negative, hostile, or resistant. Another reason for asking a member to leave the group is that a particular member's needs may be so contrary to the purpose of the group that he would receive no benefit from it. For example, if a member kept bringing up personal problems dealing with his self-concept, marriage, and weight in a parent education group, it would be best if that member were not a part of that group. After determining that a member should not be a part of the group, the next consideration is how and when to tell that member. Sometimes, the task can be quite easy. For example, the leader could meet with the member after the group and say something like the following:

Leader: Warren, it seems that the things you really need from a group are not what this group is about. Maybe you have even wondered whether or not this group could be helpful to you. Given that your needs will not be served by this group, I think it might be best if we found you another alternative. Perhaps we could locate a more appropriate group for you or refer you to someone whom you could see on an individual basis. What do you think?

Another reason for asking a member to leave is that she has been very disruptive. Certainly, there must be attempts to bring the disruptive member under control before asking the member to leave. However, if these methods have little or no effect and the member continues to disrupt and intrude on the rights of the other members, the leader should ask that member to leave the group. Ideally, it is best to do so at the end of a session or during a dyad. This prevents a power struggle from occurring in front of the other members. For example, at the end of a session, the leader could say, in private, something like:

Leader: *(Calmly)* Patty, I must speak to you very frankly for a moment. Whether or not you are aware of it, you are disrupting the group to the point that I'm afraid the other members are not receiving any benefit. All attempts to halt your disruption have been to no avail. I think it would be best if you did not return. It is my responsibility to refer you to another group or to an individual therapist, and I will do so.

If the disruption is so severe that waiting until a break or the end of the group is not possible, the leader must act immediately so that the session may resume and be of benefit to the other members. In this case, the leader must explain the action to the entire group and then say something like, "Steve, I must ask you to leave," or "Steve, you have disrupted the group too much; please leave."

Of course, these strategies mentioned apply to group situations in which the members are removable; that is, they are volunteers for the group, or the setting gives the leader the freedom to remove a member if necessary. In a setting where the members must attend and there is no freedom to remove a member, the leader may ask that the member sit in silence or sit outside the circle of working members.

Dealing with Prejudiced, Narrow-Minded, or Insensitive Members

Every now and then, a leader must deal with a member who has a very narrow or prejudiced view of the world and who tries to act as a moralist or preacher. This is a difficult situation because one purpose of most groups is to hear different points of view and learn to be tolerant of others. However, there is a point when a member who cannot refrain from preaching and judging others may have to be removed from the group. It is not good leadership to always let members have their say. For instance, if a woman is talking about having an affair and another member starts in about how evil and wrong it is, the leader should quickly cut off that member. In a case like this, the leader would have to ask the member politely to try to understand that others have different views. If this does not work, and the member insists on being heard, the leader may need to ask the member to leave the group. The leadership rule is to be tolerant of members' differences and only intervene when a member's comments are so prejudiced that they could be harmful. In the following example, the leader did not hesitate to quickly cut off the member who was being insensitive.

◆ E X A M P L E

Susan: I know I am young and all, but for the last year or so, I have been really questioning if there is a god. I am not sure how others of you feel, but I don't think I believe in God. This has me worried, and I end up often fighting with my mom about this.

Donna: *(Angrily and with a condescending voice)* How can you not believe in God?!

Susan: I am confused, and it does not feel good since all my life I have thought of God as an important part of my life, and now, I don't know what to think. It just doesn't make sense to me, especially when I talk with these friends of my brother who are in college and studying world religions.

Donna: That's crazy. What do they know compared to what older people know? Where do you think we came from?

Leader: *(In a calm, caring voice)* Donna, try to be helpful to Susan. Tune in to her.

Donna: Maybe you are just going to the wrong church. You should come to my church! I just can't believe you are questioning if there is a God. My father says that anyone who doesn't believe in God is—

Leader: *(Firmly)* Wait a minute. Donna, if you cannot tune into her pain, then you need to be quiet. Your comments are not helpful. Susan, I want you to look at other members and realize that we do understand how hard this was for you. *(She looks around and sees very concerned faces; Donna is staring down.)* I feel that we can help you. Are you willing to talk about it some more?

Susan: Yes.

In this example, the leader had to intervene quickly since the member was being insensitive to the situation. If the member persists, the leader may have to talk with the member or even ask her to leave the group if she is not open to viewpoints different from hers.

Concluding Comments

As a group leader, you will be faced with many difficult situations and many difficult members—such as the chronic talker, the dominator, the distractor, the negative member, the resistant member, the crying member, or the member who is out to "get the leader." For each of these situations, there are different skills and techniques that can be of help. For resistant clients, it is important to distinguish whether the resistance is in regard to being in the group or the fear of changing. For crying members, the leader has to know when the tears should be supported and when they should be ignored. A very important thing to understand is that there will be times when you will have to ask a member to leave the group because of the dynamics that he is creating. We suggest that, when faced with situations that we have described (and you will be faced with them if you lead groups), you refer back to this chapter and not feel the problems are unique to your group or a reflection on your leadership.

CHAPTER SIXTEEN

Working with Specific Populations

Often, group leaders work with specific populations. For each population, there are some unique leadership considerations. In this chapter, we have selected nine populations that we feel present some special challenges. The purpose of this chapter is to touch on some of the group counseling issues concerning the nine selected populations, but by no means are we attempting to cover the topic thoroughly. We discuss mainly support, growth, counseling, and therapy groups within each of the following populations.

- ✦ Children
- ✦ Adolescents
- ✦ Couples
- ✦ Chemically dependent clients
- ✦ Older clients
- ✦ Clients with chronic diseases or disabilities
- ✦ Survivors of sexual abuse
- ✦ Divorced or divorcing clients
- ✦ Adult children of alcoholics (ACOAs)

Children

Many kinds of groups can be conducted with young children. Groups valuable for almost any child are those that deal with values and self-concept. Some excellent resources are available if you are considering leading groups with children; they offer specific group activities and exercises that are interesting and helpful (Morganett, 1994; Smead,1995; Vernon, 1993).

In addition to values and self-concept groups, groups with a specific theme or purpose can be formed. Topic groups on anger, siblings, shyness, and friends are excellent for children. Many elementary school counselors conduct groups for children whose parents are going through or have recently gone through a divorce. Counselors also set up groups for children living in stepfamilies or foster care. These groups offer valuable support for children—the children learn that they are not alone in their feelings. Another common type of group is for children of alcoholic parents. These groups provide information, support, and therapy for kids living with an alcoholic. For each of these kinds of groups, the leader would need not only group leadership skills but also knowledge of specific topics such as the effects of divorce, stepfamily living, or living with a chemically dependent person.

The skills needed for leading groups with children are basically the same as those needed for adult groups. One of the main differences is that the leader may need to take more responsibility for the group than in a group composed of adults. That is, children often do not come each time with something they want to talk about. Exercises, short stories or skits, and the use of puppets, drawings, and other props all are helpful tools for the leader. If the proper tone is established, children usually will be more than eager to talk. In fact, the leader may frequently need to cut off members in order to let others share.

The length of the sessions and the number of participants should be different than for adults. Depending on the age group, anywhere from 30 to 45 minutes is appropriate. The best number of participants for most groups for children seems to be 5 or 6, although classroom guidance can be effective with as many as 35.

In workshops for elementary school counselors, participants have commented that they had too much "fluff" (fun and games) in their groups and not enough depth. Granted, with young children it is sometimes hard to take the group deeper, but if the leader is clear about the group's purpose, she can have a productive session. By using props, creative ideas, and good leadership skills, the focus can be held and taken to a level that is meaningful for the members. Usually, the counselor will not do individual work for any length of time because the other children would probably become restless, but the focus on a topic can go to a 7 or a 6 level. Often, a group session can lead to an individual follow-up session.

If you are planning to lead groups with children, we suggest that you read Rosemarie Smead's book (1995) in which she describes setting up and conducting groups with children. She also discusses such aspects as working with principals and teachers, obtaining permission from parents, confidentiality, and preparing for the group.

Adolescents

Adolescence is a difficult period in a young person's life. Voluntary growth, discussion, education, counseling, and therapy groups can be quite valuable at this stage. Groups can help with identity problems, sexual concerns, and problems with friends, parents, and school. Groups for pregnant teenagers, drug users, teenage parents, potential school dropouts, and runaways can be extremely helpful. Other valuable groups are those for adolescents who are having problems due to their parents' divorce, remarriage, or alcohol abuse.

A group leader working with adolescents should like and respect teenagers, want to learn more about their immediate world, and understand the kinds of struggles they go through while trying to grow up. Teenagers are very aware of phony attempts by the leader to be one of them or of a one-up attitude that suggests an adult knows more. They will often test the leader's level of acceptance of their values. Unfortunately, it is common for group leaders of teens to sound like parents. Hidden agendas—such as wanting the members to study harder in school, stop using drugs or drinking, or behave better in class—are quickly spotted, thus causing the members to lose respect for the leader. Leaders of adolescent groups often will be confronted if they are dishonest or not open about their intentions.

Any discussion of adolescent groups would be remiss if it did not touch on the nonvolunteer adolescent group. Many groups for adolescents are not voluntary. These groups may be school ordered, court ordered, parent ordered, or agency ordered. Many schools have mandatory groups for those caught with drugs, those with too many absences, those with poor grades, or those who want to quit school. Courts sometimes order teenagers to participate in group therapy with an agency. Many residential settings have mandatory group attendance. Leading any of these groups is extremely difficult. The leader will have to be creative and innovative to turn the negative energy around. With adolescents, especially in the initial sessions, the leader must plan interesting and relevant activities. The use of role plays, moral dilemma exercises, sentence completions, and common readings are all helpful to get members interested and involved. Starting with a formal presentation of the rules is *not* the way to start a nonvolunteer group—this sets a negative tone for members who are already negative. During the first couple of sessions of a nonvolunteer group, the leader should expect negative behavior, both verbal and nonverbal. Sometimes, it is a good strategy to allow members time to complain during the initial session. One counselor we know started her after-school group for adolescent drug users by dealing with the anger.

Leader: I know you do not want to be here, so we can take 10 minutes to complain about it, but after that we'll get focused on what we are doing here. If you want to complain, I am going to put this trash can in the center of the group. In 10 minutes, after you have dumped much of your anger, I'll remove it and we'll get started.

Problems with confidentiality can often occur in groups with adolescents. Sometimes, the leader can avert these problems by carefully screening the members to avoid placing in the same group members who do not get along. Because confidentiality is so important, the leader must make clear to the members the consequences of breaking that confidence. The consequences may be discussed and agreed on by the entire group, or the leader may simply state the consequences, such as removal from the group. The leader also needs to inform the members that she may have to tell parents about certain things that are said if she feels the person is in danger of hurting him or herself or is engaging in behaviors that are very harmful or self-defeating. Agency or school policy plus state laws may dictate what you can and cannot keep confidential.

Sessions with adolescents should last between 40 and 90 minutes. The size of any kind of growth, support, counseling, or therapy group should be no more than eight members, with six being ideal. Depending on the group's purpose, the leader may want to lead all males, all females, or a mix of both. The value of the coed group is that there is a lot to learn about the opposite sex during the adolescent years, and the group can be a very good place to do so. The disadvantage to mixed groups is that members may be inhibited when the opposite sex is present.

Couples

Several kinds of groups involve couples: marital enrichment groups, groups for abusive relationships, premarital counseling groups, or group therapy for couples. Groups for gay couples, interracial couples, and interfaith couples have been found to be very valuable for the participants. Other groups that have involved couples include groups for parents of young children or teenagers, parents of children with special needs, parents of babies who died suddenly, and couples who are caring for a mentally ill person or someone with Alzheimer's disease. In this section, we mainly focus on couples therapy groups.

Groups for couples offer some special challenges to the group leader. The leader is not only dealing with the dynamics among six or eight members but also with three or four relationships that have their own dynamics. Couples groups, therefore, are very complex and usually are difficult to lead. In a therapy group for couples, members may have different agendas. One member of a couple may be coming to the group hoping that the relationship can be improved or saved while the other is perfectly satisfied with the status quo or wishes to negotiate a divorce. Groups of this nature can become quite intense because the two members will often air their differences in the group. Sometimes, this is very painful for the couple as well as for other group members who are watching.

Because the needs of couples wishing to participate in a group experience can vary considerably, it is important for the leader to be clear about the purpose of the group. Through screening interviews, the leader can inform couples about the purpose and assess their individual and mutual needs. Meeting with the couple as well as with each partner individually provides a chance for the leader to get a broader perspective on the relationship. If one of the partners is not committed to working on the relationship, the leader may suggest couple counseling before or in addition to the group experience. Often, during screening, it will be evident that one of the partners needs some intensive therapy rather than a couples group experience. Other problems that may arise during the screening or during the group itself include the following:

- One or both partners may be reluctant to share personal thoughts and feelings in front of the other.
- One partner may feel the need to conceal an affair.
- Couples may use the group to vent powerful, negative feelings they have held in for a long time.
- One or both partners may try to use the group as a jury to vindicate their behavior in some way.

- One member in the relationship may try to enlist the group to change the partner's behavior.
- One partner may use the group to search for a new relationship.
- Members may compare themselves or their partner with others in the group and feel bad because he or she does not compare favorably.

The format for couples groups can vary. Many enrichment groups are held on an extended basis, for a full day or a weekend, with the idea that this allows time for partners to explore more fully the dimensions of their relationships and to work more intensely on issues (Corey & Corey, 1992). Full-day or weekend sessions also allow more sharing with and learning from other couples. A drawback to this format is that couples may leave the session with a group "high," feeling renewed and excited about their relationship, only to reenter the real world of kids, work, traffic, money, and in-laws. Their enthusiasm and renewed commitment may carry them along for days or weeks, but long-standing, underlying problems can surface again for some couples under the pressure of everyday living. Many leaders who conduct such marathon couples groups hold follow-up meetings to support the couples' changes and to help strengthen areas they have worked on.

A weekly or biweekly group session format can also be used with couples. One drawback to this format is that a couple, especially if they are parents, may have a problem getting free to attend a 2- or 3-hour group session on a regular basis for several weeks or months. If couples are willing to make this commitment, however, much can be done to help them look at their relationship. Couples can work on improving intimacy, handling disagreements, making decisions, and so forth, as well as have the opportunity to discuss and handle daily issues that might arise for them, such as parenting, money, personal time scheduling, sex, in-laws, and vacations. Weekly or biweekly sessions allow couples to try out communication and problem-solving techniques over an extended period of time; if they run into snags, the group is there to help work them out. This format takes into consideration that personal change—especially when two people are involved—is often slow and erratic, requiring continued reinforcement to be lasting.

There are many excellent exercises available for leaders working with couples groups (Corey & Corey, 1992; Jacobs, 1992; Stevens, 1972). Such exercises are helpful because they encourage couples to look at the broader issues that many people in relationships share, rather than to focus only on their own specific disagreements. Exercises help couples examine such areas as sex-role problems in the relationship, dependency, the need for innovation to keep relationships interesting, the need for separate identities, games that interfere with intimacy, and the role of childhood experiences in shaping values about relationships and marriage. Hearing other couples discuss their reactions to the exercises is very valuable for the members. Dr. Pat Love, in Austin, Texas, has conducted some outstanding weekend workshops with couples regarding sex and intimacy.

Chemically Dependent Clients

Many groups are available to the addicted client. Education groups can provide valuable information. Support groups can be very helpful for those in recovery. Twelve-step support groups, such as Alcoholics Anonymous and Narcotics Anonymous, have benefited millions of people. Therapy groups are beneficial for those who are in denial or are still struggling with their addiction and its consequences. In this section, we focus mainly on therapy groups dealing with those who have problems with alcohol and drugs, although most of our discussion is also relevant for groups that are dealing with sex addiction, eating disorders, gambling addiction, and other addictions.

There are many voluntary and nonvoluntary groups for those who have some addiction that greatly affects their lives. Those addicted who want help often volunteer for recovery and relapse prevention groups. The nonvoluntary groups consist of those who were caught driving under the influence, or those who were mandated to attend by their employer, school, or some other outside force. The initial sessions of any nonvoluntary group for alcoholics are difficult to lead because the members are not attending by choice, and many of them do not see themselves as having a problem. The leader must be prepared to deal with the members' anger at being forced to be in the group and the anger members feel when the leader refers to the fact that alcohol and drugs are creating problems in their lives. There are no easy solutions to the problems of working with nonvoluntary alcoholics. Leaders must be patient and understand that they will not see quick and dramatic results.

Nearly all groups dealing with chemically dependent people have to deal with their denial, which makes leading quite difficult. In addition to having a thorough knowledge of addiction and group leadership, the leader has to have the courage to be confrontive because there is a tendency both to deny the problem and to attempt to manipulate others into believing that the problem is not a significant factor in the member's life. The use of confrontation requires skill and sensitivity. The leader must always remember that effective confrontation involves confronting a member about inconsistencies, rather than a personal attack. This confrontation can be done by the leader or by another member.

Leaders can easily become frustrated with members who deny their problem and may use confrontation in a punitive way. Punitive confrontation attacks, belittles, and humiliates the member. Punitive confrontation is inappropriate, and if a leader finds himself feeling anger toward a member, he should examine his own expectations for the member and perhaps talk with a colleague about his frustration. Constructive confrontation is valuable and often necessary. It involves statements like: "You tell us you are going to go straight, yet you have no real plan for how you are going to do it. That's why none of us believes it will work."

Careful planning must be done for most groups of substance abusers. For any nonvolunteer group, the leader should realize that the members often are going to be defensive about their substance abuse and hesitant to talk about any of their issues. The leader has to plan relevant, interesting exercises and discussions to get members involved and committed to trying to benefit from the group.

One other skill that is absolutely essential when leading groups for addicted persons is cutting off. The leader will need to use cutoff skills because alcoholics often want to tell their "story" over and over again. Many leaders who have worked with alcoholics have said that cutting off the long-winded stories has proven very valuable in allowing them to get more sharing and interaction going and being able to focus on a topic in depth without having to listen to one story after another.

Always keep in mind that this population is extremely difficult to work with. The success rate is not as high as group leaders might find with members who have other types of problems. Group leaders in the substance abuse area should not expect rapid, large-scale behavioral change. Leaders should be especially careful to avoid burnout by having realistic expectations, not leading an excessive number of groups in a given day or week, and not feeling personally unsuccessful when members later return to the treatment program for the same abuse problem.

Older Clients

As with other special populations discussed so far, there are some special considerations to be aware of when working with groups of older persons. Although we speak of "older persons," this label cannot possibly accurately describe all those over a certain age because many people in their 80s function in the same way as those in their 50s. As group leaders, we must be aware that the needs of the elderly are similar to the needs of us all; that is, they are very diverse. Older persons may feel they have less personal power now than when they were employed, had children who sought their advice, or had friends who relied on them. This may lead to feelings of lowered self-esteem or alienation. Older people may have less contact with family members, siblings, or children than in former years. They may also have fewer social contacts, as many friends have died or moved away. This can lead to feelings of isolation and depression. Older people, having realistic concerns about physical and mental infirmity and death, can benefit greatly by being in a group in which they can talk about these feelings. The group leader must be comfortable with dealing with thoughts and feelings about death.

Older people are often preoccupied with past events. They tend to reminisce and tell stories of past adventures. Although such storytelling may become boring for other members, it is often a healthy way for people to process their lives and feel good about themselves. A very common activity in groups with older clients is reminiscing about different aspects of their lives. For example, the leader might allow a certain number of minutes for each member to recall his or her most memorable holiday, a particularly happy moment with a spouse or friend, or the most rewarding experience he or she can recall. These exercises can elicit memories that might lead to the member's wanting to do some personal work.

Goals and Kinds of Groups for Older Persons

While older persons can benefit from personal growth and counseling groups, the leader may find as much interest and response among older members for task, support, and education groups. A recent development being tried is to bring older people together, teach them about computers, and show them how they can communicate with others around the country. So far, this has been very successful.

Any of five possible goals may be established for different groups.

- The first goal involves providing information about various matters such as finances, health and medicine, housing, or insurance. The leader can either present the information or arrange for guest speakers.
- Another goal is what we call "making things happen." Older people, especially if they are living in a residential facility, often do not have the resources or the influence individually to make things happen, such as changing a schedule, planning a Christmas party, improving living conditions, and so forth. A task group may take on such goals to improve the general quality of life. Such a group can also provide an opportunity for members to learn or relearn effective assertiveness skills.
- A third goal involves working through personal issues. A personal growth or counseling group can help members deal with unfinished business from the past, such as guilt about not being a better parent or spouse, anger at a former friend or employer, or sadness at not having accomplished something during their lifetime. Issues such as their treatment by children or other family members or their concerns about the future, infirmity, or death are also potential areas for personal work. Members also will benefit from simply sharing these concerns and finding support within the group.
- The fourth goal for groups with older persons is developing and maintaining social contacts. As people grow older, family contacts may be less frequent because of distance or their family's preoccupation with their own lives. Friends move away or die, neighbors change, longtime neighborhood hangouts close, and the opportunity for continued social contact seems to diminish. Making new friends can seem difficult, and therefore some older people tend to become more introverted and preoccupied with themselves and the past. This can lead to diminished social skills and initiating behavior. A support group can provide a place for members to socialize; that is, to regain former social skills, as well as to meet others with whom they may form more lasting relationships.
- Finally, we have found that groups can be very useful in helping older persons explore new goals in life. Such groups may have characteristics of an education group, a support group, and possibly even a growth group as members shift their preoccupation from the past to focus more on the present moment and the future. The leader and other members may provide information and ideas for specific projects such as arts and crafts work or community activities such as joining a foster grandparent program. New goals may involve writing to old friends, establishing closer ties with other family members, or pursuing goals

formerly abandoned, such as writing or taking college courses. Members can learn that, whatever their health restrictions, it is possible to generate a new and continuing interest in life.

Settings

There are four primary settings in which groups for older persons might be held: (1) the community, (2) minimum-care residences or retirement facilities, (3) nursing homes, and (4) institutions.

The Community

There are older persons in most communities who do not have contact with family or friends and who may live a rather isolated life. Some may be in touch with local social agencies. A group program may be developed for such persons to pursue any or all of the goals previously discussed. Such groups may be sponsored by the community mental-health center, schools or colleges, local churches, or senior citizen centers. The problem of transportation must be addressed for members who wish to attend such group sessions.

Minimum-Care Residences

Standard living facilities designed for older persons also provide a setting in which such groups might be run. While such facilities may have professional staff qualified to lead groups, it is more likely that a group leader from the community will provide this service.

Nursing Homes

Nursing homes need some kind of group program. The severity of a person's physical illness will obviously place some constraints on involvement; however, the need may be just as great. Members should be screened for both their physical ability to participate and their mental status.

Institutions

There is a great need for groups for older persons in institutional settings. Many of the goals discussed here can be pursued effectively in such a setting. Institutional living can be very difficult and, coupled with medical and psychiatric problems, can lead patients to become depressed and socially isolated. A group program can go a long way toward helping with resocialization, developing a support network, and providing information and guidance. Corey and Corey (1992) provide a warm description of the contributions Marianne Corey made to a group of older residents in an institutional setting.

Clients with Chronic Diseases
or Disabilities

Groups for persons with chronic diseases or disabilities can be formed on a community basis or in hospitals or rehabilitation centers. Such groups are especially important in light of the stress generated by the onset of a disability or long-term illness. Clients are often uncertain of the course or prognosis of their condition. They must deal with a change in lifestyle, may feel out of control, and often are physically separated from the support of family and friends. The focus of their lives for many weeks or months shifts from the day-to-day business of making a living, attending school, socializing, and being involved with family and recreation, to medical examinations, treatments, and waiting with some degree of uncertainty.

Given the uncertainty of medical factors, the need for emotional support, and the struggle of working through lifestyle changes, there is an important place for different kinds of groups in this population. Groups can provide education and information on health-related issues and help clients deal with psychological issues such as loss of identity, anger, and the grieving process. Groups can also provide support and help with problem solving.

Two groups that deserve special mention are people with AIDS and those with cancer. Many excellent support groups are being led with each of these populations. If you are planning to lead these kinds of groups, you should be aware that literature discussing different approaches to each is increasingly available. We suggest you consult group journals and medical journals that deal with either AIDS or cancer.

It is usually best to form homogeneous groups based on one particular illness or disability because the illness or disability is the common denominator about which patients have concerns. There will be times, however, when this is not possible or when it is helpful to involve group members with different medical concerns. The leader must give a great deal of thought to who is let into the group and must be especially sensitive to the intense anxiety, depression, and anger that people may experience following the onset of a long-term illness or disabling condition. As people move from the acute medical stage to the rehabilitative stage, many begin a grieving process that has some generally predictable phases: (1) denial, (2) anger, (3) bargaining, (4) depression, and finally, (5) acceptance (Kübler-Ross, 1969). It is important for the group leader to understand the phases of this grieving process, both in terms of selecting members for a group and in terms of actually leading the group. Members who are dealing effectively with their medical condition can provide information, lend support, and serve as role models for those who are still in the angry or depressed stages.

Group Dynamics

Groups with members who have a chronic disease or disability are led both as open and as closed groups. Most hospital groups are open because of the need to accommodate new people arriving in the unit who are suffering from the same illness or disability. Groups for family members of people with certain illnesses are also being conducted with great success.

Leaders of groups that deal with a disease or disability need to be prepared for many different dynamics. Because of the sense of injustice members feel at the onset of a chronic illness or disability, they will often have a strong need to express powerful feelings—frustration and anger, in particular. For this reason, group leaders must feel comfortable handling hostility, some of which will be displaced onto them. The anger will often take the form of finding fault with the medical staff, nurses, schedules, and so forth. It is important for the group leader to recognize this anger as an important aspect of the grieving process and to help the member work through it.

Members often become intensely focused on their medical condition to the exclusion of other aspects of their life. They may need to be encouraged to look beyond their medical condition to the possibility of future employment, socializing again with friends, regaining a role in the family, and so forth. The leader may also find that this intense focusing of members on their own condition and anxiety about their prognosis may cause some to try to dominate the discussion, especially in support groups. Effective cutting-off skills are important to use, along with exercises that structure how the members share. For example, a sentence-completion exercise is helpful since the leader can focus members on certain aspects of their lives and illness by the sentences he uses.

Leaders, especially beginners, need to understand that clients with a chronic disease or disability often become quite knowledgeable about their condition. Rather than be threatened by the members' knowledge, leaders should try to learn from them. Certain members may try to use their superior knowledge about their condition to manipulate the leader, attempting to dominate the discussion or discount the leader's effectiveness because of lesser knowledge. The leader may need to use confrontation skills to make sure that such members do not sabotage the purpose of the group.

Having as much knowledge as possible about the disease or disability is always helpful. For example, when working with young men with spinal cord injuries, sexual dysfunction is frequently a major topic that members wish to discuss. Banik and Mendelson (1978) point out the high degree of misinformation that circulates among such patients about sexual problems. The leader will need to have—or make available through medical staff—sound information on the disability and sexual dysfunction. Also, he needs to anticipate the anxiety surrounding this topic. Group members who have had a stroke may experience mood swings caused by their physical condition, depending on the nature and extent of brain damage. It is important for the leader to be aware of the cause of such mood swings, to make sure the affected member knows the cause, and to ensure the other group members understand. Stroke patients may also experience difficulty expressing themselves at times or fully comprehending others' ideas. A lot of support and encouragement must be given such members to keep them involved in the group. Cardiac patients may develop a preoccupation with death and a concern about how much physical energy they can expend safely.

Again, misinformation is common; even accurate information is often not comprehended fully because of these patients' high anxiety levels. Education, along with support and encouragement, is important when working with cardiac patient groups.

A final consideration in working with group members with problems of chronic disease or disability in a residential treatment program is the effect the setting may have on members' outlook and behavior. Most hospitals and rehabilitation facilities regiment behavior and foster dependency. Patients are frequently told when to get up in the morning, when to eat, what activities to attend, when, if, and how often they may use a telephone, and so forth. Patients may even develop a belief that their lives are literally in the hands of the medical staff. Regimented thinking and dependency may lead to apathy on the part of such group members. Leaders may need to work with both staff and group members in countering this apathy.

Survivors of Sexual Abuse

Sexual abuse of children and adolescents is a significant mental-health problem. One way therapists are dealing with this problem is to form groups for survivors. Many mental-health centers lead groups for youngsters. For adult survivors, both men's and women's groups are being conducted in such places as mental-health centers, abuse shelters, and drug and alcohol rehabilitation centers. Leaders of survivors groups should have considerable knowledge of the issues surrounding incest and sexual abuse. Classes, readings, workshops, and leading under the supervision of a more experienced leader should be aspects of the leader's preparation. If the leader is also a survivor of sexual abuse, she should consider the progress she has made in her own healing. As is true in leading any group, personal issues that the leader has yet to resolve could interfere with the leader's role or effectiveness. In the remainder of this section, we focus mainly on working with therapy groups for survivors.

Survivors of sexual abuse are likely to benefit from one of two kinds of groups: support or therapy. Support groups provide an opportunity for survivors to speak of their pain, perhaps for the first time, with others who have also been victimized as children or adolescents. These discussions can be empowering because they validate the abusive experiences and cut through the veil of secrecy that most survivors were subjected to as children. The chance to speak openly in a supportive, confidential setting often helps survivors gain courage to work more productively in their individual therapy.

We usually recommend that a potential member become involved in individual counseling before joining a survivors therapy group. Individual therapy gives survivors a chance to gain an initial understanding of what happened to them. It is not unusual for survivors to deny or rationalize their abuse or to feel overwhelmed with shame. Survivors are likely to benefit more from a therapy group when they have passed beyond their denial and are firmly committed to exploring their abusive experiences.

Individual interviews with the leader before the first group session are especially important in a survivors group. Members should be informed of the purpose of the group, its goals, the frequency and length of sessions, the ground rules, and the techniques that will be used to help members work therapeutically on their issues. The interview should serve as a time for potential members to decide whether they feel ready to be in a therapy group. A member who is not committed to open discussions or is ambivalent about being in the group may feel too vulnerable to participate.

Survivor work in groups may take many sessions. However, because of the pain and distress survivors may experience, it is important to keep members motivated to work on issues. We suggest setting up groups on a time-limited basis, such as in 6- or 8-week blocks. Although the group will likely continue for many months, these benchmarks allow members to assess their progress and decide whether they wish to continue or take a break. We especially want leaders to avoid ongoing groups in which the members and the leader become comfortable with meeting but are not doing the work that is needed.

Therapy groups for survivors focus in depth on the pain of the individual members. However, this does not mean that the members must discuss details of their experiences in the group setting. The extent of detail discussed will depend on the skill of the leader, the comfort level of the members, and the therapeutic needs of each member. Members gain much from sharing about their early family life, relationships with their abusers and other family members, expectations of them as children, and so forth.

Because of the potentially intense reaction of individual members when exploring their abuse, we recommend that the group leader work with one member at a time rather than—as might be true in other kinds of therapy groups—attempt to take the entire group to a deeper level. Even the most skilled leader will be ineffective trying to deal with the severe pain of four or five group members simultaneously. Leaders will soon discover that most members of survivors groups can benefit greatly from watching other members explore their issues.

We support the idea that those in a survivors therapy group either remain in individual therapy or at least maintain periodic contact with their therapist. In many instances, the individual therapist will be the group leader. It is important for members to have a "safe person" to process their experiences if the group experience becomes overwhelming.

Divorced or Divorcing Clients

Recovery and "starting-over" groups are offered for those who are divorced or divorcing. When setting up a divorce group, the leader must be clear as to the group's type and purpose. If the leader is not clear, then the composition of members may be such that the group cannot be successful. Divorce recovery groups consist of members who are currently going through a divorce or are recently divorced and are still very much grieving the loss. For these groups, the leader will want to make sure the member is not in so much pain that he or she would not be ready for the group. Some people need time with an individual counselor before joining a recovery group. Starting-over groups are for people who have worked through the initial pain and loss on their own, with a therapist, or in a group, but who are still looking for help and support in fully letting go and getting on with their new life.

Recovery groups are usually short term, lasting 6 to 8 weeks. Many people who complete a recovery group go on to a starting-over group. These groups can last for several months if they are closed, or they can be open and last indefinitely. Recovery groups can also be either open or closed. Ideally, they would be closed, but because clients at an agency may need such a group, having an open group might work best for the population being served.

A leader of a recovery group must have a thorough knowledge of grief counseling and not be afraid of the emotional pain that will be exhibited. Also, the leader must be skilled at individual counseling because the leader often works with one member at a time. One-on-one work is usually quite effective if the leader uses theories that the other members can apply to their own situation. REBT is quite useful in recovery groups because most of the members are telling themselves a number of the core irrational sentences about approval, failure, and unhappiness. Many say to themselves that they don't think they can live without their partner or that they never will be happy again. Also, much of the anger and blame directed at themselves or their partners needs to be discussed and challenged. The skilled leader can use Impact Therapy and REBT to dispute these ideas. Also, it is important for the leader to be strong in theory since he cannot rely heavily on the members for helpful input because they all are feeling many of the same things.

A starting-over group is a support group in which members help each other by sharing their attempts at new behavior. The leader's role is to make sure that important issues—such as dealing with an ex-spouse, anger, issues with children, meeting new people, dating again, and sex—are discussed. The leader has many options in the way this kind of group is conducted. She can let the members direct the focus of the group by letting them bring up topics that are relevant for them, or she can use a format in which she brings up relevant topics at each session. Some leaders who prefer the latter model use one of the many books or workbooks that have been published about divorce. One excellent book we have found is *Rebuilding* by Bruce Fisher (1992).

Adult Children of Alcoholics (ACOAs)

Many adults who seek counseling come from families where alcohol was a problem when they were young. There are three basic kinds of groups for adult children of alcoholics: leaderless support groups, leader-led support groups, and therapy groups. All three groups are valuable and have helped millions who have been involved with one or more of them. Our discussion will focus on leader-led support groups and therapy groups.

Leaders of support groups for ACOAs will want to make sure the members are ready to be in such a group. If screening is not conducted, leaders may find they have members who actually should be in individual therapy rather than a support group. A support group can come early in a person's recovery and can help the person become aware of the issues that he has, or it can come when a person is in a later stage of recovery. The leader would probably not want to mix these because the needs of the members would be vastly different.

Leaders definitely should screen for a therapy group to make sure the members are appropriate. The leader will want to make sure that any potential member is able to function in a group. In addition, a potential member should not be in such great need that individual therapy would be more helpful than group therapy.

Any leader of ACOA groups must have extensive knowledge about alcoholism and its effects on family members. A leader definitely needs to understand issues such as trust, intimacy, shame, guilt, and abandonment that plague most ACOAs. The leader must be prepared to deal with much emotional pain and anger. Gestalt techniques of talking to an empty chair that represents the alcoholic have proven very effective. Using TA seems to give members a better understanding of themselves now and when they were living with an alcoholic parent. Activities such as family sculpture or psychodrama are extremely valuable if led by a skilled leader who can deal with the emotional material generated. Too often, we hear of mental-health workers leading ACOA groups when they do not have the knowledge or the individual counseling skills essential for leading such groups. If you plan to lead these groups, be sure to get the necessary skills and knowledge. Many excellent books have been written on this subject, and many workshops are presented that deal with working with ACOAs in groups.

Concluding Comments

In this chapter, we discussed considerations and skills involved when leading groups for nine different client populations: children, adolescents, couples, addicts, older persons, those with chronic diseases or disabilities, survivors of sexual abuse, those who are divorced, and ACOAs. Leading groups for each of these populations requires specialized knowledge. Our comments here are meant to introduce you to the issues and considerations involved. As you work in the counseling field, you will be asked to lead groups from these and other populations. In many cases, you will want to do additional reading and attend workshops on the specific groups that you will be leading.

CHAPTER SEVENTEEN

Issues in Group Counseling

In this chapter, we discuss co-leading, ethical and legal issues, evaluation and research in group counseling, training of group counselors, and the future of group counseling.

Co-leading

Leading groups with one or more colleagues can be very advantageous, especially for the beginner. A major advantage is that it is often easier than leading a group alone. Co-leading can be very enjoyable and valuable. A co-leader can provide additional ideas for planning the group and can share the responsibility for leading during the session. Co-leaders can provide support and relief for one another, especially when working with intense therapy groups or with difficult groups; if one leader gets stuck, drained, or off track, another leader is available to take the lead for awhile. Co-leaders often bring different points of view and varied life experiences to the group, providing members with alternative sources of opinion and information on issues. Differences in the interpersonal style of each co-leader can also create variations in the flow or tone of the group that make it more interesting. There may be occasions when a co-leader with more specialized knowledge about a given population is needed. For example, in an educational group for pregnant teenagers, a co-leader with a thorough knowledge of prenatal care can add valuable, relevant information to the group.

Co-leaders can serve as models for members of the group. Effective interaction skills and cooperation are demonstrated by co-leaders who work well together. Opposite-sex co-leaders may serve as role models and may be particularly effective in working with couples groups or groups with marital concerns. In certain kinds of groups, male and female teams can also serve as parental figures in helping members work through unresolved family issues. It should be pointed out that it is not essential that co-leaders be of the opposite sex. Many groups are led successfully by co-leaders of the same sex.

One last advantage of co-leading is that leaders get feedback from another leader. Also, leaders learn from watching each other handle various situations. For maximum awareness of nonverbal cues, co-leaders should sit across from one another in the circle. This provides an opportunity for them to easily maintain eye contact with each other while allowing observation of the members from different vantage points.

Disadvantages and Problems of Co-leading

A number of disadvantages and problems may occur due to co-leading. One disadvantage for some agencies and settings is that co-leading takes time away from other counseling duties and can add stress to an already demanding work schedule. Therefore, co-leading may not be a good use of staff's time.

Problems with co-leading groups arise mainly from differences in attitude, style, and goals of the leaders. Co-leading becomes a disadvantage when two leaders do not see group leading the same way. As Corey and Corey (1992) state, "The choice of a co-leader is important. If two leaders are incompatible, their group is bound to be negatively affected" (p. 28). The leaders can confuse the members because they each are wanting to direct the group in a certain direction.

◆ E X A M P L E

Leader 1: To get started this evening, we'd like each person to share how the week went. I think it is important to start with comments about your week so that everyone is aware of how you are progressing.

Leader 2: You might also have some questions from last week's session. We'll be glad to answer them, too.

Stacy: I had a good week. I exercised three times at the track!

Leader 1: That's great Stacy. John, you were going to visit your dad. How did that work out?

John: Great. When he asked me if I had decided if I was going to medical school, I just said I was still thinking about it instead of arguing with him.

Leader 2: That's something we talked about last week—not arguing with parents. Instead, it is often better to simply acknowledge what they have said. Let's talk some more about arguing with parents.

Sally: What about teachers? Can we discuss them?

Leader 2: Sure.

In this example, Leader 2 is working at cross-purposes with Leader 1. While Leader 1 is looking for self-reports about significant events that occurred during the week, Leader 2 shifts to focusing on handling authority figures. Although Leader 2's focus is not necessarily wrong, it is poorly timed. The members were ready to share events of the week and then were forced to shift their thinking. Leader 1 has a difficult decision: to abandon the original goal and allow Leader 2 to pursue this new direction, or to try to get back to processing the week and risk a power struggle with the co-leader in front of the group. These co-leaders are not working well together and will need to correct this problem if they are to continue to share the leading.

Problems also arise in co-leading when the following happens:

- ◆ Each leader wants to be in charge.
- ◆ The two leaders openly dislike each other.
- ◆ The two leaders view group leading in totally different ways.

If either or both co-leaders feel a need to compete or dominate, co-leading will be difficult, and the members will suffer. Co-leaders must work as a team. The process of co-leading should add to, rather than detract from, the group experience. Co-leaders should be secure in their relative position in the group and must like and respect each other in order to have a good working relationship.

When two leaders have distinctly different styles of leading or opposing views on how to proceed in the group, co-leading is not recommended. Differences can be valuable, but totally different styles usually will cause friction, frustration, or both. For instance, if one leader was trained to focus mostly on process and the other to focus mostly on content, each leader would be frustrated by the other's style of leading.

Another necessary component of co-leading is that the co-leaders must be willing to set aside time to plan each session and share feedback. The advantage of co-leading breaks down if the co-leaders are unwilling to take the necessary time for planning. Experience suggests that co-leaders who try to go to the sessions without having prepared jointly run the risk of not "flowing" well together. This may lead to conflict and bad feelings. Co-leading requires the joint commitment of leaders to work together for the benefit of the members.

Co-leading Models

Three models of co-leading are presented here: the alternate leading model, the shared leading model, and the apprentice model. Each of these models assumes that the co-leaders are committed to discussing goals and activities for each session. The model used will depend on the purpose and goals of the group, the experience of the two leaders, the individual styles of the co-leaders, and the degree to which the co-leaders feel they can coordinate their efforts.

Alternate Leading

The alternate leading model is one in which co-leaders alternate taking the primary leading role. Alternating roles are usually decided upon during the planning of a given session. For example, one co-leader may be responsible for this week's session and the other co-leader for next week's, or one co-leader may be responsible for the first half of the session and the other leader for the second half. With experience, co-leaders who work well together find that shifting roles goes smoothly.

The alternate co-leading model may be appropriate if co-leaders differ somewhat in their approaches and find themselves pulling the group in opposing directions. Alternate leading allows one co-leader to have primary responsibility for directing the group for a specific period of time without worrying about interruptions from the co-leader. This does not mean that the second co-leader is totally inactive. On the contrary, the co-leader may offer supporting comments, clarify, or summarize as necessary to be helpful to the group.

Shared Leading

The shared leading model is one in which co-leaders share the leadership, with neither designated as the leader during a specific time period. Leaders "flow" with each other and lead jointly. Although in this model they lead together, at times one co-leader will take charge, such as when conducting an exercise or working with an individual. Also, the other leader is ready to step in at any appropriate point and continue in the same general direction.

◆ EXAMPLE

Leader 1: Maybe to get started with the group this evening we'll ask for people to report on how the week went. *(Pause)*

Leader 2: John, you were going to visit your dad. How did that work out?

John: It was great. When he brought up my going to medical school, I just told him I was still thinking about it instead of arguing with him. We got along a lot better.

Leader 2: I'm really glad you found avoiding an argument helpful. What happened with other people?

Amy: I went ahead and told my mom I was going to work at the beach this summer. She took it pretty well, but I know she'll bring it up again.

Leader 1: I'm glad you went ahead and took that risk. Maybe we'll talk more about how you'll handle your mom if she brings it up again.

Leader 2: Amy and John had a chance to handle some important issues for them this week. Did others of you do something similar?

In this example, the co-leaders are actively working together, drawing out and encouraging members. Both leaders have a common goal in mind—getting members to share events that happened during the week in the expectation that a worthwhile topic or some individual work may emerge. If this does not happen, the leaders will move on to an activity they have planned for the session.

❖❖❖

When using the shared leading model, co-leaders should be careful not to echo each other's words; that is, one leader will say something, and then the other leader will say something that is very similar to the first leader's comments. Also, it is important for the leaders not to get into one commenting, then the other, then the first leader commenting again, thus creating a dialogue with one another to the exclusion of the members.

The Apprentice Model

In this model, one leader is much more experienced than the other; the group is led mostly by the more experienced leader. The co-leader is present to learn by watching and by trying her hand at leading at various times. One benefit of this model is the less experienced leader knows someone is there to help out if necessary when she is leading. The more experienced leader benefits by having someone to plan with and to debrief with after the sessions. Also, most skilled leaders enjoy teaching others how to lead groups effectively.

In summary, whether or not you choose to co-lead will depend on a number of factors. Among the most important are your style of leadership, the needs of your group members, and the availability of a compatible co-leader who is willing to make the commitment to plan and cooperate in this joint venture. Regardless of the co-leading model selected, it is important for co-leaders to maintain a consistent tone in the group and work toward common goals. This requires careful listening to each other, along with an awareness of each other's nonverbal cues. In addition to paying attention to each other, co-leaders should watch the members for clues to the impact of their co-leading styles. If members seem confused or if momentum fails to build, the co-leaders should consider their co-leading as a possible cause.

Ethical Considerations

Over the last 10 years, much has been written about ethics in counseling and ethical behavior in group work (Corey 1995; Gladding, 1995). Most ethical problems and situations deal with therapy groups and growth groups, although ethical standards apply to leaders of all kinds of groups. Leaders' ethical behavior centers on their competency and behavior with the members.

Ethical Standards

All professional associations, such as the American Counseling Association, the National Association for Social Workers, or the American Psychological Association, have ethical standards regarding working with clients in groups. Aside from these organizations, there are special organizations that consist of professionals who do group work—the American Group Psychotherapy Association and the Association for Specialists in Group Work (ASGW). These associations have their own codes of ethics. It is very important that you become familiar with the standards of any organization in which you are affiliated. We have found that many people who lead groups are unfamiliar with these organizations and therefore do not realize that any ethical standards exist. The ethical standards for ASGW can be found in the appendix. (ASGW is currently revising the 1989 standards.)

Lanning (1992) discusses ethical codes as guidelines for responsible decision making. He talks about counselors using a "systematic process of ethical reasoning" (p. 21). We agree with Lanning that many ethical situations are not so cut-and-dried as some make them out to be. In the following discussion, we try to present a realistic view of ethical behavior and situations that group leaders might encounter.

Leader Preparation and Qualifications

The fundamental ethical principle for leading groups is found in the ASGW (1989) guidelines: "Group counselors do not attempt any technique unless thoroughly trained in its use or under supervision by a counselor familiar with the intervention." Just as it is unethical to practice dentistry or surgery without training, it is unethical to practice any kind of counseling without proper preparation. Helpers must realize that it is unethical to lead groups, especially therapy groups, without proper preparation. ASGW spells out in great detail excellent standards for the training of group leaders. If every group counselor had this kind of preparation, there would be no question as to whether the person had been properly trained. Unfortunately, most group leaders are not prepared at this level, yet many feel qualified to lead groups because they have a degree in one of the helping professions.

We want to emphasize that a degree alone does not make one qualified to lead groups. We have talked with many therapists with master's or doctorate degrees who are leading groups but have no understanding of what it takes to lead an effective group. It is the ethical responsibility of any group leader to understand group dynamics, group process, group leadership skills, and group development. Also, the leader needs to have thorough knowledge of the subjects being discussed in the group. So often, we have heard leaders at our workshops say they did not realize there was so much to leading groups. They thought you just "went in and did a group—just let the members take charge and go with the flow." This is unethical leadership!

Leaders in private practice should understand that they must have the necessary skills for conducting any group they establish. Although the same standard applies in agencies, this is not as clear as it may first seem. Confusion results because administrators in agencies, hospitals, schools, and prisons force their employees (the helpers) to violate the ethical standard of being properly prepared by mandating that the helpers conduct group counseling even though they lack the qualifications and knowledge to do so. Often, the helpers have never been trained in group work or have had only minimal training. Every day, counselors, nurses, social workers, and drug and alcohol therapists are required to conduct groups even though they are not qualified. This is unethical according to the standards of all the professions previously mentioned.

If you are asked to lead groups and do not feel qualified, you should make sure you get training before you start. If you are currently leading groups without proper training, it is important that you seek training immediately. Also, if you are not properly trained, you need to be aware that you and your agency are at risk of being charged with an ethics violation. More and more clients are becoming aware that therapists have ethical standards that they should abide by; thus, an increasing number of clients question the ethical behavior of professional helpers.

Knowledge

It is unethical to lead a group without having a good grasp of the material being discussed. Too often, we hear of leaders who have little or no knowledge of the subject of the group they are leading—such as groups on eating disorders, panic attacks, anger, or grief. In each of these groups, there exists the potential for members to get into some deeply emotional material; it is the leader's ethical responsibility to know how to deal with such material. The leader cannot count on the members to know how to help other members with such complex issues as these.

Another area of knowledge that is crucial is the understanding of the cultural and gender issues of the members. It is unethical for a helper to lead a group when she is not familiar with issues that may be unique to the members due to their gender or cultural background.

Personal Growth

Leaders should not use a group for their own personal growth. We see the need and value for therapists to experience personal growth through groups, but this should not be done in the group that the person is leading. We have heard of many instances of leaders drawing attention to themselves and using the group for their own therapy. This is unethical.

Dual Relationships

For group work, we define a dual relationship as a relationship that exists in addition to the therapeutic relationship established between the leader and the members. Dual relationships are not harmful in and of themselves; many dual relationships can be very beneficial to group members. We feel that often dual relationships cannot be avoided because helpers have more than one relationship with their clients. For instance, some group leaders are also the group members' residential house counselor or the person who takes them to the movies, on hikes, or bike trips, or plays on the same sports team. There are times, especially in small towns, when group leaders will find themselves at the same party as members of their group. We do not feel that the leader is being unethical if he socializes with a member of his group as long as he is aware that potential problems could arise. *It is the leader's responsibility to make sure that the therapeutic relationship is not being jeopardized.*

Our position is that any dual relationship should be entered into with caution and any exploitative dual relationship is unethical and should be avoided. By *exploitative*, we mean any relationship in which the group leader uses a group member for his own advantage. The dual relationship that creates the most concern is one of a sexual or romantic nature. Other dual relationships that can be exploitative involve social or business relationships between the leader and group members. Any time a leader enters into a dual relationship, the leader must proceed with great caution to ensure that it is not harmful to the member or the group.

A different kind of dual relationship exists when the group leader sees a member for individual counseling. Some argue that group leaders should not conduct individual counseling with members of their therapy groups. We disagree with this position and, in fact, think it is unethical not to provide therapy if it would be in the best interest of the member. The purpose of group therapy is to help clients get better, and if individual therapy aids in the client's improvement, then it should be seen as a valuable tool in the therapeutic process. Also, many times groups are formed as a result of clients being in individual counseling with the leader, and the leader deciding that a group would be beneficial. For a more detailed discussion of dual relationships as they relate to group work, see Herlihy and Corey (1992).

Confidentiality

There are two issues regarding confidentiality that any group leader should understand: the leader's ethical responsibility for keeping material confidential and the leader's lack of total control regarding member confidentiality.

It is unethical for the leader to divulge information to anyone about any member of the group. Leaders must be very careful not to give a member's friends, family members, or business associates any information, including whether or not the person is a member of the group. There are exceptions to this rule, when breaching confidentiality is required by law, such as when a member is threatening harm to himself or others. Also, in certain institutional settings, the leader may be required to write notes in a file that is open to other staff members. The best way to deal with such a situation is to inform the members what is required of you by law and the administration so that the members understand from the beginning what your requirements are regarding confidentiality. Corey (1995) states, "Generally speaking, you will find that you have a better chance of gaining the cooperation of group members if you are candid about your situation than if you hide your disclosures and thereby put yourself in the position of violating their confidences" (p. 33).

Regarding members' keeping what is said confidential, it must be understood that leaders cannot guarantee complete confidentiality because they have no control over what members say once they leave the session. The best way to prevent any breach of confidentiality is to stress its importance and discuss the subject whenever it seems necessary (Corey, 1995).

Informing Members about the Group

Prospective members have the right to know the purpose of the group and how it will be conducted. *Ethical Guidelines for Group Counselors* (ASGW, 1989) clearly states that members should be informed of any possible risks they might encounter, such as a heightened awareness of unpleasant material from their past or the desire to make decisions that could lead to stressful consequences, such as getting a divorce. For voluntary groups, informing the potential members will give them a chance to decide whether they want to join a group in which such activities and explorations will occur. It is best, whenever possible, for the leader to use a screening interview to determine if a person should be a member of the group and to have an open exchange about the risks involved. For nonvolunteers, who do not have a choice about being in the group, explaining what is going to happen and what is minimally expected prevents any disgruntled member from saying he was never told how the group was going to be conducted and what was expected of him.

During the first session of therapy groups or any groups in which emotional material is going to be discussed, leaders should discuss the various potential risks. Members should be warned about the danger of disclosing too much too soon and the tendency to feel pressure to disclose. Members should be reassured that they do not have to disclose anything that they are uncomfortable talking about. Members also should be warned about the danger of demanding that significant people in their world act like the group members, who may be warm, accepting, caring, open, or attentive. In other words, it is unethical not to inform the members about how the group will affect them both during the session and while they are living their daily lives. Any concerns about these matters should be thoroughly discussed during the early sessions.

The Ethical Use of Exercises

Leaders should keep several ethical considerations in mind when using structured activities or exercises during a group session. Most ethical problems involving exercises result from a lack of expertise or sensitivity on the part of the leader. Leaders may use exercises that generate reactions they are unable to handle due to their lack of experience and theoretical background. Any leader who goes beyond his skill level in this respect is operating unethically. The following are examples of operating without adequate skills:

- Conducting an exercise on death—such as writing your own epitaph—and then not being able to deal with the pain and other emotions that arise
- Conducting an exercise on guilt and shame and then not being able to deal with the material that surfaces, such as incest, child abuse, or extramarital affairs
- Conducting a feedback exercise and allowing one member to be viciously attacked by the rest of the group

Additional leader behavior that is considered unethical includes the following:

- Not informing members of what they are about to experience if they participate in any group exercise. Any potential risk must be pointed out.
- Forcing a member to participate in any exercise. If, for whatever reason, a member states she does not want to take part in a given activity, the leader must allow the member this right. (It is not unethical to encourage participation, however.)
- Demanding continued participation. Members must be allowed to stop participation at any time.
- Tricking a member into revealing something personal that he might not want to reveal. For example, for an exercise called "Secrets," members write anonymously on an index card a secret that might be hard for them to reveal to others. These cards are then shuffled, and the leader or each member picks a card and presents the issue as if it were his or her own. If the leader lets members reveal which was their secret, by elimination, a member's secret can become known to everyone.
- Using exercises that lead to "heavy" emotional material without leaving adequate time for processing. In other words, it is unethical to "unzip" members and leave them unzipped.

The Leader's Role in Making Referrals

It is the ethical responsibility of the group leader to make sure members are made aware of proper follow-up treatment possibilities. The leader may see members for follow-up counseling or refer members to other therapists. Follow-up is important in therapy groups, since very often members need additional individual, group, or family counseling. Too often, this ethical standard is violated in that no follow-up treatment is outlined.

Legal Issues

Group leaders can become involved in lawsuits if they do not use due care and act in good faith. Therefore, as a leader, you will want to be sure to practice within your limits of expertise and not to be negligent in performing your duties as a group leader. A leader who uses techniques and practices that are very different from those commonly accepted by others in the profession may be considered negligent. It is your obligation to make sure members are not harmed by you, the other members, or the group experience. Paradise and Kirby (1990) list the obligation to protect the client and other members as one of the main legal issues in group work. We have heard stories of members being harmed by the leader's inappropriate use of exercises or the use of very powerful exercises when members were not ready for such experiences. We also have heard of groups in which members were allowed to viciously attack other members. These practices are not considered ethical, and the counselor could be brought up on charges of malpractice if a member felt harmed by such experiences.

The most important point to remember regarding legal issues is that you should know the laws in your area regarding counseling, clients' rights, and the rights of parents and minors. Also, it is important that you do not practice outside your level of training and that you demonstrate at all times care and compassion for your group members. If you desire more information regarding the legal issues of group work, we found two books to be very informative: *The Counselor and the Law* (Hopkins & Anderson, 1990) and *Ethical and Legal Issues in Counseling and Psychotherapy* (Van Hoose & Kottler, 1985).

Evaluating Groups

Most group leaders do not evaluate their groups because either it takes extra time or it forces them to look at the outcome of their professional work. Professionals can more easily believe that their work with clients has been helpful when they lack data to the contrary. While group leaders should not become preoccupied with evaluating their groups, periodic evaluation can give them useful feedback about their approach to groups as well as information on the kinds of experiences that are most helpful in meeting the goals of their members.

Three kinds of evaluations are possible: (1) evaluation of the changes that actually occur in members' lives, (2) evaluation by the group leader, and (3) evaluation by the members. There are advantages and limitations to each, and each type of evaluation serves a particular function.

Evaluation of the Changes in Members' Lives

Probably the most important type of evaluation is the assessment of how the group experience has had an impact on the members' behavior. Do students get better grades in school or have fewer reported incidents of misbehavior? Do spouses communicate more effectively? Do teen mothers provide better care than they would have if they had not been in the group? Do unemployed workers from the group get jobs sooner than those not in the group? Do members who experience much guilt and anxiety cope with life better after being in the group? Some of these questions are rather easy to answer, and some are difficult to answer, but there is an increasing demand for outcome-based evaluation. Agencies and institutions want to see data showing that the group work is effective in bringing about changes.

Some groups will easily lend themselves to outcome-based evaluation; with others, it may be difficult to quantify changes in members. Members' self-reports are one method of determining whether they are actually changing. Throughout the life of the group, the leader should ask members to comment on changes that they are making. Of course, such responses are not always accurate, but the leader can often get some idea of the impact the group is having on the members. Another method of evaluating behavioral change is to have other people in the members' lives give a more objective evaluation. These outside evaluators may be teachers, employers, parents, spouses, friends, probation counselors, primary care medical treatment staff, or individual therapists. The leader may receive informal comments or anecdotes such as "Yes, Billy is definitely paying more attention in class" or more formal feedback through the use of a written behavioral checklist. Presuming that Billy's behavior in class had a negative impact on his academic work, checking Billy's grades at the end of the next full marking period would also be a way to evaluate the influence of the group.

To produce data measuring the outcome, the leader must follow a procedure that includes these steps:

1. Collect pre-group data—for example, the number of panic attacks, number of days skipped, number of fights at work, number of work days missed.
2. Determine the outcome goals of the specific group—for example, students stay in school, students reduce the number of days of skipping school, grades improve, members stop smoking, members have fewer panic attacks, members get jobs. For some groups, the leader may need to determine goals for each member.
3. Focus the group sessions on the desired outcome goals. Allow members to work on their goals.
4. Develop an appropriate form for members to complete regarding their progress toward the established goals. It is very important that the form contain questions that facilitate measurement of the outcome of the group.
5. Determine whether people other than the members can be involved in evaluating outcome and, if so, obtain permission from the members and contact those people.
6. Collect data periodically, using the form.
7. Collect data at the end of the group using the form.
8. Plan for follow-up data collection by either mailing forms to the members (and others, if appropriate) at certain intervals, or giving members extra forms and asking them to send the completed forms at designated intervals. Collecting data at 3 months after the group ends, then 6 months, then 1 year, would be an excellent way to evaluate the group based on lasting changes in the members.

The Leader's Evaluation

Many leaders do a self-evaluation after each session. Usually a self-evaluation is simple and straightforward. The leader will want to recall any dynamics that seemed especially important and evaluate his role in the group. For example, "My instructions for doing the 'Family Sculpture' exercise were confusing," or "I could have cut off Dan earlier and kept the group from getting so restless," or "Sarah attacked Bill, and I didn't do anything about it." The leader can ask himself these questions:

- How closely did I follow my plan?
- When I deviated from my plan, was it because I thought of a more appropriate strategy at the moment or because I felt lost or overwhelmed by the group?
- How closely was I able to meet the needs of the individual members?
- Did things happen in the group that I did not plan for or anticipate?
- Could I have second-guessed these with more forethought?
- What have I learned from the session that I can implement next time?
- On a 1–10 scale, how would I rate my overall satisfaction with the session? Is this rating higher, lower, or the same as my rating for the last session?

The leader should keep these self-evaluations and periodically review them to observe the progress that he is making. If there are areas in which the leader feels he is not improving, he may wish to give them special attention or ask a fellow group leader or supervisor for help.

The Members' Evaluations

The leader will find it helpful to have members evaluate the group. An informal evaluation can be done as part of the closing of any session. The leader might say, "What happened in the group during this session that was particularly valuable for you?" A more formal evaluation can be done one-third of the way or halfway through the group. This might involve a checklist with questions about the process that takes place in the group as well as its content and the ways in which the group has been helpful. An evaluation that is done midway through the group allows the leader to make changes that seem desirable based on the members' feedback. A final written evaluation is also helpful for the leader in planning future groups.

A useful evaluation form for the end of groups could contain the following questions, plus some additional ones that are specific to the given group.

- What was the most important thing you gained from being in this group?
- What activities, discussions, and topics stood out for you?
- What did you like most about the group?

- What did you like least about the group?
- What would have made the group better for you?
- What could the leader have done differently that would have made the group better for you?

A leader should exercise caution when reading member evaluations. Some members may not like her and thus give inaccurate feedback; or members may have a need to please and therefore give only positive feedback. Some members give dishonest feedback due to feeling threatened or concerned for the leader. For example, if the leader continually asks members if they like the group or if it is being helpful to them, members may conclude that the leader is fishing for positive feedback and may be reluctant to offer constructive criticism. Some members develop what can be termed a "groupie" mentality; they identify so strongly with the power of the leader that no matter what happens in the group, they believe it is for the good of the group. Since it is natural to look for positive feedback, such feedback may lull leaders into thinking that their groups are terrific when, in fact, there are problems that should be corrected.

The benefit of evaluating your groups cannot be stressed enough. Much can be learned from evaluations, using any of the methods of evaluation previously mentioned.

Research

Horne (1996) states that during his tenure as journal editor for ASGW "... there [was] little or no increase in research-based, evaluative studies in group work" (p. 66). Gladding (1995) sums up the research section in his recent book by saying, "Overall, research on the effectiveness of groups needs to be greatly expanded to reach the level of sophistication that has been established on the effectiveness of individual counseling" (p. 418). Numerous articles have been written on why group research is difficult and why there is so little quality research in the group field (Bednar et al., 1987; Morran & Stockton, 1985; Robison & Ward, 1990). Cited as reasons are lack of time, lack of money, and lack of interest. Another major reason for the lack of research is the difficulty of designing a research project in which the variables can be controlled enough to study different aspects of group counseling.

Although there have been many articles published encouraging group research, no one has come to the front with ongoing quality research, either on the training of group leaders or on the effectiveness of group work. As Corey and Corey (1992) state, "Current research efforts are addressing questions that have been answered before" (p. 253). With greater emphasis being put on group therapy, we remain hopeful that more research will be conducted both at the university level and in the private sector.

Training of Group Counselors

We have been group educators for several years and currently conduct workshops throughout the United States and Canada on group counseling. The major deficiency in training that we have identified is that trainees do not get to practice using specific skills such as cutting off, drawing out, holding and shifting the focus, deepening the focus, and introducing and conducting an exercise. Many beginning counselors report that their group course consisted of being a member of a group, with part of the class time being spent on processing the group. Being a member of a group does not prepare someone to lead groups. Some workshop participants reported having had courses with a practice component consisting of leading a group with their peers. It is definitely beneficial to practice, but unfortunately this kind of practice usually does not accurately simulate what counselors will be doing in work settings after they graduate. Also, the students usually only get to practice once or twice during a semester. Much practice is needed to acquire the skills necessary to be a group leader.

Our belief is that group skills can be taught like individual counseling skills; that is, the skill is described, demonstrated, and then practiced. We believe that effective training should include delineating specific skills, practicing those skills, and practicing leading groups similar to those the student will be leading after she graduates. Toth and Stockton (1996) agree: ". . . This tends to indicate that the education of group leaders may well be enhanced, encouraged, and perhaps even accelerated through the development of certain skill-based approaches that use didactic, observational, and experiential methods" (p. 107).

Another area of training that seems lacking concerns the ability to plan effective groups. As we said in Chapter Four, good planning is essential for good leading, yet, at our workshops, many counselors comment that they did not learn how to plan their groups. The planning of quality sessions can and should be taught to anyone leading a group.

Our last concern about training deals with requiring a group experience during a graduate program. If a group experience is required, it should be productive, and the leader should model some of the skills necessary for leading groups in various settings. Too often, we hear workshop participants describe a boring or bad group experience at the graduate level. They complain of "just sitting there with the leader doing nothing." Workshop participants have said that a combination of lack of adequate training and their poor graduate group experience turned them off to groups.

The Future

Most experts seem to agree that group work will continue to be a major force in the field of counseling. Gladding (1995) is very excited about the potential for groups: "There is little doubt that in the future, group work will be robust and permeate almost all segments of society" (p. 421). Corey and Corey (1992) have listed the increase in short-term structured groups for special populations as one of the major trends of the last decade. We are finding more and more professionals seeking training in leading specific kinds of groups in which the leader takes much responsibility for what happens in the group. Many school districts are requesting training in group leadership because the counselors see the need for many different kinds of groups in the schools. Teachers are also being trained to lead support groups. More training in group leadership skills is what we see as the next trend.

We believe that the future of group work lies in the integration of counseling theories with an active, multisensory, intrapersonal model of leading. We also believe leaders need to learn more ways to involve the members in the therapeutic process while using counseling theories and the intrapersonal model. Therapists will need and demand better training as they become more aware of the legal and ethical issues surrounding group work.

Final Thoughts Regarding Leading Groups

Now that you are at the end of this book, we hope you feel much better prepared to lead groups and are excited about trying to master the skills presented. At the beginning, we commented that we thought this book would give you an understanding of group dynamics and the skills necessary to allow you to lead almost any kind of group. We hope the book has been thorough enough to provide you with the basic tools for leading a group. We enjoy leading groups and have enjoyed the challenge of writing about what we do. We would like to hear your comments. Please contact us if you have any questions, comments, or reactions to share.

Ethical Guidelines for Group Counselors

ASGW 1989 Revision,
Association for Specialists in Group Work

PREAMBLE

One characteristic of any professional group is the possession of a body of knowledge, skills, and voluntarily, self-professed standards for ethical practice. A Code of Ethics consists of those standards that have been formally and publicly acknowledged by the members of a profession to serve as the guidelines for professional conduct, discharge of duties, and the resolution of moral dilemmas. By this document, the Association for Specialists in Group Work (ASGW) has identified the standards of conduct appropriate for ethical behavior among its members.

The Association for Specialists in Group Work recognizes the basic commitment of its members to the Ethical Standards of its parent organization, the American Association for Counseling and Development (AACD) and nothing in this document shall be construed to supplant that code. These standards are intended to complement the AACD standards in the area of group work by clarifying the nature of ethical responsibility of the counselor in the group setting and by stimulating a greater concern for competent group leadership.

The group counselor is expected to be a professional agent and to take the processes of ethical responsibility seriously.

ASGW views "ethical process" as being integral to group work and views group counselors as "ethical agents." Group counselors, by their very nature in being responsible and responsive to their group members, necessarily embrace a certain potential for ethical vulnerability. It is incumbent upon group counselors to give considerable attention to the intent and context of their actions because the attempts of counselors to influence human behavior through group work always have ethical implications.

The following ethical guidelines have been developed to encourage ethical behavior of group counselors. These guidelines are written for students and practitioners, and are meant to stimulate reflection, self-examination, and discussion of issues and practices. They address the group counselor's responsibility for providing information about group work to clients and the group counselor's responsibility for providing group counseling services to clients. A final section discusses the group counselor's responsibility for safe-guarding ethical practice and procedures for reporting unethical behavior. Group counselors are expected to make known these standards to group members.

Ethical Guidelines

1. *Orientation and Providing Information:*
Group counselors adequately prepare
prospective or new group members by
providing as much information about
the existing or proposed group as necessary.

Minimally, information related to each
of the following areas should be provided.
   a. Entrance procedures, time parame-
   ters of the group experience, group
   participation expectations, methods
   of payment (where appropriate), and
   termination procedures are explained by the group counselor as appropriate to the level of maturity of
   group members and the nature and
   purpose(s) of the group.
   b. Group counselors have available for
   distribution, a professional disclosure statement that includes information on the group counselor's
   qualifications and group services that
   can be provided, particularly as related to the nature and purpose(s) of
   the specific group.
   c. Group counselors communicate the
   role expectations, rights, and responsibilities of group members and
   group counselor(s).
   d. The group goals are stated as con-
   cisely as possible by the group counselor including "whose" goal it is (the
   group counselor's, the institution's,
   the parent's, the law's, society's, etc.)
   and the role of group members in
   influencing or determining the
   group's goal(s).
   e. Group counselors explore with group
   members the risks of potential life
   changes that may occur because of
   the group experience and help members explore their readiness to face
   these possibilities.
   f. Group members are informed by the
   group counselor of unusual or experi-
   mental procedures that might be expected in their group experience.
   g. Group counselors explain, as realisti-
   cally as possible, what services can
   and cannot be provided within the
   particular group structure offered.
   h. Group counselors emphasize the
   need to promote full psychological
   functioning and presence among
   group members. They inquire from
   prospective group members whether
   they are using any kind of drug or
   medication that may affect functioning in the group. They do not permit
   any use of alcohol and/or illegal
   drugs during group sessions and they
   discourage the use of alcohol and/or
   drugs (legal or illegal) prior to group
   meetings which may affect the physical or emotional presence of the member or other group members.
   i. Group counselors inquire from prospective group members whether
   they have ever been a client in counseling or psychotherapy. If a prospective group member is already in a
   counseling relationship with another
   professional person, the group counselor advises the prospective group
   member to notify the other professional of their participation in the
   group.
   j. Group counselors clearly inform
   group members about the policies
   pertaining to the group counselor's
   willingness to consult with them between group sessions.
   k. In establishing fees for group counseling services, group counselors consider the financial status and the
   locality of prospective group members. Group members are not charged
   fees for group sessions where the
   group counselor is not present and
   the policy of charging for sessions
   missed by a group member is clearly
   communicated. Fees for participating
   as a group member are contracted
   between group counselor and group
   member for a specified period of time.
   Group counselors do not increase fees
   for group counseling services until the
   existing contracted fee structure has
   expired. In the event that the established fee structure is inappropriate
   for a prospective member, group
   counselors assist in finding compara-
   ble services of acceptable cost.

2. *Screening of Members:* The group counselor screens prospective group mem-

bers (when appropriate to their theoretical orientation). Insofar as possible, the counselor selects group members whose needs and goals are compatible with the goals of the group, who will not impede the group process, and whose well-being will not be jeopardized by the group experience. An orientation to the group (i.e., ASGW Ethical Guideline #1), is included during the screening process.

Screening may be accomplished in one or more ways, such as the following:

a. Individual interview,
b. Group interview of prospective group members,
c. Interview as part of a team staffing, and,
d. Completion of a written questionnaire by prospective group members.

3. *Confidentiality:* Group counselors protect members by defining clearly what confidentiality means, why it is important, and the difficulties involved in enforcement.

a. Group counselors take steps to protect members by defining confidentiality and the limits of confidentiality (i.e., when a group member's condition indicates that there is clear and imminent danger to the member, others, or physical property, the group counselor takes reasonable personal action and/or informs responsible authorities).
b. Group counselors stress the importance of confidentiality and set a norm of confidentiality regarding all group participants' disclosures. The importance of maintaining confidentiality is emphasized before the group begins and at various times in the group. The fact that confidentiality cannot be guaranteed is clearly stated.
c. Members are made aware of the difficulties involved in enforcing and ensuring confidentiality in a group setting. The counselor provides examples of how confidentiality can nonmaliciously be broken to increase members' awareness, and help to lessen the likelihood that this breach of confidence will occur. Group counselors inform group members about

the potential consequences of intentionally breaching confidentiality.
d. Group counselors can only ensure confidentiality on their part and not on the part of the members.
e. Group counselors video or audio tape a group session only with the prior consent, and the members' knowledge of how the tape will be used.
f. When working with minors, the group counselor specifies the limits of confidentiality.
g. Participants in a mandatory group are made aware of any reporting procedures required of the group counselor.
h. Group counselors store or dispose of group member records (written, audio, video, etc.) in ways that maintain confidentiality.
i. Instructors of group counseling courses maintain the anonymity of group members whenever discussing group counseling cases.

4. *Voluntary/Involuntary Participation:* Group counselors inform members whether participation is voluntary or involuntary.

a. Group counselors take steps to ensure informed consent procedures in both voluntary and involuntary groups.
b. When working with minors in a group, counselors are expected to follow the procedures specified by the institution in which they are practicing.
c. With involuntary groups, every attempt is made to enlist the cooperation of the members and their continuance in the group on a voluntary basis.
d. Group counselors do not certify that group treatment has been received by members who merely attend sessions, but did not meet the defined group expectations. Group members are informed about the consequences for failing to participate in a group.

5. *Leaving a Group:* Provisions are made to assist a group member to terminate in an effective way.

a. Procedures to be followed for a group member who chooses to exit a group prematurely are discussed by the counselor with all group members either before the group begins, during a prescreening interview, or during the initial group session.

b. In the case of legally mandated group counseling, group counselors inform members of the possible consequences for premature self-termination.

c. Ideally, both the group counselor and the member can work cooperatively to determine the degree to which a group experience is productive or counterproductive for that individual.

d. Members ultimately have a right to discontinue membership in the group, at a designated time, if the predetermined trial period proves to be unsatisfactory.

e. Members have the right to exit a group, but it is important that they be made aware of the importance of informing the counselor and the group members prior to deciding to leave. The counselor discusses the possible risks of leaving the group prematurely with a member who is considering this option.

f. Before leaving a group, the group counselor encourages members (if appropriate) to discuss their reasons for wanting to discontinue membership in the group. Counselors intervene if other members use undue pressure to force a member to remain in the group.

6. *Coercion and Pressure:* Group counselors protect member rights against physical threats, intimidation, coercion, and undue peer pressure insofar as is reasonably possible.

a. It is essential to differentiate between "therapeutic pressure" that is part of any group and "undue pressure," which is not therapeutic.

b. The purpose of a group is to help participants find their own answer, not to pressure them into doing what the group thinks is appropriate.

c. Counselors exert care not to coerce participants to change in directions which they clearly state they do not choose.

d. Counselors have a responsibility to intervene when others use undue pressure or attempt to persuade members against their will.

e. Counselors intervene when any member attempts to act out aggression in a physical way that might harm another member or themselves.

f. Counselors intervene when a member is verbally abusive or inappropriately confrontive to another member.

7. *Imposing Counselor Values:* Group counselors develop an awareness of their own values and needs and the potential impact they have on the interventions likely to be made.

a. Although group counselors take care to avoid imposing their values on members, it is appropriate that they expose their own beliefs, decisions, needs, and values, when concealing them would create problems for the members.

b. There are values implicit in any group, and these are made clear to potential members before they join the group. (Examples of certain values include: expressing feelings, being direct and honest, sharing personal material with others, learning how to trust, improving interpersonal communication, and deciding for oneself.)

c. Personal and professional needs of group counselors are not met at the members' expense.

d. Group counselors avoid using the group for their own therapy.

e. Group counselors are aware of their own values and assumptions and how these apply in a multicultural context.

f. Group counselors take steps to increase their awareness of ways that their personal reactions to members might inhibit the group process and they monitor their countertransference. Through an awareness of the impact of stereotyping and discrimination (i.e., biases based on age, disability, ethnicity, gender, race, religion, or sexual preference), group counselors guard the individual rights and personal dignity of all group members.

8. *Equitable Treatment:* Group counselors make every reasonable effort to treat each member individually and equally.
   a. Group counselors recognize and respect differences (e.g., cultural, racial, religious, lifestyle, age, disability, gender) among group members.
   b. Group counselors maintain an awareness of their behavior toward individual group members and are alert to the potential detrimental effects of favoritism or partiality toward any particular group member to the exclusion or detriment of any other member(s). It is likely that group counselors will favor some members over others, yet all group members deserve to be treated equally.
   c. Group counselors ensure equitable use of group time for each member by inviting silent members to become involved, acknowledging nonverbal attempts to communicate, and discouraging rambling and monopolizing of time by members.
   d. If a large group is planned, counselors consider enlisting another qualified professional to serve as a co-leader for the group sessions.
9. *Dual Relationships:* Group counselors avoid dual relationships with group members that might impair their objectivity and professional judgment, as well as those which are likely to compromise a group member's ability to participate fully in the group.
   a. Group counselors do not misuse their professional role and power as group leader to advance personal or social contacts with members throughout the duration of the group.
   b. Group counselors do not use their professional relationship with group members to further their own interests either during the group or after the termination of the group.
   c. Sexual intimacies between group counselors and members are unethical.
   d. Group counselors do not barter (exchange) professional services with group members for services.
   e. Group counselors do not admit their own family members, relatives, employees, or personal friends as members to their groups.
   f. Group counselors discuss with group members the potential detrimental effects of group members engaging in intimate inter-member relationships outside of the group.
   g. Students who participate in a group as a partial course requirement for a group course are not evaluated for an academic grade based upon their degree of participation as a member in a group. Instructors of group counseling courses take steps to minimize the possible negative impact on students when they participate in a group course by separating course grades from participation in the group and by allowing students to decide what issues to explore and when to stop.
   h. It is inappropriate to solicit members from a class (or institutional affiliation) for one's private counseling or therapeutic groups.
10. *Use of Techniques:* Group counselors do not attempt any technique unless trained in its use or under supervision by a counselor familiar with the intervention.
    a. Group counselors are able to articulate a theoretical orientation that guides their practice, and they are able to provide a rationale for their interventions.
    b. Depending upon the type of an intervention, group counselors have training commensurate with the potential impact of a technique.
    c. Group counselors are aware of the necessity to modify their techniques to fit the unique needs of various cultural and ethnic groups.
    d. Group counselors assist members in translating in-group learnings to daily life.
11. *Goal Development:* Group counselors make every effort to assist members in developing their personal goals.
    a. Group counselors use their skills to assist members in making their goals specific so that others present in the group will understand the nature of the goals.

b. Throughout the course of a group, group counselors assist members in assessing the degree to which personal goals are being met, and assist in revising any goals when it is appropriate.

c. Group counselors help members clarify the degree to which the goals can be met within the context of a particular group.

12. *Consultation:* Group counselors develop and explain policies about between-session consultation to group members.

a. Group counselors take care to make certain that members do not use between-session consultations to avoid dealing with issues pertaining to the group that would be dealt with best in the group.

b. Group counselors urge members to bring the issues discussed during between-session consultations into the group if they pertain to the group.

c. Group counselors seek out consultation and/or supervision regarding ethical concerns or when encountering difficulties which interfere with their effective functioning as group leaders.

d. Group counselors seek appropriate professional assistance for their own personal problems or conflicts that are likely to impair their professional judgment and work performance.

e. Group counselors discuss their group cases only for professional consultation and educational purposes.

f. Group counselors inform members about policies regarding whether consultation will be held confidential.

13. *Termination from the Group:* Depending upon the purpose of participation in the group, counselors promote termination of members from the group in the most efficient period of time.

a. Group counselors maintain a constant awareness of the progress made by each group member and periodically invite the group members to explore and reevaluate their experiences in the group. It is the responsibility of group counselors to help promote the independence of members from the group in a timely manner.

14. *Evaluation and Follow-up:* Group counselors make every attempt to engage in ongoing assessment and to design follow-up procedures for their groups.

a. Group counselors recognize the importance of ongoing assessment of a group, and they assist members in evaluating their own progress.

b. Group counselors conduct evaluation of the total group experience at the final meeting (or before termination), as well as ongoing evaluation.

c. Group counselors monitor their own behavior and become aware of what they are modeling in the group.

d. Follow-up procedures might take the form of personal contact, telephone contact, or written contact.

e. Follow-up meetings might be with individuals, or groups, or both to determine the degree to which; (i) members have reached their goals, (ii) the group had a positive or negative effect on the participants, (iii) members could profit from some type of referral, and (iv) as information for possible modification of future groups. If there is no follow-up meeting, provisions are made available for individual follow-up meetings to any member who needs or requests such a contact.

15. *Referrals:* If the needs of a particular member cannot be met within the type of group being offered, the group counselor suggests other appropriate professional referrals.

a. Group counselors are knowledgeable of local community resources for assisting group members regarding professional referrals.

b. Group counselors help members seek further professional assistance, if needed.

16. *Professional Development:* Group counselors recognize that professional growth is a continuous, ongoing, developmental process throughout their career.
    a. Group counselors maintain and upgrade their knowledge and skill competencies through educational activities, clinical experiences, and participation in professional development activities.
    b. Group counselors keep abreast of research findings and new developments as applied to groups.

REFERENCES

Adler, A. (1927). *Understanding human behavior.* New York: Greenberg.

American Journal of Community Psychology. (1991). *19*(5).

Association for Specialists in Group Work (ASGW). (1989). *Ethical Guidelines for Group Counselors.* Alexandria, VA: Author.

Bandura, A. (1977). *Social learning theory.* Englewood Cliffs, NJ: Prentice Hall.

Banik, S. N., & Mendelson, M. A. (1978). Group psychotherapy with a paraplegic group. *International Journal of Group Psychotherapy, 28*(4), 123–128.

Bednar, R. L., Corey, G., Evans, N. J., Gazda, G. M., Pistole, M. C., Stockton, R., & Robison, F. F. (1987). Overcoming obstacles to the future development of research on group work. *Journal for Specialists in Group Work, 12*(3), 98–111.

Berne, E. (1964). *Games people play.* New York: Grove Press.

Blaker, K. E., & Samo, J. (1973). Communications games: A group counseling technique. *The School Counselor, 21,* 46–51.

Blatner, A. (1988a). *Acting in: Practical applications of psychodramatic methods* (2nd ed.). New York: Springer.

Blatner, A. (1988b). *Foundations of psychodrama: History, theory, and practice* (3rd ed.). New York: Springer.

Capuzzi, D., & Gross, D. R. (1992). *Introduction to group counseling.* Denver, CO: Love.

Carroll, M. R. (1986). *Group work: Leading in the here and now* [Film]. Alexandria, VA: American Counseling Association.

Casriel, P. (1963). *So fair a house.* Englewood Cliffs, NJ: Prentice Hall.

Cavanaugh, M. E. (1990). *The counseling experience.* Pacific Grove, CA: Brooks/Cole.

Cheng, W. D. (1996). Pacific perspective. *Together, 24,* 2.

Conyne, R. K., Harvill, R. L., Morganett, R. S., Morran, D. K., & Hulse-Killacky, D. (1990). Effective group leadership: Continuing the search for greater clarity and understanding. *Journal for Specialists in Group Work, 15,* 30–36.

Corey, G. (1995). *The theory and practice of group counseling* (4th ed.). Pacific Grove, CA: Brooks/Cole.

Corey, G., & Corey, M. S. (1992). *Groups: Process and practice* (3rd ed.). Pacific Grove, CA: Brooks/Cole.

Corey, G., Corey, M. S., Callanan, P. S., & Russell, J. M. (1988). *Group Techniques.* Pacific Grove, CA: Brooks/Cole.

DeLucia-Waack, J. (1996). Multiculturalism is inherent in all group work. *Journal for Specialists in Group Work. 21*, 218–223.

Dinkmeyer, D., & Muro, J. (1979). *Group counseling: Theory and practice* (2nd ed.). Itasca, IL: F. E. Peacock.

Donigian, J. (1994). Group reflections. *Together, 23*, 6.

Dyer, W., & Vriend, J. (1980). *Group counseling for personal mastery.* New York: Sovereign.

Egan, G. (1994). *The skilled helper* (4th ed.). Pacific Grove, CA: Brooks/Cole.

Fisher, B. (1992). *Rebuilding* (2nd ed.). San Luis Obispo, CA: Impact.

Gazda, G. M. (1989). *Group counseling: A developmental approach* (4th ed.). Boston: Allyn & Bacon.

George, R. L., & Dustin, D. (1988). *Group counseling.* Englewood Cliffs, NJ: Prentice Hall.

Gibran, K. (1923). *The Prophet.* New York: Knopf.

Gladding, S. T. (1995). *Group work: A counseling specialty.* New York: Merrill.

Gladding, S. T. (1996). *Counseling: A comprehensive profession.* New York: Merrill.

Hackney, H., & Cormier, L. S. (1994). *Counseling strategies and interventions* (4th ed.). Englewood Cliffs, NJ: Prentice Hall.

Hansen, J., Warner, R., & Smith, E. J. (1980). *Group counseling: Theory and practice.* Chicago: Rand McNally.

Harvill, R., Masson, R., & Jacobs, E. (1983). Systematic group leadership training: A skills development approach. *The Journal for Specialists in Group Work, 8*(4), 16–20.

Herlihy, B., & Corey, G. (1992). *Dual relationships in counseling.* Alexandria, VA: American Counseling Association.

Hershenson, D. B., & Power, P. W. (1987). *Mental health counseling.* New York: Pergamon Press.

Hopkins, B. R., & Anderson, B. W. (1990). *The counselor and the law* (3rd ed.). Alexandria, VA: American Counseling Association.

Horne, A. (1996). Ending—or beginning somewhere else. *Journal for Specialists in Group Work, 21*(2), 66–68.

Hulse-Killacky, D., & Page, B. J. (1994). Development of the corrective feedback instrument: a tool for use in counselor training groups. *Journal for Specialists in Group Work, 19*(4), 197–210.

Hulse-Killacky, D., Schumacher, B., & Kraus, K. (1996). Meetings: A group work design. Pre-publication draft.

Ibrahim, F. A., & Arrendondo, P. (1990). Ethical issues in multicultural counseling. In B. Herlihy & L. Golden (Eds.), *Ethical standards casebook* (4th ed.). Alexandria, VA: American Counseling Association.

Jacobs, E. (1992). *Creative counseling techniques: An illustrated guide.* Odessa, FL: Psychological Assessment Resources.

Jacobs, E. (1994). *Impact Therapy.* Odessa, FL: Psychological Assessment Resources.

Johnson, D. W., & Johnson, F. P. (1997). *Joining together* (6th ed.). Boston: Allyn & Bacon.

Kees, N., & Jacobs, E. (1990). Conducting more effective groups: How to select and process group exercises. *Journal for Specialists in Group Work, 15*(1), 21–30.

Kemp, G. C. (1964). Bases of group leadership. *Personnel and Guidance Journal, 43*, 760–766.

Kormanski, C. (1991). Using group development theory in business. *Journal for Specialists in Group Work, 16*(4), 215–222.

Kottler, J. A. (1994). *Advanced group leadership.* Pacific Grove, CA: Brooks/Cole.

Kübler-Ross, E. (1969). *On death and dying.* New York: Macmillan.

Lakin, M. (1969). Some ethical issues in sensitivity training. *American Psychologist, 24*, 923–928.

Lanning, W. (1992). Ethical codes and responsible decision making. *Guidepost, 35*(7), 21.

Lewis, H. R., & Strelfeld, H. S. (1972). *Growth games.* New York: Bantam.

Maples, M. F. (1988). Group development: Extending Tuckman's theory. *Journal for Specialists in Group Work, 13,* 17–23.

Masson, R., & Jacobs, E. (1980). Group leadership: Practical pointers for beginners. *Personnel and Guidance Journal, 58*(3), 52–55.

Moreno, J. (1964). *Psychodrama: Volume 1* (rev. ed.). New York: Beacon Press.

Morganett, R. S. (1990). *Skills for living: Group counseling activities for young adolescents.* Champaign, IL: Research Press.

Morganett, R. S. (1994). *Skills for living: Group counseling activities for elementary students.* Champaign, IL: Research Press.

Morran, D. K., & Stockton, R. (1985). Perspectives on group research programs. *Journal for Specialists in Group Work, 10*(4), 186–191.

Newlon, B. J., & Arciniego, M. (1992). Group counseling: Cross-cultural considerations. In D. Capuzzi & D. R. Gross (Eds.), *Introduction to group counseling* (pp. 285–307). Denver, CO: Love.

Ohlsen, M. M., Horne, A. M., & Lawe, C. F. (1988). *Group counseling* (3rd ed.). New York: Holt, Rinehart & Winston.

Paradise, L. V., & Kirby, P. C. (1990). Some perspectives on the legal liability of group counseling in private practice. *Journal for Specialists in Group Work, 15*(2), 114–118.

Perls, F. (1969). *Gestalt therapy verbatim.* Lafayette, CA: Real People Press.

Pfeiffer, J. W., & Jones, J. E. (1972–1980). *A handbook of structured exercises for human relations training* (Vols. 1–8). San Diego, CA: San Diego University Associates.

Phillips, T. H., & Phillips, P. (1992). Structured groups for high school students: A case study in one district's program. *The School Counselor, 39,* 390–393.

Posthuma, B. W. (1996). *Small groups in therapy settings: Process and leadership* (2nd ed.). Boston: Allyn & Bacon.

Price, G. E., Dinas, P., Dunn, C., & Winterowd, C. (1995). Group work with clients experiencing grieving: Moving from theory to practice. *Journal for Specialists in Group Work, 20*(3), 132–142.

Project Adventure 1992 Workshop Schedule (1992). Hamilton, MA: Project Adventure.

Riordan, R. J., & White, J. (1996). Logs as therapeutic adjuncts in group. *Journal for Specialists in Group Work, 21* (2), 94–100.

Robison, F. F., & Ward, D. (1990). Research activities and attitudes among ASGW members. *Journal for Specialists in Group Work, 19*(4), 215–224.

Rogers, C. (1958). The characteristics of a helping relationship. *P&G Journal, 37*(6), 6–16.

Rogers, C. (1961). *On becoming a person.* Boston: Houghton Mifflin.

Rogers, C. (1970). *Carl Rogers on encounter groups.* New York: Harper & Row.

Roland, C. B., & Neitzschman, L. (1996). Groups in schools: A model for training middle school teachers. *Journal for Specialists in Group Work, 21*(1), 18–25.

Shapiro, J. L. (1978). *Methods of group psychotherapy and encounter: A tradition of innovation.* Itasca, IL: F. E. Peacock.

Shulman, I. (1984). *The skills of helping: Individuals and groups* (2nd ed.). Itasca, IL: F. E. Peacock.

Simon, S., Howe, L., & Kirschenbaum, H. (1978). *Values clarification.* New York: Hart.

Smead, R. (1995). *Skills and techniques for group work with children and adolescents.* Champaign, IL: Research Press.

Starak, Y. (1988). Confessions of a group leader. *Small Group Behavior, 19,* 103–108.

Stevens, J. (1972). *Awareness.* Lafayette, CA: Real People Press.

Toth, P. L., & Stockton, R. (1996). A skill-based approach to teaching group counseling interventions. *Journal for Specialists in Group Work, 21*(2), 101–109.

Trotzer, J. (1989). *The counselor and the group* (2nd ed.). Muncie, IN: Accelerated Development.

Van Hoose, W., & Kottler, J. (1985). *Ethical and legal issues in counseling and psychotherapy* (2nd ed.). San Francisco: Jossey-Bass.

Vernon, A. (1993). *Counseling children and adolescents*. Denver: Love.

Vorrath, H. (1974). *Positive peer culture*. Chicago: Aldine-Atherton.

Yalom, I. (1995). *The theory and practice of group psychotherapy* (4th ed.). New York: Basic.

TO THE OWNER OF THIS BOOK:

We hope that you have found *Group Counseling: Strategies and Skills* useful. So that this book can be improved in a future edition, would you take the time to complete this sheet and return it? Thank you.

School and address: ————————————————————————

Department: ————————————————————————

Instructor's name: ————————————————————————

1. What I like most about this book is: ————————————————

——

——

2. What I like least about this book is: ————————————————

——

——

3. My general reaction to this book is: ————————————————

——

4. The name of the course in which I used this book is: ————————

——

5. Were all of the chapters of the book assigned for you to read? ————————

   If not, which ones weren't? ————————————————————

6. In the space below, or on a separate sheet of paper, please write specific suggestions for improving this book and anything else you'd care to share about your experience in using the book.

——

——

——

——

——

Optional:

Your name: _____ Date: _____

May Brooks/Cole quote you, either in promotion for *Group Counseling: Strategies and Skills* or in future publishing ventures?

Yes: _____ No: _____

Sincerely,

Ed. E. Jacobs
Robert L. Masson
Riley L. Harvill

FOLD HERE

FOLD HERE

Brooks/Cole Publishing is dedicated to publishing quality books for the helping professions. If you would like to learn more about our publications, please use this mailer to request our catalogue.

Name: _____

Street Address: _____

City, State, and Zip: _____

FOLD HERE

NO POSTAGE
NECESSARY
IF MAILED
IN THE
UNITED STATES

BUSINESS REPLY MAIL

FIRST CLASS   PERMIT NO. 358   PACIFIC GROVE, CA

POSTAGE WILL BE PAID BY ADDRESSEE

ATT: *Human Services Catalogue*

Brooks/Cole Publishing Company
511 Forest Lodge Road
Pacific Grove, California 93950-9968

FOLD HERE